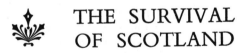

THE SURVIVAL
OF SCOTLAND

Books by Eric Linklater

THE SURVIVAL
OF SCOTLAND

*A Review of Scottish History from
Roman Times to the Present Day*

Eric Linklater

HEINEMANN · LONDON

William Heinemann Ltd
LONDON MELBOURNE TORONTO
CAPE TOWN AUCKLAND

First published 1968
Copyright © 1968 by Eric Linklater

Maps © William Heinemann Ltd 1968

434 42550 8

Printed in Great Britain by
Morrison and Gibb Ltd, London and Edinburgh

Contents

Maps

(redrawn by Harold James Blackman)

Book One

THE EMERGENT KINGDOM

Chapter I

OF the early inhabitants of Scotland, the first to be isolated by name and immortalised by reported speech, was Calgacus, a chief who commanded the Caledonian army which opposed Agricola's formidable invasion of the Highlands in the year A.D. 82.

Agricola, most famous of the Roman governors of Britain, was so fortunate or far-seeing as to marry his daughter to the historian Tacitus; by whom his exemplary character and martial achievements were recorded, with great distinction of style, for the admiration of posterity. Agricola, who arrived in Britain in A.D. 77, fought three victorious campaigns in those southern parts of the island which are now England or Wales, and in the year 80 marched as far north as the narrow waist between the estuaries of Forth and Clyde, in the country which subsequently became Scotland, and there built forts and established garrisons to protect his thinly occupied colony against the savage tribes of the farther hills.

In the following year he took measures to fortify the north-western shores of England against attack from Ireland, and subsequently launched his ambitious assault on the Highlands. His strategy was imaginative and well designed, for a fleet accompanied his army to reconnoitre harbours and carry supplies and reinforcements, but there may have been some carelessness in his tactical dispositions; for a night attack surprised the Ninth Legion in camp, and an incipient panic was only checked by Agricola's masterly deployment of cavalry and light infantry to engage his impetuous enemy from the rear. The defeated Caledonians fled from the encirclement of Roman arms, their retreat covered by woods and marshes, but with unbroken spirit regrouped to meet Agricola's triumphant, still advancing columns on more favourable ground.

The site of the great battle which followed has not been identified. Tacitus called it *Mons Graupius*; and the Grampian Hills, the mountain-mass that dominates the middle part of Scotland, got their name from a sixteenth-century misreading of Tacitus; but on what slope of the hills the Romans won their battle, no one can say with any certainty. There are those who prefer Strathmore, on the south-eastern flank, while others find evidence that Agricola preceded the wild Gordons— that legendary clan of later years—and far to the north marched through Strathbogie.

Tacitus, who was sublimely indifferent to geography, gives no help whatever. He offers, instead, a curious indictment of imperialism and wars of conquest, and in an epigram of searing brilliance epitomises much of Scotland's subsequent history. He discovered or invented a Caledonian spokesman—for Calgacus may have dropped from no womb but his imagination—and lets Calgacus denounce the expansive policy of Rome in a speech of passionate eloquence which rises to the bitter heights of a phrase that has lived in memory for nearly two thousand years. 'They make a desert,' said Calgacus, 'and they call it peace.'

Tacitus was no geographer, but he cannot be denied his place among the prophets of our world, for in the centuries that followed there were many attempts to pacify the intractable people of Scotland by desolating their land. His narrative, moreover, is almost a summary of the success and failure of Roman arms in north Britain. Agricola won his battle but found it impossible to exploit success. The mountains of the west and farther north were impermeable, and the Ninth Legion with its auxiliaries retired to winter quarters.

That Agricola had shown military genius of a very high order cannot be disputed. He defeated, in a locally decisive battle, the united Caledonian tribes, and to bring them to battle he had marched a disciplined army through country of appalling difficulty. Even to this day there are parts of the Scottish Highlands where an invading army would find progress hampered by natural obstacles, and in Agricola's time every river rose in a marsh, every hillside was clothed in scrub and forest. No roads led forward, no view promised ease of access or safe retreat. To the north and the west rose heights still striped with snow, even in high summer, and the eastern lowlands grew no crops to sustain the invaders. Wolves whimpered in thickets on the foothills and tribesmen crept as stealthily to cut off the laggards of a marching host.

In a set battle the tribesmen had been outmatched, and in open country could be outmanoeuvred by Roman discipline. Their weapons were primitive. They used long, unwieldy swords, with no points to sharpen their attack, and their shields were small. But they knew their own country. They could live on its scanty produce, and their skill in sudden foray, from the natural defences of a starkly inhospitable land-scape, gave them an elastic strength that remained unbroken. It must be admitted, however, that Caledonia's immunity owed much to the difficulties that Rome was encountering elsewhere.

At Inchtuthil, a few miles north of Perth, Agricola built a legionary fortress, covering some fifty acres, that commanded the northern route through Strathmore, and some material evidence of the magnitude of his intention—perhaps of preparation for a new campaign—was revealed, only a few years ago, when a hoard of a million nails was found on the site of his camp. Had Agricola remained in Britain, he might have led another march to build a permanent road through the hills, but the Emperor Domitian, engaged in heavy fighting on the Danube, reduced the garrison under his command and Agricola was recalled. Inchtuthil and the long nails that might have fastened bridges and defensive walls were abandoned, and Roman ambition recoiled.

Retreat was gradual but the evacuation of Inchtuthil made it inevit-able, and within less than forty years the south of Scotland was rid of its invaders and Roman policy had become defensive.

The great Emperor Hadrian built a wall from the Tyne to the Solway, and though that massive rampart became a monument to the magnitude of the emperor's intention and his military skill, it was primarily evidence of the formidable nature of the enemies whom it was built to contain. For seventy miles it reached across country, some eight or ten feet thick and twenty feet high, built of stone with a core of rubble where there was stone to be found, and initially of sods and clay on the western side. A thirty-foot ditch protected it in front; along its course stood sixteen stone forts garrisoned by regiments of auxiliaries; and between the forts were mile-castles and signal towers. It was not built to withstand the ponderous assault of a large, well-organised army, but to keep out raiding parties, foragers, plundering tribesmen; and the labour of building such a wall may be regarded as directly proportionate to the numbers and strength of the spoilers beyond it.

Hadrian's Wall was probably completed about the year 128, and a dozen years later Roman policy again became aggressive when Lollius Urbicus—governor of Britain under the Emperor Antoninus Pius—advanced to the waist between Forth and Clyde and built the Antonine Wall along the line of Agricola's old forts. It was a smaller, cheaper copy of Hadrian's Wall, though protected by a larger ditch, but apparently it was built to mark a new frontier, and the necessity for a new frontier was due to an alarming increase, in numbers and activity, of the tribes who lived between the walls in the southern uplands. The uplands had been opened, to some extent, by roads that Agricola built in his first incursion, and now the tribes were raising hill-forts in the upper basins of the rivers Annan and Clyde and Tweed. It seems clear that the Romans discerned a purposive menace in this fortification of the hills, and Lollius dealt drastically with it by a campaign, or series of campaigns, in which large numbers of the upland dwellers were seized and deported to Germany. The Antonine Wall, finished by 144 and stiffened by nineteen forts, thus became the frontier of a roughly pacified, emasculated land, and its garrison could rely, if there was need, on ready support from the greater wall behind.

But the Antonine Wall was not invulnerable. Overrun from the north, it was reoccupied, but finally abandoned before the great disaster which befell Roman Britain when its incompetent, vain governor, Clodius Albinus, withdrew much of its garrison to have himself proclaimed emperor at Lyons. Speedily defeated by the African, Septimius Severus, Clodius committed suicide and Hadrian's Wall, left undefended by his folly, was wrecked in a furious insurgence of the native people whom its frowning ramparts had too long confined. The tribes of south-eastern Scotland, known as the Maeatae, overran the northern parts of Roman Britain, but a new governor bribed them to go home again, and rebuilt the wall. Much of it, razed to the foundations, had to be built anew.

In 208 the Emperor Severus came into Britain to repeat the policy which Calgacus had denounced: to make a desert in the north and call it peace. His campaign was arduous, he may have marched as far as the Moray Firth, but he failed to bring the Caledonians to decisive action. They had learned guerrilla tactics, they harried and tormented his army and wore it down. Severus, old and exhausted, died in York in 211; but for nearly a hundred years Hadrian's Wall was firmly held and that frontier was maintained. Though the grim African had not defeated his enemies in battle, he had disabled or daunted them.

Towards the end of the century new names appear in history, and those who then broke through the wall—when another would-be usurper had withdrawn its garrison—are called Picts and Scots. The Scots came from Ireland; the origin of the Picts has been much disputed, but both made a permanent habitation of the land they came to, and in the latter part of the fourth century, when Roman Britain was increasingly perplexed by barbarian assault, the Picts attacked from the north, the Scots from the west, and Saxons in the south-east. The Emperor Theodosius and the regent Stilicho made valiant efforts to restore a civilised authority, but it was no longer possible to hold the Wall. Claudian, the last Latin poet of any distinction, wrote in praise of Stilicho in the year 400, declaring that his stout rule had dispelled from

[6]

Britain all fear of Pict or Scot or Saxon; and Stilicho may indeed have established his power as far north as York. But that success was evanescent, and by the end of the first quarter of the fifth century Rome's power in Britain had gone for ever.

Scotland had never been part of the Roman province. Agricola and Severus had penetrated far into the Highlands, and for fifty years the lands south of Forth and Clyde had lain behind the Antonine Wall; but fleeting contact with the legions and a brief occupation of the south had left no imprint of Roman civilisation. Rome had inured the Maeatae and the Caledonians to war, and let them acquire, perhaps, a fleeting acquaintance with the advantages of coalition. It seems probable, also, that Roman influence in the extreme south-west allowed the missionary bishop Ninian to establish an outpost of Christian teaching at Whithorn in Galloway. Roman benefaction went no further.

Chapter 2

How long had Scotland been inhabited before the Romans came, and who were its first people, are matters for the archaeologist. By their scanty remains and the relics of their burial-places he can identify some of them and trace their progress. All that may be said here is that there is evidence of a boldly wandering people of the New Stone Age who adventured out of the Mediterranean and found a coastwise route, by Spain and Portugal to Brittany and the shores of Ireland, and so to the northernmost parts of Scotland where, on the mainland of Orkney, they built the chambered tomb called Maeshowe, which is the ultimate triumph of megalithic architecture. A little while later a migration that probably began about 1800 B.C. brought a round-headed race to the east coast, whose burial habits were distinctive and who furnished their short grave-boxes with pots or beakers.

Mobility must be accepted as a characteristic of pre-history, and as trade-routes were established the use of metal was introduced, and metal users mingled with or ousted their neolithic predecessors. In comparison with many parts of the continent the Bronze Age made little impression on Scotland, but the Iron Age, which may have had its beginning about 300 B.C., greatly increased its population, facilitated agriculture, and possibly created a ruling class and a taste for war. There are gaps and guesses in the archaeological timetable, and the theories of any one generation are liable to change or modification by later discovery. It is commonly accepted, however, that about the time of Julius Caesar's reconnaissance in force in 55 B.C. all Britain was inhabited by people who spoke a Celtic language; the two main variants of which have provided philologists with endless matter for disagreement.

That a common language need not imply racial unity is made evident by Tacitus, who explicitly states that the Caledonians were distinguished by reddish hair and large limbs; the Silures of South Wales were swarthy of countenance with hair that curled; and the people of eastern

England resembled the Belgae of Gaul. Under a generalised Celtic culture, that is, the island of Britain contained a hotch-potch of peoples, many related in origin, others of different stock, and among comparatively recent arrivals there still survived elements, most probably interbred, of previous cultures. But the hotch-potch was not static. Popular movement was not halted by the coming of the Romans, and the ethnic tides still flowed.

In the year 297 the presence in the north of the Picts and Hiberni —the Scots from Ireland—was recorded by a Latin writer called Eumenius; and as no Roman after Severus ventured into the remoter parts of Scotland—and Severus certainly went no farther than the Moray Firth—the Picts, who were associated with the Caledonians of the north, may well have been domiciled in Caithness and Sutherland for many generations. Dispute about their origin has fomented endless, inconclusive, and often irascible debate, and their very name is suspect. *Picti* may be Latin for the name by which they called themselves, or a Roman epithet for those who painted or tattooed their skins; tattooing seems indeed to have been their habit. They made their home in the extreme north and the eastern Lowlands of Scotland, and by the early years of the eighth century they had so grown in power and numbers that the Venerable Bede recognised them as one of the four peoples of Britain; the others being the Britons, the Scots, and the Angles. It is clear, therefore, that an attempt must be made to explore the Pictish background.

The two main variants of the Celtic language are known as Goidelic or 'Q' Celtic, the mother-tongue of Irish and Scottish Gaelic; and Brittonic or 'P' Celtic, spoken by the people of Gaul and Roman Britain, and the mother-tongue of Welsh and Breton. The majority of Celtic scholars now believe that Pictish was a 'P' Celtic language and, among other sources, find evidence for their belief in the numerous survival of non-Goidelic place-names in that part of Scotland between the Forth and the Moray Firth which has been called the Pictish heartland. The prefix *Aber*, as in Aberdeen, is not Goidelic, and the many names which begin with *Pit*—as Pittenweem and Pitsligo—may derive from the early 'P' Celtic of the tribes who later divided to settle in Gaul and Britain. Such philological argument has been used to propose, if not to prove, an origin for the Picts in the Iron Age Hallstatt culture. At Hallstatt in the Austrian province of Salzburg a rich lode of ethnic ore has been uncovered, and migrants endowed with its culture went to the south-east and east coasts of England from where they may later have moved to those parts of Scotland beyond the Forth-Clyde waistline.

The philologist, however, may not ignore the historian who has discerned a foreign habit in the system of succession practised in the Pictish kingdom, which was matrilinear; descent was registered through the mother, and that was not a Celtic custom. The historian, moreover, can find embarrassing evidence that Pictish, so far from being a variant of the Celtic language, was a foreign tongue. In the latter half of the sixth century St. Columba undertook many journeys into the lands of the northern Picts to essay their conversion, and on the authority of Adamnan, his biographer, he had, on at least two occasions, to employ an interpreter. Columba spoke 'Q' Celtic, and if 'P' Celtic had been the language of the Pictish king they could surely have debated without an intermediary. But Adamnan, whose life of Columba was written in the last years of the seventh century, is as unequivocal about the need for interpretation as was the Venerable Bede, some thirty years later, when in his *Ecclesiastical History* he asserted that Pictish was a language distinct from Gaelic, Brittonic, and English. Now Bede, in his monastery at Jarrow, had had many dealings with the Gaelic-speaking church of Iona, and in his time the Picts were an important nation that had often met the Northumbrians in bloody conflict. Bede, a scrupulous historian, knew what he was talking about.

He himself believed the Picts had come into Scotland, by way of Ireland, from Scythia: but where he would have located Scythia is not known, for as a geographical term it had no fixed frontiers and the Scythians, whoever they were, were always nomadic. According to an obscure Roman-British writer called Gildas, who probably died in 570, the Picts were people who came overseas from the north; and Nennius, a British churchman born in the latter half of the eighth century, declared they came first to Orkney, and from those northern islands laid waste many regions and occupied a third of Britain. It must be admitted that neither Gildas nor Nennius inspire any confidence in their writings, but their ascription of a boreal origin for the Picts coincides with the opinion of Roman authors, who always associated them with the Caledonians of the north; and there is archaeological evidence, of a very striking sort, for the arrival of seaborne aggressors —powerful, unidentified, but they may have been Picts—in the farthest parts of Britain during the last century B.C. and the first century A.D.

In Caithness, Orkney, Shetland, and the Hebrides there are the numerous remains of those ingeniously and laboriously constructed forts, called brochs, which have provoked almost as much argument as the Picts themselves. Only one survives, in the Shetland island of

Mousa, in approximately its original shape, and the Mousa broch is a round tower with double walls and no opening in its outer wall but one guarded door. It rises to a height of over forty feet and has a diameter, at ground level, of about fifty feet. The number of ruined brochs has been estimated at about ninety in Shetland, a hundred in Orkney, perhaps two hundred and thirty in Caithness and Sutherland, and forty in the Hebrides. If all had survived as successfully as the Mousa broch the north-eastern corner of Scotland and the islands beyond it would be guarded by four or five hundred shrewdly designed, well constructed, and impressively tall forts whose primary purpose was manifest. They were built to defend the land against a seaborne enemy; their distribution makes this assertion incontestable.

It used to be thought that the Picts were the builders of the brochs, but the assumption became untenable when the distribution of the brochs was compared with the distribution of the many sculptured stones whose elaborate carving has preserved not only the distinctive *motifs* of their ritualistic art, but the manner of their costume and the spirited style of Pictish horsemen. In later centuries the Picts practised an intricate and formal art. They were strangely addicted to carving symbols which resemble a looking-glass and a comb and crescent moons, often filled with mushroom shapes, which are split by thunder-bolts or branching arrows. Fish, falcons, snakes, geometrical designs, and figures not unlike an embryonic elephant may accompany the crescent moons; and beside cavaliers on high-stepping horses go the hieratic figures of a grim priesthood. But these bewildering and splendid relics are chiefly found between the Moray Firth and the river Tay, and there are no brochs there. The broch-builders lived only in the far north and the islands, but the Picts took all the land from Shetland to the Forth-Clyde waistline.

It is tempting to assume that Picts or proto-Picts were indeed the seaborne aggressors against whom the brochs were raised, and whose assault the Iron Age broch-builders failed to withstand. There is indeed no other people of known importance capable of major enterprise before the third century who can be charged with so momentous an invasion; for the Romans offered no menace from the sea that could have provoked the building of such a palisade of fortresses. Though the philologists will not be persuaded that the Picts were a northern, mari-time people, and though philological argument cannot lightly be dis-regarded—for it is gravely academic and almost as elaborate as Pictish sculpture—the archaeologists have deciphered what may be evidence that the incomers were indeed of alien stock.

On a sculptured stone, discovered in Lunnasting on the mainland of

Shetland, there is an inscription carved in the Ogham script which has been transliterated as: *ettocuhetts ahehhttannn hccvvevv nehhtons*.[1]

The last word is a Celtic name, but the others—if the transliteration is accurate—bear no resemblance to any known tongue. It may be a relic of a Bronze Age language that Celtic invaders from the south, enriched with the Hallstatt culture, superstitiously preserved for some inconceivable ritual; but perhaps more probably it is the ancestral language of a seaborne people who spoke a non-Indo-European language and kept it alive—after finding a more accommodating vocabulary—as the speech of a haunted priesthood.

It could only have been spoken, one feels, with considerable difficulty, and if the Picts were burdened with such a jargon they may have been quick to recognise the advantage of abandoning it in favour of 'P' Celtic.

[1] *The Problem of the Picts.* F. T. Wainwright.

Chapter 3

O<small>F</small> the four peoples identifiable in the early years of the eighth century in what is now Scotland, the Picts lived beyond the waist; the Angles occupied the northern part of the Northumbrian kingdom that stretched from the Humber to the Forth; the Britons of Strathclyde had the lands between Dumbarton on the Clyde and the Solway, with possibly some territory farther south; and the Scots, who had come from Ireland, had established the kingdom of Dalriada, which roughly consisted of Argyll and the nearer isles.

It was probably in the fifth century that the Scots of northern Ireland invaded Argyll and began to rule their new-won lands from the rude strongholds of Dunadd, at the root of the long peninsula of Kintyre, and Dunollie, opposite the Sound of Mull. But Dalriada got its greatest strength, and sanctity too, from Columba, the princely abbot of Iona who, after excommunication by an Irish synod, went with twelve disciples to that small green island off the Ross of Mull—an island facing the Atlantic over a white fringe of sand—and made of its loneliness one of the great creative centres of learning and Christianity.

Born of the royal blood of Ireland, Columba was a man of aggressive temper, active and authoritarian, with a voice—it is piously recorded— of miraculous power. He was in his early forties when he arrived in Iona, in the year 563, and for thirty-four years he laboured to convert the northern Picts and established the ecclesiastical rule of a monastic church in which abbots enjoyed a larger jurisdiction than bishops, though bishops were clearly of a superior grade to presbyters. The most famous of his deeds among the heathen is his conversion of Brude, king of the northern Picts, in his capital on Loch Ness; and the rulers of Dalriada seem to have acknowledged his authority in the secular affairs of their kingdom. When Conall the king died in 574, his successor was Aidan, whom Columba chose and ordained in preference to his brother; and under Aidan the Scots revealed an ambitious spirit and pursued an expansive policy.

They thrust eastwards into farther lands, along the valley of the Forth, and seem to have won much territory from the southern Picts. They launched an attack on Orkney, which must indicate a northward extension of their power on the west coast; and they fought, but lost their battle, against the Pictish people of Angus. Aidan's adventurous reign came to an end, however, when he challenged Ethelfrith of Northumbria, and in 603 was utterly defeated in the southern uplands. For an appreciable time—for a matter of seventy or eighty years—Northumbria seemed likely to become the predominant power in all Britain, and so great were its subsequent achievements, in scholarship and art and polity, that one may even regret its failure. A middle kingdom between the Humber and the Forth, that divided Britain into three, might have given the island a happier future and societies more contentedly based on ethnic relationship. But that was not to be. Northumbria grew, then shrank again, and the country that was to become Scotland, having contributed to its growth, finally despoiled it of half its territory.

Ethelfrith, who discomfited Aidan, defeated the Britons at Chester, in or about the year 613, and thereby extended his dominions to the west coast and separated the Britons of Wales from those of Strathclyde. But Northumbria was a union of two kingdoms, Bernicia in the north and Deira in the south, and again and again dynastic rivalry divided it. Ethelfrith, a Bernician, was defeated by Edwin, of the royal house of Deira, and Edwin ruled or dominated the greatest confederation yet seen in England. But when he fell in battle with the Britons he was succeeded by Oswald of Bernicia who, in his years of exile, had been sheltered in Iona and there had received Christian baptism. From Iona he brought monks to restore Christianity in Northumbria, and for a few years was recognised as overlord of England. He too died in battle, but his victor, Penda of Mercia, was in due course killed by Oswald's brother Oswiu, who in his turn became overlord and propagated the faith brought from Iona among the heathen Saxons.

Under his son Ecgfrith Northumbrian expansion to the south was halted, but both Oswiu and Ecgfrith took large slices of Pictish territory, and according to Bede the Scots of Dalriada and the Britons of Strathclyde both recognised the supremity of Ecgfrith. But in 685 Ecgfrith, quite literally, went too far, and in Nechtanesmere, near Forfar, he was killed and his invading army totally defeated. Aldfrith, an illegitimate son of Oswiu, succeeded to a diminished kingdom, defended its narrowed frontiers, and preserved its cultural heritage to enrich the great age of Bede. Aldfrith, like Oswald before him, had lived in Iona, and in Northumbria reinforced its sturdy growth of Celtic scholarship and piety. After him the succession became erratic, but learning survived and by the second half of the eighth century English teachers exerted great influence in foreign parts. The Church established by Columba and nurtured in Northumbria had spread its doctrine far.

Northumbria was still a single state, with its northern frontier on the Firth of Forth, in 840, when the Picts and Scots were about to become united under Kenneth mac Alpin, king of Scots. Little can be said with certainty about the unification of the Picts themselves, who at the time of Columba's arrival were recognisably two peoples; pagan in the north, but in the south the heirs, at long remove, of St. Ninian's Christian teaching. It is possible, however, that a dominant king was already recognised, for there is a *Pictish Chronicle*—parts of which are considered trustworthy by modern scholars—that preserves a royal catalogue from about 550, and much of it is corroborated by Irish chronicles. By 685, when the Picts under Brude mac Bile so decisively beat Ecgfrith and his Northumbrians at Nechtanesmere, it is fairly certain that Pictland was a single kingdom, though the geography of Scotland must dispel any thought of a centralised government that exercised a uniform authority, and in the circumstances of the time it would be foolish to suppose that all men lived peacefully with their neighbours.

The Irish *Annals of Tigernach* declare that in 736 Angus, son of Fergus, king of the Picts, laid Dalriada waste and took the old Scottish fortress of Dunadd; and twenty years later Symeon of Durham reports that another Angus, in alliance with a Northumbrian monarch, marched against Dumbarton and forced the Britons to accept their terms. That the Picts were the major power in Scotland is evident from the extent of their territory, which was much larger than Scottish Dalriada; but their rulers became less Pictish than their kingdom, and the Pictish monarchy was weakened by the rule of matrilinear succession. It was the females of the royal house who carried the seed of kingship, and when a nameless queen married a foreigner—as often she did—her son's Pictish blood would be diluted, and with her heir might be born dynastic rivalry. The Pictish queens were apparently unconscious of racial differences, for the mother of Talorcan, who was king in 653, had married a son of Ethelfrith of Bernicia; Brude mac Bile was the son of a British king of Strathclyde; and Dalriadic Scots probably fathered other of the Pictish monarchs. It may be, indeed, that the royal ladies of Pictland were persistently exogamous, and that would explain, in some degree, this union of Picts and Scots under Kenneth mac Alpin; though as he became king in Dalriada in 841, and king of the Picts in 843, his acceptance was probably enforced by his own soldierly strength and aptitude. For several years there was resistance to his rule, and it was not until 850 that the united kingdom was established and Kenneth, the son of forty kings in Dalriada—if his genealogy can be trusted—ruled all the land beyond Forth and Clyde.

We know nothing, except by inference, of the people he ruled; but their relative antiquity must not prompt the inference that they were a savage, primitive people. That they were not civilised in any fashion comparable with those anciently established in Egypt and Mesopotamia must be accepted; for the Celtic ethos was averse from the habits of close association and purposive industry that prompt the building of cities and the interlocking associations of urban life. But authority, both temporal and spiritual, was recognised, and the catalogue of the kings, of both Picts and Scots, proves their sense of a proud identity, of continuity from a distant past, and there is no extravagance in believing that bards and genealogists provided much of their entertainment when the weather was too harsh for hunting.

The Scots of Dalriada shared the legendary tales of Ireland, but no trace survives of a Pictish epic, and that is doubly unfortunate; for even fragments of a Pictish *Beowulf* would illuminate, if only with a small and flickering light, the puzzle of their origin. But no clue remains to the temper of a vigorous people, save the intricate and masterly designs carved into their sculptured stones; and they are incontrovertible evidence that the Picts had a culture which found expression in vivid works of art. It was an art that embraced a stylised naturalism—in its depiction of animals, horsemen, and archers—a stereotyped symbolism, and elaborately formal ornamentation; and what is one to make of that? Perhaps their habit of speech was also formal and ornate.

Families, it is probable, lived together in small groups, not in isolation. Their lives were dominated by the seasons and social obligation, by agriculture or their flocks and herds, by hunting and fishing; and their thoughts by superstition, weatherlore, gossip, and ancestral tales, and the faith brought from Ireland by Columba. In its dawn the Christian message that death had been defeated and sin forgiven may have wakened a mood of generous exhilaration—the Pictish horsemen indeed prance with fine assurance on their stones—and the permissive exogamy suggested by a custom of matrilinear succession would surely preclude too harsh a definition of sexual morality. The masculine dignity of Pictish sculpture may have been happily accompanied by the liberalism of a society in which women had much freedom as well as the inescapable burden of daily toil.

Chapter 4

THOUGH Kenneth mac Alpin may be granted military skill of a high order, his acquisition of a united kingdom was facilitated by the arrival of a new and very unruly element in Scotland. In 794 the Annals of Ulster record the 'devastation of all the islands of Britain by the gentiles'—the Norsemen, that is—and though Celtic imagination must be chided for exaggeration, the Norsemen went far to justify it in subsequent years. Iona and Skye were pillaged in 795, other Hebridean islands in 798; and in 802 and 806 the pirates came again to Iona, to burn and slay. These early raiders were followed, after an interval of some thirty years, by more purposive attack. In 836 Kenneth sent to Ireland for assistance—though Ireland too was being plundered—and in 839 there was a battle in Argyll in which Picts and Scots, fighting together against the Norsemen, were heavily defeated. It is probable that Norse or Danish vikings had also plundered and fought on the east coast; and if Pictland was menaced on one side, Dalriada on the other, a defensive coalition under a strong king would be the natural response.

The Norse explosion was about to change the face and condition of all western Europe, and Scotland's geographic situation invited early attack. The two northern archipelagos of Orkney and Shetland were probably colonised by peaceful settlers before 800, and thereafter used by vikings as advanced bases for assault on the Hebrides, the Isle of Man, and Ireland. Within a hundred years of the first settlers' arrival Orkney became the seat of a Norse earldom that substantially influenced affairs in the north, and by 900, or thereabout, the far corner which is now Caithness and Sutherland had been conquered and was temporarily held by Sigurd of Orkney and Thorstein the Red, a viking of noble family whose grandfather, Ketil Flatnose, had lately established himself in the Hebrides.

Of the constitution of the early kingdom of Scotland little is known beyond a tradition that it was divided into the seven provinces of Atholl, Strathearn, Fife, Angus, Mar, Moray, and Caithness, each under

[17]

a kinglet who acknowledged the high king of Kenneth's line. If this can be accepted as a loose description of the administrative divisions of the kingdom in the latter part of the ninth century it must be admitted that Kenneth's regality had already suffered loss, for there is no mention of Argyll and the Western Isles. In the north and east the provincial rulers were later known as *mormaers*, a title that may be translated as steward, and the appointment of a *mormaer* in Lennox—the lands north of Dumbarton that face the estuary of the Clyde—suggests an explanation of these stewardships. It seems probable that they were created to tighten administration of the kingdom and stiffen its defences: the Western Isles had been lost, and if Argyll was so closely menaced as to prevent effective government, then the stewardship of Lennox was the defended frontier that guarded the Clyde; while in the north the *mormaers* of Caithness and Moray were guardians of the lands threatened by the growing power of the Norse earldom of Orkney.

For some time the kings of Kenneth's line appear to have observed a rule of succession that Pictish habit may have influenced, for brother was followed by brother, uncle by nephew or cousin by cousin. In the reign of Constantine II—seventh in succession from Kenneth—the kingdom was humiliated by an English invasion when Athelstan, grandson of Alfred the Great, revealed a heroic ambition and crossed the border. Athelstan, who styled himself *Rex totius Britanniae*, had already, in 927, exacted recognition of his supremacy from Constantine and the king of Strathclyde, and won possession of York, a city that the Danes had taken in 866. His authority was acknowledged by the Welsh, he defeated the rebellious Britons of Cornwall, and when confronted by the powerful alliance of resurgent Scotland, Strathclyde, and the Norsemen of eastern Ireland, he broke their strength in the great battle of Brunanburh; a site not certainly identified, though probably it was somewhere on the Solway. According to the *Anglo-Saxon Chronicle* he had, before the battle, led his army on a triumphal march as far as Fordun in Kincardineshire, while his fleet went farther still and harried the coast of Caithness; but as a triumph is more usually the sequel to a victory, it seems preferable to ante-date Brunanburh and ascribe the march rather than the battle to the year 937.

The English triumph had no material consequences, but in the magnification of hindsight it can be recognised as an early demonstration of the insecurity in which Scotland was destined to live. Had Northumbria survived there would have been a buffer state between the northern kingdom and the larger power of England; but Northumbria had shrunk and the collapse of the Norse kingdom of York—which used to be the Anglian kingdom of Deira—had opened the way to aggression from the south. Then, on two occasions, the Scots enlarged their danger by the voluntary acceptance of territories below the line of Forth and Clyde. In 945 Malcolm I, who succeeded Constantine II, accepted from Edmund, king of England, a lease in Cumbria of lands south of the Solway when Edmund needed an ally to prevent the Norsemen of Ireland from joining their cousins in Northumbria; and at some time after 971 Kenneth II received from Edgar, king of England, Edmund's son, the astonishing gift of Lothian: the land, that is, between the Forth and the Tweed. Edgar was a great king, a man of peace, devoted to the reform of the church and its benefactor. He, like Athelstan before him, had asserted his suzerainty over Scotland and shortly after his coronation Kenneth II, with the kings of Strathclyde and Cumbria and the ruling princes of Wales, had all submitted to him at Chester. Why, then, did he yield Lothian, the richest part of Northumbria, to the Scottish king? The apparent answer is that Edgar, a man of peace, wished to secure his kingdom by allegiance rather than war; but if the Scots still maintained, through alliance with Strathclyde, their influence in Cumbria, then Lothian was outflanked and virtually lost to England already.

To the great-grandsons of Kenneth mac Alpin and to their sons and grandsons, death came in battle or at the hands of the cousinly rival who succeeded them. An exception to that dismal rule was Malcolm II, son of Kenneth II, whose enterprising reign had a peaceful conclusion. Malcolm succeeded in 1005, and in the early years of his reign Sigurd, earl of Orkney, known as Sigurd the Stout, defeated Findlaec, *mormaer* of Moray. Sigurd was the son of Earl Hlodver and Edna, daughter of the Irish king Kjarval; and Sigurd married a daughter of Malcolm II by whom he had a son, Thorfinn, who became the greatest of the Orkney earls and took large parcels of Scotland for his own. In Malcolm's time England was sorely perplexed by the most worthless of its kings, Ethelred the Unready, and the persistent attack of Danes and Norsemen; and Malcolm saw an opportunity to add to his dominions. In 1006 he crossed the Tweed with a numerous army and laid siege to Durham. English Northumbria was ruled by Earl Waltheof —at some time a Norse or Danish adventurer had married into the ancient native family—and though Waltheof was too old for war, his son Uhtred was able to rout the invaders so decisively as to warrant a vainglorious celebration of victory. The palisades surrounding Durham were decorated with the severed heads of the Scots, all washed and neatly combed.

Malcolm's unscrupulous gamble had failed, but in 1018, at Carham on the Tweed, he and Owen, king of Strathclyde, defeated

Uhtred and reasserted Scotland's title to that perilous frontier on the river. With ruthless severity, indeed, he did what he could to safeguard it by laying waste all the lands between Tweed and Tees; and though in 1031 the great Cnut of Denmark—who had become king of England in 1016—invaded Scotland and according to the *Anglo-Saxon Chronicle* secured Malcolm's submission, that submission, if indeed it was made, was no more than a gesture; for Cnut made no attempt to regain Lothian and Scotland's frontier was still the river-line. Owen of Strathclyde died soon after the battle at Carham and Malcolm set Duncan, his grandson, on its throne as 'king of the Cumbrians'; and in 1034, when Malcolm died and was buried in Iona, the Irish *Annals of Tigernach* lauded him as 'the honour of all the west of Europe'.

Duncan succeeded to a kingdom that included all the mainland of what is now Scotland, except that province in the north which the earls of Orkney ruled; some parts of Argyll; and perhaps most of Galloway. Also in his domain was an undefinable portion of Cumbria, south of the present border; but on none of his territories was his hold as secure as Malcolm's had been, and for this insecurity Malcolm was to blame.

Malcolm made Duncan his heir in defiance of custom. Had the conventional pattern of succession been maintained—by which succession alternated between different branches of the family tree planted by Kenneth mac Alpin—the throne would have gone to the line of his cousin, Kenneth III, whom Malcolm had killed. Kenneth was survived by a nameless grandson, who was conveniently murdered on the eve of Duncan's enthronement, and a granddaughter, Gruoch, who married Gillecomgan, *mormaer* of Moray. He too met a violent death, and his son, Lulach, was a child whose claim could not seriously be entertained.

Now Malcolm had three daughters, of whom Bethoc—married to Crinan of Dunkeld—was the mother of Duncan; Donada married Findlaec of Moray, the uncle of Gruoch's husband, Gillecomgan, and their son was Macbeth; and the third daughter (name unknown) was the mother, by Sigurd of Orkney, of Earl Thorfinn. The dispute that followed was a family affair, exacerbated by the fact that Malcolm, after killing Gruoch's grandfather, had had her brother murdered; and the dispute was palpably thickened, the quarrel sharpened, when Gruoch married Macbeth, her first husband's cousin. Macbeth was also cousin to Duncan and to Thorfinn of Orkney, and by his marriage he acquired responsibility for the feud that Gruoch had inherited.

Duncan fell out with his cousin Thorfinn, and there was war between them in which Duncan's strength was deeply bled. Then Macbeth, with his own claim to the throne and a family feud to encourage it, took up the quarrel, and Duncan was defeated and killed in battle near Elgin. Macbeth succeeded and for seventeen years ruled well, but ruled a diminished realm; for in the south Strathclyde and its Cumbrian appendage seem to have been held for Duncan's sons, and a great part of the north—all, perhaps, north and east of the Tay —lay within Thorfinn's realm.

Then Duncan's line revived. He had married, it seems, the sister of Siward, a Danish earl of Northumbria, who probably gave his sons shelter; and in 1054 Siward made war on Macbeth, but died before his offensive had much effect. It may be presumed, however, that Malcolm, Duncan's elder son, continued to get help from Northumbria, for in 1057 he invaded Scotland in sufficient strength to defeat and kill Macbeth in battle near Lumphanan in Aberdeenshire. He succeeded to the throne as Malcolm III and fortified his title by marrying Ingibjorg, daughter of Thorfinn of Orkney. She probably brought him a handsome dowry, for Thorfinn, who may have lived till 1065, is said to have ruled nine earldoms in Scotland, all the Western Isles as well as Orkney and Shetland, and a great realm in Ireland. But his large dominion fell into pieces when he died, and on the mainland most of it seems to have resumed allegiance, without serious contest, to the Scottish king.

Malcolm III, known as Malcolm Canmore, or Great-head, was to reign for thirty-five years, and in that time Scotland emerged from the obscurity of its formative years, and entered the more brightly illuminated, yet still perilous epoch that Duke William of Normandy initiated when he defeated Harold of England at the battle of Hastings.

Chapter 5

MALCOLM II's bold resolve to discard a devious rule of succession in favour of the right of primogeniture—which had darkened Duncan's reign with a family feud—was triumphantly justified by Malcolm Canmore's inheritance of the kingdom. Malcolm's only rival, by blood, was Gruoch's son, Lulach, whose abilities were slight —he was known as Lulach the Fool—and he was killed a year after the fall of Macbeth. Then, before 1070, Ingibjorg, Thorfinn's daughter, died; and Malcolm was free to marry a young woman whose distinguished ancestry was matched, or overmatched, by her own remarkable character.

Margaret, who became his queen, was the daughter of Edward the Atheling and granddaughter of the warrior-king of Wessex, Edmund Ironside. Fleeing from the hostility of Cnut, the Danish conqueror of England, Edward found refuge in Hungary and there married Agatha, a lady of the imperial house—possibly a granddaughter of Stephen, king of Hungary—who bore him a son and two daughters. In 1056 he returned to England, where his uncle, Edward the Confessor, was king; but the Atheling was mysteriously prevented from going to court and soon died of an unknown cause. His son Edgar was the natural heir to the English throne, but when the Confessor died in 1066 Edgar was still a boy, and in the circumstances of the time, with war imminent, his claim was overshadowed by military necessity. After William of Normandy's victory at Hastings, Edgar took an oath of loyalty to him, but two years later he and his mother and his two sisters fled from England and, by the arbitration of foul weather, arrived in the Firth of Forth and found shelter at the court of Malcolm Canmore. Within a year or two his sister Margaret was married to the Scottish king and Edgar had become a guest whose political ambition was perhaps less embarrassing than his native ineptitude.

Though Edgar's presence at the Scottish court invited the hostility of England's Norman king, Malcolm had needed no extraneous excuse for warlike enterprise. Five years before the conquest of England he had invaded Northumbria, and that was the first of five incursions. He and William both made fearful havoc in the north of England, and William may have had a better excuse for the barbarity of his warfare. Malcolm tried to create a new frontier south of the Tweed, and when England was still at odds after the Norman conquest, he would have been better advised to seek his purpose by negotiation and alliance rather than by war. But William, when he devastated Yorkshire and the north, was impelled by fear for the safety of his troubled realm.

In 1069 Sweyn Estrithson, king of Denmark, who still cherished a claim to the English throne, sent a great fleet into English waters, and in Yorkshire an English army gathered to face it; one of its leaders was Edgar the Atheling. William had to buy peace from the Danes, but the English dissidents were fearfully punished and much of the north of England was left a blackened desert. Then Cumbria was laid waste by Malcolm, and so many English captives were driven over the border that there was hardly a house in Scotland—or so said an English chronicler—that had not an English slave.

On two occasions Malcolm was punished for his depredations, and forced to make submission to an English king. In 1072 William the Conqueror invaded Scotland, and at Abernethy on the Tay Malcolm did homage and gave as his hostage Duncan, his eldest son by Ingibjorg, old Thorfinn's daughter. And nineteen years later, when William's abominable son, William Rufus, was on the throne of England, another English invasion compelled Malcolm to do homage again. On neither occasion, however, can the nature of his submission be clearly defined. Malcolm was possessed of estates in England, and for them he could have done homage without invalidating the independence of his kingdom. There were debatable lands, on either side of an uncertain border, to which, without much gravity in his submission, he may have acknowledged England's superior claim. It was certainly not the homage of a liegeman that he pledged—the admission of obligation to military service, that is—and simple homage seems often to have been little more than formal obeisance to the victor in a tourney. It is difficult, indeed, to resist the suspicion that an oath of allegiance, exacted under duress, was sometimes as easily uttered, and usually as frangible, as a politician's promises in the happier days of modern democracy; but on this occasion Malcolm was given no opportunity to break his word. William Rufus was the first to act, and in defiance of his own terms of peace he marched north, took Carlisle, and those parts of Cumbria south of the border, which he colonised from the south of England despite Malcolm's protests.

In his previous campaign a new castle had been built on the Tyne, and now another was raised at Carlisle. On both east and west, England had a guard against invasion, and when William Rufus fell ill, the fear of death induced in him a pacific mood to which Malcolm, in his old age, was ready to respond. Malcolm was invited to Gloucester, but by the time he arrived William had recovered both his health and his notoriously foul manners, and the Scottish king was refused an audience. He returned to his own country, led a last furious raid into Northumbria, and was killed in a Norman ambush with his son Edward beside him. Three days later Margaret his queen, already ill, died of grief in Edinburgh.

Nothing in Malcolm Canmore's life was of more abiding significance than his marriage to this remarkable woman. He by modest warfare had achieved nothing; in thirty-five years he had invaded the north of England five times, with never more than a limited objective, and the only consequence was the advancement of England's frontier, the building by England of defensive outposts at Newcastle and Carlisle. But Margaret, the English princess with a Hungarian mother, was an innovator, and despite the rebellion that followed her death, her innovations left their impression on her adopted country. She was a devout churchwoman, sympathetic with the rigorous and splendid rule of the Cluniac Benedictines, and she found much to deplore in the laxity and corruption of the Scottish church. With her continental background and her youthful memories of the court of Edward the Confessor, she saw Scotland as a poor and backward country, in sore need of discipline and charity, and like so many English women in similar circumstances, in the centuries that were to follow, she imposed her discipline and organised her charities. She insisted on a closer observance of the Sabbath than was customary in Scotland at that time, and on stricter marriage regulations. She complained that Lent had been shortened and the Easter Communion neglected; and because she had chosen the great Lanfranc, archbishop of Canterbury, as her spiritual father, she had the authority of his scholarship to support her demands and reinforce her argument.

There was no Norman blood in her, but she had her full share of the Normans' delight in splendour and in lavish donation to their church. She and Malcolm gave rich gifts to the cathedral of St. Andrews, repaired the ruined church of Iona, founded and handsomely endowed the abbey of the Holy Trinity at Dunfermline. Her court was furnished with many-coloured, ornamental cloths, and her table set with vessels of gold and silver. Foreign traders were encouraged, and new fashions evolved from the elegant materials of their commerce. But her charities were equally munificent, and the monk Turgot—subsequently bishop of St. Andrews and Margaret's biographer—records some incidents in her life which, if true, reveal an impulsive, warm-hearted woman more agreeable by far than the Cluniac disciplinarian who would suffer no profanation of the Sabbath.

Turgot's biography is overstuffed with pious reflection and fulsome adulation of the dead queen, and his account of the magnificence of her court is certainly exaggerated; though a few coloured hangings and some silver cups must have shown brightly against her Scottish background. But he describes her habit of supplementing her gifts to the poor by purloining what belonged to the king when her own store of clothing and money was exhausted, and that has a ring of truth unlike most of his sanctimonious panegyric. The king, says Turgot, was not offended by her well-intended robberies, and it can hardly be doubted that in her private charities, as in her public benefactions and reform of the church, she enjoyed Malcolm's complaisance and support. That her influence ruled their domestic life seems probable from the fact that of her six sons, four were given English names, the other two were Alexander and David after the heroes of Macedon and Israel. None had a Gaelic name, but *Alexander* and *David* were thereafter naturalised in Scotland; and Margaret herself was elected to sanctity by popular esteem before a pope had time to canonise her.

The death of Malcolm and his English queen was followed, however, by a Celtic revival or revolt of a sort that was to recur throughout Scottish history. Not yet had a Highland Line been drawn, to divide the people of the north and west from those of the south and east, but Margaret's reforming zeal, and Malcolm's youthful acquaintance with the southern parts of England, had brought about their court, not only new fashions in wear and worship, but new men, clerics, and others who spoke the French of Normandy and Brittany; and their influence was sufficient to create, in obstinately Celtic minds, a menace to the older habit of life, and determination to preserve it. Malcolm was succeeded, not by his eldest surviving son, but, in the ancient Celtic fashion of succession, by his brother Donald Bane; and a popular rising drove out 'all the English who before were with King Malcolm', as the *Anglo-Saxon Chronicle* has it.

Donald Bane had been living in the Hebrides, remote from his brother's anglicised court, and he was joined, surprisingly, by Malcolm's son Edmund; a young man in revolt against his parents rather than progress. The others fled to England, where their half-brother Duncan—Ingibjorg of Orkney's son—had lived since William the Conqueror took him as a hostage for his father's good behaviour.

He, with the approval of William Rufus, enlisted an army of Normans and English, and early in 1094 drove out Donald Bane, and got himself precariously crowned. He promised to dismiss his alien followers, and the Celtic revengers took advantage of his weakness to ambush and kill him. Donald Bane regained his throne and named as his successor his nephew Edmund.

Inexplicably he then embroiled himself in English politics, and joined a Northumbrian rebellion against William Rufus. Donald was an old man of sixty who should have had more sense. But having become a king he apparently thought it incumbent on him to behave in a kingly way, and interfere with his neighbours. He chose the wrong side and suffered for it. The Northumbrians were defeated, and William Rufus, with what appears to be uncharacteristic generosity, gave his support to Edgar, the fourth son of Malcolm and Margaret, who marched north and after hard fighting took his Celtic uncle prisoner. While passing through Durham, Edgar is said to have been promised victory by St. Cuthbert, who appeared to him in a dream, and when Donald became his prisoner, he treated his uncle with relative leniency. Donald was not executed, but merely blinded and held in servitude.

Chapter 6

EDMUND, the renegade son of Malcolm, was allowed to die in a monastery. His brother Edgar took the Scottish throne, and was followed in turn by Malcolm's youngest sons, Alexander and David. It is significant that they have been generally regarded, or written of, not as their father's heirs, but as the sons of Margaret.

They were good kings, and by historians have been rightly praised. But they were, in fact, usurpers; for Edgar was given his throne by Anglo-Norman power, and the true heir was William, son of Duncan, Malcolm Canmore's eldest son by Ingibjorg of Orkney. But Edgar, despite the violence of his arrival, lived gently and ruled without tyranny. He died, unmarried, after nine years' reign in which the most memorable event was, perhaps, his gift of an elephant to the high king of Ireland. His mother's brother, Edgar the Atheling, had gone crusading and become friendly with the emperor of the Greeks: from him, it may be, Edgar of Scotland received that embarrassing gift, and courteously passed it on to Ireland.

At Edgar's death his brother Alexander became king, and David, as heir presumptive, acquired Cumbria and parts of Lothian. Seven years before, in November, 1100, their sister Maud had married Henry I of England, William the Conqueror's youngest son, and to that marriage the sons of Margaret owed much of their good fortune. Henry still felt the need to reinforce his title to the realm which his father had won by force of arms, and it could be substantiated, in a way, by marriage to a girl who was called, rather dubiously, an English princess and whose Scottish father might be ignored by stressing the fact that her great-grand-uncle was Edward the Confessor. Her brothers, who had spent part of their youth in England, were regarded with favour, not merely because of an acquired relationship, but also because they could guarantee the security of his northern frontier. For most of his reign, Henry I of England was bitterly engaged in the defence of his duchy of Normandy, and the friendship of Scotland was vital to his interest overseas. Alexander had not succeeded without acknowledging, in some degree, Henry's superiority and accepting some sort of vassalage; his queen, Sibylla, was one of Henry's many illegitimate daughters, and the marriage was childless.

His brother David was luckier in all ways. Apparently more gifted by nature, and more easily at home in the high fashion of Norman society, he was signally favoured, and richly endowed, in the politics of royal marriage, by alliance with Maud, widow of the earl of Northampton and daughter of the Conqueror's niece Judith, who had married Waltheof, earl of Northumbria, son of Siward the Dane. Waltheof, beheaded in reprisal for a revolt in which he took no part, was later venerated as a martyr; and Judith, daughter of the Conqueror's sister Adèle and the greatest heiress in England, brought to her second husband the two great earldoms of Northampton and Huntingdon.

David's junior share in Scotland—Cumbria and perhaps most of Lothian—gave him no trouble large enough for memory, but Alexander, ruling the lands beyond the Forth, was less fortunate. His northern and western frontiers may not have been very exactly defined, for Ross and Moray under their *mormaers* were almost independent, as was Argyll in the west. In the farthest north Caithness and Sutherland were still part of a Norse earldom, and in 1098 the late King Edgar had formally ceded the Hebrides to Magnus Bareleg, the adventurous king of Norway. Within its uncertain boundaries the heart of Scotland was still open to the assault of Celtic emotion, and early in his reign Alexander was attacked in his castle at Invergowrie by a Highland host, which he dispersed by a charge of horse and pursued through the hills to remote fastnesses in Ross. He had some aptitude in war, and was notably devout. Authoritarian by temper, he was extravagantly generous to his churches and monasteries, and to these Norman characteristics he added political sympathy with the Norman oligarchy at whose apex sat Henry of England. In 1114 Alexander joined his royal brother-in-law in a Welsh campaign against the king of Gwynedd, a campaign in which he had no interest other than his loyalty to the throne that his sister shared.

Under the sons of Margaret the Normanisation of Scotland proceeded with a curious lack of opposition; or, perhaps it would be more accurate to say, with no such opposition as to be remembered in a country which had not yet taken to writing its history. Normanisation meant the introduction of knight-service, the tenure of land by an acknowledged duty to the king. It implied the building of churches and castles, the stricter administration of church lands, and development of the monastic system. It was feudalism adapted to the Scottish climate, and therefore

[28]

a feudal structure looser than its English model; for the native Scots—
the original hybridisation of Pict and Celt—were less amenable to
discipline than their southern neighbours, and the incomers, the king's
new tenants, did not march in as conquerors, but as the king's friends.
To provoke unnecessary disturbance would have profited neither them
nor their master; and they were probably shrewd enough to refrain
from demanding too much from an alien people whose unknown
tongue let them preserve an essential independence. Beginning, as was
natural, in the south, Normanisation marched north over the Forth,
into the eastern Lowlands and eventually into the lowland parts of
Moray and Ross; but it never penetrated the true Highlands, unless
thinly by remote example. The origins of the clan system are obscure,
but Celtic monasticism was based on tribal ownership of a monastery,
and heredity governed the election of its abbots. From such ecclesiastical
beginnings the clan system may have come into being, and as early as
the eleventh century it appears to have become the pattern of an evolv-
ing society in the north and west. The chief of a clan derived authority
from his blood—the blood of preceding chiefs—and from election by
his clansmen or family; but the power of the chiefs may have been
enhanced, as if by infection, by the great power of Anglo-Norman
nobles in the neighbouring lowlands. If this were so, it was the
only feudal infection to penetrate the Highlands; for the clan system
must have included from the beginning some obligation of military
service.

While Alexander ruled the old heartland of Scotland, David, after
his marriage in 1114 to the Countess Judith's daughter, spent much
time in his English earldoms, and in the hunting-field found companions whom he would later bring to Scotland as its new nobility.
There were 'new men' in Northumbria, whom King Henry had
enfeoffed with broad acres to preserve the peace of an ever-turbulent
countryside, and among them, when David was in his own lands of
Lothian, he met those who, in the course of time, were to breed the
governing families of Scotland. There was the son of a Robert de Brus,
a Norman of the Cotentin peninsula, to whom the Conqueror had
granted many Yorkshire manors; and a neighbour of his was Bernard,
lord of Bailleul in Picardy. The Balliols and the Bruces were already
approaching the country in which their descendants would compete for
a doubtful throne, and as the Normans advanced, so did the outposts of
their feudal church. William of Normandy had established the close
relationship of state and church, and by his followers and their successors his policy was maintained. It was David, Norman by inclination
and a true son of Margaret, who brought Augustinians over the border

to found, at Jedburgh, a priory which, by mid-century, became an abbey.

At Alexander's court there were Norman officers of state, and he too showed favour to incomers from the south, and brought Augustinians to Scone when he rebuilt its old Culdee monastery. Shortly before his death he installed a French bishop at St. Andrews, and in token of his grant of land to its church he presented also his Arab charger,[1] which was led to the altar, richly caparisoned, and bearing his shield and armour: a symbol of the Norman chivalry that he represented in a country which had not been conquered, but parts of which would be absorbed into the contemporary feudal system.

He died, and David succeeded him in 1124. He inherited a kingdom which had been well prepared for the introduction of its new rulers. Norman theory and some degree of Norman practice had been domesticated. What now was required—in the opinion of David, earl of Huntingdon and Northampton—was organisation. He had learnt much from his brother-in-law, Henry of England, whose turbulent genius showed most clearly in the success with which he had imposed a feudal discipline by installing men of his own choice in positions of dignity, where they enjoyed the remuneration of the lands he had given them under a dominating awareness that all they held, they held by grace of the king, and owed him their service in return. To organise, with comparative success, a Norman state in Scotland, a new influx was required of men trained and taught in the Norman tradition. The Norman clerks and officials, and the few landowners—or tenants of the king—who were already established, had to be reinforced, and the influx had to be planted in lands removed, by an arbitrary judgement, from their native owners or tenants. David had abundant sources of such in his English earldoms, in the north of England, in his companions of the chase; but to bring them to Scotland, and install them in their territorial dignities without raising wide and bloody opposition, must have been a task to daunt anyone less than a king who had learnt, from Henry of England, both arrogant assurance and a royal skill in the choice of his subordinates.

The old centre of government was at Scone, not far from Perth, where from ancient times the kings had taken their seat—or, perhaps, set foot—on the Stone of Destiny which, by tradition, had been brought from Ireland by the earliest Scots conquerors. The Scottish kings were neither crowned nor anointed, but inaugurated in office with some forgotten ritual; and with a Celtic ritual, against which he protested, David was given his royal authority to introduce an alien

[1] *The Normans in Scotland*. R. L. G. Ritchie.

[30]

rule. One of the first, and probably the very first, of the 'new men' by whom his rule was to be established, was Robert de Brus, to whom he granted the vast lands of Annandale about the river Annan, that runs from the southern uplands to the inmost parts of the Solway Firth. The grant apparently included land beyond the Solway, in what is now England, and Robert de Brus became master of the western approach to Scotland. Also in attendance on David, when he took his seat or set his foot on the Stone of Destiny, were Randolf de Soules and Guillaume de Sommerville: the former was given the border lands of Liddesdale, the latter acquired a great territory in Lanarkshire.

These grants were the beginning of a wholesale redistribution of Scottish land, not only as vast estates but in small parcels in recompense for minor services. A troop of Norman names was domiciled that clerks and local pronunciation changed gradually into such familiar shapes as Gifford, Melville, Lindsay and Oliphant, Comyn and Crichton, Seton and Herries. A rebellion in Moray, by stubborn Celtic supporters of the old royal house, was easily suppressed and all Moray, falling into David's hands, was re-settled. A Fleming called Freskyn acquired a huge territory there, and founded the family *de Moravia* which was to play a vital part in the War of Independence; and related to him was the ancestor of the great house of Douglas. But the incomer whose descendants meant most to Scotland was Walter fitz Alan, the son of a knight of Brittany whose father had acquired lands in Norfolk and Shropshire. Alan was sometime sheriff of Shropshire, and when Walter, his second son, followed David to Scotland he became his dapifer or steward. He was given land which corresponds to the modern county of Renfrew, his office became hereditary, his successors took it as their name, and the fitz Alans of Brittany and Shropshire eventually became the royal Stewarts or Stuarts.

Except in Moray there is no evidence that military action was a preliminary to change of ownership or tenancy, and the explanation of the peace in which so vast a transference was effected is threefold or fourfold. David's manifest authority—an armed authority not to be gainsaid—must obviously explain much, and the indeterminate title by which a native or Celtic proprietor held his land may have been nearly as helpful. No native magnate held a written title; his authority may have rested only on the remembered strength of his father's or his grandfather's right hand; and in theory he had no right at all to claim ownership of land which originally was the common possession of a family or clan or tribe. A major factor was that neither the native magnate nor his tenants were, in general, expelled from their lands— the exception was Moray—but were merely obliged to accept the

[31]

imposition of new superiors, whose duty to the king would compel them to show reasonable consideration for his humble, working subjects; and though the presence of foreign authority might vex the spirit, there would be material benefit in a new security for life and goods that a king's officer could promise. Some of the re-allotted lands, moreover, may have been derelict and unoccupied; and others in the possession of heiresses who were glad to be given a Norman husband.

The Highland rebellion which had provoked the clearance and resettlement of Moray was led by Angus, earl of Moray, and Malcolm MacHeth, who are said to have commanded 5,000 men. The size of their army was probably exaggerated, but the nature of their revolt is not to be despised. In motive it was akin to the Celtic resentment which briefly set Donald Bane on the throne after the death of Malcolm Canmore and Margaret his queen; for Angus was a grandson of Lulach the Fool, of the old royal house, whom Malcolm Canmore had killed, and the rebel Malcolm was probably related to him. Highland opposition to the forces of enlightenment was still alive, though it had not the strength to resist the charge of Norman horsemen. This northern adventure was trivial, however, in comparison with David's campaigns in England after the death of Henry I, in 1135, had opened the way to civil war and anarchy.

Henry's daughter Matilda—at his death his one surviving legitimate child—had first married the Emperor Henry V, and subsequently Geoffrey of Anjou. After long debate Henry had named her as his heir, and David had sworn to support her. But William the Conqueror's daughter Adèle had married the count of Blois and borne him a son, Stephen, in many ways an excellent young man who, when of age, married Maud of Boulogne, who was the daughter of David's younger sister Mary. Stephen, rallying support with great promptitude, got himself crowned before Matilda reached England, and with the prospect of civil strife in England, David of Scotland found himself in the delicate position of an uncle whose two nieces were about to be at war with each other. At first he honoured his oath to Matilda, and simultaneously served the cause of his own country by invading the north of England, nominally in opposition to the usurper Stephen, but more usefully to seize the English fortresses of Newcastle and Carlisle, and all the land between. David had a son, the Earl Henry, who thought his mother—daughter of the martyred Waltheof and the Countess Judith—could claim Northumbria; and when, after negotiation, Stephen appeared to admit his claim, David established his headquarters in Carlisle.

There he conceived a bold and statesmanlike idea, which was nothing less than the recovery, for Scotland, of those northern parts of England which were regarded as its lost provinces. From all corners of his kingdom he mustered a great army, and advanced as far as Cowton Moor, not far from Northallerton, in Yorkshire. But there he was halted by the embattled Church of England, that feudal estate which William the Conqueror had so carefully nurtured. Thurstan, the archbishop of York, had commanded a muster of all the Norman landowners in the north, and at the Battle of the Standard—a standard which bore on its summit, above holy banners, the sacred Host—the Scottish king was defeated. Normans fought against Normans, and Norman archers on the English side were perhaps the deciding factor.

David returned to Carlisle, and there, by a family agreement, he and his son, the Earl Henry, were given what war had failed to give them. Maud, the wife of Stephen and daughter of David's younger sister, moved as it seems by affection for her Scottish uncle and his son, established peace by securing the grant of Northumberland to the Earl Henry and southern Cumbria, with Carlisle, to his father. The Scottish frontier ran, where Kenneth mac Alpin had hoped to establish it, from the Tyne to Derwent Water. The civil war in England went to and fro, and ten years later, in 1149, when the party of the sometime Empress Matilda was again dominant, there was a new agreement between David and Matilda's son, Henry of Anjou—subsequently Henry II of England—by which Henry swore that should he become king he would give David all the land between Tweed and Tyne, and southern Cumbria on the west.

But the Earl Henry died in 1152, his father David in 1135, and when Henry of Anjou became Henry II of England in 1154, he took a more realistic view of his deserts, and conveniently forgot his sworn oath. Malcolm IV, Earl Henry's son, was a boy eleven years old, and when Henry complained that he had been defrauded of a great part of his kingdom, Malcolm yielded the northern counties, and was poorly recompensed by confirmation of his titles to his father's earldom of Huntingdon. The Scottish border was withdrawn to the Tweed and the Solway, and that, for Scotland, was a disaster the effect of which would be felt for the next four hundred years. By the line from Tweed to Solway Scotland was too narrowly confined for the effective defence of some of its richest land, and of its capital city, when its capital was finally established in Edinburgh. With a frontier reaching from Newcastle to the high hills of the Lake District it would have added to its strength people of the same stock as their neighbours in

Lothian and northern Cumbria, and a territory permitting manoeuvre against English invasion. But a border between Berwick and the innermost corner of the Solway gave no such room, and a perpetual insecurity was Henry II's legacy to Scotland when he foreswore himself at the Treaty of Chester in 1157.

Chapter 7

W HEN the Earl Henry died, Malcolm, his eldest son, though only a boy, was formally presented, in the several provinces of Scotland, as heir to the kingdom. That was done by express command of King David, and may be taken as confirmation of the law of primogeniture. Malcolm IV, known as Malcolm the Maiden, announced his devotion to chastity, in the temper of Edward the Confessor, and revealed a spirited addiction to the ideals of chivalry. In his reign, of a dozen years, he suppressed another rising in the north; he went with Henry of England to war in France and was knighted at Tours; and returned to crush rebellion at home and discipline the turbulent, intractable men of Galloway. The alien temper of Argyll and the Western Isles was revealed when a seaborne army landed in Renfrew and sacked Glasgow; its leader was Somerled, a petty king of mixed Norse and Celtic blood, who had lately invaded the Isle of Man and defeated Godfrey its Norse king. Somerled's army was repulsed, and he himself killed, by Walter the Steward; but his title to a Hebridean dominion lived longer than he, and was claimed in succession by his descendants in Clan Dougall and Clan Donald, whose chiefs called themselves Lords of the Isles.

Malcolm died, unmarried, in 1165, and was succeeded by his brother William, a robust, red-haired young man, of martial spirit, romantic temper, and maladroit habit, who in his maturity is said to have become pious and peaceful. His benefaction to the church was limited to a single endowment, and his royal ability was equally modest. When the sons of Henry II discovered the typical Plantagenet difficulty of living amicably with their father, and rose in revolt, they were joined by William who invaded the north of England and by sheer folly got himself taken prisoner; caught at a disadvantage, he might well have escaped, but chose instead to charge. His horse went down, and William became an English captive.

Henry II, who had subdued family dissension, showed William no mercy. The Scots king was carried to Falaise in Normandy, and there Henry demanded that William should become his liege for Scotland and his other lands, and to ensure obedience, took the castles of Edinburgh and Stirling, Berwick, Roxburgh and Jedburgh, and garrisoned them with English troops at Scottish expense. William had no choice but to comply. His younger brother was also an English prisoner, neither was married, and long captivity would have been equivalent, not only to abdication, but also, in all probability, to extinction of the dynasty established by the sons of Margaret. So William submitted, and for fifteen years, till Henry's death, Scotland lived in feudal subjection to the English king.

William returned to a disaffected kingdom. Galloway, that remote, intransigent province, discovered cause for war within its own borders. The Scottish bishops refused to accept the Treaty of Falaise in so far as it commanded them to make submission to York and Canterbury, and were upheld by Pope Alexander III. In the conservative north a claim to the throne was put forward on behalf of Donald MacWilliam, a great-grandson of Malcolm Canmore and Ingibjorg of Orkney, and before he could effectively deal with that recurrent trouble, William had again to submit to humiliation. He, at the age of forty, had planned to marry, but Henry II, his feudal lord, disapproved of his choice and offered instead a French lady, Ermengarde de Beaumont, whom William was obliged to wed. Then he gathered an army to subdue the northern rebellion, and because Galloway was now pacified, or at least quiescent, a noble of that province marched with him and achieved the royal purpose by killing Donald MacWilliam near Inverness.

In 1198 Scotland emerged from feudal inferiority when Henry II died and the pope preached a holy war in reply to Saladin's capture of Jerusalem. Henry was succeeded by Richard Coeur-de-Lion, who was resolved to join the crusade, but could not afford it. William offered him 10,000 marks of silver for a charter renouncing the rights granted to Henry, and Richard released him from all his obligations. Scotland was again a free country, and when Richard went on his crusade he left the northern border of his kingdom secured by friendship.

Ten years later Richard died, and his brother John, that bad but not unskilful king, took the throne though the heir-of-line was Arthur, son of Geoffrey, his deceased elder brother, who had married Constance, the daughter of William's sister Margaret. John was accepted by England, but William apparently tried to take advantage of the dubious nature of his succession by claiming Northumberland. John temporised, Arthur was murdered, and in 1209 John, in aggressive

[36]

mood, marched north to demand satisfaction for Scottish opposition to some English castle-building; and William bought peace for 15,000 marks, a sum designed also to secure suitable marriages for his two daughters, perhaps to the sons of John. War with England was avoided, the princesses did not get their promised husbands, and again the north rose in revolt. The two kings remained on uneasy terms, and William Comyn, earl of Buchan, suppressed the northern insurgents. William the king was old and ill and died at last, in the last month of 1214, at the great age of seventy-two, leaving as his heir, Alexander, a boy of sixteen.

Alexander II supported the indignant barons of England against kingly irresponsibility in the revolt sealed by Magna Carta, and was meagrely rewarded with the assurance that his sister's interests would be safeguarded. Again there was dissension on the border, and the English harried Lothian; but after John's death, Alexander married his eldest daughter Joan, sister of Henry III. He revived Scotland's claim to the northern counties of England when Henry's barons rebelled against him, but war was again avoided and at York, in 1237, a lasting peace was concluded between the two countries. Alexander abandoned the old claim to Northumberland, Cumberland, and Westmorland, and the border was finally established on a line from Tweed to Solway, with wardens of the east, middle and west marches, three on either side, to preserve its peace if they could. Peace, in a general way, came into being, and though menaced from time to time, endured till the outbreak of the War of Independence in 1297. The most serious threat occurred in 1255, after the marriage of Alexander III, a boy of ten, to Henry III's daughter Margaret, a child of eleven. Henry tried to assert an authority over the young couple and their country, for which a parental relationship was the specious excuse, and on the Scottish side of the border there disconcertingly appeared a pro-English party inclined to accept his pretensions. Under the leadership of the Comyns, however, the Scottish party prevailed, with the help of a Welsh alliance when the Welsh were in revolt against Henry, and by wise counsel, or a common regard for self-preservation, a coalition of the two parties established a board of regency.

Under Alexander II an attempt was made to extend Scottish dominion to the Hebridean islands, over which Norway still claimed suzerainty, and in the following reign this led to the visible enlargement of Scots sovereignty, and Norwegian defeat at the so-called battle of Largs. The major achievement of the two kings lay in the material improvement of the kingdom, where sound administration brought some degree of prosperity, and law took advantage of prevailing peace

[37]

to extend its jurisdiction; but the acquisition of the Western Isles was a notable feat that expelled a rival power whose near presence had for long been humiliating and occasionally a menace.

Alexander II made two attempts to win the Hebrides, both unsuccessful. He sent a mission to Norway to ask its king, Hakon IV, if he would sell his title; and Hakon, a powerful and successful monarch, replied tersely that he was in no need of money. Then, in 1249, Alexander gathered a fleet and set out to take by force what he could not buy. But while his ships lay in the Sound of Kerrera, near the modern town of Oban, he caught a fever and died.

His son, Alexander III, renewed his father's claim. In 1261 he sent ambassadors to Bergen, and simultaneously, as it seems, despatched the earl of Ross to harry the Isle of Skye, and encouraged some of the island chiefs to renounce their allegiance to Norway. Hakon was alarmed by the Scottish threat, and commanding the mobilisation of men and ships, prepared to assert his continuing suzerainty by a massive display of strength. The Norwegian empire had lately grown by the acquisition of Iceland and the earldom of Orkney, and he was in no mood to relinquish the Hebrides. For some three hundred years Orkney and Shetland had retained at least their semi-independence, but had lost a decisive battle to Hakon's grandfather; Iceland, that fiercely individualistic republic, had been betrayed by internecine war, and acknowledged Hakon as its king; and already, in 1230, Hakon had sent a small fleet, half of it recruited in Orkney, as far as the Isle of Man to reassert the title so forcefully re-established by Magnus Bareleg in 1098. And now he gathered a much greater fleet, to punish Alexander's presumption, and early in July set sail with 'so great a host that an equally great army is not known ever to have gone from Norway'; or so say the *Annals of Iceland*.

But Hakon in 1263 was an old man, and either the delays attendant on old age, or bad weather, retarded his voyage, and it was not until 10th August that he left Orkney and sailed down through the Hebrides, where he was joined by Magnus, king of Man, and other chiefs. They were delayed by adverse winds, and it was already late in the season before his great fleet doubled the Mull of Kintyre and reached Arran in the Firth of Clyde. There he was in a position to strike hard and perhaps decisively, but wasted time on discussions that came to nothing. Alexander, whose dispositions are unknown, sent Dominican friars to offer peace, and with great good sense and a sound knowledge of their climate, the Scottish emissaries protracted negotiation until autumn gales should come to their assistance.

Hakon issued an ultimatum, and took his fleet far up the Firth, to

[38]

an anchorage between Largs and the Isle of Bute. He sent forty ships up Loch Long to plunder and replenish his harness-casks, and raiding parties penetrated far inland, perhaps as far as Stirling. But when they returned to their ships they were imprisoned by a wild gale blowing up the loch. It was on the last day of September that the main fleet was struck by the gale, and suffered much damage. Fighting on a minor scale began when Scots came down to plunder some half-dozen ships that had been driven ashore, and when eight or nine hundred Norwegians were on land, a Scottish army was seen to be approaching. But there was no general action, and it is clear that the greater part of the army was not involved in the skirmishing that followed. It appears, indeed, that the Scottish plan was to defer action until Hakon should assemble his whole force, and no attempt was made to prevent the discomfitted Norwegians from returning to their ships. The great fleet that had sailed so proudly, and been battered so grieviously by the south-westerly gale, was in no condition to mount a major battle.

The weather moderated, the survivors of the fleet from Loch Long rejoined the king, and he sent them ashore to burn his wrecked long-ships on the shore near Largs. Then he sailed over to Arran, and plundering where he could to feed his hungry men, began his melancholy retreat to the north. His purpose had failed, and Alexander had neither been persuaded into acknowledging Norway's claim to the Isles, nor beaten into submission. Foul weather still attended Hakon, and in Orkney he fell ill, and in mid-December died.

Three years later peace was written between the kingdoms in terms recorded in the *Annals of Iceland*: 'Alexander, king of the Scots, should take under his power and dominion Man, and all the Hebrides; and should pay from this year onwards a hundred merks of refined silver every twelve months to the king of Norway: and moreover 4,000 merks of refined silver during the next four winters.' Alexander is said to have paid in advance the 4,000 merks, but no more is heard of the annual tribute, and the hard facts of geography discouraged any thought of coming to claim it.

In later years the fighting at Largs was grotesquely magnified, and in the sixteenth century George Buchanan, the great Latinist, wrote that Hakon had landed a force of 20,000 men of whom 16,000 were left dead on the beach beside 5,000 of their opponents. So history is made when the facts of history are obscured by time. It is much to be regretted that nothing is known of Alexander's dispositions, for he did indeed win a great victory; though without much fighting. He knew the danger he was in, but could only guess at the point of attack. Hakon might well have landed his large army somewhere in the

Moray Firth, and had he been more expeditious, or had better luck with the weather, he could have offered battle, in great strength, on the shores of the Firth of Clyde. Alexander, who took certain measures to guard the Moray coast, had to create a mobile defensive force, and the army that showed itself near Largs—in which, according to Hakon's saga, there were nearly 500 armoured horsemen—was presumably the mass of manoeuvre held in readiness to meet the main assault wherever it might be made. Military success need not always be measured by the butcher's bill, and Alexander should probably be given credit for a victory won by strategic disposal of his forces, and a wise procrastination in committing them.

It would be agreeable to record that prudence brought a proper reward and crowned his reign with seemly triumph; but such was not the case, and headstrong passion ended all his good work, and his kingdom too.

That statecraft, in those early centuries, was often the plaything of family relationships has already become broadly evident, and it was the ill fortune of Alexander's domestic life that brought disaster to his realm. The wife he had married in childhood was Margaret, daughter of Henry III and sister of Edward I of England; she died in 1275, and Alexander did not remarry until ten years later, when his three children were dead. A boy, David, died in 1281; the elder son at the age of twenty, in 1284; and their sister Margaret, married to Eric II of Norway, in 1283, after giving birth to a daughter also called Margaret. Then, in 1285, Alexander married Yolande, daughter of a Comte de Dreux. He needed a male heir, and he was still only forty-four. The marriage might have been fruitful if its motive had only been political, but Alexander, unfortunately, fell in love with Yolande.

In March, 1286, he held a council in Edinburgh, which sat till late on a day of boisterous weather. He supped with his nobles, and after supper determined to rejoin his young wife, who was at Kinghorn on the other side of the Firth of Forth. If the day had been rough, the night was tempestuous, but Alexander could not be dissuaded from his purpose. He rode to the ferry, crossed safely against a northerly gale heavy with snow, and rejected a plea that he should spend the night at Inverkeithing. He took horse to ride east to Kinghorn, and somewhere in the darkness lost touch with his guides, and fell from a little cliff to his death.

Chapter 8

WHEN writing of Scotland's early history it is almost obligatory to quote the little epicedium on Alexander's death that is often said to be the earliest surviving fragment of Scottish verse:

> Qwhen Alexander our kynge was dede,
>   That Scotland led in lauche and le,
> Away was sons of alle and brede,
>   Of wyne and wax, of gamyn and gle.
> Our golde was changit into lede.
>   Crist, borne into virgynyte,
> Succoure Scotlande and ramede,
>   That is stade in perplexite.[1]

In the dark years that followed it was, of course, both easy and natural to look backwards at an imagined golden age, and mourn its passing. But there is evidence of substance in that sad memory, and Alexander's people, or many of them, may indeed have enjoyed an abundance of ale and bread, of wine and wax for tapers in the dark, and gaming and glee, with gold in the king's treasury, which vanished utterly when war crossed their constricted frontier.

Very gradually, in some localities, the appearance of Scotland was changing. The wooden castles built by the Norman incomers had been replaced by stone towers that still stood, it is probable, among subsidiary wooden buildings. Churches and abbeys and monastic buildings, some with tall castle-like towers rising above plain Cistercian walls, had been built in many places from the rich grazing-ground of the borders to both shores of the Moray Firth. And small towns were growing up, not merely in size and prosperity, but into the dignity of royal burghs with the privileges accorded to their new status. The power of the king and the strength of his law were explicit in the burghs, whose burgesses were exempt from feudal obligation and whose increasing wealth endowed them with a new freedom.

[1] For glossary see p. 361.

The institution of the sheriff and his sheriffdom, as officers and areas of the king's government, had by the end of the thirteenth century been extended as far as Kintyre and Skye: the sheriff, tenant of a royal castle, was charged with civil and criminal administration, and the collection of rent and taxes. There was the nucleus of a central government in the king's court, the *curia regis*, whose principal officers were the chancellor, the chamberlain, and the justiciar; and in 1293 a full meeting of the king's council was called, for the first time, a parliament. Such a parliament would not presume to question the king's supremacy, but the word had made its appearance. More important, perhaps, was the establishment, in certain cases, of the jury system, that David had first introduced. Before Alexander died the king's justice was recognised, if not always effective, from the borders to the Moray Firth; only the far north and west retained immunity from its benign interference.

The first of the royal burghs were Berwick and Roxburgh, which owed their status to David. They represented a new conception of life in which man could expect to earn a living, not only by tilling the soil, but by trade and manufacture. Commerce began with the export of hides and wool, the import of iron and spices, and in David's reign silver pennies were minted to expedite commerce. Trade was conducted by the burgesses of the new burghs, who enjoyed their own laws and privileges and were, to begin with, incomers like the new system; they were Flemings, Normans, English or Anglo-Danes. By the end of David's reign there were fifteen burghs and they continued to increase, prospering from the monopolies they were granted, and largely self-governing within defensive walls. Over the Court of the Four Burghs of Berwick, Edinburgh, Roxburgh, and Stirling, their ruling body, the king's chamberlain presided.

The growth and increasing endowment of the church under David has already been observed, and the introduction of the great continental religious orders, and their discipline, was of the utmost importance, not only to the spiritual welfare of the kingdom, but to its economy. The pure and withdrawn worship of God in a monastery did not preclude the intensive working, by its lay brothers, of monastic lands that had lain barren until they came, and in the borders, where Melrose was the first Cistercian foundation, great flocks of sheep provided the wool which made Berwick the chief trading town in the country. There were ten dioceses in Scotland, each of which was supposed to be divided into parishes under a parish priest, but parochial clergy could not always be provided, and as progressively the monastic system was favoured by the king and his nobles, many parish churches, with their lands and tithes, were granted as part of its endowment to a

[42]

nearby abbey or monastery. The abbey of Holyrood, for example, was enriched by holdings in Stirling, Berwick, and Renfrew, as well as in Edinburgh, by certain fishing-rights, by neighbouring churches and churches as far away as Galloway; and in the endowment of the abbey of Arbroath were no fewer than thirty-four parish churches.[1] The church, indeed, became a feudal institution in which the humble parts were subject to its great officers, and supported them; but the Cistercians, in particular, made more of their tributary lands than mere parish priests could have done.

Of the beginnings of literature there was, as yet, scant sign of promise. In Gaelic-speaking parts of the country the old Irish legends undoubtedly survived, but elsewhere the newer languages had not found sufficient roots. Between Inverness and the Humber there was a spoken English that did not differ greatly from north to south, and French was the language of the court, Latin of the church. There may also have been a *lingua franca* that allowed Flemish merchants, Anglo-Danes, and the offspring of the Norman lords to converse with their Celtic neighbours, but a *lingua franca* is no foundation for literature or scholarship. In the thirteenth century there are two names only that suggest an interest in polite learning, Michael Scott and the nebulous Thomas of Ercildoune, called Thomas the Rhymer. Michael Scott, scholar and reputed wizard, became astrologer to the Emperor Frederick II, and Thomas of Ercildoune, of whose writings nothing remains, held land in the parish of Earlston in Berwickshire. To these, perhaps, should be added the names of Devorgilla of Galloway and her husband John Balliol, who in 1262 founded a college for Scots students at Oxford.

Of the common people of the time, very little can be said that known facts will verify, though a good deal can be inferred. The majority lived by primitive agriculture and husbandry in a communion with nature so close that only their gift of memory and laughter, their innocent faith in the validity of the Christian doctrine, removed them, with any decision, from their kinship with domesticated animals and the feral beasts of a nearby oppressive hinterland. They were hardy, because their weaklings died in childhood. The seasons governed their existence, but they believed in the omnipotence of God, in the risen Christ, and in the magical properties of certain herbs and incantations to cure toothache, backache, and the other common ills to which they were subject. They knew satiety at harvest-time, and hunger after a late spring. They enjoyed, beyond question, their Celtic heritage of music, dancing, and song.

[1] *Scotland from the Earliest Times to 1603.* William Croft Dickinson.

It is, moreover, worthy of note that among the exports on which dues were levied were the skins of wild animals such as foxes, weasels, and martens; wild cats, beavers, ferrets, squirrels, and others; while provision had still to be made against the depredation of wolves. In the immediate neighbourhood of humanity wild animals existed in enormous numbers, and the human population was small. Man was still in the minority. And that, perhaps, was a symptom of health which we have long since lost.

Book Two

THE WAR
OF INDEPENDENCE

Chapter 1

THE infant Margaret, Maid of Norway, granddaughter of Alexander III, had been recognised as his heir in 1284, after the death of his surviving son; so deeply rooted now was the rule of primogeniture. A little more than two years later she became queen of Scots, at the age of three, and six guardians were appointed to govern in her name: the earl of Fife, James the Steward, the bishops of Glasgow and St. Andrews, and two members of the formidable house of Comyn, which fetched its descent from Donald Bane, who briefly wore the crown after the death of Malcolm Canmore and Margaret his queen. Some fifty years earlier, when Alexander II was still childless and about to engage in war, the magnates of the kingdom had chosen as his successor, should Alexander fall in battle, Robert Bruce, the great lord of Annandale, whose grandfather was a grandson of King David I; and his son, another Robert, made a show of resistance to the election of the child Margaret and her guardians, and entered his own claim to the throne; but was somehow dissuaded from pressing it.

Three years later the child's father, Eric of Norway, being anxious about his daughter's prospects, made a diplomatic approach to Edward I of England—whose sister was the Maid's grandmother—and at his suggestion discussion ensued between delegates of England, Norway, and the guardians of Scotland, with the purpose of finding her a husband and securing the peace of her kingdom. It was agreed that the Maid should go to England untrammelled by any contract of marriage, but Edward was already negotiating privately with the pope for a dispensation to marry her to his son, who became the second Edward; because young Edward's father and the Maid's grandmother were brother and sister, the children were within the prohibited degrees of canon law.

Edward I, who was to play a dominating part in the affairs of Scotland for nearly a score of years, must be accepted as one of the great kings of England, and cannot avoid the charge of ruining the happiness of his neighbours to gratify a cruel but natural ambition. He ruled the largest and most powerful of the British principalities, and to such a man the temptation to subjugate the whole island was irresistible; and once he had yielded, it became an obsession. He made war in France, he conquered Wales. He reformed the administration and justice of his own land; he defended feudal rights, but prevented their incursion into the royal prerogative; he ensured the preservation of large estates by entail, a measure that secured a rich inheritance for eldest sons and left younger brothers to look after themselves. He is said to have been faithful to his wife, Eleanor of Castile, by whom he had four sons and nine daughters. Arrogant in his youth, his arrogance was tempered in later life, and a legalistic mind inspired the valuable laws he enacted. Tall and handsome, he was, in the spirit of his ancestors, devoted to hunting and military exercise. But his ambition to unify Britain under his single rule created in Scotland, not only poverty where prosperity had been, but a warlike spirit which, when it had repelled English aggression, turned in upon itself to tear Scotland apart.

The pope acknowledged the royal authority of his plea for freedom from the usual prohibition of canon law, and his proposal to marry his young son to the Maid was joyfully accepted by the magnates of Scotland, with the proper reservation that the independence of the kingdom must not be impaired.

In 1290 the poor child Margaret, Maid of Norway and queen of Scots, set sail from her own land and died at sea, or in Orkney, perhaps from sea-sickness or a surfeit of the figs and gingerbread with which the vessel was provisioned. The prospect of a peaceful union between England and Scotland vanished, and would scarcely reappear for three hundred years. Edward's politic plans crumbled and were blown away, and Scotland was left with an empty throne and no claimant to it whose claim could avoid dispute.

There were claimants or competitors in plenty. They numbered thirteen in all, and included Eric of Norway, who as father of the Maid had what may have been a good legal title; but only four of the competitors were given serious consideration. They were John Balliol, Robert Bruce, John Hastings, and Florence, count of Holland; the first three were descendents of the three daughters of David, earl of Huntingdon, the younger brother of Malcolm IV, and Florence pretended that Earl David had renounced his claim to the throne in favour of his sister Ada, from whom Florence was descended. There was, for a little while, some danger of civil war between the Bruce and his supporters, and Balliol and his faction, most notable in which was John Comyn, Balliol's brother-in-law and himself a minor competitor. The bishop of St. Andrews then wrote to Edward of England, pleading for his help as adjudicator, with the laudable purpose of avoiding war, and for the furtherance of his own favourite, who was Balliol. Edward's response was immediate. The Scottish magnates were invited to meet him at Norham on the Tweed, and to ensure that he would be received with proper respect he mobilised the northern levies of England.

Edward's apparent magnanimity was explained when the Scots were told that he had come as their lord paramount, and must be recognised as such before he could adjudicate. That, of course, was reiteration of an old pretension to which the complications of feudalism had often given a specious appearance of legality. The Scottish kings had for long been possessed of great estates in England, and for these they had always acknowledged the superiority of the English king. But English monarchs had as often pretended that their feudal duties, in respect of an English estate, covered the whole realm of Scotland; and the maladroit William I, when an English prisoner, had in fact done homage for his kingdom. But Richard I of England had, for a price, freed William from that humiliating compact, and when Alexander III did homage for his English lands he expressly excluded his kingdom, which he held, as he boldly declared, 'of God alone'. But now, with supreme contempt for the elements of good faith expected in an arbitrator, Edward sought only his own advantage and with cynical perspicacity saw how to take it from a multifarious conflict of opposing loyalties, and self-interests as naked as his own.

The *communitas* of Scotland—the assembled magnates, that is, speaking with a single voice—rejected his claim, but the competitors, including Bruce and Balliol, accepted Edward as their superior, and agreed to abide by his judgement. Robert Bruce and John Balliol were the final contenders, the former being the son of Earl David's second daughter, the latter the grandson of David's eldest daughter; and judgement was given in favour of Balliol. He was installed as king on the Stone of Destiny at Scone, and did homage to Edward for the realm of Scotland. Edward, as Scotland's sovereign lord, immediately began to humiliate its puppet king. He declared his right to hear appeals, in his own court, from Scottish judgements; Balliol was asked to account for a wine-bill left unpaid by Alexander III; and in 1294, less than two years after his accession to a meaningless throne, he and certain of his barons were summoned to attend Edward on a military expedition to Gascony.

Balliol refused, and a council of the realm made a treaty of alliance with France. Edward marched north to deal with rebellion, and towards the end of March, 1296, crossed the Tweed. He laid siege to Berwick, quickly took it, and massacred its inhabitants. The English are said to have been infuriated by the barbed invective shouted from its walls by a doomed but dauntless garrison; the true reason for its destruction, however, was that Berwick was the richest port in Scotland and a serious rival to England's trade with the continent. The increased prosperity of Scotland, lately grown under the benign rule of Alexander III, was a menace to English commerce, and the king of England was as determined to destroy his neighbour's wealth as he was to dominate its throne. A month after the taking of Berwick a Scottish army was utterly defeated at Dunbar, and in July Balliol again made surrender of his kingdom. The 'Toom Tabard' he was called—the Empty Coat—and nothing, indeed, can be said in his defence except that he was a weakling whom vanity and cruel fortune had pushed into an untenable position.

Edward in triumph marched as far north as the Moray Firth, and on his return took from Scone the Stone of Destiny, the Black Rood of St. Margaret which was said to contain a fragment of the True Cross, and such national documents as he could find. At Berwick he held a parliament, at which two thousand lords and landowners, bishops, and other churchmen signed what was called the Ragman's Roll and did him homage as king of Scotland. Among the signatories were Robert Bruce, son of the competitor now dead, and his son Robert, earl of Carrick, a young man of twenty-two. Scotland was on its knees, and, as it seemed, finally defeated. English officials took over its government under John de Warenne, earl of Surrey, and Hugh Cressingham, and English garrisons manned all its castles of importance. When Edward left Scotland he left a sullen, conquered land, held in subjection by the armed force of alien governors. '*Bon bosoigne fait qy de merde se deliver,*' he said to Surrey, but flattered himself in thinking he had got rid of the filth he had been so eager to acquire.

Chapter 2

NOT everyone of note had made submission at Berwick. In Moray, in the stubborn, conservative north, there were still recalcitrants, and in Renfrew a young man called Wallace, son of a simple knight, was wholly disinclined to accept English domination. So, indeed, were most of the ordinary people of the middle and lesser classes. In the north, in Ross and Moray and Aberdeen, and in Argyll in the west, the signs of discontent were quickly manifest, and the bishop of Glasgow, with the young Robert Bruce and James the Steward, impulsively took the field, but failing to agree, either in policy or tactics, capitulated to an English force that was slightly superior in strength. In the summer of 1292 Cressingham reported that all the land was in a state of turmoil, save only some parts of Lothian and the borders; but Scotland, though insurgent, was still lamentably divided between the supporters of Bruce and Balliol. Both Wallace and Andrew of Moray, the leader of rebellion in the north and descendant of Freskyn the Fleming, were Balliol's men; but William Wallace, when he emerged from obscurity by a sudden act of violence, became the acknowledged champion of a Scotland that utterly rejected its leaders' obeisance to Edward, that demanded freedom and asserted its birthright to independence.

William Wallace, son of Sir Malcolm Wallace of Elderslie, one of the minor landed gentry, is said to have been educated by an uncle who was a priest, from whom, by repetition of the Latin tag, *Dico tibi verum libertas optima rerum*, he early acquired his belief that liberty was the best of human conditions. Legends accumulated thickly about him, and it is difficult to disengage truth from romantic fiction. The English regarded him merely as a brigand, and it is possible that by brigandage he began a personal revolt that, as it gathered momentum, attracted popular support and grew into the War of Independence. In 1297 he attacked the English garrison at Lanark, and having killed William Hazelrig, the sheriff, advanced on Perth and drove out the English justiciar. Then, with a numerous company, he occupied the Forest of Selkirk, and a little while later is said to have moved northward to besiege Dundee.

Wallace caught the imagination of Scotland, and out of an age when the perilous virtue of patriotism was a still uncommon concept, he may be accepted as Scotland's first overt and dedicated patriot. Long before Wallace, Scotland had acquired its sense of identity, and shown a readiness to fight for its preservation. But those who resisted English aggression had been men whose own fame or well-being demanded independence; and Wallace, so far as can be judged, lifted his head above the heads of acquiescent neighbours with a pure sense of the necessity of rebellion against alien domination. Though petty brigandage was the beginning, the final booty he sought was independence, and his name deserves, not only the popular adulation it has always been given, but the honour proper to a creative spirit. If Edward, by a policy of suppression, exacted the response of an indignant nationalism, it was Wallace who first gave it voice and direction.

He who made the movement effective, however, was Andrew of Moray. From the great provinces of the north which had so long been independent of kings, Andrew of Moray led his Highland forces from conquest of the castles of Urquhart in the Great Glen, of Inverness and Aberdeen, to Montrose and Forfar, and when he and Wallace joined hands, the greater part of the old Celtic kingdom was theirs and no longer under English command. Arrogant as ever, Edward refused to believe that the threat to his domination was serious, and went off to war in France. Warenne and Cressingham, his vice-regents in Scotland, were more realistic and took the field against Wallace and Andrew of Moray. They met at Stirling.

Over the river Forth, which rises from twin sources on the eastern slopes of Ben Lomond, and meanders leisurely, looping and re-looping in 'the links of Forth' through the flat carse of Stirling to tidal waters, the castle of Stirling stands majestically on a steep crag that frowns, like a natural keep, against the opposing Highland hills. Stirling, the gateway to the Highlands, was a strategic centre whose importance had been firmly established by geography. Below the castle a narrow bridge crossed the river in the direction of an abrupt elevation now called the Abbey Craig. On its southern slope Wallace and Moray stood with their army: an army which must have been heterogeneous and only partially trained, but showed itself remarkably susceptible to control.

There was some parleying and inconclusive negotiation before battle was joined, and on the English side there may have been altercation, between Cressingham and Warenne, about tactics. The upshot was rash and unsoldierly, for a frontal attack was ordered across the narrow bridge on to ground on which heavy cavalry could not easily deploy, and the embattled Scots shrewdly waited for the critical moment at which to launch their counter-attack. Their leader, whether Moray or Wallace, showed an admirable tactical sense—as well as an established authority over voluntary troops who by nature were indifferent to discipline—and having waited till a large and significant minority of the English army had crossed the bridge, launched his Scottish spearmen in a devastating attack down the causeway which led to the river. A moiety of the English army, more or less, was assailed on the narrow ground by impetuous Highlanders and the enthusiasts of the southern Lowlands, and while half of Warenne's force watched impotently from the Stirling bank, their comrades on the farther shore were cut to pieces.

The English and their Welsh bowmen fought bravely, and Cressingham with knightly fervour rode valorously into battle to be killed by a Scottish spear. Such was the hatred he had earned that his dead body was flayed, and fragments of his skin distributed through the country as little symbols of victory against an enemy who could not, and would not be tolerated. But the Scots had lost a leader more valuable than Cressingham, for Andrew of Moray had been wounded, and before long was dead of his wounds.

Warenne, from disaster, fled in haste to the border. He left his lieutenants to hold Stirling castle, which hunger soon forced them to surrender, and his army's wagon-train was cut off where the marshes of the meandering river were intersected by deep, slow-running rivulets called 'pows', and the triumphant Scots added an appreciable booty to a success which, though it brought no decisive advantage, was of supreme psychological importance. An English army which included armoured knights on heavy horses, and could almost be called professional, had been beaten by provincial infantry who were capably led and inspired by indignant patriotism. The War of Independence had achieved reality, and the embattled commoners of the country, both Highlanders and Lowlanders, had tasted blood and drunk the heady air of victory. They would need, before long and for a long time to come, all the encouragement they could summon from their memory of that September day in 1297 on Stirling Bridge.

Wallace made no attempt to exploit success by claiming the leadership of his resurgent country. He was still Balliol's man, despite John Balliol's abdication, which the Scots held to be invalid, and until Andrew of Moray's death in November he and Moray jointly commanded an army dedicated to the liberation of a constitutional kingdom; thereafter Wallace styled himself Guardian of the kingdom.

Letters were despatched to Hamburg to tell German merchants that a liberated Scotland was again open to trade, and Wallace appears to have based his authority, after summoning a national assembly, on consent of the *communitas*. To English eyes he seemed a rebel, but in Scotland he stood for its chosen king and legal government.

Edward of England was in France, fighting vainly against Philip the Fair, and his realm was disturbed by the dissidence of the great earls of Norfolk and Hereford. Wallace took advantage of his enemy's pre-occupation and led a large, unruly army into Northumbria. The Scots plundered at will, spread terror by murderous assault—though Wallace tried to restrain them—and before Christmas were driven home by the chilling onslaught of winter. They failed to capture Edinburgh, New-castle, or any of the border castles, but except for punitive raids by Warenne and Sir Robert Clifford they won respite from further war until the summer of 1298. Wallace, as the acknowledged Guardian of Scotland, had that larger title fortified by the honour of knighthood; there were magnates of the realm who now were willing to follow him in battle.

King Edward acknowledged the menace of the north by returning from France and establishing his headquarters in York. He mobilised a powerful army of some 2,000 horse and perhaps 12,000 infantry, most of the latter being Welsh. Wallace was now regarded as much more than a brigand: he was both an ogre and an insult to the majesty of England. It was essential to defeat him, and the English army advanced with inexorable purpose and arrogant unconcern for the dubious loyalty of its Welsh archers. From Roxburgh the road to victory lay through Lauderdale, bypassed Edinburgh, and the army pitched its tents near Kirkliston, a few miles to the west. The anticipated victory there seemed uncertain, for the transports expected at Leith were delayed by contrary winds and the army grew hungry, the Welsh rebellious. There was no sight or rumour of the Scots army, and Edward was about to fall back on Edinburgh when his loyal henchmen Patrick, earl of Dunbar, and Gilbert de Umfraville, the English earl of Angus, rode in with news that the Scots were only a dozen miles away, in a wood near Falkirk.

The advance was immediately resumed, through Linlithgow, and on the morning of 22nd July the Scots were discovered on a hillside east of Falkirk, arrayed for battle in four schiltrons, or spear-rings. Wallace's main strength—almost his only strength—lay in his infantry. He had a small force of cavalry, all but a few of indifferent quality, and between the schiltrons stood his archers from the Forest of Selkirk. But his only hope of success rested on the endurance of his spearmen, their discipline and strength to repel the charge of armoured knights. 'I have brought you into the ring, dance if you can,' said Wallace to his doomed patriots.

The earls of Norfolk and Hereford, their quarrel with the king now healed, led a charge of horse, and the Scottish archers were cut down. Then the English bowmen, and the French crossbowmen who stiffened them, shot their shafts and bolts into the defenceless schiltrons, and when great gaps appeared in the solid ranks, the king's feudal cavalry charged again. The battle was long, but the stubborn spear-rings, breached by the hail of arrows, were no match for knights on covered horses, and the Scottish horse had been driven from the field. Wallace's immobile army suffered grievous losses, and Edward's victory was sufficient to give him revenge for Stirling Bridge.

Wallace and other of the Scots leaders escaped, but Wallace's brief fame as a fighting general was foremost among the casualties of the day. It is, indeed, impossible to resist the thought that if Andrew of Moray had survived his wound, there might have been a different end to Edward's invasion. The English king had joined his army at Roxburgh early in the month, and marched through Lauder on 9th July. For more than two weeks, while threatened by a growing shortage of provisions and the indifferent loyalty of his Welshmen, he must have been vulnerable to surprise attack, to ambush, and the harassment of forces trained and disposed for guerrilla warfare. But Wallace, who had started his career by enlightened brigandage, had abandoned his older practice and chosen to fight a pitched battle, without cavalry to dislodge the English archers, or such advantage of the ground as he had had at Stirling. His was the blunder that brought defeat. He resigned his position as sole Guardian of Scotland—or was relieved of it—and was succeeded by Robert Bruce, earl of Carrick, and John Comyn, the younger, of Badenoch; both of whom had presumably fought in the lost battle.

After a foray to the west, Edward retired to his own country in September, and for four or five years the English domination of Scotland was largely restricted to the south-eastern parts of the country between Stirling and the border. The English garrison at Stirling castle was starved into submission in 1299, and the new Guardians, still ruling in the name of John Balliol—who was now in papal custody—-re-established in their sorely smitten country something like orderly and constitutional government. But at the apex there was antipathy between the two Guardians that could not for long remain undeclared. Fortunately for Scotland, Edward had difficulties of his own; his great nobles were out of sympathy with their king.

In the summer of 1298 Wallace went abroad, apparently to look for help from Philip the Fair, king of France, and to plead Scotland's cause in Rome. The English were ardently soliciting the favour of Pope Boniface VIII, but for some years the papacy had shown its friendship to the Scots, and Boniface, who believed in its supremacy over all kingdoms, accused Edward of interference with a papal fief. Neither Scotland nor the English king, however, could accept so large a claim. At Carlisle, in the spring of 1300, Edward again gathered his feudal host, and having taken the great castle of Caerlaverock, marched westward into Galloway. He rejected the terms of peace that were offered—they included the restoration of John Balliol—and by the tidal waters of the Cree, near Wigtown, a Scottish army was briskly beaten and quickly scattered. But little was gained by the victory, and the glittering array of English chivalry, under its bright, heraldic colours, rode ponderously and inconclusively home again, having granted the Scots a seven months' truce.

The twin guardianship of John Comyn and Robert Bruce had been enlarged by the addition of William Lamberton, bishop of St. Andrews, but his addition had not given it stability. At a council held in Peebles, in 1299, there had been a violent quarrel, in which the Red Comyn 'leaped at' the earl of Carrick, and a few months later Bruce resigned. He was replaced by Sir Ingram de Umfraville, kin to John Balliol and friendly with the Comyns. Still unable to agree, the three Guardians resigned before May, 1301, and he who took their place was Sir John de Soules, descendant of a Norman knight who had followed David I, and whose castles of Hermitage and Liddesdale commanded the south-western gate to Scotland. The offensive against England was renewed, and the prospect of Balliol's restoration brought closer. He was released from papal custody, and given protection by Philip the Fair of France.

Edward, despite papal rebuff, was still stubbornly intent on Scotland's subjugation, and in 1301 led a new army to the north. The king commanded its eastern division, which from Berwick marched through Tweeddale to the Clyde and laid siege to Bothwell castle; the other division, under Edward, prince of Wales, advanced from Carlisle into the south-west, but made little progress. A Scottish force of considerable strength, and vigorously led by de Soules and Ingram de Umfraville, harried both divisions of the English army and prevented their intended juncture near the mouth of the Clyde. They were forced instead to winter at Linlithgow, and in January, 1302, Edward agreed to another truce. But then occurred a strange and momentous event, for Robert Bruce submitted to the English king and was received into his peace.

He had been active in the western campaign against the prince of

[56]

Wales, for the Carrick men were out in force, and only he, as earl of Carrick, could have summoned them to service. From the abortive rising in which, with the Steward of Scotland and the bishop of Glasgow, he had led the insurgents of the west, he had fought or argued for independence since 1297. Why, then, this sudden and bewildering *volte-face*?

Chapter 3

THE record of these years is scanty, their history obscure; but certain things show clearly enough. The heavy defeat at Falkirk had neither diminished the Scottish hunger for independence, nor dissolved the will to fight. It had turned a reckless enthusiasm into a stubborn purpose, it had given policy and tactics a cloak of seemly caution; for Scotland could not afford another Falkirk. The brigandage of Wallace's first beginnings, moreover, had grown into a movement, a warlike intention, that all sorts and classes had joined. As closely involved as the sturdy peasantry of Wallace's schiltrons were such doughty churchmen as Wishart, bishop of Glasgow, and Lamberton of St. Andrews; and there is no lack of noble names in the forces of resistance. The Red Comyn, John of Badenoch, and the earls of Atholl and Menteith were on the patriotic side; there were Grahams and Keiths and the Steward; there were John de Soules and Simon Fraser of Tweeddale, and many others. A whole nation appeared to be renewing itself in the union of resistance, and with that renewal there seemed an ever-nearer prospect of the restoration of the Toom Tabard, that empty man, John Balliol.

From papal custody he had gone, by favour of the French king, to the old castle of the Balliols in Picardy; and some said he was about to return to Scotland with a French army behind him. If that were to happen, and French arms were successful, Bruce's earldom of Carrick and his father's broad lands of Annandale might well be in danger. The Comyns were pledged to Balliol and the Red Comyn was Bruce's open enemy. A Scottish triumph, at that time, would have meant the triumph of Balliol and the Comyns—and the probable eclipse of the Bruces.

It must be remembered that feudalism was, to some extent, a denial of nationalism and its obligations; for a feudal baron might owe allegiance, for certain of his lands, to the king of another country; as did Robert's father for the Honour of Huntingdon. To modern eyes a turncoat, Robert must have seemed to many of his contemporaries—and certainly to the king of England—a shrewd, indeed an honest man, who had discovered the propriety of reverting to an older loyalty. Robert himself may have thought that Edward would recognise his claim to the Scottish throne, in the justice of which he himself unquestionably believed. His father, the Competitor's son, had retired from politics, and was within a year or two of his death. Would Edward favour Robert in preference to the incompetent Balliol? It is conceivable, too, that Robert saw the possibility of marching with Edward against Balliols and Comyns; and then, having used England's strength to destroy them, the enticing prospect would be visible of a new patriotic rebellion with himself as its undisputed leader. It is not unthinkable that he turned away, in simple disgust, from the humiliation of taking service under the Toom Tabard; but so simple a motive is improbable.

If he hoped to be given the throne as a reward for diligence in Edward's service, and to occupy it as Edward's vassal, he was no more than an energetic fortune-hunter. There is some reason, however, for believing that his motive was larger and more perilous—that he proposed to make use of Edward, and having overwhelmed his rivals with English aid, to claim a throne to which his right could not be denied; and if that were his policy, then Robert was long-headed, far-sighted, cool, determined, and unscrupulous. In the summer of 1304, when he was high in Edward's favour, he made a secret and solemn agreement with Lamberton of St. Andrews by which they promised mutual friendship 'in view of future dangers'. They were, at the time, with the English army at the siege of Stirling. It was an improbable situation in which to pledge themselves, in a clandestine pact, to an alliance whose objective could have been nothing less than Scotland's independence. Lamberton, the friend of Wallace and of Wishart of Glasgow, was a dedicated patriot; and Bruce was no less resolved though his ways were devious and the Scotland of his vision was a land ruled by himself. In the month of June, 1304, only dedicated and resolute men would have contrived so desperate an alliance.

Two years earlier, under the walls of the Flemish town of Courtrai, a great French army had been utterly defeated by the people of Ypres, Bruges, and Courtrai; and when France ceased to menace England she could no longer be regarded as an effective ally. A political mission of uncommon strength went to Paris, to seek safeguards for Scotland, unavailingly, should peace be concluded between the two larger countries; and William Wallace came home to help, if not to lead, his threatened people. An English foray was defeated by Comyn and Simon Fraser, and in the summer of 1303, after England had made peace with France, Edward led another massive army across the border.

A young man called Sir William Oliphant held Stirling castle, and refused to surrender. But Edward bridged the Forth on pontoons, and leaving Stirling behind him, marched as far north as the Moray Firth, where tradition has it that he had to fight hard for the castles of Urquhart and Cromarty. He wintered in Dunfermline, and in May, 1304, laid siege to Stirling. He had a formidable artillery, and for three long months pelted the castle walls with boulders and Greek fire thrown out by cumbrous engines known by such arrogant or facetious names as *Lup-de-guerre* and *Tout-le-monde*, the *Parson*, and the *Robinet*. Hunger at last forced young Oliphant to surrender, and Edward, with the rancorous and vile display of temper that sometimes discoloured his reputation, refused to let the garrison march out with military honours, but threatened to hang and disembowel the starving men and their brave captain; and when those about him protested against the proposed massacre, his fifty-odd captives were despatched to English prisons.

It was during this siege that Robert Bruce, in the service of England, and Lamberton, lately returned under safe conduct from Paris, made their clandestine alliance against future perils; and long before Oliphant surrendered all but three of the magnates and leaders of Scotland had made submission to Edward. Wallace, encouraged by Lamberton, was still in the field, as were the Red Comyn and Simon Fraser of Tweeddale. To the latter, when they yielded, Edward was not ungenerous, and other leading men suffered no worse than short periods of exile or the forfeiture of estates which could be re-purchased at a stated price. But there was to be no clemency for Wallace; no terms of peace were to be offered him, other than absolute submission to the royal will. Wallace had never accepted English rule, and he was still—or had again become—the very symbol of resistance. Wallace lay beyond the farthest frontier of forgiveness.

Except for Wallace, all Scotland was apparently defeated. The magnates had made their submission, and though resistance still smouldered, there were no flames to light a new campaign. To bring about a final settlement a parliament elected ten representatives to meet the English parliament and frame a constitution. No longer a kingdom, Scotland got John of Brittany, Edward's nephew, for lieutenant, and English officials, with Scottish adjutants and English garrisons to support them, settled down to rule a conquered land. It may well have been Edward's intention that they should govern it justly and without undue harshness; but to one man he remained unalterably vindictive.

Wallace was captured, not far from Glasgow, on 3rd August, 1305, and taken to London. On the 23rd, in a procession that included the lord mayor, sheriffs, and aldermen, he was led on horseback to Westminster Hall to be charged with treason and other crimes. A vast crowd had gathered to mock him as he passed, and the judgement on him was a mockery of justice itself. He was not guilty of treason, because he had never been in the king's peace, and had never sworn allegiance to Edward. But revenge supplanted justice, and Wallace, bound to a hurdle, was pulled behind a horse from Westminster to the Tower, to Aldgate and thence to Smithfield, where sentence was carried out. He was hanged, cut down alive, disembowelled, and beheaded. His head was raised high above London Bridge, his quartered body divided, for exposure, between Newcastle upon Tyne, Berwick, Stirling, and Perth. Mutilated as badly were the name and honour of a great king, for all the baser part of Edward's nature was exposed to history as pitilessly as Wallace's severed head and limbs to the winds that blew on Thames and Tyne, on Tweed and Tay.

Less than six months later, Robert Bruce broke the unhappy peace of his country, and committed it to revolution, by stabbing and killing the Red Comyn in the church of Greyfriars at Dumfries. There is no discoverable connexion between this desperate act and Wallace's execution, but it is possible that Bruce had been falling out of the king's favour, and that his fall began about the time of the trial at Westminster Hall. In the campaign that brought about Scotland's total subjugation he had been actively engaged on the English side; active, indeed, against Wallace. But previously he had been friendly with Wallace, and Wallace's brother, Sir Malcolm, had belonged to Bruce's party. When Wallace was captured, he had in his possession documents in which were details of certain 'confederations and ordinances made between him and the magnates of Scotland'. Bruce's name may have been included. Manifestly he had not recently been in league with Wallace, but a record of earlier collaboration could have roused Edward's suspicion. In the Ordinance of September, 1305, which settled the affairs of Scotland with apparent finality, there occurs, side-by-side with the sentence of four years' exile on Sir Simon Fraser, the curious injunction that 'the earl of Carrick shall be commanded to put Kildrummy castle in the keeping of such a man as he himself will be willing to answer for'. It is a sinister command that indicates little trust in Bruce, and no more in his nominee.

After his father's death in 1304, Robert had done homage for the great English lands he had inherited; some debts due to the exchequer were respited by Edward; and when Bruce petitioned the king for the forfeited Carrick estates of Sir Ingram de Umfraville, his request was granted. But in October, 1305, Sir Ingram was reinstated in his lands, and in the same month, when four temporary Guardians were appointed for Scotland—because the king's nephew, nominated lieutenant for the country, was still absent—Bruce was not among them. He had been one of the king's chosen advisers when plans were being made for the settlement of Scotland, he was a member of the Scottish council chosen to assist the lieutenant; but in the new team of Guardians whom Lamberton led, Bruce had no place. He was, it is true, permitted to remain in Scotland, but the very fact that Edward, after April, 1305, seems not to have summoned him for consultation or advice, may be further proof of some disagreement between them that appears, on the slender evidence of chronology, to have had its beginning about the time of Wallace's capture.

If disagreement there was, it became a breach that nothing could bridge when John of Badenoch, the Red Comyn, was killed in Dumfries; and what led to that fatal meeting, and reckless act, is cloaked in darkness. Romantic tales were invented of Bruce's sudden escape from England—when apparently he was living in Scotland—and of Comyn's treachery, when politics made it expedient to blacken Comyn's name. The simplest explanation, however, is that both Bruce and Comyn were meditating, if not plotting rebellion; and when Bruce heard that Comyn's prospects were improving, or his plans taking shape, he decided to call his rival to a meeting. That Comyn was a formidable rival cannot be disputed. John Balliol's claim to the throne had not survived the French defeat at Courtrai and the consequent treaty and peace between France and England. Comyn was heir to the factional interest which had supported Balliol, and his own claim was fortified by the great possessions of the family that recognised him as their chief. He had served as a Guardian of the realm, and played a distinguished part in the war of resistance. He could trace descent from Donald Bane, king of Scots in the last years of the eleventh century.

Bruce, it is probable, had reason to suppose that Comyn might precede or hinder him in an attempt for the Scottish throne. He sent two of his brothers from his own castle of Lochmaben, in Annandale, to Comyn's castle of Dalswinton, some eight or nine miles to the west, with a suggestion that they meet in Dumfries. And there, in the church of the Friars Minor, a quarrel occurred or recurred. Seven years before, at Peebles in the Forest of Selkirk, a council of the realm had been interrupted by fighting between Sir David Graham 'of Sir John Comyn's following, and Sir Malcolm Bruce of the earl of Carrick's following'; and in the ensuing brawl 'John Comyn leaped at the earl of Carrick and seized him by the throat'. Now, in Dumfries, it appears that Robert Bruce, earl of Carrick, was the first to leap; and whoever restarted dispute, it was the Red Comyn who was the slower with sword or dagger. And Bruce, with sacrilege to stain his soul, for the killing was done before the high altar, and with murder as a possible blot upon his name, found himself condemned to years of the most arduous endeavour in pursuit of a patriotic aim that enlisted, after much tribulation, the sympathy and heartfelt support of all Scotland.

Chapter 4

IN the bottom drawer of Scotland's literary heritage lie two long narrative poems that celebrate the two great heroes of the War of Independence. The earlier, and infinitely the better, is *The Bruce* by John Barbour, archdeacon of Aberdeen, who lived from 1320 till 1395 and had written his poem by 1376. There were, at that time, living men who could remember Bannockburn and King Robert, and though *The Bruce* is a chronicle of national triumph, much ornamented and fattened by tradition, it cannot be denied considerable value as an historical narrative.

The other poem, Blind Harry's *Wallace*, was probably written not later than 1460 by a wandering minstrel whose aim was to compose a panegyric on a hero and exploit his undoubted patriotism. About Wallace's historical reality and actual deeds Blind Harry knew little and cared less. He wooed popular favour, and won it, by gross and ridiculous exaggeration of Wallace's achievements, and by fierce invective against the English oppressors; from whose practice Scotland, by the fifteenth century, had suffered long and deeply. Blind Harry's verses acquired a far wider renown than Barbour's poem, and till the nineteenth century were highly regarded in most of the humbler houses of Scotland. As the worse poem got a larger fame than the better, so did the lesser man it eulogised; but despite popular opinion there can be no doubt that Bruce, in an historical context, is of greater importance than Wallace. Though Wallace's patriotism burned with a purer, brighter flame—though his courage and dedication were absolute—he was, historically speaking, only the herald or precursor of the man who recreated, out of the chaos of defeat, the national independence and the enduring kingdom of Scotland.

No one can deny the possibility that Robert Bruce killed the Red Comyn in premeditated assault; though that is improbable. It is far more likely that he killed in the heat of a quarrel forced upon him. But it does not greatly matter. It matters no more than his tergiversation, and the motives for it, of the preceding years. What is of moment, alike in estimation of his character and assessment of what he made and did, is his behaviour in the years that followed. And no praise is too high for that.

At the time of this major crisis in his life he was about thirty years of age, and he lived for long in the rough atmosphere of sheer adventure. He survived hardship and danger, he suffered the loss of friends and brothers, he endured calamity and the eclipse of fortune; but his spirit did not falter, his purpose was never abandoned. His story took on the likeness and proportions of an epic, and Robert grew in stature to match the greatness of its theme. He was the supreme soldier of his time and he became a king whose kingliness seemed inborn. He was a man of profound piety and in his ordinary habit of life he appears to have been humane and even genial.

When he left the church of the Friars Minor, however, and came out into that cold February day, he had, to help him in his urgent task, no more than two obvious advantages, apart from the strength of his own mind and body. The Red Comyn had been removed from the scene, and his secret pact with Lamberton assured him of the church's support. The blow that killed Comyn seems to have been ill-timed. The English king was old and ailing and it would have been prudent to await his death. Then Robert could have struck more safely, for the prince of Wales was a man of easier temper than his father. But had the pact moved forward to become a plan for the restoration of a Scottish king, and were some of the planners already prepared for action? What followed the killing was done so quickly and so expediently that it cannot all have been improvisation.

The castle of Dumfries, where English justices were in session, was seized by Robert's followers, and the people of the town rallied to his side. Dalswinton and other strongholds were quickly taken. Rothesay castle had been one of Hakon of Norway's prime objectives before the battle of Largs, and Dunaverty stood at the southern tip of the long peninsular of Kintyre: when Robert's followers had captured them, they commanded the Firth of Clyde. Robert rode to Glasgow, whose good bishop Wishart gave him absolution, exacted his promise to revere the church in Scotland, and preached a crusading sermon for him. Then Robert went to Scone, where he was to be crowned. Lamberton of St. Andrews, the presiding Guardian of Scotland, was in Berwick; and a little while before the coronation he too rode to Scone, where Robert demanded formal recognition of his right and title to the throne.

Though the Stone of Destiny was now at Westminster, Scone was

Scotland, showing the earldoms and divisions of the land in about 1300.

still recognised as the seat of royalty, and in a double ceremony—on Friday, 25th March, 1306, and on Palm Sunday, two days later—Robert was enthroned and crowned in the presence of three bishops and three earls: the bishops of Glasgow, St. Andrews, and Moray, the earls of Atholl, Lennox, and Menteith. Duncan, earl of Fife, who should have been there, was in Edward's power, but his young sister Isabel, wife of the earl of Buchan, escaped from her husband in England, stole his horses, and by Palm Sunday was in Scone. It was she, by family right, who installed Robert on a makeshift throne. Also present were his four brothers: Edward, of reckless bravery and little judgement; Nigel, who was to be one of the first casualties of the war; Alexander, a brilliant scholar, master of arts at Cambridge and dean of Glasgow; and Thomas, who lived little longer than Nigel. Others are named as having attended the coronation, and two who won fame beyond the rest, save the king himself, were Thomas Randolph, later earl of Moray, and young James Douglas. Randolph was Robert's nephew, and Douglas, now landless, the son of Sir William, a magnate of the south-west and kin to the great family of Moray. Sir William was a violent man who had died a prisoner in the Tower of London; his son was to become famous as the Black Douglas.

Edward, surprised and infuriated by the news from Scotland, appointed as his lieutenant Aymer de Valence, who for reconquest of the country had, for a secure base, all Lothian from Berwick and Roxburgh to Edinburgh and Stirling. Edward's instructions were positive and ferocious. All who were in arms against England were to be pursued and taken, dead or alive, and those who gave no aid to pursuit were to forfeit their estates and be imprisoned. All who had a share in Comyn's death were to be hanged and drawn. All taken in arms against King Edward, and all who sheltered them, were to be hanged or beheaded. Bruce's estates in England were declared forfeit; his castle of Lochmaben, his lands of Annandale, were given to the earl of Hereford; Henry de Percy got his earldom of Carrick. Almost daily came messengers from the fierce old king bearing letters urging de Valence to more feverish activity. He was commended for burning Simon Fraser's property in Tweeddale; he was ordered to burn the manor and destroy the lands of Sir Michael Wemyss, in whom 'we have not found either good word or service'; and 'if possible do worse' to Sir Gilbert de la Hay.

Robert gathered what force he could, and probably found the greater part of his strength in his own territories of the south-west. He went into Galloway—always a divided land—to put down local hostility, and elsewhere had to deal with supporters of the Comyns, or be rebuffed by them. Scotland was very far from being united behind him, and de Valence, as energetic as he, moved with great speed and resolution. Both Lamberton and Wishart were taken, and sent to English prisons. De Valence took Perth, and in June Robert was tempted to attack him there. But his army was untrained and de Valence, moving first, took him by surprise at Methven, and the patriots were routed. Robert, fighting in his shirt, narrowly escaped capture, and fled with a few hundred men; but his nephew Randolph, and many others, were made prisoner.

With Robert were Marjorie, his daughter by his first wife, Isabel of Mar, and his Queen Elizabeth, daughter of Richard de Burgh, earl of Ulster, whom he had married after his submission to Edward in 1302. When the remnants of the defeated army, seeking safety in wilder, higher country to the west, were approaching Tyndrum—between the head of Loch Lomond and Rannoch Moor—they were again attacked, by John Macdougall of Lorne, and seemingly lost cohesion. The queen and the lady Marjorie, with other women, were mounted on what horses remained, and with an escort led by the earl of Atholl and Nigel Bruce set out across the mass of the Grampians to the castle of Kildrummy in Aberdeenshire. Built in the reign of Alexander II, Kildrummy was the ancient seat of the earls of Mar, and the noblest of northern castles. But despite its strength, its great curtain walls and four round towers, it was unprotected against treachery, and when de Valence and the prince of Wales marched up the river Don from Aberdeen, it had to yield to treachery. The queen and her women had fled north again before the English approach, almost certainly with the intention of seeking refuge in the Norwegian islands of Orkney; Robert's sister Isabel was dowager queen of Norway, and Scotland and Norway were on friendly terms. But the fugitives got no farther than Tain on the Dornoch Firth, where in the sanctuary of St. Duthac they were taken prisoner by the earl of Ross, a man of Balliol's faction.

The renewal of war, and the opportunity for vengeance that the rout of Methven gave him, provoked Edward to reprisals so ferocious that the old king's sanity must seem in doubt. As well as indiscriminate terrorism, there were many instances of specific punishment of insensate savagery. Simon Fraser was executed in London; after evisceration and the burning of his entrails he was hanged, beheaded, and his head was set up above London Bridge beside the weathered mask of William Wallace. The earl of Atholl was hanged—an unheard-of punishment for an earl—but his rank was recognised by a gallows-tree thirty feet higher than Fraser's. Nigel Bruce, with many others, was drawn, hanged, and beheaded at Berwick. A few months later, Robert's younger brothers, Thomas and the scholarly Alexander, were defeated and captured at Lochryan in Wigtownshire. They were taken to hear sentence from Edward himself, who was then at the priory of Lanercost in Cumberland. By his command Alexander was hanged; Thomas was roped to horses, pulled through the streets of Carlisle, hanged, and then beheaded.

Even women were not immune from Edward's senile fury. For Robert's sister Mary, and the Countess Isabel of Buchan—who at Scone had installed him on his throne—cages of wood and iron were made, and in these they were suspended from the castle walls at Roxburgh and Berwick. Lest the king be accused of barbarity, however, his prisoners were allowed the use of a *chambre cortoise*. At the Tower of London another cage was ordered for Robert's daughter Marjorie, who was still a child; but then Edward relented and Marjorie was sent to a nunnery in Yorkshire.

After the women of his party had taken horse for Kildrummy, Robert and those who remained with him sought means of escape. Five months after his coronation, Scotland had become too dangerous for its sudden king. The Macdougalls of Lorne were Balliol men and his bitter enemies, but the earl of Lennox and his followers were loyal, and most of the Macdonalds of Islay and Kintyre, who had lately been on the English side, were opposed to the Macdougalls and therefore inclined to favour Robert. He also had Campbell supporters in Kintyre, and at the southern tip of the peninsula was the castle of Dunaverty, which he had ordered to be taken soon after the murder of Comyn, and which was still held for him. By devious ways, then, Robert and his companions made their way down by Loch Lomond into the Lennox country, and crossing to Bute, sailed to Dunaverty. There he stayed for three days, and warned of danger, left before two of Edward's officers, thinking he was still within its walls, laid siege to the castle. But Robert, before their siege-train had settled down, was in the island of Rathlin, some fourteen miles west of the Mull of Kintyre and about four miles from the north coast of Ireland.

Barbour's statement, that Robert spent the winter of 1306 on Rathlin, has often been repeated, but is manifestly untrue. It is a small island, dignified by handsome cliffs, and there was no cover on it for a fugitive now hotly pursued. It is probable that Robert went there with the intention of using it as a stepping-stone to refuge in Ireland. His father-in-law was Richard de Burgh, earl of Ulster, and his loyal friend James the Steward, now an old man, had married Richard's sister. The earl, it is true, was of Edward's party, but to Robert it may have seemed that family ties would prove stronger than political allegiance. Perhaps

Possible routes taken by Bruce and Queen Elizabeth after the murder of
Comyn and the Battle of Methuen.

he was disappointed, for if he did go to Ireland, he did not stay. There has been much speculation on where he spent the following months, and there is good reason for believing that when, or if, Ireland failed him, he turned about and made his way to Orkney. It was in early September that Kildrummy was taken by de Valence and the prince of Wales, and the queen and her party had fled before then, with the apparent intention of crossing to the northern islands. News of their flight, and its goal—but not the news of their capture in Tain—may well have reached Dunaverty by 22nd September, when the castle was besieged and Robert escaped to Rathlin. He would have been less than human if, in the desperation of those friendless days, he had not been tempted to seek the company of his queen, his daughter, and the small escort that went with them.

English chroniclers, writing two centuries later, say that Robert went to Norway, but as he was in Carrick again by early February, that is unlikely; for winter was not the proper season for crossing the North Sea. If, however, 'Norway' can be extended to include its possessions, then Orkney may be accommodated within the chroniclers' statement. For what it is worth, an Orkney tradition not only preserved the belief that Robert had spent the winter there, but named his host, the udaller Halcro, who was said to have fought with him at Bannockburn. Robert certainly renewed a former grant of £5, payable from property in Aberdeen, to the cathedral of St. Magnus in Kirkwall; and according to legend the blessed St. Magnus himself appeared to the citizens of Aberdeen after the battle of Bannockburn. Of more solid worth than legend or tradition, however, is the undoubted fact that the loyal bishop of Moray, who had attended Robert's coronation, was in Orkney early in 1307; and Edward wrote to Hakon, king of Norway, to ask for his arrest.[1] If Orkney gave refuge to a bishop, it may well have offered safety to a landless king.

It is unlikely, however, that Robert spent all the winter there. The chronicler John of Fordun, who died in 1385, says that the hardships of his wandering months were alleviated by a noble lady, 'Christiana of the Isles', and by her help he was enabled to return to Carrick. The noble lady has recently been identified[2] as Christina of Mar, whose husband was a brother of Robert's first wife. She had inherited from her father the Hebridean islands of Rum and Eigg, Uist and Barra, and most of the opposite mainland shore. She obviously had the means to help Robert, and if, in Orkney, Robert had learnt of the capture of his wife and daughter—if, instead of finding the comfort he expected,

[1] *The Scottish War of Independence.* Evan Macleod Barron.
[2] *Robert Bruce.* G. W. S. Barrow.

he had been told they were Edward's prisoners—he would have had a new and urgent reason for seeking help to re-awaken war from the abyss of defeat. The hypothesis is that Ireland had failed him; Orkney had succoured him but given him news that impelled him to attack again, with whatever strength he could muster, his intolerable enemy; and Christina of Mar provided him with a force sufficient to essay a small offensive.

Before the end of 1306 Robert sent secret agents to collect his Carrick rents. Towards the end of January, 1307, he returned to Kintyre with a little army of Hebrideans. His brothers Thomas and Alexander were with him, and may have been with him throughout his wanderings. He had gathered elsewhere a few stubborn adherents, and the Lanercost Chronicle, written in nearby Cumberland, asserts his alliance with an Irish kinglet who had brought a large following. He had men enough to divide his small force into two divisions. One, commanded by Thomas, Alexander, and the Irish kinglet, was sent to exploit or sup-press some obscure trouble in Galloway. Dissidence was endemic in Galloway, and from divided loyalties a hazardous profit might be won. But the brothers and the Irishmen were too weak to force an entrance. Near Lochryan they were defeated, and Thomas and Alexander made prisoner by the Gallovidian chief Dougal Macdouall. By him they were delivered to Edward's justice, and their fate has already been described.

Robert himself, with his other division, made a desperate attempt to secure a foothold in his own earldom. With him were young James Douglas and the loyal and valiant Robert Boyd. According to Barbour these two crossed over to Arran and intercepted a company newly landed to relieve or reinforce the commander of Brodick castle. They took a useful booty and when Robert joined them a spy was sent over to Carrick with orders to light a fire on Turnberry Point if conditions favoured an attack. A fire was lighted, but not by the spy, and when Robert crossed the broad firth he was given a dispiriting report. The country swarmed with English troops, Turnberry castle was strongly held by Henry de Percy, and there was no hope of raising local support. Nevertheless, it was decided to attack, and before daybreak the little force stormed the village below the castle, where many of the garrison were billeted, and waking them with the sound of breaking doors, put them to the sword. The castle was too strong to be taken but Percy and his men were extremely alarmed by the invasion of their peace, and remained within its walls. Robert and his men withdrew, taking some prizes of war, and Percy, shaken by the surprise attack, made no attempt to retaliate.

Barbour's account may be substantially accurate, and if it is, the inference is clear. Robert's attack was not only premature, but delivered without proper reconnaissance or knowledge of the enemy's strength and disposition. It was strategically indefensible, and tactically unsound. His motive could not have been his calculation of success, and must have been emotional. But if, for once, Robert allowed himself to be dominated by natural feeling—by hatred of the oppressor and an obsessive desire to take revenge for the injuries done to his family— he was quick to realise that self-indulgence of that sort was quite impermissible in one who, though he had no land to rule, no people to obey him, still felt upon his brow the obligations of the crown he had put on at Scone. Emotion, and the recklessness it bred, were dismissed from his mind, and by cold calculation he devised a plan of campaign in which orthodoxy had no part and there was no room for the pomp and circumstance of royalty.

He embarked on a clandestine, almost subterranean resistance such as came into being in several German-occupied countries in the Second World War. Throughout Scotland the castles which dominated the country were held by English garrisons or Scottish commanders in yoke to England. The English forces were far too strong to be confronted in battle, but by guerrilla warfare he might reduce their effectiveness, curtail their fields of action, and any success, however small, would not only advertise the fact that the Scottish cause was still alive, but bring him recruits to advance the cause. Scotland was not a whole, united land, but most of its people were held in a stubborn, invisible union by their passionate desire for independence and the measure of freedom it would give them. The *communitas*, in whose name its leaders had so often spoken, was indeed a community, of all ranks, with an underlying sense of identity, with a common hope and an ever-emergent purpose, that were of far greater import than the many cracks and divisions, of class and policy, that scored its surface. There was a kingdom of the mind, real though inchoate, with shadowy foundations in the Scotland of Alexander III, and a temper toughened under the hammer of Edward of England. It was the reality of this kingdom, and Robert's conviction of its reality, that justified his continuance of the war and his prosecution of what must have seemed an impossible task.

Within a very few months his fortune had improved, and he was beginning to show himself on the surface of his kingdom. The story of this dark period is told with much detail and an infectious spirit of delight by John Barbour. Much of Barbour's tale must be dismissed, regretfully, as the accumulation of a legend, but there are incidents which may be true, for in folk-memory a picturesque anecdote may remain fixed in shape and colour while the greater events make no impact whatever.

Robert's immediate plan was to retire to the wild hill-country between Carrick and Galloway, but before or while he was withdrawing, young Douglas—if Barbour can be trusted—took the opportunity to visit, with two companions only, his estates in Lanarkshire, where he perpetrated a picturesque outrage that captured people's attention, though its military significance was negligible. Coming with circumspection into Douglasdale, he found in Thomas Dickson, a man of substance, a loyal friend who secretly mustered a small company of sympathisers, and a plot was made to surprise the English garrison of the castle during their worship in St. Bride's chapel—Palm Sunday was conveniently near. The English soldiers, carrying their green branches, entered the church, and Douglas followed in a countryman's disguise. One of his supporters raised the battle-cry too hastily, and the English had time to adopt a defensive formation in the chancel. They offered a stout resistance, but the Scots, with Thomas Dickson first in the attack, overpowered them and killed the greater part. Then Douglas and his followers, returning to the castle, which was inadequately garrisoned by the cook and the porter, ate the dinner that had been prepared for English consumption, and kindled a fire whose abominable fumes made a pillar of smoke that was much regarded. It was useless to try to hold the castle, so having set aside the portable loot—weapons, clothing, and silver—Douglas ordered the remaining stores to be collected in the wine-cellar, and barbarously executing his prisoners threw their bodies into the foul mess of malt and meal and wine, and burnt the castle above them. This bonfire of groceries and murdered men was known as the Douglas Larder.

Meanwhile the English and their allies of Lorne and Galloway were building a human barricade round Robert's retreat in the south-western uplands, and for some weeks there was a game of perilous hide-and-seek about Loch Trool, which lies in a circuit of hills rising to 2,500 feet and more. In a defile called the Steps of Trool Robert won a small but useful victory when an English advance was halted in a well-contrived ambush and this success gave him a little freedom of movement and confidence to venture into the Ayrshire lowlands. There, it seems, he recruited rapidly, for on 10th May he gave battle to de Valence at Loudon Hill, a dozen miles east of Kilmarnock.

Robert, choosing a position between two peat-mosses, strengthened it by digging trenches that would guard his flanks from cavalry. Barbour estimates his strength at six hundred fighting-men and as many 'rangale' —ill-armed, undisciplined supporters, that is—while the English, he says, were three thousand strong, which is certainly an exaggeration. But though they were no more than a third of that, they had the advantage of heavy cavalry, mail-clad knights on covered horses, enough to make a handsome spectacle as they rode to the attack. It was a mass of light and colour that moved towards the trenches. Chivalry clad itself in gay hues. De Valence's shield of blue and white bars, on which sat ten little red birds the shape of doves, had shields as cheerfully painted on either side of it. So glittering an army—helmets burning in the sun, hauberks 'white as flowers', bright spears, gay pennons, and multi-coloured shields—so shining a troop they were they looked the angels of heaven's host, says Barbour.

But the Scottish pikes had no respect for a handsome appearance, and the Scottish position was strong. Before nightfall the English were defeated and de Valence was in full flight for the castle of Ayr. Three days later Robert discomfited another English force under Sir Ralph de Monthermer, who also fell back upon Ayr. Then Robert, following up his victories like a good general, laid siege to Ayr, but was compelled to raise the siege when English reinforcements—de Valence's army, re-formed, and counter-attacking, perhaps—threatened his position. So strong was the English offensive that Robert was forced to seek his old retreat in the hill-country of Galloway, and for the next couple of months he was again on the defensive. The English forces and their allies in the south-west, roused by a succession of small defeats, took once more the upper hand. De Valence reinforced the garrison and strengthened the castle of Ayr; led punitive expeditions into Carrick and Glentrool; and vigorously searched the hills. In face of this offensive the Scottish king, biding his time, waited for time to help him.

Time helped him nobly, and in early summer King Edward died. From October of the previous year to the spring of 1307 Edward had been at Lanercost in Cumberland, old and sick and fretting for vengeance. When the days grew longer his strength, for a little while, returned. He was dissatisfied with de Valence's conduct of the war in Scotland, and he resolved to cross the border himself. He sent to London for his tents, and on Whit Sunday reviewed his troops. Four hundred horsemen, decked with green leaves, rode past him, and the old king was well pleased with the display and grew merry to see his fine soldiers again. He gave his travelling-litter to Carlisle cathedral, as a thank-offering, and rode northwards. But he had outlived his strength. Dysentery attacked him again, and on 7th June, at Burgh-on-Sands, he died, being sixty-eight years old. His *idée fixe* was not diminished by the approach of death: he bade the prince of Wales send his heart to the Holy Land with an escort of a hundred knights, but carry his bones from place to place, wherever he should march against the Scots, unburied till his ancient enemy were utterly subdued. Edward II, however, declined this unpleasant legacy, and having taken his father's body to York, handed it over to the archbishop for burial in Westminster Abbey.

The new king of England then returned to Carlisle and crossed the border early in August at the head of a magnificent army. He advanced as far as Cumnock in Ayrshire, where he remained for two or three weeks. But his appearance was more warlike than his intentions, and on 25th August, very peaceably, he led his army home again, having accomplished nothing.

No sooner had he gone than the Scots raided Sir Dougal Macdouall's lands in Galloway. They wrought such destruction that the earl of Richmond, now lieutenant of Scotland in de Valence's place, was hurriedly ordered to go to their defence with all the strength at his disposal—Sir Dougal's lands were largely garrisoned by English troops. It is not certain that Robert himself accompanied this punitive expedition against the man who, six months before, had sent his brothers to their death. The strategic centre of the war was no longer in Carrick or Galloway. At last the time had come for him to go northwards, to consolidate his strength in the Highlands, and perhaps he set out for Inverness immediately after Edward had started his retreat to England. If he waited to revenge himself on Macdouall first, he can have waited only till his raiders got their teeth into Galloway, and then he must have travelled north at speed: for by Christmas he had two more victories to his credit, one secured by negotiation, the other by frontal attack. He took with him his brother Edward, the earl of Lennox, Sir Gilbert de la Hay, and Sir Robert Boyd; and he left Douglas as his lieutenant in the south-west.

Douglas celebrated his new command with another brisk dramatic exploit: he recaptured his castle in Douglasdale, that had been rebuilt since the burning of the Larder, by means of a second ruse. Having concealed a sufficient force in the neighbourhood of the castle, he tempted the garrison by sending forward fourteen men, disguised in country frocks, who led horses laden with fodder. The castle gates opened and the garrison happily came out to commandeer the hay of which their stables were badly in need. Then the fourteen countrymen threw off their bundles of hay and mounted their horses: Douglas and his men came out of their ambush: and the castle garrison, attacked in front and rear, was quickly defeated. The castle was again demolished, but this time, more merciful than he had been, Douglas spared the lives of his captives and set them free.

Chapter 5

EDWARD II was 'not industrious, neither was he beloved by the great men; albeit he was liberal in giving, and amiable far beyond measure towards those whom he loved, and exceedingly sociable with his intimates. Also in person he was one of the most powerful men in his realm'.[1] He was assuredly a more amiable person than his predecessor, but as a reigning monarch he was ill-equipped for the fourteenth century. During the old king's lifetime he had regularly been forced to attend his father's campaigns in Scotland, and the glittering prizes of a military career had been scrutinised, enumerated, and extolled, for his benefit, with such hot earnestness, such prolixity, that he had grown weary of their tedious dazzle. As soon as he became his own master he avoided unnecessary warfare and no longer pretended even to find pleasure in the dust and bruises of a tournament. It is true that on sundry occasions—notably in 1310 and 1314—Edward II violently remembered his inherited claim to the Scottish throne and, with the occasional brief zeal of an easygoing man, undertook and commanded a new campaign against the ever-growing strength of King Robert. Once, it is true—in 1314—he moved against Scotland with all the strength he could muster. But except for these periods of unusual energy the character of the war changed after 1307. Till then there had been a steady offensive, unremitting and remorseless, against every manifestation of Scotland's independent existence; after 1307, with brief exceptions, England was on the defensive and the initiative passed to Robert, whose attack became as unremitting and remorseless as Edward's had been. But to emphasise the comparatively static position of England under its new king is not to depreciate Robert's achievement. The English defensive position was enormously strong. In 1307 every Scottish castle of importance was still held by England or English partisans; and in mediaeval warfare the castles were dominant factors. Robert was still a king without a

[1] *Scalacronica.* Sir Thomas de Gray.

kingdom, for in all Scotland there was no strip of land he could call his own, no walled town where his standard flew. He had survived the loneliest part of his struggle, he had won the little battles of Glentrool and Loudon Hill, he had gathered a small but gallant army, he had strong friends waiting his arrival in the north, and England's policy was no longer a forward policy: there is the sum of his credit balance. But against him were castles studding the land from Berwick to Inverness, strongly garrisoned, impregnable except to siege-train or starvation or Douglas's tactics; and in the north, where his friends were, were also his enemies the earl of Ross and John Comyn, earl of Buchan.

Robert's strength in the north lay chiefly in the great province of Moray, that separated, like a wedge, the northern earldoms of Ross and Sutherland from the north-eastern earldom of Buchan. Under their gallant young leader, Andrew de Moray, the men of that province had played a notable part when Wallace was the spearhead of Scotland's battle for independence; the bishop of Moray preached the same cause when the Bruce became its leader; and now, as the English commander at Forfar had written, the people were 'all ready at his will more entirely than ever'.

It is probable that the castle of Inverness had already been taken and destroyed when Robert arrived there after his raid on Galloway: the tasks that confronted him were the subjugation of Ross and Buchan. Robert dealt first with the northern earldoms—Sutherland was temporarily under the influence of the earl of Ross—and quelled their opposition by a very imposing display of strength. Ross was admitted to a six months' truce; early in December he wrote to Edward II, apologising for his deflection, and explaining that Robert had come with an army of three thousand men who, at the earl's expense quartered themselves on the marches of Ross and Sutherland, while Robert threatened to lay waste all his territories unless he made peace with him till Pentecost next, 1st June, 1308. The earl afterwards became one of Robert's faithful adherents, and his son Walter fought and was killed at Bannockburn.

Having brought Ross to terms, Robert turned to Buchan. Here his difficulties were greater. The Comyns were still the most powerful family in Scotland, and the blood feud between them and the king made quite untenable any hope of friendly or diplomatic agreement. 'The earl of Buchan desires, more than anything else, to take vengeance of you, Sir King, for the sake of Sir John the Comyn that was slain in Dumfries,' says Barbour. And the king replies: 'I had great cause to slay him.' Therefore to fight and to beat them decisively was Robert's only chance of securing himself against their otherwise constant menace. He marched to Inverurie, prepared to give battle. There, however, he fell seriously ill, and a great sadness took the heart out of his men. 'There was none in that company,' says Barbour, 'who would have been half so sorry to see his brother dead before him as he was for the king's sickness: for all their hope lay in him.' But Edward Bruce, Robert's brother, rallied them, and for greater security they carried the king in a litter to Slivoch, sixteen miles north-west of Inverurie.

News of their whereabouts and of the king's illness reached Buchan, who promptly advanced against them in strength. He was accompanied by Sir John de Mowbray and Sir David de Brechin. Apparently the king's army had dwindled to a fraction of its former strength—it would have been tempting providence as well as the earl of Ross to leave Moray unguarded—for Barbour declares that Buchan's following was as two to one. The king's men, however, found so strong a position in front of a wood that Buchan hesitated to attack. He sent forward his archers to worry the royalist force, and Edward Bruce replied by throwing out his own archers to form a defensive screen. For three days there was sniping between the rival bowmen, but there was no hand-to-hand fighting. This gingerly battle took place 'after the Martinmas, when snow had covered all the land'. The inclemency of the weather, doubly unkind to the defending army, was aggravated by lack of provisions, and after three days the royalists were threatened by starvation. They found security in audacity, and, bearing the king's litter in their midst, marched off in close formation in the very face of the enemy. And so bold was their front that Buchan dared not attack, though his army had steadily been growing in numbers during the three days of competitive archery.

The magnificent effrontery of this movement can be safely ascribed to Edward Bruce, whose talent for war consisted largely of reckless determination and belief in the efficacy of rapid movement; and the fact that he withdrew his force in safety suggests that it was well armed and well disciplined: that is to say, that it still consisted of the small company (Lennox, de la Hay, Boyd, and their people) who had accompanied Robert from Galloway, together with certain gentlemen of Moray and their immediate followers; it was an army, not an assembly of rustic loyalists.

Having marched to Strathbogie, and stayed some little time there, the king returned to Inverurie and went into winter quarters. Barbour says his army then numbered nearly seven hundred men, and

> thai wald ly in to the plaine
> The wynter sesone; for wictaile
> In till the plaine mycht thaim nocht faile;

but unless Inverurie and the neighbouring country were well-disposed to Robert—despite the shadow of Buchan upon them—the problem of feeding so large a force must have been difficult. Buchan, however, did not leave them long at peace. He gathered a 'full great company' and advanced as far as Old Meldrum. On Christmas Eve, in the morning, his lieutenant, Sir David de Brechin, made an armed reconnaissance and near Inverurie cut to pieces an outlying party of royalists. When Robert heard of this he rose from his sick-bed and, disregarding all protests, prepared to lead an immediate counter-attack. 'Their boast has made me hale and sound,' he said, 'for no medicine would so soon have cured me as they have done.'

This swift offensive took Buchan by surprise. His outposts, however, warned him of the king's approach 'with banners waving to the wind', and he had time to order his battle and station his camp-followers in support. His men made a goodly show, says Barbour. But Buchan, who had already shown his unsoldierly quality at Slivoch, now revealed entire lack of leadership. The king advanced in determined fashion; Buchan's line wavered; Robert pressed his attack harder; Buchan's front line began to give ground; then his supporters, seeing their masters falter, turned and fled; the panic spread forward, the knights turned tail, the battle became a pursuit, and the beaten army was chased as far as Fyvie, where there was a castle with an English garrison. Some time later Edward Bruce is said to have conclusively beaten the earl near Old Deer.

Robert now proceeded systematically to destroy the power of the Comyns. Barbour says that he

> gert his men bryn all Bowchane
> Fra end till end, and sparyt nane;
> And heryit thaim on sic maner
> That eftre that, weile fyfty yer,
> Men menyt 'the Herschip of Bowchane'.

But there was more in the Herschip[1] than setting fire to crops and cottages and driving cattle; and there was more than personal vengeance in it. The Comyns held the castles of Kinedar, Slains, Rattray, Dundarg, and Kelly; their allies held three others; and there were English garrisons in Aberdeen, Aboyne, Fyvie, and Kintore: all these strongholds had to be reduced before Robert could safely leave the north-east corner behind him and turn to other tasks of conquest, pacification, and consolidation. No general can afford to leave an unconquered enemy in his rear, and the Comyns were enemies of peculiar danger. They were

[1] Harrying.

strong, they were implacable, they represented the Scottish opposition to Robert; their survival meant the persistence of internecine warfare, their destruction meant the reinforcement of Robert's prestige, the rallying to his standard of prudent sitters-on the-fence and well-wishers whom fear of the Comyns had previously immobilised. The Herschip, in all its ruthlessness, was justified by necessity. Its strategic value was obvious and its moral effect was tremendous.

In June the defeated earl was appointed Edward's warden of Galloway: he must have fled his own country not later than March. In July the citizens of Aberdeen joined King Robert in his successful assault upon the castle of Aberdeen. Before autumn every castle in Aberdeenshire and the country north and west of it had been captured save one: Banff was still held for England.

A swift campaign in Argyll; the subjugation of Galloway; and cease-less war against the castles, the strong-walled outposts of England—these were the tasks that now confronted Robert.

The Macdoualls of Argyll and Lorne were kin to the Comyns: Alexander of Argyll was the Red Comyn's uncle. Alexander was an old man, however, and the enmity of his son, John of Lorne, was the principal menace to Robert in the west. Having temporarily pacified that part of Scotland north of Inverness; having destroyed all opposition in Aberdeenshire; and the loyalty of Moray being assured, the conquest of the west—the scotching of John of Lorne, that is—was clearly the next step in Robert's process of consolidation, and he essayed it, apparently, very soon after the reduction of Buchan. July, 1308, is the probable date of his marching against Argyll. His army was large, and he was accompanied by Douglas, who had recently come north with an important prisoner, Thomas Randolph, the king's nephew: John of Lorne, after being defeated, said that Robert's army numbered between ten and fifteen thousand, figures which, though they cannot be taken as a serious estimate, may be regarded as a tribute to the imposing appearance of the royal forces.

The size of the advancing army made its progress comparatively slow, and John of Lorne had time to place an ambush in the Pass of Brander, a narrow defile that gives access to the south-east shore of Loch Etive—a sea-loch—from the north-west shore of Loch Awe. The north-east wall of the Pass rises to the abrupt magnificence of Ben Cruachan. John of Lorne had his galleys in Loch Etive, and himself lay in one of them to wait the result of the battle—a result disastrous for him. His ambush was dislodged from above, and his Highlanders were defeated on their own ground. Douglas led the king's archers over the top of Ben Cruachan, and from the heights looked down on Lorne's ambush; the main army entered the Pass and was assailed from both sides; the men of Lorne shot arrows and trundled boulders down the slopes; but the king's men were lightly armed and light of foot themselves, and he promptly ordered a heather-stepping uphill attack that spoilt the enemy's defensive scheme. Then Douglas, heralding his approach by a storm of arrows, led a downhill charge, and though the men of Lorne offered sturdy resistance the two-sided attack defeated them, and presently they broke and fled through the Pass. From his galleys John of Lorne was able to see their headlong flight.

After his settlement of the west, Robert marched north to conclude his negotiations with the earl of Ross, who in November or December of the preceding year had agreed to a six months' truce. Since that time Robert's position had grown very much stronger; he had destroyed the power of Buchan and pacified the west; his star was plainly rising. His new prestige had its proper effect upon Ross, who, at Auldearn in Moray, on 31st October, 1308, made full surrender and tendered his homage to the king. Robert accepted his surrender with a liberal gesture: he not only established Ross in all his former lands and tenements, but granted to him the additional lands of Dingwall and Ferncrosky, and in return for this wise generosity, 'I, William,' said the earl, 'for myself, my heirs, and all my men, to the said lord my king have made homage freely and have sworn on the evangel of God.'

Following the pacification of the north and the west, the conquest of Galloway was completed in the early months of 1309, after a prolonged struggle. After Buchan's defeat Edward Bruce, with Douglas, Lindsay, and Boyd, had been ordered south; on 29th June, 1308, Edward Bruce defeated de Umfraville and the men of Galloway somewhere in the valley of the Cree, and forced him to retire to the castle of Buittle; by piecemeal conquest and the capture of small castles Edward slowly continued the pacification of Galloway; and before autumn, Douglas, campaigning in the Forest of Selkirk, had captured Thomas Randolph, the king's nephew, who, after assisting at Robert's coronation, had been taken prisoner by the English, had fought most vigorously on their side and eagerly chevied Robert during his hide-and-seek days in Glentrool, and later was to rival Douglas himself in his daring exploits for the Scottish cause.

Barbour says that Douglas, coming one night to a house on the Water of Lyne, listened at the door and heard someone inside exclaim: 'The devil!' Whereupon, naturally enough:

> he persawyt weill
> That thai war strang men, that thar
> That nycht tharin herbryd war.

After a sturdy scuffle Randolph was made prisoner, and Douglas, as already recorded, took him north to the king; where Randolph, in reply to Robert's suggestion that they might now be reconciled, hardily taunted Robert with pursuing his war against England 'with cowardy and with slycht'; to which the king replied with dignified composure and committed Randolph to safe keeping.

In November Edward Bruce took the castle of Rutherglen, and returned to Galloway to meet a new English attack. One of de Umfraville's colleagues, Sir John de St. John, had gone into England after Edward's victory on 29th June, and there recruited a strong force and recrossed the border, says Barbour, at the head of fifteen hundred men. Edward Bruce, finding himself in the neighbourhood of St. John's army, withdrew his infantry and rode forward with his cavalry, who numbered fifty. One of them, Sir Alan de Cathcart, lived long enough to tell Barbour the story of the reckless work that followed. A heavy mist made visibility poor, but the little cavalry force discovered the line of St. John's march and followed him. Later in the morning the mist suddenly rose, and, less than a bowshot distant, Bruce saw the English army. Without hesitation he charged them and cut his way through. Then his gallant fifty reformed, charged again, and again broke through the English ranks. Seeing their enemy dismayed and standing in confusion, Bruce led another charge, but the English did not wait for his third onslaught. They scattered and fled, and the large remnant of the fifteen hundred took to their heels before the mad gallantry of Bruce and his fifty horsemen.

> It wes a rycht fayr poynt perfay,

says Barbour with some complacency; it was certainly an exploit that perfectly illustrates Edward Bruce's genius for audacity. He was in truth

> a noble knycht;
> And in blythnes suete and joly;
> Bot he west owtrageouss hardy,
> And of sa hey wndretaking,
> That he haid nevir heit abaysing
> Off multitude of men.

By the middle of March he was present at the parliament his brother assembled in St. Andrews. This parliament is interesting on three counts: its purpose, its constitution, and Robert's ability to convene it in St. Andrews.

Its chief purpose was to consider negotiations with France that had already been initiated, and to intimate to King Philip that Robert was now recognised as king of Scots by the nobility, church, and

[83]

communitas of the kingdom. Diplomatic conversations had been proceeding between Philip's envoys and the English court to ascertain the possibility of a truce between England and Scotland, but though Edward II was not averse from pacific measures he was not prepared to admit Robert's title to the Scottish throne, and the conversations were finally unproductive. Philip's diplomacy was revealed in the directions on the various documents in possession of the French mission: those meant to be shown in England were addressed to Robert de Bruce, earl of Carrick, and those intended for Scottish eyes were addressed to the king of Scotland.

The names of those who attended the parliament are interesting because they indicate the areas on which Robert had so far depended for assistance. In addition to 'the barons of the whole of Argyll and Innisgall', there are twenty-eight names recorded. Eight of these are southern names: Edward Bruce, Thomas Randolph, Douglas, James the Steward, Robert de Keith, Edward de Keith, Alexander de Lindsay, and Robert Boyd. The remaining twenty represent northern families: Scotland north of the Forth and Clyde was clearly the dominant factor in the earlier part of the War of Independence.

And, thirdly, the fact that Robert was able to summon his parliament to St. Andrews shows that by March, 1309, he had securely established his position in Fife. Brechin castle had fallen to him; Forfar had been captured; and now Cupar had evidently been taken, and Fife acknowledged his sovereignty. These conquests were effected by surprise attack and ceaseless vigilance that pounced on opportunity like a seagull on galley-scraps: Forfar had been captured by escalade under cover of night, and though the manner of Cupar's taking is not known, Sir Thomas de Gray, the author of *Scalacronica*, relates a couple of adventures that befell its warden—his father, a daring and skilful soldier whose service was full of gallant deeds and romantic accidents—which clearly reveal the nature of the Scottish offensive: an imaginative persistency in attack was its most notable characteristic.

By the summer of 1309 the only castles north of the Forth and Clyde still held for Edward were Banff, Dundee, and Perth: these were regularly reprovisioned and reinforced from English ships. Stirling was also in English hands. Perth and Stirling were so strong that their capture presented almost insuperable difficulties. West of Stirling the great castle of Bothwell was still an English stronghold, as were Ayr and the castles of the south-west: Lochmaben, Caerlaverock, Dumfries, Dalswinton, and others. In the south-east the English position, buttressed by Edinburgh, Jedburgh, Roxburgh, and Berwick, was numerously and strongly manned.

Chapter 6

THE proposals for peace which the St. Andrews parliament had discussed received intermittent attention during the summer of 1309. Lacking the truly questing pacifism of doves, however, these overtures rather resembled homing pigeons: they could do no more than carry unacceptable conditions and return with a diplomatic negative. What negotiation failed to effect was secured by Edward II's devotion to Piers Gaveston, and by the Scottish climate. In the autumn of 1309 Edward despatched troops to Berwick and Carlisle, but their commanders were more concerned with their king's infatuated regard for his Gascon favourite than with prosecution of the war, and they agreed to a truce with the Scots. This truce, originally intended to expire on 14th January, 1310, was subsequently extended for a material reason, for, says the *Lanercost Chronicle*, 'the English do not willingly enter Scotland to wage war before summer, chiefly because earlier in the year they find no food for their horses'.

During this interval of peace Edward reinforced his garrisons in Scotland, and the Scottish clergy, meeting in Dundee, asserted with martial emphasis their allegiance to King Robert. The ancient church of Scotland, indeed, when threatened by English discipline and patronage, ever translated their duty to God in terms of loyalty to Scotland. Bishop Lamberton, that wise and gallant prelate, was still active in diplomatic negotiations for the welfare of his country; abbots and preaching friars had supported Robert in peril of their lives, and still supported him in peril of their souls, defying his excommunication by the pope; and Glasgow's heroic bishop, blind now, lay in an English prison waiting for the victory at Bannockburn to release him.

In the summer of 1310 Edward prepared a major offensive against Scotland, and in his preliminary arrangements showed both energy and acumen. He assembled a large fleet, and by the despatch of ships and men to Perth made of that all-important outpost a base of operations in the very heart of the enemy's country. In anticipation of success the earl of Ulster—Robert's father-in-law—was given power to receive the vanquished or the malcontent to Edward's peace, and in August Edward himself reached Berwick with his invading army. But it was a smaller muster than he had ordered, and less loyal than he had hoped. His barons served unwillingly or not at all. They sent small and grudging contingents, and their contingents were late in arriving. At Berwick Edward was involved in another quarrel with the nobles, and he did not cross the border till September. His hope of forcing a decisive battle was unrealised, for Robert wisely employed guerrilla tactics and contented himself with harrying the outposts of a force too large for him to destroy. Edward, after marching as far north as Linlithgow, retired to Berwick and prepared to winter there. Seeing him in retreat, Robert followed him and did much damage in Lothian, which was in Edward's peace. Edward recrossed the border, again seeking battle, but Robert again evaded him and created a useful diversion by preparing, or at least threatening, an attack on the Isle of Man: for this marine flanking movement he relied, presumably, on the galleys of the Western Isles. Then Edward began to weary of so stern a task as the subjugation of Scotland, and renewed negotiations for peace. Robert was not unwilling to respond, but presently he was warned that the English meant treachery, whereupon he terminated the peace conference by moving into Galloway and threatening the western march of England. Edward replied by sending Gaveston to Perth with two hundred men-at-arms to hinder the advance of any reinforcements that Robert might order from the north.

Gaveston remained in Perth till April, 1311, when he returned to Berwick. In July, in London, a melancholy duty confronted Edward: he was forced to preside over a parliament whose business was to pass sentence of perpetual banishment on Gaveston. His love for the undesirable Gascon had brought England to the verge of civil war.

This *impasse* was Robert's opportunity. He, 'having collected a large army, invaded England by the Solway on Thursday before the Feast of the Assumption of the Glorious Virgin (12th August), and burnt all the land of the lord of Gillsland, and the town of Haltwhistle and a great part of Tynedale, and after eight days returned into Scotland, taking with him a very large booty in cattle. But he killed few men besides those who offered resistance'.[1] Having brought back the cattle, he returned to England by way of the eastern border and marched as far as Corbridge, 'burning the district and destroying everything, and causing more men to be killed than on the former occasion'.[1] He laid waste those parts of Tynedale which he had previously spared, and

[1] *Lanercost Chronicle.*

[86]

after harrying for fifteen days returned to Scotland, the wardens of the eastern march being powerless to hinder him. The result of this brisk invasion was that Northumberland sued for a separate peace, and after negotiations paid £2,000 for a truce till 2nd February, 1312. Certain parts of Lothian were also persuaded to buy peace till the same date. The war having become a war of aggression, Robert was now making it pay its expenses.

The Lanercost chronicler—who, having the dubious advantage of living close to the border while these events were taking place, knew what he was writing about—remarks at this point that 'in all these aforesaid campaigns the Scots were so divided among themselves that sometimes the father was on the Scottish side and the son on the English, and vice versa; yea, even the same individual might be first with one party and then with another. But all those who were with the English were merely feigning, either because it was the stronger party, or in order to save the lands they possessed in England: for their hearts were always with their own people, although their persons might not be so.'

Early in 1312, their marches being still without adequate protection, Robert again raided the north-eastern counties of England and compelled them to pay for another truce. Later in the year the strong castles of Dundee and Ayr were captured for him. In the first days of July a parliament was summoned to Ayr, and Robert made public his intention—or allowed it to become known, for it was repeated to the English king—of sending his brother Edward to invade England while he himself invested the castles of Dumfries, Caerlaverock, and Buittle, and supported his besieging forces by raiding across the border. This plan—if it was correctly reported by King Edward's correspondent—was subsequently improved: in the middle of August, Robert crossed the border with his whole army and lay for three days at Lanercost Priory. From there he advanced to Corbridge, and having plundered and laid waste the neighbouring country he sent forward a detached force under his brother Edward. Edward's column took Chester-le-Street, continued its advance, and seized and sacked the city of Durham. Having wasted the surrounding country Edward established temporary headquarters at Chester-le-Street and waited there while Douglas, continuing the advance with the spearhead of the column, advanced as far as Hartlepool, which he sacked. With a large booty and many prisoners Douglas then retired northwards, rejoined Edward Bruce at Chester-le-Street, and with him fell back on the main force at Corbridge. As a result of this well-contrived and very alarming invasion the people of Durham begged for a truce, and agreed to pay £2,000 for immunity from attack until 24th June, 1313—a period of ten months—and at the same time promised the Scots free access through the bishopric lands whenever they desired to make a raid. Northumberland secured an extension of the truce, for the same period, for a like sum, and Cumberland and Westmorland bought temporary peace for a smaller amount —they could not find so much as £2,000—and the loan of hostages. On their way home the Scots attempted to capture Carlisle, but were defeated with heavy casualties. Without wasting more time—he had, of course, no siege-train—Robert recrossed the border and with Randolph and the earl of Atholl proceeded to Inverness, where he held a parliament in the last week of October. Edward Bruce and Douglas concluded their remarkable campaign by laying siege to the castles of Dumfries, Buittle, and Caerlaverock, which were all captured by the end of March, 1313.[1]

For the sweeping success of his invasion Robert was greatly indebted to the disintegrating personality of Piers Gaveston. In the early days of 1312, defying the parliamentary sentence of banishment, the Gascon had returned to England. The barons cut off the king's supplies, Edward and Gaveston fled northwards, and for subsistence plundered York and Newcastle. Gaveston was captured in June, and by order of the earls of Lancaster and Warwick was beheaded on the high road near the town of Warwick. Edward continued his feud with the barons, and internecine dispute prevented them from paying much attention to the northern marches: in January, 1312, Edward had again offered peace, but his terms were unacceptable, and the war continued.

While Edward Bruce and Douglas were busy with their siege of the south-western castles, Robert, having dismissed his parliament in Inverness, essayed the capture of Perth, a walled and moated town, heavily garrisoned: the garrison included a hundred and twenty mounted men, so its total strength must have been very large. The strategic value of Perth was enormous, and its defences were commensurate. For six weeks Robert laid siege to it without success, and then, in full view of the garrison, who mocked his going, he marched away with all his army. But during the investment he had made an accurate survey of the moat and walls and discovered that part of the moat was comparatively shallow. After a week's absence he returned to Perth, under cover of a dark night, having armed certain of his men with ladders in addition to their ordinary weapons. The town lay before them, dark and silent and unsuspecting. Robert, in full armour, carrying a ladder and a spear, was the first to lower himself into the moat: the water was neck-high and cold, for the month was January. Hastily but in silence his men followed him, and Robert was the

[1] *Chronica Gentis Scotorum.* John Fordun.

[88]

second man to reach the top of the wall. A goodly number had climbed it before the alarm was given. The mediaeval system of depending at night on paid watchmen, rather than on sentries, was a great help to surprise attack and the town was still sleeping when the attack began. Robert, reinforcing a daring attack with prudence, kept a strong guard with him to deal with organised resistance or counter-attack. The rest of the invading force, split into small parties, set off through the streets, and the bewildered citizens, caught in their beds or fleeing in their shirts, woke to a more dreadful nightmare than any they could have contrived in their dreams. There was no massacre, however. Robert had given orders that life was to be spared as far as possible: the majority of those within the walls were of the same blood as those who came from without, and except for some more valorous than reasonable in their defence, and others who were notorious enemies of Robert, few, it seems, were killed. Barbour says that Robert was merciful to the townspeople; the Lanercost chronicler says that he let the English garrison go free; Fordun declares that known traitors, English and Scots, were executed. One may reasonably infer that killing was selective and judicious, not haphazard. But there was widespread looting, and many gallant invaders who had climbed the wall in stark poverty were by sunrise richly clad, with money in their new pockets and new armour on their backs. Then the walls of Perth were demolished, its towers were razed, its moat was filled, houses were burnt or pulled down—

> He levyt nocht about that toun,
> Tour standand, na stane, na wall,

says Barbour, and the Lanercost chronicler declares that Perth was utterly destroyed. Its strength had been too great, its strategic value too obvious, to leave anything that might tempt the English to counter-attack, recapture, and rebuild it.

Four months later, in May, that is, Robert invaded and captured the Isle of Man. His activity was unceasing, his genius for effective movement astonishing: the secret of the art of war, as he practised it, was significant mobility. Consider the record of ten months, from July, 1312, to May, 1313: in July he had held his parliament in Ayr and made his plans for the invasion of England; he had led his army across the western march and then eastwards to Corbridge; from there he had sent Douglas and his brother Edward on swift offensives against Durham and Hartlepool; returning to Scotland, he left Douglas and Edward in charge of operations on the border and proceeded to Inverness, where he held another parliament; this progress, that flattered his friendly relations with the north, enabled him to give personal attention to any difficulties that had arisen from Argyll to Buchan, from Sutherland to Aberdeen; then, presumably with northern troops, he captured Perth, and returned to the south-west in time to receive, from his old enemy Sir Dougal Macdouall, the surrender of the castle of Dumfries; and a few weeks later he invaded Man. He conquered Scotland by forced marches and ruled it from the saddle.

The Island of Man was a Scottish possession by right of purchase from Norway, but actual tenure went backwards and forwards, between England and Scotland, like a shuttlecock. Robert now presented it to his nephew Randolph, whom, in generous recognition of his conversion, valour, and loyal service, he had recently created earl of Moray. The island would have been an excellent base for commerce-raiding on the west coast of England, but unfortunately Randolph was unable to hold it: it was recaptured in 1314 by John of Lorne—whom Edward had made his Admiral of the Western Seas—and Randolph had great difficulty in regaining possession.

The truce with the northern counties of England having by this time expired, Robert made plans to cross the border again. But his threatened invasion was averted by a timely bid for peace. The price offered was acceptable, and another truce was sold. The north of England was now guaranteed against attack till September, 1314.

The next phase in the war was the reduction of Lothian, which was still held for England. It was guarded by strong castles, its officials were English nominees, and a majority of its leading families were still adherents of England. By 1313, however, the English tenure had grown very insecure, and the condition of the people was acutely unhappy. They were subject to spoliation by the Scots and by their own nervous garrisons, and south-eastern Scotland was in a state of barely suppressed anarchy. Its conquest for Robert was distinguished by three famous exploits: Douglas's capture of Roxburgh castle, Randolph's capture of Edinburgh, and the taking of Linlithgow peel by William Bunnock, a farmer.

In the meantime Edward Bruce, having laid siege to Stirling—it is not known on what date—had made a compact with de Mowbray, its constable, by which the latter agreed to surrender it should no relief come before midsummer, 1314. This impolitic agreement was, of course, an open challenge to England: it would be incredible were it not that compacts in the age of chivalry were often impolitic, and that Edward Bruce was notorious for light-hearted recklessness. Robert's comment on the bargain, as reported by Barbour, is sensible enough to be authentic, though its moderation is remarkable: 'That wes unwisly doyn perfay!' He then points out the folly of giving the English king time in which to prepare his attack, who from his wide territories could muster an army far more numerous than Scotland's defence: the Scottish cause has wantonly been put in danger. But Edward takes the wind out of his reproof by stoutly declaring that though all the English come, and more than all, 'We sall fecht all!' Whereat Robert 'prisyt him in hys hart gretumly'.

The English chroniclers say that Edward Bruce did not attack Stirling till after the fall of Edinburgh, and that Edward II's campaign for its relief was consequently hurried. It is known, however, that Edward had begun to make warlike preparations before news of the capture of Edinburgh could have reached him: the English chroniclers may have been a little inclined to post-date the challenge, as Barbour, who ascribes it to the summer of 1313, was surely guilty of ante-dating it. But whatever its date, the compact was made, and Stirling was Edward's goal when he invaded Scotland.

Once again he showed unusual and commendable energy, and circumstances favoured him more than they had in 1310. In reaction against the murder of Gaveston the majority of the barons were, for a little while, loyally disposed towards their king, and Edward, stirred by the Scottish challenge, summoned a feudal muster without waiting to obtain the consent of his parliament. Eight earls and eighty-seven barons, with their retainers, received writs of summons and—after some delay—proceeded towards Scotland.

On 24th March, Edward summoned 21,500 infantry from Wales, the north of England, and the Midlands. Four thousand archers and other infantry were also ordered from Ireland. Mobilisation proceeded slowly, however.

On 27th May, Edward issued third writs of summons in which he peremptorily declared: 'We had ordered the men to be ready by a date already past. The enemy is striving to assemble great numbers of foot in strong and marshy places which it is very difficult for the cavalry to reach. Therefore you are to exasperate and hurry up and compel the men to come.'

This command was more liberally obeyed, and early in June Edward was in command of a very imposing army: 'Six or seven days before the Feast of St. John he left Berwick with more than 2,000 armed horse and a very numerous infantry. There were enough men there to march through the whole of Scotland, and some thought that if all Scotland were collected together it could not resist the king's army. The multitude of carts stretched out in a line would have taken up twenty miles. The king, in his confidence, hastened day by day towards his goal. Short time was allowed for sleep, shorter for meals.'[1]

The English army took the inland route to Edinburgh, up Lauderdale and by Soutra Hill. The Scots made no attempt to harass it as it crossed the moors. They were waiting for it at Bannockburn. On Saturday, 22nd June, Barbour says the English marched from Edinburgh to Falkirk, full twenty miles. This was fine marching but poor preparation for battle.

[1] *Scalacronica.*

Chapter 7

THERE has been much discussion about the true site of the battle of Bannockburn, and this is not a matter of merely academic interest. The nature of the ground determined, to a large extent, the manner in which the battle was fought, and its outcome. To-day one looks down from the commanding height of Stirling castle at country which has been changed utterly in appearance by progressive farming and industrial development. Coal-mines, railway tracks, and recent building disguise the castle's old environment, and fields drained by modern agriculture look nothing like the rough, waterlogged meadows of the fourteenth century. It is, moreover, not impossible that natural forces have altered the battlefield. Running approximately eastward from the castle is the meandering river Forth—looping and re-looping in its tidal course—and from high ground south and south-west of Stirling the Bannock burn, in some places between high banks, cuts an even more tortuous channel on its way to the river. It was one of many burns that drained the higher land, and in the way of natural drainage they sometimes ran in furious spate, scouring deep holes, and sometimes in sluggish peace. Now all streams and rivers tend to alter course and find new channels, and six hundred and fifty years ago the Carse of Stirling—the low ground south of the convolutions of the Forth—may have looked very different, not only from the present scene, but from an observer's view of it before industry and agriculture disguised the surface. This is important, because the final dispositions for the English army were largely dictated by the course of the streams and the river. An attempt, therefore, to map the battlefield can only be made in the knowledge that the basic terrain—a terrain unaltered by modern development—may have suffered unrecorded changes since the day when Robert and his divisional commanders looked out from the entrance to New Park, and the glittering column of Edward's chivalry rode from Falkirk through the Torwood.

The castle rock, some four hundred feet high, falls precipitously to the north and west, but towards the south-east slopes gently down, by a glacial tail, to a shelf, from fifty to a hundred feet in height, that separates the Carse from the rising ground to the south and west. A mile or two south of the rock was New Park, a timbered expanse reserved for hunting, perhaps two miles in breadth. Some of the Park was the open valley of the Bannock, and south again were the old trees and rocky outcrop of the Torwood. From Edinburgh the high road marched through Falkirk, and then north-westward to the wood, and through it on the line of an old Roman road some two hundred feet above sea-level. It was on Sunday, 23rd June—presumably in the late afternoon—that the vanguard of the English army came out of the wood, and looked at what lay before them. It was not yet certain that they would have to fight for the castle. The governor, Sir Philip de Mowbray, rode out to greet his king—manifestly by permission of the Scots—and suggested that as he had arrived by the date agreed upon, honour had been saved. An advance through New Park would be difficult, he said, as all the paths had been blocked. But the battle had already begun.

A problem more difficult of solution than discovery of the exact site of the battle is assessment of the numbers engaged. Barbour, poet and patriot but no statistician, declares that Edward's army was 100,000 strong, and Bruce commanded 30,000. The modern scholar, on the other hand, has sometimes been afflicted with a kind of ascetic incredulity, and as the old historian, for glory's sake, affected a magnanimity of belief that led to fabulous exaggerations, so has he, for virtue's sake, favoured too drastic a diminution. These extremes must be avoided, and it is reasonable to start with the known fact that Edward ordered the mobilisation of more than 21,000 infantry. It is not to be supposed, however, that so large a number assembled, and it may not be cynical to suppose that no more than two out of three responded, or were rounded up. Give him, then, 14,000 infantry.

His cavalry were more important, and an English chronicler estimates them at more than 2,000. In this respect Barbour himself is not unreasonable, and of covered horses—the heavy horse that carried armour of its own as well as an armoured knight—counts 3,000. It is true that Edward was able to persuade only three of his earls to follow him, who were Humphrey de Bohun, earl of Hereford; Gilbert de Clare, earl of Gloucester; and Aymer de Valence, now earl of Pembroke. But the lesser nobility were there in greater numbers, and Edward had summoned, or invited, certain Scottish and Irish knights and others from Gascony, France, and Brittany. Most famous of all his volunteers was Sir Giles de Argentine, reputed the third best knight of his time, who had been a prisoner at Salonika but obtained his release by Edward's favour. According to a very scholarly estimate,[1] the English heavy

---

[1] *Bannockburn.* J. E. Morris.

cavalry probably numbered between 2,000 and 2,500. It was they, not the infantry, who bore the brunt of the fighting.

The Scots had no heavy horses, and their light cavalry numbered 500. That has never been disputed. Of their infantry it must be said at once that if their numbers were low, their quality was high. They were the veterans of seven years continuous warfare, and their leaders were men who had accustomed them to success; no soldier would ask for a leader with better qualifications than that. Except for a few hundred archers, they were spearmen, armed also with sword or axe, and they had been drilled to advance in their schiltrons like huge, iron-bristling hedgehogs. They were disposed in four main divisions, each under a famous captain, and it is improbable that a moving mass of men, capable of movement in close order and responsive to command, could have greatly exceeded in numbers the old-style infantry battalion of about a thousand rank and file. It may be permissible to enlarge the schiltron to 1,200 or 1,300, but probably not more. Four schiltrons would then amount to about 5,000 spearmen. Add to them 500 light horse and an equal number of archers, and the Scottish army numbers 6,000 against England's 14,000 infantry and at least 2,000 heavy horse. In open country, armoured knights on covered horses were almost the equivalent of light tanks in the Western Desert: but King Robert gave them no chance to ride at will.

The Scottish army assembled in the Torwood, mobilisation having begun in May. On Saturday, 22nd June, when Edward was advancing from Falkirk, the Scots were disposed in four brigades, commanded by Randolph, earl of Moray; old James the Steward's heir Walter, whose lieutenant, and the real leader, was the boy's cousin, James Douglas; the king's brother, Edward Bruce; and Robert himself. In the king's brigade were the men of Carrick, Argyll, Bute and the Isles, and of Lowland parts that Barbour does not name. Randolph's brigade was presumably drawn from Moray, Douglas's from Strathclyde, and Edward Bruce's contingent may have come from many districts, from Galloway to Fife. The Torwood was not to be the site of the battle, and on Saturday, with Randolph leading the van and Robert commanding the rearguard, the army marched to New Park. The road entered the Park half a mile north of the Bannock, and there Robert halted his brigade under cover of the trees. Randolph took up his position beside St. Ninian's kirk, little more than a mile from the castle, and the other two brigades halted between them.

The entry to the Park was protected, on either side of the road, by a honeycomb of dug potholes covered with grass and brushwood. Barbour makes it quite clear that Robert fully appreciated the strength of the site he had chosen, for he records, at some length, what the king told his brigade commanders. The relief of Stirling castle was the enemy's intention, and to reach the castle the English must either go through the Park or across the Carse. Among the trees of the Park the Scottish infantry would have an advantage over mounted men, and cavalry on the Carse would be confused on ground so scored and channelled by many streams. And now the entry to the Park was restricted by concealed potholes.

Early on Sunday morning the Scottish army heard Mass and broke its fast on bread and water. The 'small folk' who attended the army, gillies and others, were sent under cover behind Coxet Hill. Keith, who commanded the light cavalry, and James Douglas led a reconnaissance through the Torwood to see what progress the enemy was making. They were deeply impressed by the magnificence of the invading host. Burnished armour shone in the sun, flaming banners and bright pennons flaunted their colours through the dust thrown up by the thunder of the horses' tread. The helmets and the helmet feathers burned like myriad flames above the endless host that marched against the 'few folk of ane sympill land'. Douglas and Keith galloped back to the king and delivered their report in private. Robet wisely forbade them to tell the men what they had seen, and let a story go round that the English were advancing in disorder.

The story, as things turned out, was not far from being true. About the time when Mowbray rode from the castle to meet his king, the vanguard of the English army under the earls of Hereford and Gloucester came through the Torwood and beyond the open ground of the valley of the Bannock, saw, near the entry to New Park, a number of Scots in apparent retreat. There was rivalry and ill-will between Hereford and Gloucester, and neither, as it seems, heard anything of Mowbray's news; they ignored their orders to halt south of the burn. They cantered forward—rivalry, it may be, quickened their pace—and Hereford's nephew, Sir Henry de Bohun, in advance of all the rest, saw that he who was dressing his ranks, a little way in front of the trees, was the Scottish king. Mounted on a 'gray palfrey', Robert was armed only with an axe, and a high crown surmounted his leather-capped helmet. Levelling his lance, de Bohun charged. At the crucial moment Robert pulled his pony aside, and rising in his stirrups as de Bohun thundered past, struck with his battle-axe—

> And he raucht till him sic a dynt
> That nothyr hat, nor helm, mycht stynt
> The hewy dusche that he him gave,
> That ner the heid till the harnys clave.

De Bohun fell dead, and Robert sat holding the broken shaft of his axe.

There were those who, with justification, rebuked the king for his recklessness, but the infection of that first blow filled the watching soldiers with exuberant confidence, and when the impetuous Englishmen, in disarray, pressed their attack, the Scottish spearmen hotly engaged them. Edward Bruce's brigade may have come to his brother's assistance, for the English horsemen were driven back, and as they regrouped to withdraw, the Scots pursued. But discipline ruled them, and they were recalled before they had gone too far.

Hereford and Gloucester had advanced in defiance or neglect of orders. But about the same time another cavalry division was attempting to outflank the Scots and ride to Stirling by a route east and north of New Park. Between the road and the watery, stream-cut Carse, there was firm ground above the shelf that defined the Carse, and three hundred horsemen, under Sir Robert Clifford and Sir Henry Beaumont were seeking a way to the castle that would avoid New Park and bring them in behind the Scots. The English did not believe that the Scots would stand to fight. The father of Sir Thomas de Gray, who wrote *Scalacronica*, rode in Clifford's division, and according to him Clifford and Beaumont's intention was to ride round New Park towards the castle. The *Lanercost Chronicle* explains that Clifford's purpose was 'to prevent the Scots escaping by flight'. Whether Clifford was acting independently, or in accordance with instruction, is not known, but he and his men made a dangerous advance. They went as far as St. Ninian's kirk without opposition, and Randolph, whose brigade stood by the kirk, was with the king when the English movement was first observed. In the excitement of Robert's encounter with de Bohun, and the brisk engagement that followed, some inattention to other events was not unnatural, but Randolph was sharply rebuked, and returned hurriedly to his brigade.

Promptly he led his spearmen to the attack, and that he was in time to do so may be explained by the probability that Clifford's heavy cavalry had had some difficulty on broken ground east of St. Ninian's where the Pelstream, a tributary of the Bannock, runs down into the Carse. When the English saw the schiltron advancing out of the trees, they gave it ground—they let it come into the open before charging—and then ensued a very fierce and stubborn fight. The Scottish spears took a heavy toll of horses, the English lances failed to break the iron-thorned hedge of a disciplined and implacable infantry. Infuriated by their impenetrable resistance, the horsemen hurled swords and maces into the midst of the schiltron, and unhorsed knights, encumbered by their armour, were helpless in the mêlée.

The force of the attack failed and was broken, the schiltron still advanced, and the English fled, some towards Stirling, and some, with tidings of discomfiture, back to the main body of their army. But the fight had been a close-run thing, and while it was still in doubt Douglas had begged the king to let him go to Randolph's assistance. With sound judgement, Robert refused. There was little darkness at midsummer, and the English might yet mount another attack. In the event they did nothing more aggressive than look for a night's harbour on ground that would give them some protection against a night attack, and let them water their horses. The Scots had a little leisure to enjoy their first instalment of victory, and all ranks must have felt the infection of success, and a sturdy growth of confidence from their discovery that a marching schiltron could defeat heavy cavalry.

The English horse, and some part of their infantry, crossed the Bannock and found a harbour in the upper part of the Carse under the rising contour of its defining shelf. About this, Barbour is explicit. They spent the night down in the Carse, he says, and cleaned their weapons ready for battle. And because the ground was channelled by 'pows' or sluggish streams, they broke down houses and roofs to make bridges. Some illuminating discoveries have lately been made about the nature and environment of the battlefield,[1] and much that was previously obscure, now seems clear. The Carse was earlier known as *Les Polles*—or in Scots, 'the pows'—because of the many slow streams that cut it; and an inhabited locality, too scattered to be called a village, bore the name of Bannock. It lay about that part of the Bannock burn which, through a small but steep-sided ravine, ran down into the Carse. The burn got its name from the inhabited locality, and the battle was named, not after the stream, but after the place. Therefore, argues Professor Barrow—and the argument seems convincing—the battle of the second day, which was the major battle, must have been fought near the *place*, rather than in the vicinity of some undistinguishable part of the *stream*. He cites a fifteenth-century chronicle in which the battle was still called 'of Bannok'. The second day's engagement, he suggests, took place on the higher, drier land called Balquhiderock, above the shelf, and north of the scattered 'village'; and the English army, or a large part of it, bivouacked for an uncomfortable night in the adjacent area of *Les Polles* that was called the Carse of Balquhiderock. This appears to be an acceptable definition of the battle and bivouac areas if it is remembered that the shape of the terrain may have been substantially different six hundred years ago, and both areas may have been larger than they now appear.

[1] *Robert Bruce.*

Barbour says that men from the small English garrison in the castle came to help the bridging of 'the pows' by carrying doors and window shutters from Stirling; but the distance makes it improbable that they gave much assistance. The proximity of the village or inhabited locality of Bannok, however, would make bridging feasible, and as many of the English infantry must have crossed the burn, to patrol and to screen the cavalry, there would have been no shortage of labour. How much of the enormous English baggage-train was brought forward is not known, but one may assume that Edward and his greater nobles were enabled to rest, however briefly, in some comfort.

For the majority, however, it was a night of gross discomfort, and it is easy to believe a report that many of the English infantry found relief in hearty drinking. The Scottish leaders, on the other hand, were anxiously debating strategy. Robert had spoken to his men, and after telling them how well they had done, and confessing his belief that so good a beginning should have a good ending, bade them decide whether to continue the battle or prudently retire. Their answer, natural in that exultant hour, was that they would fight. But for seven years Robert had won success by guerrilla tactics, and he seems to have seriously considered retiring to the wilder country of the Lennox, where ambush and sudden assault might gradually destroy the invader without exposing the Scots to a major defeat. In view of Edward's overwhelming strength, there was much to be said for such a plan. But during the night a deserter from the English service, Sir Alexander Seton, came into the Scottish lines with useful information. According to Sir Thomas de Gray, Seton, now a prisoner of the Scots, told the king: 'Now is the time, if ever, to win back Scotland. The English have lost heart and are discouraged. They expect nothing but a sudden, open attack. I swear on my head that if you attack in the morning you will defeat them easily and without loss.'[1] So the decision was taken to fight.

Very early on Monday, the feast of St. John the Baptist, the Scots again heard Mass. The English, moving up from the Carse on to firm ground above the shelf, saw the army advance out of New Park to kneel in prayer. Still incredulous of their intention to fight, Edward is said to have exclaimed, 'They kneel to ask mercy.' He was answered, if Barbour may be believed, by Sir Ingram de Umfraville, sometime a Guardian of Scotland, but now in England's service. 'But not of you,' said Sir Ingram. 'They ask it from God, and yon men will win or die.' 'So be it,' said Edward, and all his trumpets sounded.

The English charge was delayed by dispute between Gloucester and Hereford about the honour of leading it. When they encountered the

[1] *Scalacronica.*

Scots, Edward Bruce's brigade, on the right of the Scottish line, was the first to come into action, 'and the great horses of the English dashed upon the Scottish spears as upon a dense forest, and there arose a great and horrible din from the broken lances and the wounded horses, and so for a time they stood locked together.'[1]

Now Randolph's brigade came up on Edward Bruce's left, and Douglas on the left of Randolph. Opposed to them was the great mass of the English army, cavalry in front, infantry behind, and few of them with proper room to fight. They were committed to battle on ground too narrow for the full deployment of their strength, and they could not break through the forest of the Scottish spears. Then, for relief, some unknown leader succeeded in extricating a company, or several companies, of archers, and bringing them to a flank from which they could direct their fire against the schiltrons. The Scots had no protection against the hail of arrows—their own bowmen were out-shot—but Robert had foreseen the danger, and Keith's five hundred light horsemen were ready to counter it. Keith charged so fiercely and so compactly that the archers broke and fled, and by their flight added to confusion as they sought safety among the crowded ranks of the English infantry.

In the main battle Gloucester had been killed, old Clifford had fallen, and John of Badenoch, son of the Red Comyn, lay also among the dead. Impeded by dead or riderless horses, the English charge was halted in confusion, and slowly the advance of the schiltrons continued in the grotesque and dreadful uproar of close-locked battle. Having watched the defeat of the English archers, Robert committed his own brigade, perhaps on his brother's right. The battle had spread a little wider, and all four Scottish schiltrons were now in line. Before the pent-up fury of the king's Highlanders the English gave ground, and though many still fought stubbornly, confusion began to melt into flight. Nothing is told of the great mass of the English infantry, most of them still south of the Bannock, but evidently there was no one capable of taking command and forming a rearguard.

Now, while the chivalry of England wavered, there erupted from the back of Coxet Hill the excited mob of 'small folk', the gillies and others who had been ordered to take shelter there; and to an army more than half beaten, they may have seemed a reinforcement impossible to resist. Flight became general when it was decided that Edward must evade death or capture. It may have been Aymer de Valence, now earl of Pembroke, who insisted that he leave the field, for Edward, who had had a horse killed under him, was a brave man who had not shrunk

[1] *The Bruce.* John Barbour.

from the heat of the battle. But despite his protests he was hurried away with a great escort of five hundred knights. They rode, not across the Bannock where there was still savage fighting, but by Clifford's route to Stirling; and when Sir Giles de Argentine saw that the king was safe, he turned about and with heroic egotism rode to his death on the spears of Edward Bruce's schiltron.

Retreat became a panic flight. Men were drowned in the meandering loops of the Forth, and the little ravine of the Bannock was filled full of dead men and horses. Robert's victory was complete, and became a lasting memorial to his brilliance as a general. His strategy had been impeccable, his tactics precise and successful, and the solid foundation of his victory was the drill and discipline which had made the traditional stationary schiltron capable of offensive movement. The spoils of battle were enormous, for many of the English discarded arms and armour and all their baggage-train was taken; but Edward escaped. His capture might have concluded the war.

He was refused admittance to the castle, whose constable was ready to surrender, and rode round the west side of New Park, closely pursued by Douglas and a small body of horse. A swarm of English infantry had followed their king, and gathered under the castle rock. They were so many that Robert was compelled to hold his troops in check in case they re-formed and launched a new attack. This prevented a more effective pursuit, and Edward and his large escort got safely to Dunbar, where Earl Patrick, always an English adherent and still loyal, put him aboard a ship that carried him to Bamburgh. Most of his five hundred knights rode on to Berwick.

Many men of rank were made prisoner and held for ransom. The lordliest of the prisoners was the earl of Hereford, who was exchanged for fifteen Scottish captives in English hands. They included Robert's queen, his daughter Marjorie, and the old blind bishop of Glasgow. The large remnant of the army that had gathered under the castle rock surrendered at will, and some thousands of the Welsh contingent, harried by country folk, were led by Pembroke to Carlisle. Mowbray surrendered Stirling castle, which was demolished. There seems to have been no great slaughter of the fugitives: a sufficiency of loot may have assuaged the Scottish army's wrath.

'And now Robert de Bruce was commonly called king of Scotland by all men, because he had acquired Scotland by force of arms.'[1]

[1] *Lanercost Chronicle.*

Chapter 8

ROBERT had won Scotland by the sword and forged a sceptre in war, but until sovereignty and the independence of his people were recognised in the councils of Rome and England, his work was unfinished. In the diplomatic conversations of 1309 a formula had been proposed which, had it been acceptable to both parties, would have brought peace: it was, quite simply, the recognition of Scotland's independence and Robert's sovereignty. But Edward refused to admit these allied facts, and the war went on. Bannockburn should have taught him and his barons the truth, but it did not. After Bannockburn Scotland was ready for peace and solicited peace: King Robert wrote to King Edward saying there was nothing he so earnestly desired as a permanent good-understanding between the two kingdoms. But the formula for peace was unchanged, and the rulers of England still refused to do business on such terms. Now and again England, or the northern parts of England, were forced to appeal for a truce. But for thirteen years there was no lasting peace. From time to time olive branches waved in the wind, but no fruit fell, and Robert discovered that the only way to get the olives was to beat the trees.

A few weeks after Bannockburn, Douglas and Edward Bruce were over the border again, spoiling the northern counties; and the history of the next thirteen years is a history of raid upon raid, of punishment implacably repeated until at last the English were driven to admit the obvious force of King Robert's claims and the manifest status of Scotland.

It is unnecessary to record in detail the repetition of hammer-strokes that Robert and Douglas and Randolph dealt on the cringing counties beyond the border. Year after year the Scots raided Northumberland and Cumberland, Durham and Yorkshire, carrying fire and sword as they went, cattle and the purchase price of a new truce when they turned home again. They did not always come back unscathed, and though now they went openly as conquerors—no longer raiding with desperate audacity, but descending on the fold with the bold and peremptory air of Victory's favourites—victory did not always come to them at the first easy summons. They made a most determined attempt to capture Carlisle, Robert himself leading his troops, and despite their furious attack and ingenious device, Carlisle refused to capitulate: Sir Andrew de Harcla, its constable, was a gallant knight and a good soldier. They were beaten back from the walls of Berwick, and though on a later occasion they captured the town by assault, the castle yielded only to starvation. And the castle of Norham, commanded by the indefatigable Sir Thomas de Gray, survived eleven years of constant peril and diversified a stubborn defence with romantic incidents such as the knight of Marmion's adventure, who for love of a lady came there, as to the most dangerous place in Britain, to do battle against the Scots in a golden helmet, and went home a plainer and a wiser man, for the Scots, it is said, made shipwreck of his face— *ly naufrerent hu visage.*

There is indeed such a number of stirring episodes in the tale of these years that their more prosaic aspect of fear, starvation, and misery on the one hand, and stern policy on the other, is apt to be forgotten. Douglas laying his ambush among the birches by the Jed; Douglas's duel with de Neville, the Peacock of the North; the bishop of Dunkeld throwing off priest's raiment—he wore armour beneath it—to rout the English invaders in Fife; Simon Spalding keeping watch on the walls of Berwick—these lively events rise like bubbles to the surface of the years, but underneath were poverty and plague and dread: underneath them was Robert's unyielding resolution to establish the independent sovereignty of Scotland beyond doubt or question, beyond legal quibble or the tortuous claims of politicians and land-hungry monarchs.

The remorseless punishing of the northern counties of England was his simplest weapon, and may, indeed, have been more than a weapon. It may have been an economic policy dictated by poverty: after many years of war, internecine as well as national, it is quite improbable that Scotland was able to feed herself. Scorched earth grows no corn, and men at war have little time for husbandry. As early as 1310 Scotland had been buying meat and meal from Ireland, as well as arms and armour, and victory at Bannockburn can have done little to increase its harvests. The raiders drove cattle back from England to assuage their neighbours' hunger, and as economic policy it is likely that raiding was temporarily successful. But as a weapon to compel England's recognition of Robert's sovereignty it was blunted by the fact that southern England, where the power and riches of the kingdom lay, cared little for distresses suffered by the north. To the south of England, that before the Norman Conquest was dominated by Wessex, the north was almost a foreign land. In Rome, moreover, no manifestation of Scotland's power in arms was sufficient to influence Pope John XXII, who regarded Robert as a mischief maker.

It may be assumed that the quest for a new position of strength, from which to coerce the stubborn English, was the principal motive behind Edward Bruce's attempt to conquer Ireland. In 1315 Edward was offered the Irish crown by some Ulster chieftains who had no power to bestow it; and the excuse advanced for his ill-advised and ill-fated venture was a pledge to free the Celtic people of Ireland from their English masters. Edward Bruce was a reckless, aggressive man, of no great wisdom, and an unruly ambition was probably persuasion enough for him. But his brother Robert was a cautious man, and it is difficult to understand why he consented to so rash an undertaking unless he was persuaded, by Irish emissaries, that Ireland was indeed ready for revolt and willing to accept Scottish leaders. Then indeed he could have seen the prospect of establishing himself in a position from which he could threaten England with invasion through a resurgent Wales, and compel recognition of his sovereignty.

At first the venture went well. Edward Bruce and Randolph easily defeated the Anglo-Irish in Ulster, and won other victories over English forces. Within a year Edward was crowned king in Ireland at Dundalk, and Robert himself was persuaded to bring large reinforcements for his brother; but plague and famine joined a confused war in horrible alliance, and the winter campaign of 1317 and 1318 became a disaster mitigated by Robert's brilliant conduct of a long retreat from Limerick. The whole project was a lamentable mistake, which Scotland could ill afford, and came to its unhappy but inevitable conclusion when Edward was killed at Dundalk in 1318, and many of his army fell with him.

Edward's death necessitated a new Act of Succession. A parliament held in May, 1315, had declared that Robert's daughter, Marjorie, was the heir-apparent, but that—failing the birth of a son to Robert—she had agreed, in view of the special difficulties of the time, to be passed over in favour of Edward Bruce. Three years later Edward was dead, and Marjorie, married to the Steward of Scotland, had died in childbed leaving a son. By an Act of 1318 this son was made heir to the crown unless Robert himself should leave male issue, and in the event of his minority Randolph was named his guardian. The same Act carefully defined the principle of succession, decreeing that succession should go first to the male issue of the sovereign in the order of birth, next to the female issue, and, these being exhausted, to collaterals in the same fashion. Six years later, after twenty years of marriage—seven of which had been spent in prison in England—Robert's queen bore him a son, David, to whom, when he was two years old, the clergy, nobility, and people took oaths of fidelity at Cambuskenneth in presence of their king: and it was decreed that, should David die without issue, the succession should go to Robert, the Princess Marjorie's son.

The king's scrupulous care in nominating heirs to the throne and defining the law of succession was largely dictated by his natural desire to establish succession in his own family—dynastic motives had influenced him before patriotism moved him—but he also remembered the chaos of 1290, when there was a dearth of heirs and a glut of claimants, and these Acts were designed to prevent the recurrence of such disastrous confusion.

In 1317 the Papal Court again became actively interested in Scottish affairs. At Edward's instance the pope issued a bull commanding, under pain of excommunication, a two years' truce between England and Scotland: it was addressed to 'our dearest son in Christ, the illustrious Edward, king of England, and our beloved son, the noble Robert de Bruce, acting as king of Scotland'. Two cardinals came to England with the bull, and the cardinals sent two messengers to Scotland:

'The king graciously received them and heard them with patient attention. After having consulted with his barons, he made answer, that he mightily desired to procure a good and perpetual peace, either by the mediation of the cardinals, or by any other means. He allowed the open letters from the pope, which recommended peace, to be read in his presence, and he listened to them with all due respect; but he would not receive the sealed letters addressed to "Robert Bruce governing in Scotland". "Among my barons," said he, "there are many of the name of Robert Bruce, who share in the government of Scotland. I can receive no letters which are addressed to me under that title, unless with the advice and approbation of my parliament. I will forthwith assembly my parliament, and with their advice return my answer."

'The messengers attempted to apologise for omission of the title of king; they said that Holy Church was not wont, during the dependence of a controversy, to write or say anything which might be interpreted as prejudical to the claims of either of the contending parties. "Since, then," answered the king, "my spiritual father and my holy mother would not prejudice the cause of my adversary by bestowing on me the appellation of king during the dependence of the controversy, they ought not to have prejudiced my cause by withdrawing that appellation from me. I am in possession of the kingdom of Scotland; all my people call me king, and foreign princes address me under that title; but it seems that my parents are partial to their English son. Had you presumed to present letters with such an address to any other sovereign prince you might, perhaps, have been answered in a harsher style; but I reverence you as messengers of the holy see." He delivered this sarcastical and resolute answer with a mild and pleasant countenance.

'The messengers next requested the king to command a temporary cessation of hostilities. "To that," replied the king, "I can never consent without the approbation of my parliament, especially while the English daily invade and spoil my people."

'The king's counsellors told the messengers that if the letters had been addressed to the king of Scots, the negotiations for peace would have instantly commenced. They imputed the slighting omission of the title of king to the intrigues of the English at the Papal Court, and they unguardedly hinted that they had this intellegence from Avignon.'[1]

Robert, who was busy with preparations for the siege of Berwick, continued work on his engines, unmoved by papal interference: 'I will listen to no bulls,' he said, 'until I am treated as king of Scotland and have made myself master of Berwick.'

When he heard of Robert's refusal to receive the bull, and of the way in which his messengers had been treated—for subsequently they were robbed of all their documents—his Holiness was shocked and astounded, and his cardinals were ordered to excommunicate the Scottish king and all his adherents. The orthodox channels of excommunication were closed, however, as the patriotic clergy of Scotland declined to serve such hostile papers on their king, and the papal fulminations, echoing from beyond the border, were strangely inoperative. Then the Papal Court grew angrier still, and more active. The excommunication was repeated, and papal denunciation, commination, invective and thunder-loud reproof continued to impugn the cause of Scotland. In 1319, moreover, when Edward II, roused by the fall of Berwick and momentarily at peace with his prime enemy the earl of Lancaster, made large preparations to renew the war, the archbishop of York was authorised by the pope to advance him £2,500 out of funds collected for a crusade.

The English attempted to recapture Berwick. Their army was large, their attack determined, and their equipment elaborate. Mobilisation orders for 8,000 men were issued, ships were prepared to co-operate in the assault, and a monstrous movable engine called The Sow was constructed. The Scots, under Walter the Steward and with the assistance of a Flemish engineer called Crab, were equally determined and

[1] *Foedera:* paraphrased by Hailes.

[106]

no less ingenious. But they were hard put to it to maintain their defence. Robert, however, created a diversion in their favour by sending Douglas and Randolph on a raid into Yorkshire. The English queen was then living in York; she escaped the raiders, but Yorkshire suffered severely at their hands; and the English clergy demonstrated their lack of martial skill. 'The citizens of York, without knowledge of the country people and led by my lord archbishop William de Meltoun and my lord bishop of Ely, with a great number of priests and clerics, attacked the Scots one day after dinner near the town of Mytton, about twelve miles north of York; but as men unskilled in war they marched all scattered through the fields and in no kind of array. When the Scots beheld men rushing to fight against them they formed up according to their custom in a single schiltron, and then uttered together a tremendous shout to terrify the English, who straightway began to take to their heels at the sound. Then the Scots, breaking up their schiltron, mounted their horses and pursued the English, killing both clergy and laymen, about 4,000, and about 1,000 were drowned in the water of Swale.'[1]

The archbishop's plate and other furniture fell into the hands of the Scots, and the knowledge that they were successfully campaigning in his rear persuaded the English king to raise the siege of Berwick. Following these twin discomfitures the English sued for a truce, and for two years they were admitted to uneasy peace.

In January, 1320, the pope summoned the Scottish king—not as the Scottish king, but as *nobilem virum, Robertum de Brus, regnum Scotiae gubernantem*—to attend with his principal clergy the Papal Court at Avignon. Robert ignored the summons and the pope pronounced new excommunication against him, and against the bishops of St. Andrews, Dunkeld, Aberdeen, and Moray. But the people of Scotland had grown tired of these vacant threats, this thunder without lightning, and a parliament sitting at Arbroath in April of that year addressed to the pope a remonstrance notable for dignity beyond the common speech of parliaments, and for its heroic conception of the Christian promise to mankind.

After a preamble relating the oppressive acts of Edward I, it averred that 'at length it pleased God to restore us to liberty, from these innumerable calamities, by our most Serene Prince, King, and Lord, Robert, who for the delivering of his people and his own Rightful Inheritance from the Enemies' Hand, did like another Joshua or Maccabaeus, most cheerfully undergo all manner of toil, fatigue, hardship, and hazard. The Divine Providence, the right of succession by

[1] *Lanercost Chronicle.*

the Laws and Customs of the Kingdom (which we will defend till death) and the due and Lawful Consent and Assent of all the People made him our King and Prince. To him we are obliged and resolved to adhere in all things, both upon the account of his right and his own merit, as being the person who hath restored the people's safety, in defence of their liberties. But after all, if this Prince shall leave these principles he hath so nobly pursued, and consent that we or our Kingdom be subjected to the King or people of England, we will immediately endeavour to expel him, as our Enemy and as the subverter both of his own and our rights, and will make another king, who will defend our liberties. For so long as there shall but one hundred of us remain alive, we will never give consent to subject ourselves to the Dominion of the English. For it is not Glory, it is not Riches, neither is it Honour, but it is Liberty alone that we fight and contend for, which no Honest man will lose but with his life.'

The nobility of the declaration is indisputable, but the threat to the king is explicit. He must on no account make any show of subjection to the king of England under pain of being expelled from Scotland and replaced with another more obedient to the will of parliament. Here is no suggestion that kings enjoyed any authority other than that of popular election and the continuity of popular support; but rather an implication that Robert was still regarded as a successful guerrilla leader who could expect no further support if he deviated from the established course of the war. It should perhaps be noted that this interpretation of his authority can be substantiated, to some extent, by the generosity with which he rewarded those who had principally aided him in the War of Independence. He made lavish grants of land in the manner of a guerrilla chieftain, rather than in the style of a securely established monarch. He weakened the resources of the crown and of the kingdom by the munificence of his gifts. But his authority was, in effect, unquestioned, and the table of succession to the throne, which he had established, was not seriously challenged.

The Arbroath manifesto created a marked impression on the Papal Court, and the pope now advised Edward to make a lasting peace with Scotland. But Edward preferred secret diplomacy—which was unsuccessful—and the Scots were endeavouring to conclude a private agreement with Edward's enemy, the earl of Lancaster. This agreement was not ratified, and presently Lancaster was defeated, captured, and executed. Edward thereupon wrote to the pope: 'Give yourself no further solicitude about a truce with the Scots; the exigencies of my affairs inclined me formerly to listen to such proposals, but now I am resolved to establish peace by force of arms.'

The Scots anticipated this promised attack by raiding eighty miles into England; Robert led one army, Douglas and Randolph the other; they returned with some useful plunder, and prepared for the English invasion by making a desert of southern Scotland. Edward crossed the border in August, 1322. So thoroughly had Robert cleared the country of crops, cattle and goods, that an old bull, too lame to be driven off, was the only booty the English won. Famine impeded their advance, and dysentery reduced their strength. They lay three days in Edinburgh, and then withdrew. Douglas harried their retreat but could not prevent them from sacking the abbeys of Holyrood and Melrose and burning the monastery of Dryburgh.

Robert, having mobilised an army from the Highlands and Islands, retaliated by invading England, and nearly succeeded in capturing Edward near Rievaulx Abbey in Yorkshire. The English were defeated there after a battle in which 'the Scots were so fierce and their chiefs so daring, and the English so badly cowed, that it was like a hare before greyhounds'.[1]

This new evidence of Edward's inability to defend his people persuaded Sir Andrew de Harcla, the heroic governor and now the earl of Carlisle and warden of the Western March, to conclude a separate peace with King Robert, thinking 'that it would be better for the commonalty of both kingdoms that each king should possess his own without homage of any sort, than that such slaughter, conflagration, imprisonments, devastation, and depredation should go on every year. ... The poor folk, middle class, and farmers in the northern parts were not a little delighted that the king of Scotland should freely possess his own kingdom on such terms that they themselves might live in peace.'[2] But Edward's view of the treaty was different from the farmers' view, and de Harcla was subsequently arrested and, with all possible degradation, executed for treason.

But Edward was again compelled to sue for peace, and on 30th May, 1323, a truce of thirteen years was proclaimed at York and ratified at Berwick. English intrigue at the Papal Court continued, however, but without much effect. Robert sent his own ambassador to Avignon—his nephew Randolph, earl of Moray—and this daring and resolute soldier now showed a certain gift for diplomacy, and by tactful insistence on his own and King Robert's desire to fight for Christianity in the Holy Land, convinced the pope that it would be desirable to recognise Robert as king of Scots. His Holiness, admitting the soldier's logic, consented to this courtesy and wrote at length to King Edward

[1] *Scalacronica.*
[2] *Lanercost Chronicle.*

explaining his reasons for yielding: Edward replied with unconcealed displeasure. But negotiations proceeded for a permanent peace, and commercial relations between the two countries were slowly renewed.

In 1326 Randolph negotiated a defensive and offensive alliance with France. Randolph was rather out-generalled, however, for it was agreed that either country should terminate any condition of peace with England in the event of the other being at war with England, and that the Scots should invade England whenever England should be at war with France. In the same year a parliament was convened at Cambuskenneth, in which for the first time representatives of the Scottish burghs sat with the barons and nobility: their principal duty was to vote a grant to the king of the tenth penny on all rents to compensate him for the depreciation of his revenue by prolonged expenditure on the war.

Edward II's unhappy reign was now drawing to a close. The baronial case against him was that he undertook 'nothing in the way of honour or prowess, but was only acting on the advice of Hugh le Despencer so as to become rich. . . . The commons of the time were wealthy and protected by strong laws, but the great men had ill will against him for his cruelty and the debauched life which he led.'[1] On the Feast of St. Hilary, in January, 1327, the bishop of Hereford preached on the text from Ecclesiasticus, 'A foolish king shall ruin his people'. On the following day the bishop of Winchester preached on a text from the story of Elisha and the Shunammite, 'My head, my head', and explained with sorrow what a feeble head England had had for many years. On the third day, in the Great Hall at Westminster, the archbishop of Canterbury took for his text, 'The voice of the people is the voice of God', and announced that by unanimous consent of all the earls, barons, archbishops, bishops, clergy, and people of England, Edward was deposed from his pristine dignity, and that the Prince Edward should succeed.

The succession of Edward III produced a new series of diplomatic interchanges, which succeeded only in irritating the Scots. The English offered to renew the truce which bore the authority of Edward II, and also proposed a treaty of more lasting peace. But as they still declined to acknowledge Robert's sovereignty their good faith was not unnaturally suspect. At the same time Henry de Percy was authorised to receive into the king of England's peace any Scots who desired that dubious benefit, and England was still intriguing against Scotland at the Papal Court. Edward Balliol, moreover, son of the puppet-king John Balliol, had three years before been brought back to England with

[1] *Scalacronica.*

great solemnity, and was living there in the state befitting an illustrious person. Robert would have required a very simple faith, a childish faith, to believe in the sincerity of England's peace offers; but he and his counsellors had long lost their innocence. On Edward III's coronation day the Scots made a hostile demonstration against Norham castle, and plans were prepared once more to raid the northern parts of England unless peace were conceded on acceptable terms.

The new king and his advisers were given ample time to make ready a suitable reception for the invaders. A feudal levy was ordered, German mercenaries under John of Hainault were engaged, and a bright-hued flock of knights gathered from Flanders and Brabant, from Artois and even from Bohemia, to win renown in the first campaign of the boy-king whose ambition was to be the mirror of chivalry. This magnificent and motley army gathered at York, and tasted war without waiting for the Scots to come near them; for the English archers quarrelled with the foreigners, and such brawling started, and such ill-will grew between them, that for four weeks the knights of Hainault and Flanders and Bohemia could scarcely stir from their lodgings by day or doff their armour by night. But presently the English army, a great host, marched northwards out of York. Their progress was slow, and they came somewhat ponderously into Northumberland, 'a savage and wild country full of deserts and mountains'.[1] At Newcastle lay another considerable force, and Carlisle was also heavily garrisoned. But neither the king nor his commander in Newcastle nor the governor of Carlisle could get any information about the movements of the Scottish army, which, swiftly riding, came burning and spoiling and crossed the Tyne before news of them reached it. 'These Scottish men are right hardy,' says Froissart, 'for when they will enter into England, within a day and a night they will drive their whole host twenty-four miles, for they are all on horseback. They carry with them no carts, for the diversities of the mountains that they must pass through, in the country of Northumberland. They take with them no purveyance of bread nor wine, for their usage and soberness is such in time of war that they will pass in the journey a great long time with flesh half sodden, without bread, and drink of the river water without wine; and they neither care for pots nor pans, for they seethe beasts in their own skins. They are ever sure to find plenty of beasts in the country that they will pass through. Therefore they carry with them none other purveyance, but on their horse: between the saddle and the pommel they truss a broad plate of metal, and behind the saddle they will have a little sack full of oatmeal, to the

[1] *Chronicles.* Jean Froissart.

intent that when they have eaten of the sodden flesh that they lay this plate on the fire, and temper a little of the oatmeal: and when the plate is hot they cast of the thin paste thereon, and so make a little cake in the manner of a cracknel or biscuit, and that they eat to comfort withal their stomachs. Wherefore it is no great marvel though they make greater journeys than other people do.'

The Scottish leaders were Randolph and Douglas: the king, though no longer in good health—he was suffering from a disease that has generally been described as leprosy—had with indefatigable spirit gone again into Ireland to examine the possibility of fomenting a new rebellion in Ulster:[1] but his hopes were defeated, and after some time he returned to Scotland having accomplished nothing. Randolph and Douglas, however, were themselves masters of mobile warfare, and under their command the raiding army baffled and bewildered the portentous chivalry of England and Hainault. The smoke of burning houses would show where they were busy, but by the time the English had armed themselves, and paraded in their proper companies, and displayed their banners, the Scots were far away and new smoke told of fresh destruction. Once they left a rhyme stuck on a church door to mock their slow-foot enemies:

> Long beardes, hartlesse,
> Paynted hoodes, witlesse,
> Gaie cotes, gracelesse,
> Make Englande thriftlesse.

It was decided that as the Scots would have to recross the Tyne to get home it would be wise to wait for them by the ford they had already used, fourteen miles from Newcastle, and discarding the greater part of their baggage the English army hurriedly marched thither and lay there in great discomfort in bad weather by a flooded river. For a week they endured all manner of discomfort, for they had set out with no more food than each man could carry for himself, and when rations arrived from Newcastle, they were poor in quality, insufficient in quantity, and a penny loaf cost sixpence. Their harness rotted in the rain, their bivouacs of green branches made but a poor shelter, and all the wood was too wet to burn. And still they heard no word of the Scots, who were snugly encamped in Weardale.

The English decided to set out and look for them again, and a reward was offered of knighthood and lands worth £100 a year to any one who should bring news of the Scots' whereabouts. A dozen knights and squires set out in search of the enemy and their guerdon. For four

[1] *Calendar of Documents.* Joseph Bain.

days the English marched southwards, scarcely knowing why or whither, and then a squire called de Rokeby came in to say he had found the Scots, and indeed had been captured by them, but they, hearing of the reward he would win for finding them, and being, they said, also eager for battle, had released him and sent him back to his king. The English immediately followed de Rokeby and discovered the Scots in a strong position on high ground to the south of the river Wear. King Edward issued a formal challenge: let the Scots come down from their hill and fight fairly on level ground. The Scots, less chivalrous and having no more than a third of the English numbers, replied that they intended to stay where they were, and to stay as long as they pleased. At twilight they blew their trumpets as though 'all the devils of hell had been there',[1] and they lay that night, still defiant, in the warmth of enormous camp-fires. For three days the armies faced each other across the river, and light skirmishing relieved the monotony of their watch. The Scots were short of rations, and starvation, it was hoped, might bring them to reason. But on the fourth morning they had vanished. In the darkness they had quietly withdrawn from their hill and found another position, two miles away, where woods and marshes protected them from attack. That night Douglas led two hundred horsemen on a sudden raid into the English camp, and nearly captured the king. Having roused the whole camp, he sounded the retreat and safely withdrew. Randolph asked how he had fared: 'Sir,' said Douglas, 'we have drawn blood.'

A day and a night of most discreet activity followed. The English were ill at ease and fearful of another raid when darkness fell. In the Scottish lines camp-fires burnt brightly, and behind the lines the Scottish army was silently going home by a wet road through the protecting marsh. In the morning the English again woke to find an empty camp before them: till mid-day they stood to arms, fearing a trick; then they realised that the Scots had really gone, and their boy-king wept bitterly for his enemy's escape. It was no use to follow them. The campaign was over, and at York, on 25th August, 1327, the magnificent army was ingloriously disbanded.

Froissart, describing the retreat of the English, says 'they were nigh so feeble that it should have been great pain for them to have gone any farther', and though it is not clear whether he refers to the knights or merely to their horses, it is true that a weary inclination for rest, not merely from marching but from war, now became apparent in England. The Scots, however, showed no signs of fatigue. Robert had returned from Ireland, and brisk arrangements were made for a new

[1] *Chronicles.*

The battle sites of the War of Independence.

campaign. Robert laid siege to Norham castle; Durham was raided; Randolph and Douglas, having invested Alnwick castle, behaved with some levity and relieved the tedium of the siege with 'great jousts of war by formal agreement'.[1] Victory was assured, and they knew it, and now they could afford the time for a few tournaments.

The English parliament met at Lincoln. Depressed by the thought of having to pay their recent mercenaries from Hainault for services that had been signally unprofitable, and urged to pacific measures by Roger Mortimer, the queen-mother's paramour, they agreed to offer Robert a marriage alliance between his son, the infant Prince David, and the Princess Joan, King Edward's six-year-old sister. This proposal, signifying peace with honour, was delivered to King Robert under the walls of Norham castle. The siege was abandoned, and negotiations began without more delay. This was victory indeed, for Joan's dowry was the recognition of Scotland's independence.

Edward summoned his parliament to York, and issued safe-conducts thither for Scottish commissioners and representatives. There, on 1st March, 1328, a statement was published in which King Edward asserted that he did 'will and grant by these presents, for us, our heirs and successors whatsoever, with the common advice, assent, and consent of the prelates, princes, earls and barons, and the commons of our realm in our parliament, that the kingdom of Scotland within its own proper marches as they were held and maintained in the time of King Alexander of Scotland, last deceased, of good memory, shall be retained by our dearest ally and friend, the magnificent prince Lord Robert, by God's grace illustrious king of Scotland, and to his heirs and successors, separate in all things from the kingdom of England, whole, free and undisturbed in perpetuity, without any kind of subjection, service, claim, or demand. And by these presents we renounce and demit to the king of Scotland, his heirs and successors, whatsoever right we or our predecessors have put forward in any way in bye-gone times to the aforesaid kingdom of Scotland.'

Subsequent to this proclamation a treaty was framed, concluded in Edinburgh on 17th March, and ratified by the English parliament at Northampton on 4th May. Provision was made for the royal alliance; for the employment by England of her good offices on behalf of Scotland at the Papal Court; for the adjustment of various disputes with regard to private property sequestrated during the war; for the prohibition of Scottish intervention in Irish affairs; for the payment by Scotland of an indemnity of 30,000 marks in respect of damage sustained by the northern counties of England; for the restoration to

[1] *Scalacronica*.

Scotland of the Stone of Destiny; for perpetual peace between the two kingdoms, subject to the eminently fair provision that if Scotland, according to the terms of its treaty with France, should find it necessary to make war in England, then England should be at liberty to make war in Scotland.

The marriage of Prince David and the Princess Joan was celebrated at Berwick in July. Not all the clauses of the Treaty of Northampton were so scrupulously regarded, however, for the citizens of London refused to part with the Stone of Destiny, and the Scots do not appear to have paid the promised indemnity of 30,000 marks. But the infraction of peace treaties is not so rare a phenomenon as to deserve special comment. The Treaty was, and remains, King Robert's patent of victory.

Eleven months later, by a bull dated at Avignon, 13th June, 1329, Pope John XXII granted to Robert, the illustrious king of Scotland, and to his successors, the right to receive anointing and coronation. This right, conferring a sanctity that no civil ceremony or claim in primogeniture could bestow, had never belonged to the Scottish kings since Rome dispossessed the church of St. Columba. By it the Catholic church acknowledged what secular power had been forced to concede, and the claims for which Robert had fought so long received the sanction of the ultimate power in Christendom.

But the promise of anointing oils came a little too late: supreme unction had preceded them, for Robert had died six days before the issue of the papal edict.

A little evening of peace had preceded the king's death, and the record of his last days has room to tell of building a castle, and a house, and a ship to sail on the Clyde. He built his castle at Tarbet in Kintyre, where, two hundred and thirty years before, Magnus Bareleg's galley had been pulled across the heather to mark his dominion of Kintyre and the Isles: it was a strong castle but not luxurious, for in time of ceremony carpets of birch-boughs were laid. His house was at Cardross, near Dumbarton, where there was more comfort and some show of royal eccentricity: for as well as falcons he kept a lion in a cage, and planted a garden, and glass windows lit his painted rooms.

He was in his fifty-fifth year when he died, and his queen had predeceased him by a few months. A life of constant strain and much hardship had aged him prematurely. Before burial, his heart was taken from his body, embalmed, and closed in a silver casket. Two years later, Douglas, in obedience to the king's request, set out to carry it in war against the enemies of Christ, and then to bury it by the Holy Sepulchre.

He voyaged to Spain, where Alphonso of Castile was fighting against the Moors of Granada, and joined the Christian host. In a battle on the marches of Andalusia, thinking 'rather to be with the foremost than with the hindmost, he struck his horse with the spurs, and all his company also, and dashed into the battle of the king of Granada, crying "Douglas, Douglas!" thinking the king of Spain and his host had followed, but they did not; wherefore he was deceived, for the Spanish host stood still. And so this gentle knight was enclosed, and all his company, with the Saracens, whereas he did marvels in arms, but finally he could not endure, so that he and all his company were slain. The which was great damage, that the Spaniards would not rescue them.'[1]

Robert's heart was recovered and brought home with Douglas's body. The one was laid in Melrose Abbey, and the other in St. Bride's Chapel of Douglas. The Good Sir James, says Barbour, was not so handsome that we need speak much of his beauty: his face was somewhat grey, and he had black hair. He had great bones, broad shoulders, and finely shaped limbs; his body was well-made and lean; when he was blithe he was lovely, and meek and sweet in company, but all-another countenance he showed in battle. He spoke with a slight lisp that suited him well, and so deft was he in arms that after all his fighting his face was unscarred. Of his loyalty, unfailing courage, skill in war, and wisdom in council, history tells in plain words, and the magnanimity of his spirit has never been questioned. Only great kings are served by such as Douglas: only the greatest would not find their glory dimmed by such a friend.

Of Sir James—lisping a little, dark-hued, lovely when blithe and terrible in battle—we can make something of a picture; but Robert escapes us. Barbour says nothing of his appearance, and whether his features were as kingly as his life cannot be told. His physical strength was surely prodigious: only strong hands kept his head on his shoulders in the wilds of Galloway, and only a blacksmith's arm could have split de Bohun's helmet from the little height of a pony; but strength was allied to speed, for that swerve from de Bohun's path was quick as a matador's. 'In the art of fighting and in vigour of body, Robert had not his match in his time, in any land,' says Fordun.

Nor can his greatness as a true king, a leader of men, be denied. The essence of his statesmanship was a clear conception of Scotland's right to independent sovereignty, an unyielding determination to achieve it, and his earnest desire for peace as soon as the victory at Bannockburn had in fact established such a sovereignty. The minor

[1] Chronicle.

attributes of a statesman, his social intelligence, a gift of speech, a suavity of manner, may be discovered in the story of his reception of the papal messengers in 1317:[1] he smiles upon them, he is blandly non-compliant, he exposes their want of logic, he is helpful with suggestions that can be of no help whatever, and he is most courteously intransigent. A diplomat, one says, having read the story, and adds to the picture of the hero-king the complication of fine manners and a cultivated intelligence: a pretty addition to his qualifications as a guerrilla chief.

To the church, whose priests and bishops had always been his true friends and most daring allies, he showed a boundless liberality. The Scottish church had helped him with heart and voice, in body and in spirit, and he rewarded it with open hands. He never forgot his friends, and often he forgave his enemies. The monks of Lanercost observed that his progress through Cumberland had been strangely merciful, and they were the English chroniclers who recorded his clemency after Bannockburn. There was no unnecessary cruelty in his policy. His military virtue was supreme, his temper humane and genial. He re-created a nation, he unified a people that has always shown a genius for disunion, and he won for Scotland a few years of rarest triumph. But the glory did not endure.

[1] Pages 105–6.

Book Three

THE ROYAL STEWARTS: ROBERT II TO JAMES IV

Chapter I

THE glory did not endure. In the long perspective of history it seems to have vanished overnight, and much of what followed was both shameful and ludicrous.

Robert's son David, now David II, was only five years old and already married, in accordance with the terms of the Treaty of Northampton, to Joan, sister of Edward III. The purpose of the marriage was to 'assure and confirm' the peace between England and Scotland; but in England it was unpopular. An Act of 1318 had named Thomas Randolph, earl of Moray, as regent during David's minority; but that prudent, strong, and valiant man died in 1332, and James Douglas was already dead in Spain.

Donald, earl of Mar, was then elected regent, and almost simultaneously Scotland was invaded by Edward Balliol, son of John the Toom Tabard, at the head of a small army whose chiefs were commonly called the 'Disinherited'. They were barons who, having chosen to fight on the English side, had forfeited their estates; but with them were English lords in quest of Scottish land, and undoubtedly the army had been helped and encouraged by the English king. Edward III had already received Balliol's homage, not as a private person, but as king of Scotland.

At Dupplin, near Perth, the regent Mar, in command of a large army, was surprised and defeated by the invaders, and in September, 1332, Scotland got a second king when Balliol was crowned at Scone. His reign was brief, for before Christmas he was chased over the border by the earl of Moray, son of Thomas Randolph, and Archibald Douglas, a younger brother of Sir James. But Scotland's weakness had been disastrously revealed. Under the prolonged stress of war much of its administrative system had collapsed, and the unity it had shown under strong leadership had insufficient foundations to maintain itself without leadership. The only common interest was detestation of the English, and even to that ruling emotion there were exceptions.

Balliol returned to Scotland, and Edward III now openly supported him. Berwick was besieged, and in an attempt to relieve it the new regent, Archibald Douglas, gave battle at Halidon Hill, not far from the town. His army was destroyed by the English archers, whose fire-power was deadly. Within four years of Robert's death Scotland had tumbled into an abyss of defeat. At a parliament in Edinburgh Balliol surrendered Berwick to Edward III, Lord Paramount of Scotland, and the following year, at Newcastle, granted by charter to the English king the southern counties from Haddington in the east to Dumfries in the west. English sheriffs were appointed, English garrisons occupied the castles, and the 'Disinherited' returned to their forfeited lands. English barons became earls of Buchan, Mar, and Strathearn; Annandale and Liddesdale got English lords. Balliol again did homage for the kingdom he had pawned.

Yet Scotland refused to accept the manifest fact of its defeat. The boy David and his queen found safety in France. Again and again Edward had to cross the border to help his puppet king, whose kingdom was so dangerous that neither castle nor town could promise him security. The English king was not to be resisted but as soon as his back was turned, his lieutenants were in peril. And then, in 1338, Edward perceived a richer prize across the Channel, and crossing to the Low Countries laid claim to the throne of France, and began the Hundred Years' War. That paragon of tenacity the countess of March—a daughter of Thomas Randolph, familiarly called Black Agnes—had held the castle of Dunbar against a five months' siege, and now the English garrisons in Edinburgh and Perth were driven out. In the west Sir William Douglas, a natural son of the Good Sir James, took the field; and Balliol again retired to England.

David II came home from France, and in 1346 rashly listened to a French appeal for help against the common enemy, and invaded northern England. He was a king who did neither credit nor service to Scotland, but he was brave enough, and in battle at Neville's Cross, near Durham, he was twice wounded and fought with his captor before he was subdued. The Scots were again defeated by the English bowmen, and David was led in triumph to the Tower of London. He was to be a prisoner for eleven years, and for those eleven years the regent of Scotland was Robert the Steward, son of Walter and David's half-sister Marjorie. Robert had been present at Neville's Cross, and was under some suspicion of having deserted his king.

After long delay it was decided that a ransom of 90,000 marks, to be paid in instalments, was the proper price for David's freedom, but the French, alarmed at the prospect of peace between England and Scotland, sent men and money to their deluded ally, and a Franco-Scottish force recaptured Berwick. Edward III, who had returned from France, took immediate and terrible revenge. He marched to Berwick, and from Roxburgh to Edinburgh laid waste the whole country, leaving so black a desolation that this punitive march—which coincided with the Feast of the Purification of the Virgin—was known as the Burnt Candlemas. A year later, however, in 1357, a new treaty re-assessed David's ransom at 100,000 marks—a mark was two-thirds of a pound sterling—and Robert Bruce's worthless son returned to freedom in an impoverished land whose poverty he aggravated by witless extravagance. He pawned the crown jewels, he spent on his own pleasure the money painfully wrung from a straitened people to pay his ransom. He drove his nobles to revolt, and in 1363 Robert the Steward, William Douglas—a nephew of the Good Sir James and now earl of Douglas—and George, earl of March, led a rebellion which was defeated or pacified. David celebrated that local victory by riding to London and making with Edward III a scandalous agreement to surrender, to Edward or one of his sons, the succession to the Scottish throne in return for cancellation of his ransom; of which, in six years, only two instalments had been paid. David's first wife, Joan, had died without issue the previous year. His second marriage, to a handsome widow, was also barren.

At Scone, in 1364, a Scottish parliament indignantly refused its consent to the monstrous bargain that David had so shamelessly proposed. The land was overburdened, custom duties had been doubled and again increased, but penal taxation was preferable to a Plantaganet king, and a new effort would be made to pay the ransom. France, as it happened, came to Scotland's rescue by renewal of its war with England, and when Edward found himself in difficulties he agreed to accept reduced instalments of 4,000 marks; which were duly paid from 1369 till his death eight years later. The parliament of 1364 was doubly notable. Its sturdy regard for independence was most admirable, and for the first time its members appear to have represented the Three Estates of the realm: they included not only prelates and nobility, but commissioners from the royal burghs.

The special power of the burghs, which had their own court, had long been recognised. From the time of Alexander III, and even earlier, the merchants of the burghs had enjoyed the monopoly of trade within their own areas. They were the money-makers of the kingdom, and despite the almost endemic disease of war and the recurrent failure of administration, they had maintained a precarious trade with buyers overseas. Burghal rights and burghal law cannot be regarded as evidence of a growing democracy within the little towns of the kingdom, for in the beginning the merchants and the craftsmen who served them had enjoyed, if not equal, at least comparable rights; but with the growth of trade, and the accumulation of wealth, the importance and power of the merchants increased, and the influence of the craftsmen diminished. But recognition of mercantile power and privilege implied a division of authority, or a broadening of the base of authority, which thrust responsibility on to a new class and brought the burgesses into association with the noble and learned classes who ruled by right of inheritance or with the voice of the church. The admission to power of the Third Estate was the first dawning—though noon was very far away—of government by the people and for the people.

In 1296 the burghs of Edinburgh, Berwick, Roxburgh, Stirling, Perth, and Aberdeen had formally signified their approval of an alliance with France. Thirty years later, when crown rents had dwindled under the stress of war, the burgesses of the kingdom had agreed with its nobility to pay a tenth of their revenue to the king, who for his part undertook to pay the market price for goods required in the royal service. Then, when 100,000 marks were demanded for the ransom of their worthless monarch, the burgesses were not only summoned to help, but admitted to parliament as representatives of a third power in the land. It will be charitable to give David credit for the elevation of the Third Estate. Nothing else can be said in his favour, and his death in 1371 cannot have been regretted. As well as being frivolous, extravagant, and inept, he was unlucky; for it was in his reign that the Black Death came to Scotland. It was imported from England in 1349, when a foolish raid on Carlisle carried infection from a plague-stricken town; and in three subsequent visitations it brought fearful mortality.

David's successor was his nephew Robert, who had been regent during David's captivity. Older than the late king, Robert II was fifty-five when he succeeded by right of his mother Marjorie—wife of Walter the Steward, daughter of Robert Bruce—who had died in childbirth or soon after. Robert was a tall and handsome man, of stately appearance, but a weak and ineffectual king. Philoprogenitive to a marked degree, he fathered on Elizabeth, daughter of Sir Robert Mure of Rowallan, four sons and six daughters before marrying her. By his second wife Euphemia, daughter of the earl of Ross, he had two sons and several daughters; and his illegitimate children numbered at least eight sons. Though children born out of wedlock were legitimated by the subsequent marriage of their parents, it was thought advisable to affirm, with consent of the prelacy and nobility, that Robert's eldest son, John, earl of Carrick, was indeed heir to the throne, and recognised as such; an affirmation which, in due course, gave Scotland a king even feebler than Robert II.

The French alliance was renewed, and fourteen years' truce had been concluded with England in 1369. In the last years of his reign, Edward III —who died in 1377—had been roughly treated in France, where the constable, Bertrand du Guesclin, had driven his troops out of theEnglish possessions between the Loire and the Gironde. Edward, the warrior-king, was no longer an active menace to Scotland, and Robert II might have enjoyed a peaceful reign if his own nobility had been more tract-able. But the great men of Scotland, their possessions swollen by the munificence of Robert I, and their native arrogance enhanced by memories of successful war, were in no mood to accept the authority of an elderly king whose family was no better than their own, and whose throne was merely the heritage of his father's fortunate marriage with Marjorie Bruce. In parts of the country a noble anarchy prevailed, and on the borders recurrent warfare made mockery of official truce.

In 1378 the Scots took Berwick, but lost it again. Richard II had succeeded to the English throne, and his uncle John of Gaunt, duke of Lancaster, made a gentle foray that exacted a new promise of peace. Four years later there was some fighting in the south-west, and John of Gaunt returned with an army that made history. It marched as far as Edinburgh, and left Edinburgh intact. Shakespeare's 'time-honoured Lancaster' had, in the intervening years, thought it prudent to leave England when Wat Tyler led the Peasants' Revolt, and he had found refuge in Holyrood. He showed gratitude for the hospitality he had received by denying to his army the customary pleasure of setting Edinburgh on fire. His gentle example was not followed and the borders again erupted.

In 1385 the French endeavoured to maintain their war against England by mounting a small expedition from Scotland. The admiral of France, John de Vienne, arrived with a force of knights and men-at-arms, a lavish present of armour, and a subsidy said to amount to 50,000 francs in gold. Their incursion had unfortunate results. The Scots were jealous of their allies' wealth and splendour, the French resented the coldness of their welcome, and were contemptuous of Scotland's poverty. The admiral wanted the glory of victory in a pitched battle; he was taken on a border raid. The Scots, under the earl of Douglas, insisted on a retreat when strong opposition threatened, and when Richard II led a punitive expedition into Scotland, the French were shocked by their allies' strategy. Without opposition the English were allowed to burn Melrose Abbey. They burnt Dryburgh, Holyrood, and Edinburgh; and the Scots made no effort to defend their country. The English were exhausted by their exertions and got no military benefit from them; but Douglas recovered Teviotdale and from the north-west of England took a booty that, if one excepts the destruction of Melrose, made handsome recompense for the damage inflicted elsewhere. The English having retired, there was no reason for the French to remain in Scotland; but before returning to their own country they were, to their intense disgust, required to pay the cost of their maintenance.

Two years later, in reprisal perhaps for Richard's invasion, there was a massive raid across the border led by Douglas and the king's second surviving son, Robert, earl of Fife. The north of England was harried and plundered as far as Durham, but a reward more lasting than the common booty of war was the product of that incursion. Of all the border ballads there is none more splendid than *The Battle of Otterburn*, and it deserves quotation because the heritage of border warfare was not only hatred and wasted lands, but memories of heroic enterprise, of chivalry and hardihood. It would be false, and grotesquely false, to pretend that warfare became a game, but it became a way of life in which audacity and skill at arms had values of their own, and a name for gallantry was worth more than a stolen herd of cattle.

The ballad-maker knew the rules of chivalry, and the Douglas— James, the second earl—challenges Harry Percy, known as Hotspur, whose father was Henry, first earl of Northumberland:

> To Newcastell when that they came,
>   The Douglas cry'd on hyght:
> 'Harry Percy, an thou bidest within,
>   Come to the fight, and fight!—

> 'For we have brent Northumberland,
>   Thy herytage good and right;'

The challenge accepted, battle was joined at Otterburn between the Cheviots and the Roman Wall. Percy and Douglas met and fought till blood ran in the sweat of their brows like mist in the rain. Percy was the better man, and with a mortal blow struck Douglas to the ground.

> The Douglas call'd to his little foot-page,
>   And sayd, 'Run speedilye,
> And fetch my ain dear sister's son,
>   Sir Hugh Montgomery.

> 'My nephew good,' the Douglas sayd,
>   'What recks the death of ane?
> Last night I dream'd a dreary dream,
>   And I ken the day's thy ain.

My wound is deep: I am fayn to sleep,
    Take thou the vaward of me,
And hide me by the bracken bush
    Grows on yon lilye-lee.'

All day and all night the battle continued, till Percy and Montgomery
met:

'Now yield thee, yield thee, Percy,' he said,
    'Or I vow I'le lay thee low!'
'To whom shall I yield?' said Earl Percy,
    'Now I see it maun be so.'—

'Thou shalt not yield to lord nor loun,
    Nor yet shalt thou to me;
But yield thee to the bracken bush
    Grows on yon lilye-lee.'—

'I winna yield to a bracken bush,
    Nor yet I will to a brere;
But I would yield to Earl Douglas,
    Or Montgomery if he was here.'

So Percy yielded. Douglas was killed, and a battlefield in a country
wasted by war was illuminated, as if at dawn, by the light of a poetic
understanding which saw nothing strange in reconciliation after battle:

The fray was fought at Otterbourne,
    Between the night and the day;
Earl Douglas was buried at the bracken bush,
    And the Percy led captive away.

There is, too, something like reconciliation in the epitaph pronounced on Robert II when, at the age of seventy-four, he died in
Ayrshire. 'A tenderare hart mycht na man have': so a contemporary
wrote, and there, perhaps, lies the explanation of his enormous family
and his failure in public life.

One of his sons was Alexander, earl of Buchan, known as the Wolf
of Badenoch, who in the first year of Robert III's[1] reign made monstrous
exhibition of the anarchy in northern Scotland. His misdeeds were
notorious, he was censured with good reason by the bishop of Moray,
and retaliated by burning the burghs of Forres and Elgin and the
bishop's cathedral in Elgin; one of the noblest buildings in Scotland.
He was persuaded to do penance for his crime in the Dominican
church at Perth, but suffered no other punishment; for there was no
effective law in Scotland.

More remarkable was an instance of what must be called romantic

[1] His baptismal name was John, but he elected to be crowned as Robert.

savagery. There had long existed a Highland feud between Clan Chattan and Clan Kay, whose identification still presents some difficulty, though Highland genealogists appear confident that the dispute, finally settled in battle, was between Davidsons and Macphersons, both of whom were tribes within the kinship of Clan Chattan. A judicial combat was arranged, and an enclosure erected on the North Inch of Perth, a broad meadow beside the river Tay, within which thirty men from each clan were to fight to the death with chosen weapons. The contest duly took place, before the king and a great crowd of spectators, and those fighting as Clan Chattan were the victors. Twenty-eight of Clan Kay were killed, and out of the whole sixty either seven or eleven wounded men survived. The combat, it is said, brought peace to the Highlands for a long time; and though the barbarity, as a spectacle, of organised battle cannot be denied, it must be admitted that the willingness of the clans to submit to judicial combat is an indication of rude order in the emergent society of the north.

A family quarrel, of clouded origin and obscure conclusion, now occurred between Robert, earl of Fife, and Robert III's elder son, David, who at the age of sixteen was created duke of Rothesay; the ducal title being new to Scotland. The earl of Fife, a son of Robert II, was at the same time made duke of Albany. In his father's time Albany had acted as Governor of Scotland, and continued as such under Robert III until 1393. But in 1399 Rothesay was made Lieutenant of the realm, with power to act in the king's name. Albany's ambition was clearly evinced in his choice of a title—*Albany* was an old name for all Scotland beyond the Forth—and that he should now be jealous of his young nephew was natural enough. Rothesay's behaviour, moreover, aggravated the older man's displeasure. In rapid succession Rothesay married, and was parted from, a daughter of the earl of March, and a daughter of the earl of Douglas; and he is said to have lived a life of vice and folly. If that is true, he paid for his folly by an early death, which may have been hastened by Albany's intervention. The fact that a parliamentary inquiry into his death was thought necessary, and came to the conclusion that he 'had departed by divine Providence and from no other cause', may or may not seem to cast suspicion on Albany.

Between him and the throne there was now only Robert III's younger son James, a boy of seven. Albany resumed his former power as Governor or Lieutenant of the kingdom, and war with England was renewed. In England the troubled reign of Richard II had come to its unhappy end, and Henry IV, a son of John of Gaunt, had succeeded. He had made overtures of peace to Scotland, and been rebuffed; in consequence of which he led an army as far as Edinburgh, contemplated for some days the difficulties of assaulting it, and withdrew when news arrived of imminent trouble in Wales. He acquired as an ally, however, the earl of March, whose daughter had been ill-treated by the young duke of Rothesay. The offended earl renounced his allegiance to Scotland, and continued the offensive which Henry IV had tentatively essayed. In 1402 an army of considerable size, under Albany's eldest son and Archibald, the young earl of Douglas, marched into England, and at Homildon Hill, north of Wooler in Northumberland, was defeated in the usual way: English archers, shooting with pitiless accuracy, drove it from the field in rout, leaving as prisoners five earls, of whom Douglas was one.

The English army was led by Harry Hotspur and the renegade earl of March, and it is agreeable to record that Hotspur, having revenged himself for discomfiture at Otterburn by taking prisoner Archibald Douglas, a second cousin of James Douglas whom he had killed but who had defeated him, then became so friendly with his prisoner that Archibald went with him to battle against Henry IV, when Hotspur rose in revolt against his king. Hotspur was killed at Shrewsbury, and the spirit of the border ballads revives in the inevitable feeling that his death was a loss to both England and Scotland.

In Scotland Albany remained master of the country, but the aged king, only a little while before his death, contrived to send his surviving son, the boy James, now aged eleven, to France. This was manifestly a sensible precaution, for even if Albany was guiltless of Rothesay's death, the temptation to eliminate James might have been more than ambition could withstand. It was unfortunate indeed that the ship in which the boy sailed was captured, off Flamborough Head, by the English. Whether this was due to sheer mishap, or the timely despatch of a messenger to England, no one now can say; but the consequence was that James lived in exile from his native land for eighteen years. Robert III died a few weeks later, having dictated his own melancholy epitaph: 'Here lies the worst of kings and the most miserable of men.' Like his father he was a man of majestic stature, whose long white beard and benign expression gave him a look of fatherly devotion to his people; which, indeed, he may have felt. In one respect his reign was fortunate, for harvests had been good and the people were well fed.

In 1406 the boy James was proclaimed king, and Albany appointed regent. Albany ruled in his own name, but the kingly state he assumed rested not so much on any real power to govern as on a remarkable ability to placate his nobles and please the people. He was praised for the moderation of his rule, but no other policy was open to him. He was rich, and is said to have been generous. He had to walk warily, and is reported to have been just. His cleverness is indisputable. He persuaded Henry IV to release Archibald, earl of Douglas, who had been taken prisoner at Shrewsbury; and with Douglas he made a compact or 'bond' of mutual assistance. He induced the renegade earl of March to return to Scotland.

During his regency the first heretic was burnt in Scotland, and the university of St. Andrews was founded. After the papal schism, and the installation of a second pope in Avignon in 1378, Scottish students preferred the university of Paris to Oxford or Cambridge; but when France forsook the anti-pope, Benedict XIII, he sought refuge in Spain, a country that offered no inducement to scholars. England adhered to the pope of Rome, and Scotland, still faithful to Benedict, was in need of its own school. Benedict granted bulls that gave St. Andrews a university's privilege to teach and examine in several faculties, and the university was founded in 1411.

The papal schism was also responsible for the introduction of heresy. In England John Wyclif declared the church would do better without pope or prelates, and denying the priestly power of absolution, denounced penances and indulgences. He had previously expressed his belief that episcopal sees and monasteries should be disendowed; and he preached the dangerous doctrine that only those in a state of grace had an inherent right to property or office. His teaching spread to Scotland, and its first martyr was John Resby, who was burnt in Perth.

Midway between such disparate evidence of the coming of a more modern world, a Highland war disturbed the north. The chiefs of Clan Donald, Lords of the Isles by virtue of descent from Somerled, were virtually independent, and in 1411 Donald of the Isles claimed in his wife's name the earldom of Ross. Such addition to his power would have made him formidable indeed; but Albany had a personal interest in the earldom. His granddaughter Euphemia was the rightful heir, and Euphemia, a nun, had resigned her title in favour of Albany's son John, earl of Buchan. Faced with opposition, Donald prepared to fight and led a Highland army to Inverness, which he burnt. His intention was to seize the earldom lands in the shires of Banff and Aberdeen, and plunder Aberdeen to pay his followers. Aided by the local gentry, the burgesses made ready for battle, and found an able leader in Alexander, earl of Mar, a son of the Wolf of Badenoch and grandson of Robert II. Donald of the Isles, through his mother, was another of Robert's grandchildren, and the battle of Harlaw was rather a family dispute than a fight between Lowlands and Highlands. It was a bloody affair, fought some twenty miles north-west of Aberdeen, and for long it was remembered as 'the red Harlaw'. The upshot was that Donald was defeated, Aberdeen saved, and Albany's son got the earldom of Ross.

Albany died in 1420, at the great age of eighty-three, and his son Murdoch followed him as regent. Now Scotland again became involved in the affairs of France, and made restitution for its shabby treatment of John de Vienne and his knights in 1385. The French were in sore need of help. That brilliant soldier, Henry V of England, had soundly beaten them at Agincourt in 1415, and under the mad King Charles VI their country was bitterly divided between the rival parties of Burgundy and Armagnac. Henry married Catherine, daughter of Charles VI, and was recognised, by the Burgundians, as regent and heir to the French throne. The dauphin appealed for aid to Scotland, and in 1491 a Spanish fleet escorted to La Rochelle a Scottish army said to have numbered 6,000—but surely this is an exaggeration—which Albany's son, the earl of Buchan, commanded. As the French in Scotland had made themselves unpopular, so did the Scots in France. They ate too much, and drank too much: a still persistent habit of soldiers in a foreign country. But in 1421, at Baugé, east of Angers, they defeated Henry V's brother Clarence; and three years later, at Verneuil, they fought to the bitter end of a lost battle, their dead including the earls of Buchan and Douglas. A few years later, Scottish soldiers shared the defence of Orleans and marched under the banner of Joan of Arc. These spirited actions presaged much that is curious in Scottish history; for often, in the future, Scotland was to find good soldiers for service abroad, when few could be found for its own defence.

Henry V died of dysentery in 1422. His son, Henry VI, was only a few months old, and the child's uncles, who governed in his name, were willing to release James, the still uncrowned king of Scotland, in return for a ransom of 60,000 marks. In 1424 James married the Lady Joan Beaufort, his 'milk-white dove', a granddaughter of John of Gaunt, and in April of that year returned to the country he had not seen for eighteen years.

A century, all but a few years, had elapsed since the death of Robert Bruce, and in that century Scotland had often been humiliated, often distracted by war. Parts of it had been blackened by war, and parts wrung dry by war's exactions. The power of the throne had been dissipated by folly, and like other European countries Scotland had watched the growth of a rich and dissident nobility that threatened to unfasten the whole structure of the kingdom. Yet Scotland had survived. As it had endured the hammer-blows of Edward I, so it had endured and survived the maladministration of its own kings and the anarchic temper of its native magnates. It had, indeed, done better than survive. It had defied ill-fortune, and put on growth.

Berwick, the great seaport, a 'second Alexandria', had been lost to the English, and Roxburgh, one of the first four burghs, was still in their hands. But Edinburgh, Dundee and Aberdeen had become thriving ports, and ships were being built in Inverness. St. Andrews had acquired a university—which quickly and ungratefully transferred its allegiance from the pope at Avignon to him in Rome—and parliament, having added the Third Estate to its prelacy and nobility, had begun to acknowledge its increasing responsibilities by delegating some of its functions to what may, without too much exaggeration, be called executive committees. In many parts of the country there were signs and symptoms of increasing prosperity. Though no chronicler has recorded their activities, it is possible that the burgesses of the growing burghs had found profitable investment for the spoils of Bannockburn; and it may be suspected that the very inefficiency of those old gentlemen, Robert II and Robert III, had given the rising merchants of the towns a freedom which a closer administration might have denied them. Harvests had been good; and perhaps God had tempered the wind for His shorn lambs.

Chapter 2

THE Stewart Dynasty had made an inauspicious beginning. The old Breton family, briefly domesticated in Shropshire, from which David I had chosen a *dapifer* or high steward to accompany him to Scotland, had sired, with the initial compliance of Marjorie Bruce, two amiable but ineffectual monarchs, and no one, in 1424, could have foreseen the race of talented, high-spirited, and personally attractive kings who were to fetch their descent from the old tired loins of Robert III. Only in their unfailing misfortune were the later Stewarts to recall their progenitor. In all other ways they were the most agreeable and gifted of royal races in Europe. But in James I the family pattern of intelligence, flair, and unfailing tragedy was firmly established.

Before essaying an account of his reign, it is fitting to say something of the man himself and his accomplishments; for to the throne of Scotland he brought the novelty of a literary ability of high order. During his long residence in England he had read, and learnt to appreciate with a profound understanding, at least some of the poetry of Geoffrey Chaucer. His own long poem, *The King's Quhair*,[1] is modelled on Chaucer's translation of the famous French allegory, *Roman de la Rose*, and while the motive is the young king's love for Joan Beaufort, whom he married, the influence under which he wrote is literary; and in its grace and craftsmanship *The King's Quhair* will stand comparison with Chaucer. Imprisoned in a tower that overlooks a garden—a garden was a conventional scene, but in James's case it may have been real—he looks out and sees his young love walking:

> And therewith kest I doun myn eye ageyne,
>   Quhare as I saw walkyng under the Toure,
> Full secretely, new cumyn hir to pleyne,
>   The fairest or the freschest young floure
>   That ever I sawe, methoucht, before that houre,

---

[1] Book.

For quhich sodayne abate, anon astert
The blude of all my body to my hert.

And though I stood abaisit then a lyte,
   No wonder was, for quhy? my wittis all
Were so ouercome with plesance and delyte,
   Only through latting of myn eyen fall,
That sudaynly my hert become hir thrall
   For ever; of free wyll, for of manace
There was no takyn in hir suete face.

From time to time there has been dispute as to whether James was indeed the author of the *Quhair*; but there is no need to doubt it, and there can be no denial that poetic ability of such an order gave the Scottish throne a distinction wholly new in kind. He was not the founding father of Scottish literature, for Barbour, who made an epic poem of Robert Bruce's life, had preceded him: Barbour died some thirty years before James came back to Scotland. But James must be given some credit for the flowering of Scottish poetry that so boldly coloured the next hundred years.

It was formerly believed that he had also written two shorter poems, of a very different sort, called *Peebles to the Play* and *Christ's Kirk on the Green*; but possibly, or even probably, they date from later in the century. There is interest, however, in the fact that for a long time they were associated with James—it was considered not improbable that a king of his temperament was their author—and they are worth attention because they offer a glimpse of the ordinary people of the fifteenth century: the people who grew the crops, and shod the horses, and served the growing needs of an expanding community.

Christ's Kirk opens boisterously:

Was nevir in Scotland hard nor sene
Sic dansing nor deray,
Nowthir at Falkland on the grene,
Nor Pebilis at the play,
As wes of wowaris, as I wene,
At Chryst-kirk on ane day;
There come our Kitteis weschin clene,
In new kirtillis of gray,
                      Full gay,
At Chrystis kirk on the grene.

To dans thir damyfellis thame dicht,
Thir lasses licht of laitis;
Thair gluves wer of the raffel richt,
Thair schone wer of the straitis.

Thair kirtillis wer of lincum licht,
Weill prest with mony plaittis;
Thay wer sa nyss quhan men thame nicht,
Tha ysqueilit lyk only gaittis,
                                    Sa loud,
At Chrystis kirk &c.

Of all thir madynis, myld as meid,
Was nane sa gympt as Gillie;
As ony rose hir rude was reid,
Hir lyre wes lyk the lillie:
Fow yellow yellow wes hir heid,
Bot scho of lufe so sillie;
Thocht all hir kin had sworn hir deid,
Sche wald haif bot sweit Willie
                                    Allane,
At Chrystis kirk &c.

Scho skornit Jok and skrippit at him;
And murgeonit him with mokkis;
He wald haif lufit, sche wald nocht lat him,
For all his yellow lokkis.
He chreist hir, scho bad ga chat him,
Sche compt him nocht twa clokkis;
Sa schamfullie ane schort goun sat him,
His lymmis wer lyk twa rokkis,
                                    Scho said,
At Chrystis kirk &c.

Against the larger historical picture of war and internecine strife, of plague and disaster—the picture of preceding reigns is a picture that will recur in later years—it is necessary to study the evidence of such verses as these; and the comforting fact emerges that common life was not entirely darkened by the thundrous shadow of great events, nor wholly shattered by the destructive ambition of unruly nobles. Common life kept an appetite for jollity, and there was village junketing though the castle nursed its plots and brooded over new conspiracy. Village girls could afford leather gloves and narrow shoes and kirtles of dainty linen; and being light of heart could mock a young man despite the attraction of his well-combed yellow hair. Whoever wrote the poem—whether James or some other—he was a man of education, but not removed by education from sympathy with ordinary people; and the ordinary people were not unduly, or always, oppressed by authority.

Peebles to the Play is in rougher mood, and scatters any inclination to suppose that village life, because it had seasons of jollity, was therefore idyllic:

> Than they to the tavern-house
> With meikle olyprance;
> And spak wi' wordis wonder crouse,
> 'A done with ane mischance!
> Braid up the burde,' he hydis tyt,
> 'We are all in ane trance:
> See that our nap'ry be white,
> For we will dine and dance,
> > There out,
> Of Peblis to the play.'
>
> Ay as the gudewife broucht in,
> Ane scorit upon the wauch,
> And bade pay, ane other said, 'Nay,
> Bide whill we reckon our lauch.'
> The guidewife said, 'Have ye na dreid:
> Ye sall pay at ye auch.'
> And young man start upon his feet,
> And he began to lauche,
> > For heydin,
> Of Peblis to the play.
>
> He gat ane trenchour in his hand
> And he began to compt:
> 'Ilk man twa and ane ha'penny!
> To pay thus we were wont.'
> Ane other start upon his feet,
> And said, 'Thou art owre blunt
> To tak sic office upon hand!
> Be God thou servit ane dunt
> > Of me,
> Of Peblis to the play.'
>
> 'Ane dunt,' quod he, 'what devil is that?
> Be God, you dar not do't!'
> He start till ane broggit staff,
> Winceand as he were wood.
> All that house was in ane reird:
> And cryit, 'The haly rude!
> Help us, Lord, upon this erd,
> That there be spilt na blude
> > Herein,
> Of Peblis to the play!'

Jollifications in the fifteenth century might be rough and rowdy, but as it is unlikely that many people, of either sex, survived their

[136]

infancy except those who were robust from birth, they probably suited the majority of those who shared them. And again it must be noted that rowdy celebration of high days and holidays is proof that life was not all subject to the mischances of history; and it is possible that a self-seeking and adventurous aristocracy bore less hardly on its humble neighbours than on its king.

James was well aware of the lawlessness in the land, and the need of a strong king ruling strongly. He was in his thirtieth year when, in 1424, he came home to be crowned at Scone, and in his first parliament he made it abundantly clear that he intended to establish and maintain peace throughout his realm; to punish rebels and all who broke the law; and to assure his own income by punctual collection of all customs and burghal dues. According to a tradition that may readily be accepted he is said to have declared that if God granted him life, 'There shall be no place in my realm where the key shall not keep the castle, and the bracken-bush the cow.'

Little more than a year after his accession, he ordered the arrest of Murdoch, duke of Albany, lately the regent, and his son Alexander. Already in confinement were Murdoch's elder son Walter, and his old father-in-law the earl of Lennox, and several other distinguished dissidents. What they had done to provoke the king's displeasure is not known, but manifestly they offered menace or obstruction to his authority, for in May, 1425, having been convicted by their peers, Murdoch and his sons and old Lennox were executed on the Heading Hill at Stirling.

Three years later James turned his rigorous attention to the High-lands, where, it must be inferred, the native spirit of independence, unsubdued by the red ruin of Harlaw, had again been contumacious. To a parliament in Inverness James summoned forty or more Highland chiefs, among whom was Alexander, Lord of the Isles, the son of Donald who had fought at Harlaw. All were arrested, three were executed. The others, including Alexander, were sentenced to brief imprisonment, and for a little while there was peace. But in 1429 Alexander, unrepentant, took revenge by burning Inverness. He would have done better to admit defeat, for promptly the king marched into Lochaber, where Alexander was forced to submit. His life was spared, and in the church at Holyrood, standing in shirt and drawers before the high altar, he formally surrendered and yielded his sword to the king. After a short imprisonment in Tantallon castle, he was given his freedom; but James was less lenient to others.

After the execution of old Lennox, James took possession of his estates, and kept them. Malise, earl of Strathearn, was deprived of his

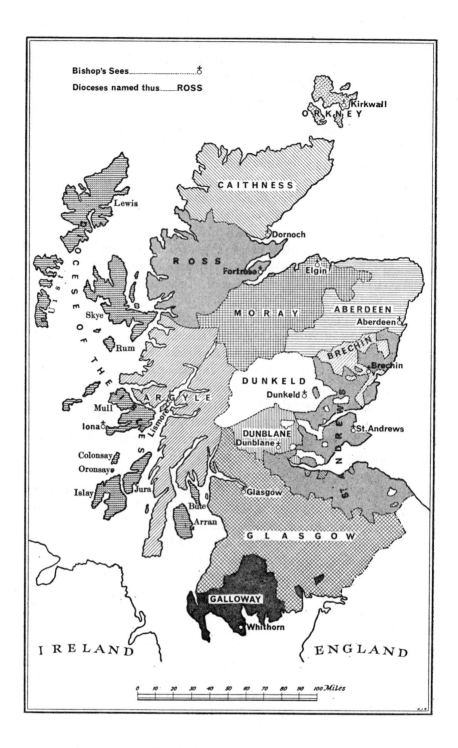

The state of the church in 1550.

earldom and sent into England as a hostage for the king's ransom. George, earl of March, son of the renegade earl, had his estates forfeited in punishment of his father's fault. James was accused of simple greed, but a better explanation lies in his deliberate policy to fortify the crown and increase its resources. Under Albany and his sons—John, earl of Buchan, who had been chamberlain, and Murdoch the sometime regent—its revenues had been mulcted, but now Buchan was dead, killed at Verneuil, and new men were made responsible for the collection of rents and other dues. The king's politic campaign to reduce the power of his nobles was much helped by the fact that several of them were still in France, fighting the English under the banner of Joan of Arc.

The French alliance was strengthened by the marriage, in 1436, of James's daughter Margaret to the dauphin who became king as Louis XI. The marriage was unhappy, for Louis was among the least pleasant of men, but the prospect of it—and it was long in prospect— may, by inducing some apprehension in England, have helped to keep an uneasy peace. Scotland was still in debt for James's ransom, and James had no wish to complicate the task of subduing his own nobility by becoming involved in war with England. There were, indeed, no hostilities until near the end of his reign, when some skirmishing near Berwick was followed by an abortive attempt, that James himself led, to capture the English fortress of Roxburgh.

Within twelve years James had done much to improve government and the administration of justice. His sheriffs in their sheriffdoms had proclaimed the supremacy of the king's law, and made it known. A court consisting of the chancellor and representatives of the Three Estates, chosen by the king, had been established to hear complaints brought from local courts which had failed to administer the law without fraud or favour, to the poor as to the rich. Attempts to secure broader representation of the people in parliament had been unsuccessful, but the business of parliament was expedited and enlarged by the introduction of a committee to determine and to prepare the appropriate measures to be put before it. This committee became known as the Committee of the Articles, and was later subject to abuse. The extension of law, the improvement of justice, were achievements that cannot be disputed, and the special provision of advocates for poor people summoned to court might be expected to have made the king popular. But popularity was denied him because he imposed taxes which Albany, who was unable to collect them, had in effect remitted.

For his strenuous efforts to elaborate and impose a sound domestic policy, James was poorly rewarded. In 1437 he was murdered. He who instigated the plot was probably Walter, earl of Atholl, or his grandson,

Sir Robert Stewart. Atholl, an old man of seventy-five, was the surviving son of Robert II's marriage to Euphemia Ross: the children of his first marriage, to Elizabeth Mure, were by many thought illegitimate, and if that indeed were so, then Atholl was the rightful king of Scotland, and because he was old his grandson could soon hope to succeed him. The conspiracy found favour among those who resented James's suppression of the nobility's former privilege, and those who had suffered under the firmness of his justice. The opportunity for murder came when a great council was summoned to receive a papal legate in Perth. The king took up residence in a convent outside the wall, and his private chamberlain, who was Atholl's grandson, let in the assassins. There were eight of them, led by Sir Robert Graham who had been imprisoned early in James's reign, when James arrested the earl of Lennox. James was discovered in a closet, and stabbed to death, his queen also being wounded. Within a few weeks the murderers were taken, and, with Atholl, put to death after fearful torment.

Graham is said to have declared that posterity would bless him for having slain a tyrant, but none applauded his deed. In general revulsion against so monstrous an act, both nobles and people proclaimed their loyalty to the widowed queen and her son, and James II was anointed and crowned at Holyrood. But he was only six years old and a throned infant was incapable of holding for long the impulsive loyalty that had approved his succession.

Chapter 3

THE succession of a child, no matter what goodwill installed him on the throne, could only undo by weakness what his father had done by strength. James I had tried to create a royal authority, endowed with sufficient revenue and adequate power, that might dominate a recalcitrant nobility and maintain, throughout his realm, an administration and a system of law capable of dealing justice without fear or favour. Exalted above all, in the sight of all, should be the power of the throne. But no throne, half-filled by an infant, could exert, by proxy, power of that sort.

James I, well taught in England in the principles both of poetry and kingly jurisprudence, was in Scotland defeated and slain by the daggers of native anarchy. The ominous threat embodied in the Arbroath parliament's declaration of independence, a hundred years before, became vocal and effective when a king dared to assume a royal power. The king was murdered, and the queen-mother who tried to take his place was derided. Her adjutants were ignored or mocked, and a self-seeking nobility asserted an hereditary right to the noble gift of freedom by using their freedom under a dilapidated throne to reap harvests of their own advantage.

Archibald, fifth earl of Douglas, was lieutenant of the realm, the bishop of Glasgow its chancellor. Within a year or two Douglas had to take action against rebels or the unruly, and anarchy appeared in high places. A Stewart of Darnley was killed by a Boyd of Kilmarnock, who was then killed by the Stewarts; and before he could prove his strength and justify his office, Douglas died. Two lesser men, of recent elevation to positions of power, then briefly dominated the scene. One was Sir William Crichton, keeper of Edinburgh castle, the other Sir Alexander Livingstone, keeper of Stirling castle. Crichton had the initial advantage when the child-king was taken to Edinburgh for safety, but by obscure means the boy was removed to Stirling, and when the queen-mother remarried—her second husband was a Stewart, known as the Black Knight of Lorne—Livingstone, with some violence, added further to his authority by making her his virtual prisoner. Crichton and Livingstone were then associated in a murderous plot against the powerful house of Douglas.

Archibald, the ineffectual lieutenant of the realm, had been succeeded by his son William, a boy of sixteen, who soon showed himself aware of the strength he had inherited: the family empire included most of the south-west of Scotland, and other lands in the east and north. William Douglas is said to have been friendly with the boy-king, who admired his high temper. He was manifestly an obstacle, if not a menace, to the ambitions of Crichton and Livingstone, who found it convenient to accuse him of a treasonable aspiration to the throne; to which he had some claim through his mother, a descendant of Robert II by his second marriage to Euphemia Ross. The young Douglas, and his only brother, rashly accepted an invitation to dine—and presumably confer—in Edinburgh castle; where they were murdered. According to the traditional story a black bull's head was put on the table; and though so macabre and ceremonious an introduction to the theme of death seems extravagant, even for the fifteenth century, there may have been some such prelude to assassination, for the murder was commemorated in a popular rhyme:

> Edinburgh castle, towne and toure,
> God grant thou sink for sinne!
> And that even for the black dinoir
> Erl Douglas gat therein.

The younger earl was succeeded by his great-uncle, called James the Gross, who showed no enmity to the murderers and may have been privy to their plot. He, in 1443, died and was succeeded by another William, with whom Livingstone made an alliance against Crichton. There ensued a limited civil war, in which each side did considerable damage to the other's property. The Douglas-Livingstone coalition was the more successful, and a general council was persuaded to 'put to the horn', or outlaw, the whole Crichton family and deprive its leader of his office as chancellor. But he still held Edinburgh castle, and after withstanding a long siege emerged with the honours of war and found a new ally in the redoubtable person of James Kennedy, a nephew of James I and bishop of St. Andrews.

William Douglas, in the meantime, had added to his territorial wealth by marrying his cousin, the Fair Maid of Galloway, and formed an alliance with the earl of Crawford, most warlike and formidable of magnates beyond the Forth. Crawford and Livingstone carried war into Bishop Kennedy's diocese, burning and looting, and the bishop retorted by excommunicating all who had done him harm. Exactly a year later Crawford was mortally wounded while trying to intervene in a family battle, near Arbroath, between Ogilvies and Lindsays; and his death was generally believed to vindicate the good bishop's excommunication. As if to show that internecine strife was not enough to satisfy the turbulent appetites of the time, war was also renewed on the border.

In 1483, soon after the accession of James II, a nine years' truce had been concluded with England. The truce expired, and the English burnt Dunbar and Dumfries. A month later the earls of Douglas, Angus, and Ormond—all of them Douglases—with William Sinclair, earl of Orkney, burnt Alnwick and Warkworth in Northumberland. Later in the year the Douglases won, in pitched battle, a decisive victory over young Percy of Northumberland at Gretna, where the river Sark runs into the sands of Solway. The eminence and enormous power of the house of Douglas were now to be challenged, however, by the only man who had a right to its obedience. The young king had grown up.

In 1449, James II, in his nineteenth year, married Mary of Gueldres, a niece of Philip the Good, duke of Burgundy; and as if to prove that he had come of age, arrested Livingstone and his sons and immured them at Blackness on the Forth. At his first parliament Livingstone was forfeited, his sons found guilty of high treason, and executed. But the inordinate power of William Douglas was again increased, for to him was given some part of Livingstone's forfeited estates. Crichton, high in the king's favour, was again chancellor, and it may be that James intended to show, by generosity to Douglas, that the appointment implied no enmity to him. But the arrogance of the great earl was not to be tempered by reward.

In 1450 he went to Rome, riding in great magnificence and numerously attended, and during his absence the king found occasion to suppress some local disturbances in the Douglas lands. What happened there, and what happened immediately after Douglas's return, are not known; but Douglas had been in communication with the king of England in circumstances that must have seemed suspicious. He found it advisable to make a formal submission to parliament, and he was restored to his lordships that may nominally have been forfeited. In 1451 he was confirmed in his lands and offices and castles, and 'the charters of confirmation show that he held: the earldom of Douglas, the earldom of Wigtown, the lordship of Galloway, the forests of Ettrick and Selkirk, the lordship of Bothwell, large estates in the sheriffdoms of Edinburgh, Haddington, Lanark, Roxburgh, Linlithgow, Peebles, and Aberdeen, and the offices of sheriff of Lanark and Warden of the West and Middle Marches. Nor should it be forgotten that his brothers, Archibald, earl of Moray, Hugh, earl of Ormond, and John of Balveny, held large extents of lands in the north and north-east. The house of Douglas, indeed, bestrode Scotland like a Colossus'.[1]

The reconciliation was short-lived. Douglas in his earldom appears to have recognised no authority but his own, and openly defied the king. Then he made alliance, or 'banded', with Alexander, earl of Crawford—known as the Tiger Earl, and son of him who died while excommunicate—and with John, Lord of the Isles and earl of Ross; and such an alliance can hardly be interpreted as anything other than a challenge to the throne. What followed was an act of desperation and, in the circumstances, no more to be blamed than Robert Bruce's killing of the Red Comyn in the church of Dumfries. It may, indeed, be condoned as a very timely murder; for it may well have saved Scotland from a destructive civil war.

Sending a safe-conduct to Douglas, James invited him to Stirling castle. There they dined, and James besought him 'to break his band' with Crawford and Ross. Douglas refused, and James in just anger exclaimed, 'If you will not, this will', and struck him with a dagger. His courtiers or servants finished what he had begun, and the rebel earl lay dead. A little while later a Scottish parliament pronounced its verdict, exonerating its king from blame and declaring that Douglas by treason and conspiracy was guilty of his own death. It is difficult to dispute the cold and precise objectivity of that judgement; and James II, by taking upon himself the guilt of murder, may deserve more credit than he has ever been given for preserving the entity of Scotland when that entity was threatened by the swollen ambition of a rival greater than he in actual power, less only by his lack of the anointing oil of royalty.

The Douglases were not yet broken. After the death of Earl William, his brother James rode into Stirling with six hundred men behind him to loot and burn, to drag the dishonoured safe-conduct through the streets at the tail of a broken-down horse, and later to renounce his homage to the king of Scots and offer allegiance to the king of England.

To that defiance James responded with admirable promptitude. He marched in force into the Douglas absolutism of the south-west, and compelled the submission of James, the ninth and last earl of the family long called the Black Douglases. But in victory he was lenient. Too lenient, indeed, for a year later James Douglas was allowed to go to

[1] *Scotland from the Earliest Times to 1603.*

[144]

London to negotiate a truce, and in London Douglas, without James's knowledge or consent, secured the release of Malise, sometime earl of Strathearn, whom James I had sent as a hostage into England.

Now Malise, grandson of David, earl of Strathearn, who was the son of Robert II and his second wife Euphemia Ross, had in the view of many dissidents a better right to the throne than James II, who was descended from Robert III the dubiously legitimated son of Robert II and his first wife, Elizabeth Mure. To counter the threat, implied or real, of a legitimist claim to the throne—or what argument could construe as legitimist—James II again took the field, and Douglas, in a manner ill-befitting the family tradition, retired hurriedly into England. There was a battle at Arkinholm, near Langholm in the shire of Dumfries, where his brothers were defeated. One was killed, another taken prisoner and executed, and the third fled to England. In 1455 the Douglas sub-regality was abolished, its last earl attainted, its estates were forfeited to the crown.

James II, still in his mid-twenties, had proved himself a worthy son of his father. A strong and resolute monarchy was what Scotland needed, and both had given determination and all their energy to the task of securing the authority necessary for the well-being of their kingdom. James II, who was to die untimely, got a little wayward epitaph in a stanza of François Villon's *Ballade des Seigneurs de Temps Jadis*:

> le roy Scotiste
> Qui demy face ot, ce dit on,
> Vermeille comme une amatiste
> Depuis le front jusqu'au menton.—

A birthmark reddened one side of his face, and a fiery cheek betokened a fiery temper. But underlying impulsive moods there must have been, as in his predecessor Robert Bruce, a calm and confident assessment of what his purpose was, and a workmanlike ability to establish kingly rule. In striking contrast with the wild anarchy that disrupted the realm while he was an infant, there is, except for his final assault on the Black Douglases, a singular absence of violence in his last years. The peace, or relative peace, of those years is some indication of the loss that Scotland suffered by the lamentable accident of his death.

In 1460 he laid siege to Roxburgh, which was still in English hands. His artillery consisted of cannon of the primitive sort that were built of parallel strips of iron enclosed and bound by iron bands. One of these, while James was inspecting its charge and firing, burst and killed him.

[145]

The loss to Scotland was incalculable. Had he lived for another twenty years his firmness of purpose, his initiative and instinctive authority, might have created, under a dominating throne, a coherent realm whose ordered life would have stimulated those good impulses, to the expansion of trade and growth of prosperity, which so hardily persisted under all the discouragement of insecurity and a faltering authority. But James, fiery of face and fiery of mood, was killed by the intimacy with which he ruled his kingdom. He was as interested in its cannon as in its constitution.

Chapter 4

JAMES II's son was a delicate child, only eight years old. His reign, in its beginning only nominal, lasted twenty-eight years, and despite a complexity of political disagreement it was a period of growth. The burghs and many of their burgesses prospered and acquired a new importance, and by the king's marriage to an amiable Norwegian princess the northern islands of Orkney and Shetland were added to his realm. It can hardly be disputed that for much of its good fortune during this period Scotland was indebted to the fact that England was distracted by the tedious and unhappy dynastic conflict known as the Wars of the Roses. The ordinary people of England were not much affected by the angry struggle between the houses of York and Lancaster, but for thirty years, from 1455 till 1485, the magnates of the kingdom were so deeply concerned in local rivalries that they had no great inclination or opportunity to interfere in the affairs of their northern neighbour. In the first years of the new reign, however, Scotland was briefly embroiled in the English war and threatened by a dangerous attempt to disrupt its still precarious unity.

A few days after the death of James II, the castle of Roxburgh surrendered and was demolished. Four months later Margaret of Anjou, Henry VI's able and delightful queen, came to Scotland seeking aid for her husband, then a prisoner in Yorkist hands. She raised an army and led it as far south as St. Albans, where the Yorkists were defeated and Henry VI regained his liberty. But the Lancastrian victory had no substance in it. Though London was little more than twenty miles away, it was the defeated Yorkists who took the city, where Edward, duke of York, was crowned as Edward IV. Margaret and her hapless husband retreated to the north and were beaten at Towton. They took refuge in Scotland, and paid for three years' shelter by surrendering Berwick and promising to cede Carlisle.

Unable to mount an open offensive against Scotland, Edward IV employed the exiled Black Douglas to foment a major insurrection. Douglas and his brother, John of Balveny, were sent into Scotland, and by a treaty negotiated at Westminster and Ardtornish on the Sound of Mull, John, Lord of the Isles and earl of Ross, with the help of his unruly kinsman Donald Balloch, undertook the subjugation of lands beyond the Forth; while Douglas was to essay conquest of the south. They became pensioners of Edward, and his liegemen. On the borders Douglas had scant success, and his brother Balveny was captured and executed; but in Inverness the redoubtable Lord of the Isles made pretence to kingly powers and gathered crown rents and customs. In 1465, however, a truce between England and France was followed by a treaty between England and Scotland that promised peace for fifteen years, and the Lord of the Isles discreetly renewed his allegiance to the Scottish throne.

For these first few years of the reign the queen-mother, Mary of Gueldres, and Bishop Kennedy of St. Andrews shared the authority of government. Mary was young, energetic, not always prudent; her early death, in 1463, may have contributed to the instability that marred the character of her son. Of Bishop Kennedy there is no adverse criticism except a suggestion that he may have been extravagant. About his probity, humanity, and wisdom all are agreed, and his foundation of St. Salvator's College at St. Andrews deserves the liveliest admiration. It was presumably a natural taste for splendour that prompted him to build a great ship, known as the Bishop's Barge, and a tomb for his own interment, each of which was reputed to have cost as much as St. Salvator's. His death, some eighteen months after that of the queen-mother, was certainly a misfortune and exposed the young king to the predatory ambition of a party led by a hitherto little known family, the Boyds of Kilmarnock.

In 1466 James III, aged fourteen, was decoyed from the palace of Linlithgow and removed to Edinburgh castle, whose governor, Sir Alexander Boyd, had been the king's instructor in military exercises. There, before the Estates of the Realm, the king was induced to proclaim that what had happened had been done by his consent, and the Estates approved a charter by which Robert, Lord Boyd, was named governor of the king's person and keeper of the fortresses of the kingdom. To their manifest audacity the Boyds added an undoubted talent, and Robert's son, Thomas, is reputed to have been a person of great charm, wisdom, and kindliness. His rise to high fortune was certainly remarkable, for in 1467 he was created earl of Arran and married the Lady Mary, the king's sister. But the family did not long retain the power it had so deftly seized.

To Robert, Lord Boyd, credit must be given for the treaty of 1468 by which James III married Margaret, the daughter of Christian I, king of Denmark, and so added Orkney and Shetland to the realm of Scotland. The Danish king agreed to a dowry of 60,000 florins of the Rhine, and when he was unable to find more than 2,000 florins in ready money, pledged the earldom of Orkney and the lordship of Shetland for the large remainder of the sum. The old Norse earldom had descended by devious ways to a noble family of Norman origin, the Sinclairs of Roslin; and in 1470 James III made a shrewd bargain with William, the third earl in that family, by which he acquired his lands and rights in exchange for the castle and lands of Ravenscraig in Fife. This transaction made James in effect master of the islands, and when in 1472 they were, by act of parliament, annexed and united to Scotland, his ownership of the earldom estates was fortified by their incorporation in the realm. Until the eighteenth century Denmark was to make recurrent claims to her right of redemption, but without consequence. It was geography that ultimately decided the issue and demonstrated that Orkney and Shetland, like the Hebrides, were Scottish soil.

Long before that decision became evident, the Boyds had fallen from favour. That kind and courteous man, the newly elevated earl of Arran, went to Denmark to bring the Princess Margaret into Scotland, and his father led an embassy to England. During their absence the young king listened to some of the many enemies of the Boyds, and for good reason or ill—because he was told the truth or because his character was unstable—he 'conceived great hatred' of Arran. Such was the news that met Arran when his ship, with the Princess Margaret aboard, came into Leith; and she who brought him the news was his wife, the king's sister. Margaret and her attendants went ashore, and Margaret was married in circumstances of uncommon magnificence at the palace of Holyrood; but Arran re-embarked, and with his faithful wife for comfort sailed back to Denmark. His father joined him from England, and the Boyds, found guilty of treason, were forfeited in life and lands. Sir Alexander, the king's old instructor in military exercises, was attainted and executed.

The king, who was only eighteen at the time of his marriage, gave no proof of having inherited his father's royal gifts of strength and authority, but for a little time his reign was fortunate. Scotland had been enlarged by the acquisition of Berwick and Roxburgh in the south, and of the two archipelagos in the north. In 1473 Margaret of Denmark had given birth to a son, afterwards James IV, and when the child was little more than a year old a marriage was arranged for him with Cecilia, the youngest daughter of Edward IV. The treaty with England, of 1465, having thus been renewed and fortified, James or his advisers had the assurance and strength to deal with John, Lord of the Isles and earl of Ross. He who had been ready to take English pay and wage war against his king, had nominally submitted a dozen years before, but in fact had maintained a partial and truculent independence. Now, however, he was brought to book, and submitted himself to the mercy of the crown. He was deprived of some of his lands in the west, of the castles of Inverness and Nairn, and of his earldom of Ross; but his title of Lord of the Isles was recognised, and as such he was to sit in parliament.

That was a rare exercise of the royal authority. More typical of James's reign are the repeated complaints of his parliament that he did not enforce the law, that he was idle, and indifferent to his country's needs. He found favourites whom the nobility despised, and took his pleasure in the company—so said his barons—of 'masons and fiddlers'. Foremost among them were Cochrane and Roger, the former an architect who made notable additions to Stirling castle, and the latter a skilful musician who is said to have founded an influential school of music. That James showed a lively interest in the fine arts will not, in these days, discredit him; but in the fifteenth century a king had need of sterner tastes. Cochrane and Roger may well have been men of great talent, and yet have given James poor advice. A knowledge of Gothic architecture, or the harp and the viol, may not preclude ignorance of the duties and arts of government. The king, moreover, had brothers, the duke of Albany and the earl of Mar, whose accomplishments were of the conventional, knightly sort, and therefore more admired by their contemporaries.

James grew jealous or fearful of his gifted brothers, and had them arrested. Mar died in prison, and the suspicion of foul play was perhaps inevitable, though there is no evidence whatever that James was guilty of his death. Albany escaped, by killing his gaolers, and fled to France. From there he went to England, and in the summer of 1482 concluded with Edward IV an unpardonable treaty by which he assumed the title of king of Scotland and asserted his willingness to do homage for his realm to the king of England. He agreed to break the French alliance, and to surrender Berwick, Lochmaben, and much land on the border; for reward he was to marry Edward's daughter Cecilia, who eight years before had been promised to James's year-old son. Edward provided him with an army, and perfidious Albany marched north to fulfil a shabby bargain and win the kingdom that he proposed to dismember and pawn.

To counter the English threat, James mobilised and led an army to Lauder, and was so unwise as to let himself be accompanied by

Cochrane, Roger, and other of his favourites: his fencing-master, his tailor, and a man described as a smith, though perhaps he was a goldsmith. He was joined by a second army, led by the earls of Angus, Huntly, Lennox, and Buchan; who, before facing the English, decided to outface their king. There was, at that time, much to provoke their anger, though James could not be blamed for a succession of bad harvests and the near-famine that afflicted parts of the country. But the consequence of bad harvests was high prices, and inflation was aggravated by progressive debasing of the coinage, a measure for which Cochrane was blamed. The angry nobles, led by Angus, were resolved that James must recall 'black money' and dismiss his favourites. James indignantly refused their demands, and Angus's response was to seize Cochrane and his wretched companions, and hang them from Lauder bridge. The nobles then arrested their king, and turning their backs upon Albany and the English, made James a prisoner in Edinburgh castle. The English, unhindered, recaptured Berwick and marched on Edinburgh.

A curious compact persuaded them to retire. Albany and his royal brother were reconciled, and Albany regained the offices and estates he had forfeited. He forgot or deferred his pretension to the throne, and ignored his promised allegiance to Edward. The English got no profit from their expedition other than the town and castle of Berwick, which thereafter remained in their hands; and James continued to live as a prisoner in Edinburgh castle. In control of administration were Albany, the archbishop of St. Andrews,[1] and the bishop of Dunkeld.

For no obvious motive Albany then decided to rescue James from his prison, and that he effected with the help of the provost and citizens of Edinburgh. But after a brief period during which the brothers appeared to be on the friendliest terms, James discovered that Albany was again in treasonable communication with the English king, and Albany found it expedient to cross the border. Edward IV, his ally and presumptive lord paramount, died in April, 1483, and Albany was again deprived of his estates. Richard III succeeded to the English throne, and he, sufficiently occupied with domestic troubles, made peace with Scotland. Albany made a last attempt against his brother's rule, but was defeated and fled to France, where he died.

James had still a few years to live and reign, and might have lived in peace had he been adroit or able to restrain his avarice; but greed and a maladroit insistence on securing for his own use the revenue of the rich priory of Coldingham brought him into conflict with the powerful border family of Home, which claimed Coldingham as its own. Allied

---

[1] St. Andrews was erected into its archbishopric in 1472.

with the Homes were the Hepburns, and as the quarrel deepened and spread they got support from the bishop of Glasgow, the earls of Angus and Argyll, and many others. The quarrel became a rebellion, and James fled to the north, where the earls of Huntly, Crawford, Erroll, and Buchan, the archbishop of St. Andrews and good Bishop Elphinstone of Aberdeen were loyal to him. The rebels captured Dunbar, and at Stirling took from its acquiescent governor the heir to the throne, James, duke of Rothesay, a boy of fifteen.

A brief pacification was followed by renewal of dispute, and near Stirling the king's army met the rebels. The loyalists of the north were on their way to join him, but without waiting for their arrival James attacked his enemies. The battle went against him, he was persuaded to flee, but was thrown from his horse and took shelter in a building known as Beaton's mill. There he was murdered by someone whose identity has never been discovered.

There can be no pretence that James III was of much service to Scotland other than by his marriage to a Danish princess whose dowry extended his dominions. But the wealth of the country increased despite the mismanagement of the currency; parliament grew in importance, its functions became more specific, despite a king who was loth to enforce its laws; and rich burgesses got recognition of their influence in the new powers accorded to their burghs. There was much building of towers and castles; the great castles of Borthwick, Craigmillar, and Doune raised their walls, and the king himself added to Stirling and Linlithgow. In Edinburgh Mary of Gueldres founded the church of Trinity College—its site now hidden beneath some railway-lines—and decorated it with the altar-piece by Hugo van der Goes that preserved portraits of James and his queen. Roslin chapel, whose exuberant masonwork is perhaps too heavily elaborate, was founded by William Sinclair, earl of Orkney, in or about 1450. Scotland's second university came precariously into being at Glasgow, where for a long time it existed like a delicate child whose relatives hardly expect it to outlive its infancy; and literature, nurtured by many poets now lost, was putting forth the *Fables* of Robert Henryson for the pleasure of town-dwellers who, in increasing numbers, lived in the comfort of stone houses. Though parliament still found it expedient to deplore 'the great poverty of the realm', its enactments included sumptuary laws that suggest some mitigation of poverty; for the wearing of silk gowns, doublets, and cloaks had to be restricted by law. The most persistent problem was the literal shortage of money. As trade increased, more money was required, and there was never enough gold and silver to mint what was wanted.

[152]

Chapter 5

THE Renaissance was both a rediscovery of the past, and a break with the past. The old world of Greece and Rome, with its treasure-houses of art and learning, had never been wholly submerged or entirely forgotten, but in Italy in the fifteenth century the revival of the arts, the renewal of learning, seemed to bring it to life again with almost the impact of such an earthquake as might force to the surface of the sea the drowned continent of Atlantis. That impact shattered the universalism of the middle ages, when life—however deeply torn by war's disaster and dynastic ambition—had been unified by general agreement about religion and society and the meaning of life. A long age of intellectual tranquillity was broken, and new ideas emerged that changed not only the style of painting and the forms of architecture, but the aims of thought and the practice of government.

The realm of Scotland lay far from Italy, and its soil was poorer than Tuscany's. In its little burghs there was no tradition nor the visible riches that would let them bear even the most distant comparison with the splendours of Venice and Florence and Naples and Milan. But the spirit of the Renaissance was pervasive and strong, it could enrich the most improbable fields, and the successor to James III—whose ineptitude on the throne had not precluded a genuine interest in music and architecture—was a king who can truthfully be called a prince of the Renaissance.

James IV was only fifteen when he succeeded to the throne in 1488, but his energy, strength, and ability soon became apparent, and he had the inestimable gift of winning popular favour. To begin with, he was probably assisted by his father's mysterious and shameful death. The monarchy was all-important. It was the linchpin that held society in place, and the disagreeable fact that James I and James III had both been murdered did not destroy or even diminish respect for the throne. The first parliament of the new reign felt it necessary to apologise for the unhappy accident at Beaton's mill, where the late king 'happinnit to be slane'.

To the acquired authority of the throne James IV added that of his own ability. It was in accordance with the new spirit of the age that a ruler should show, if not a sense of vocation, an attitude to the business of ruling that can almost be called professional. James had a sturdy body and a lively, inquiring mind. He was closely interested in guns as his grandfather had been, and he showed a passionate concern for ships and shipbuilding. He took a romantic delight in tournaments, and his scientific bent led to experiments in surgery and alchemy. His father's avarice had bequeathed him substantial riches, and his court became famous for a splendour hitherto unknown in Scotland. He was not indifferent to music, and great poets enhanced the glory of his reign. But dominating all else was his determination to rule and govern, to make law effective and his kingship real.

In the first year or two after his accession, when the earl of Angus was his guardian, some minor bickering by restless barons was suppressed without much difficulty, and an engaging adventurer called Sir Andrew Wood gave uncommon pleasure by two small victories at sea. England and Scotland were at peace, but piracy was rife about their coasts, and Wood himself, merchant and landed proprietor, had had some experience of that sort. When a fleet of five English pirates was harrying in the Firth of Forth, he received an appeal for help, and led his two ships, *The Flower* and *Yellow Carvel*, against the intruders; beat them, and brought them into Leith as prizes. Later in the year he repeated his triumph when the Englishman Peter Bull, perhaps in search of revenge, brought three stout vessels into the Firth to intercept Wood on a voyage from Flanders. A very desperate fight ensued, but Wood was again the victor and took his prizes to Dundee. Naval warfare is a rarity in Scottish history, and these encounters, of merely local significance, deserve mention if for no other reason.

James's royal policy first showed itself in aggressive action against the ever turbulent independence of the Celtic peoples of the north and west. As early as 1490 he made a Highland progress, and in 1493 the old Lord of the Isles, chief of Clan Donald, was finally defeated and deprived of power. Seventeen years had passed since his submission to James III and the forfeiture of his earldom of Ross, but one of his sons, who bitterly resented and hotly disputed that submission, had since then created great turmoil in the west. He was finally pacified by assassination in Inverness, where his own harper cut his throat; but then his father, with great unwisdom, gave dominion over his Hebridean territories to a nephew, Alexander of Lochaber. Alexander seized the castle of Inverness and ravaged the lands of Cromarty in what may have been an attempt to recapture the forfeited earldom. But he fell foul of the Mackenzies of Kintail, and between Mackenzies and Macdonalds there was bitter war. It is possible, too, that the old Macdonald was again in communication with England. For one reason or another there was urgent need for pacification and the assertion of royal authority, and when that had been achieved the king made a progress through the Isles to receive submission of the chiefs.

There can be no doubt whatever that the chiefs of Clan Donald were motivated not only by a stubborn passion for independence, but by a profound belief in their entitlement to independence. A year after the old Macdonald's submission, a Macdonald of Islay, in full view of the royal fleet, recaptured his castle of Dunaverty in Kintyre, and hanged the king's governor from its ramparts. For this insolence he and his four sons paid with their lives. But some years later Donald Dubh, a grandson of the last Lord of the Isles, escaped from prison to lead his own clan, with Macleans and Macleods and Camerons, in a new revolt that was only suppressed after hard fighting. James did not shrink from employing clan against clan to restore order, and it has to be admitted that he gave his lieutenants in the north and west, the earls of Huntly and Argyll, a power and a freedom which they sometimes used for their own advantage. But James was popular in the Isles and the western Highlands. He spoke some Gaelic, he enjoyed sport, he had the sort of character and physical abilities that appealed to a people whose military instincts were simple and deep-seated. Though he suppressed disorder with unfailing vigour, he made strenuous efforts to win the friendship of his Hebrideans, and his partial success became apparent on the bloody field of Flodden, where Celtic chiefs and their followers fought and died with their king.

For most of his reign his relations with England were friendly, and for that he was chiefly indebted to the fact that after the death in battle of Richard III, the English throne had been occupied by Henry Tudor, earl of Richmond, who succeeded as Henry VII. A man of great ability and a hard-headed politician, Henry was not the most likeable of monarchs and his title to the throne was dubious. Both insecurity and good sense inclined him to establish peaceful relations with Scotland, and in 1493 he proposed a marriage alliance. James's betrothal, at a tender age, to Edward IV's daughter Cecilia, had long since lapsed, and Henry had a young but growing daughter called Margaret. A seven years' truce was agreed, and a year or two later James broke it by receiving, and perhaps inviting, the Yorkist pretender to the English throne, Perkin Warbeck. Warbeck claimed to be the younger brother of the 'Princes in the Tower', of whose murder Richard III is commonly held guilty, though a cold scrutiny of the facts may reveal Henry VII as the likelier villain. James, it is evident, believed in the impostor's claim, and married him to a daughter of the earl of Huntly. Warbeck pretended that the English would flock to his banner, but a raid into northern England found no supporters, and the deluded king and the glib impostor were soon estranged. A few months later Warbeck and his wife left Scotland in a ship called *Cuckoo*, which James provisioned for them. After he had gone, another raid was mounted against England, with great preparation for the transport of artillery. The castle of Norham was unavailingly besieged, and when it was learnt that the earl of Surrey, with a very large force, was marching to its relief, the Scots retired, having accomplished nothing.

Henry VII showed more diplomacy. Spain had lately become his ally, and in 1496 the Spanish ambassador, Pedro de Ayala, came to Scotland to persuade James to forsake the old alliance with France. He returned a year later, and the truce with England was renewed. Ayala sent from Scotland a long report, descriptive of the king and his country, which is so flattering to both as to make it quite evident that he had fallen under the spell of James and his court.

'The king,' he wrote, 'is of noble stature, neither tall nor short, and as handsome in complexion and shape as a man can be.' He speaks Latin very well, says Ayala, and also French, German, Flemish, Italian, and Spanish. One may doubt so large an accomplishment, but the great scholar Erasmus, who tutored James's natural son, Alexander, wrote of him: 'He has a wonderful intellectual power, an astonishing knowledge of everything'; and Ayala proves his sensitive ear when he writes: 'His own Scotch language is as different from English as Aragonese from Castilian. The king speaks besides the language of the savages who live in some parts of Scotland and on the islands. It is as different from Scotch as Biscayan is from Castilian.

'He fears God,' continued Ayala, 'and observes all the precepts of the church. He gives alms liberally, but is a severe judge, especially in the case of murderers. He is neither prodigal nor avaricious, but liberal when occasion requires. He is courageous,' but he is 'not a good captain, because he begins to fight before he gives his orders.' Had Ayala accompanied him on the abortive raid into England, or ridden with him on some Highland foray? 'His deeds are as good as his words. For this reason, and because he is a very humane prince, he is much loved. He is active, and works hard. When he is not at war he hunts in the mountains.'

Of the kingdom he is calmly critical. 'The Scotch are not industrious, and the people are poor. They spend all their time in wars, and when there is no war they fight with one another.' But since the present king succeeded to the throne, 'they do not dare to quarrel so much as formerly'. Ayala was gratified by his discovery that foreigners were made welcome, but hospitality did not blind him to some defects of temper in his kindly hosts: 'They are vain and ostentatious by nature. They spend all they have to keep up appearances. They are envious to excess.' He thought better of the women, who 'are courteous in the extreme. I mention this because they are really honest,[1] though very bold. They are absolute mistresses of their houses and even of their husbands, in all things concerning the administration of their property, income as well as expenditure. They are very graceful and handsome women,' and they wore a head-dress which Ayala thought 'the hand-somest in the world', but unfortunately did not describe it. To a Spaniard whose womenfolk lived in seclusion, the easy freedom of life in Edinburgh may well have been attractive, or perhaps the pleasure he took in female society induced him to look with favour at the domestic background. 'The houses are good,' he says, 'all built of hewn stone and provided with excellent doors, glass windows, and a great number of chimneys. All the furniture that is used in Italy, Spain, and France is to be found in their dwellings.'

That, of course, cannot be accepted as an accurate picture of housing throughout the country. It is surprising, indeed, to find that houses, thus built and furnished, were apparently so numerous that Ayala could describe them as typical of the domestic circumstances in which the nobles and the richest burgesses lived. But elsewhere there is evidence of wealth and its ostentation that, in some respects, substantiates Ayala's report.

However fractional and arbitrary it may be, the most enduring record of Scottish life in the reign of James IV is the poetry of Robert Henryson and William Dunbar. Henryson, a schoolmaster in Dunfermline, had probably written most of his poems in the previous reign—he died, an old man, before 1508—and in temper and spirit he belonged to the older, pre-Renaissance world. But that world had not, of course, been thrown away like an old boot. It was still in use, and when so much of Scotland's official story is loud with anger and stained by blood it is doubly agreeable to find proof in Henryson that some of its private history was humorous and gay. He wrote a number of

[1] Chaste.

moral fables, some derived from Aesop, but all given new originality by his laughing genius. Here is the beginning of his fable of *The Frog and the Mouse*:

> Upon ane tyme (as Esope culd Report)
> Ane lytill Mous come till ane Rever syde;
> Scho micht not waid, hir schankis were sa schort,
> Scho culd not swym, scho had na hors to ryde:
> Of verray force behovit hir to byde,
> And to and ffra besyde that Revir deip
> Scho ran, cryand with mony pietuous peip.

And here, from *The Cock and the Fox*, are two stanzas that describe the mourning of Pertok the hen after Chantecleir the cock has been carried off by the fox:

> 'Allace,' quod Pertok, makand sair murning,
> With teiris grit attour hir cheikis fell;
> 'Yone wes our drowrie, and our dayis darling,
> Our nichtingall, and also our Orloge bell,
> Our walkryfe watche, us for to warne and tell
> Quhen that Aurora with hir curcheis gray,
> Put up hir heid betwix the nicht and day.

> 'Quha sall our lemman be? quha sall us leid?
> Quhen we ar sad, quha sall unto us sing?
> With his sweit Bill he wald brek us the breid,
> In all this warld wes thair ane kynder thing?
> In paramouris he wald do us plesing,
> At his power, as nature did him geif.
> Now efter him, allace, how sall we leif?'

It may be useful to note that the language of Henryson and Dunbar is not Scots, but English; a literary refinement of the Early Middle English dialect that was once spoken from Yorkshire to the Forth. As local differences developed and hardened, the English of Lothian became known, a little self-consciously, as Scots or Middle Scots; but there is no more reason to suppose that the natives of Lothian spoke as Henryson wrote, than there is for believing that ordinary Englishmen in King George III's time spoke as Dr. Johnson wrote.

Of Dunbar's poems the best known is his *Lament for the Makaris*:

> On to the ded gois all Estatis,
> Princis, Prelotis, and Potestatis,
> Baith riche and puir of al degre;
> *Timor mortis conturbat me.*

The verses with their graveyard chorus mourn the loss of more than a score of poets:

> He hes tane Roull of Aberdene,
> And gentill Roull of Corstorphin;
> Two bettir fallowis did no man se;
>   *Timor mortis conturbat me.*

> In Dunfermelyne he hes done roune
> With Maister Robert Henrisoun;
> Schir Johne the Ros enbrast hes he;
>   *Timor mortis conturbat me.*

> And he hes now tane, last of aw,
> Gud gentill Stobo and Quintyne Schaw,
> Of quham all wichtis hes pete:
>   *Timor mortis conturbat me.*

Most of those he names are quite unknown. Their work has vanished, there is no other memory of them. But Scotland at the beginning of the sixteenth century was manifestly not an unlettered country, and the long tradition of hostility to England had inspired no enmity to English poetry; for Chaucer was certainly Robert Henryson's master, and Dunbar revered him. Dunbar's humour is far wilder and more exuberant than Henryson's. His genius, indeed, was dark and explosive, his invention enormous and grotesque. He could use an immense vocabulary with the violence of gunfire, but his craftsmanship was superb and his formal or panegyric verses are like a king's banqueting hall hung with cloth of gold and gorgeous tapestries. In him the savage strength of primitive times was unabated, but clothed in a measured magnificence.

His greatest poem is a long satire called *Two Married Women and the Widow*, in which, with ferocious hilarity, he exposes the long-cherished conception of the insatiability of women's sexual appetite, and parallel to that, in pitiless mockery, the ludicrous insufficiencies of the husbands who misuse or betray them, and whom they insolently cuckold. Bawdy and bedecked with splendour, it is written with arrogant assurance, and in much of its detail substantiates Ayala's picture of a land where wealth, in certain classes, was abundant and ostentatious, and whose women were as bold as the Spaniard thought, but rather less 'honest'.

Dunbar wrote an epithalamium for James IV's wedding to Margaret Tudor, daughter of Henry VII of England. The palace of Holyroodhouse was built for her, and the marriage celebrated in August, 1503.

In Dunbar's allegorical verses the young princess—she was barely fifteen—is welcomed by the flowers and the birds of a brightly blooming garden as the Rose who came to wed the native Thistle:

> Thane all the birdis song with voce on hicht,
> Quhois mirthfull soun wes mervelus to heir;
> The mavys song, 'Haill, Rois most riche and richt,
> That dois up flureis undir Phebus speir;
> Haill, plant of yowth, haill, princes dochtir deir,
> Haill, blosome breking out of the blud royall,
> Quhois pretius vertew is imperiall.'

> The merle scho sang, 'Haill, Rois of most delyt,
> Haill, of all flouris quene and soverane;'
> The lark scho song, 'Haill, Rois, both reid and quhyt,
> Most plesand flour, of michty cullouris twane;'
> The nychtingaill song, 'Haill, naturis suffragene,
> In bewty, nurtour, and every nobilnes,
> In riche array, renown, and gentilnes.'

> The commoun voce uprais of birdis small,
> Apone this wys, 'O blissit be the hour
> That thow wes chosin to be our principall;
> Welcome to be our princes of honour,
> Our perle, our plesans, and our paramour,
> Our peax, our play, our plane relicite,
> Chryst the conserf frome all adversite.'

Ayala wrote of the good houses he had seen in Edinburgh and other towns; to qualify a too-favourable report it is useful to read Dunbar's address *To the Merchantis of Edinburgh*:

> May nane pas throw your principall gaittis
> For stink of haddockis and of scattis,
> For cryis of carlingis and debaittis,
> For fensum flyttingis of defame:
>   Thine ye not schame,
> Befoir strangeris of all estaittis
> That sic dishonour hurt your name!

> Your stinkand Scull, that standis dirk,
> Haldis the lycht fra your parroche kirk;
> Your foirstairis makis your housis mirk,
> Lyk na cuntray bot heir at hame:
>   Think ye not schame,
> Sa litill polesie to wirk
> In hurt and sklander of your name!

At your hie Croce, quhar gold and silk
Sould be, thair is bot crudis and milk;
And at your Trone bot cokill and wilk,
Pansches, pudingis of Jok and Jame:
        Think ye not schame,
Sen as the world sayis that ilk
In hurt and sclander of your name!

Municipal administration was well-intentioned but inefficient. In-numerable acts for local government were passed, admirable in purpose but ineffectual because too often they were ignored. The common town-plan was a high street running down from the castle and intersected by the lanes or entrances to farther doorways called 'vennels' and 'closes'. In the high street were the market cross, the church, and the tolbooth. The market cross was the symbol of burghal jurisdiction before which public proclamation might be made or a criminal executed. The tolbooth was both a prison and the admini-strative centre. It was, however, frequently in disrepair, and public business was often conducted in the church, whose steeple might also serve as a convenient prison. Punishment for minor offences appears to have been sporadic rather than strict, and the common sentence of banishment from the town was usually ignored. As Dunbar makes evident, the streets were encumbered on either side with middens, and when there was no other place for refuse it was thrown into the church-yard, to the inconvenience of the merchants who used it as a market-place.

There was, however, a sense of close community, and great insistence on the maintenance of open markets to offer equal opportunity in trade. There was no social equality. The rights of trading were the privilege of the burgesses, and the craftsmen of the town lived on a lower social level. Their efforts to assert rights of their own and obtain some representation on the burgh council were for long repressed, but gradually admitted, and by the latter half of the fifteenth century the craftsmen had formed associations which were grudgingly recognised. From these associations emerged what were known as the Incorporated Trades, of which in Edinburgh there were eventually fourteen. But the burgesses usually maintained vested interests, and an almost hereditary authority, by the simple process of re-electing themselves, or nominating members of their own family, to the burgh council.

Parliamentary legislation, on the other hand, was on the whole practical as well as wise. Much of it was concerned with increasing the efficiency of the judicial system. The main courts for criminal justice, called Justice-Ayres, were regularly held, and sheriffs were instructed in their proper function. The king's Privy Council became more efficient, and for judicial business was reinforced by the Lords of the Session. Edinburgh was now generally recognised as the capital of the kingdom, and the king himself, always intent on the promotion of good justice—of fair justice for all—worked hard to establish in Edinburgh a permanent court of justice. His efforts were hampered by the scarcity of good judges and the lack of money to pay them.

Money was found, however, for the creation of a navy and the development of a royal artillery. As well as Sir Andrew Wood, there was in Leith a family of notable seamen called Barton, who had profited from piratical exercise against both Dutch and Portuguese. Most famous of them was Sir Andrew who at last fell in fight against an English ship, and won the honourable epitaph of a verse in an English ballad:

> 'Fight on, my men!' says Sir Andrew Barton,
>   'I am hurt, but I am not slain;
> I'll lay me down and bleed a while,
>   And then I'll rise and fight again.'

Inspired by such men as these, James first built a ship of twenty-one guns called *Margaret*, and then the great *Michael*, which is said to have been two hundred and forty feet long and to have carried a prodigious armament; and for which he created a new dockyard on the Forth. It is certain that the *Michael* cost him more than the kingdom could afford, and she was never in action.

An enthusiast for artillery, James cast his own guns at Edinburgh castle: siege guns or bombards, and field guns of various calibre distinguished by such names as curtals, serpentines, sakers, and culverines. As well as the expense of their manufacture, the movement of these guns cost a great deal; for roads had to be levelled and smoothed to permit the passage of the ox-drawn carriages or gun-carts that bore the ponderous engines; and accompanying their gunners went expert smiths to cope with breakdown.

Foremost among James's civil advisers was the wise and good Bishop Elphinstone of Aberdeen, by whose exertions Scotland's third university was founded in 1494, and James's interest was shown in the name he gave it. The first principal of King's College was Hector Boece, a good Latinist and sometime the friend of Erasmus. Among the faculties of the new university was the first school of medicine in Britain. In the year before Flodden, where he was killed, James's son Alexander founded St. Leonard's College in St. Andrews, and a few years earlier a royal College of Surgeons was established. Printing was introduced by a patent to Walter Chapman and Andrew Myllar, burgesses of Edinburgh. The masterpiece of their press, for which Bishop Elphinstone was responsible, was the *Aberdeen Breviary* and *Legends of the Saints* in beautifully clear black and red print. To the works of Henryson and Dunbar was added, only a few weeks before Flodden, Gavin Douglas's noble translation of the *Aeneid*. That Douglas, a son of the fifth earl of Angus, was a fine and original poet, as well as translator, is shown by the prologues that he wrote to its several books, the most celebrated of which contain vivid descriptions of the evils of a Scottish winter, the enchantment of its summer.

In the clarity of hindsight it is obvious that the last years of James's reign were progressively darkened by the advancing shadow of his fatal battle. Scotland, a small country, became increasingly involved in the major politics of Europe, and in 1509 the prudent king of England, Henry VII, died and was succeeded by his bellicose son Henry VIII. France had grown too strong for the comfort of her neighbours. The great provinces of Burgundy, Anjou, and Brittany had become fiefs of the crown, and Louis XII sought new fields to conquer, especially in fragmented Italy. But in Spain, where the marriage of Ferdinand and Isabella had brought about the union of Aragon and Castile, the Moors at long last were vanquished, the Jews expelled, and the westward voyages of Christopher Columbus symbolised an ambition that even conquest of the New World would not satisfy. Spain too had interests in Italy, which were bound to bring her into conflict with France. James and Scotland, allied by marriage and a treaty of perpetual peace with England, were still by an older friendship deeply involved with France; and England, never at ease when France was strong, looked with apprehension at the new power of Louis XII. Ayala's mission to Scotland, undertaken on behalf of both Spain and England, had had, as its prime objective, the breaking of the 'Auld Alliance'.

Farther to the east the Turks were a menace to much of Europe. After the capture of Constantinople in 1453 they had extended their conquests, and when they were temporarily in difficulty some thirty years later, the notion of a restrictive crusade was hatched in Rome. The idea—the hope or the project of a crusade—was slow to develop, and never materialised. France and Spain, fighting for their own purposes, met in confused circumstances in Italy, and James, much encouraged by Pope Julius II, hoped for a unifying war against the infidels, of which he might become a leader. But in the end he had to make Scotland's traditional choice between France and England.

After the accession of Henry VIII there were border raids and

[163]

skirmishes of the usual kind, and the sea-fight in which Sir Andrew Barton was killed left his two ships in English hands. England and Scotland were nominally at peace, but Henry, with deliberate insolence, refused to give up his prizes. In the same year England joined, with Spain and Venice and the Emperor Maximillian, the Holy League that Pope Julius had formed against France; and when France was in danger, Scotland was in danger too. The Auld Alliance was renewed in 1512, and the pope, at Henry's instigation, threatened James with excommunication should he attack England. Henry reasserted the old, discredited claim of the English throne to paramountcy over Scotland, and in August, 1513, having landed in Calais, defeated the French at Guinegate in Artois. James, in a final effort to maintain peace, had sent his herald, the Lyon King at Arms, to warn Henry that war with France must mean war with Scotland; but Henry rudely dismissed his envoy.

The earl of Angus, Bishop Elphinstone, and other of his counsellors still implored James to be prudent, but the king's high temper, exacerbated by Henry's contempt, rejected their advice, and on 22nd August he led a Scottish army across the Tweed. Despite the opposition of his wiser counsellors, both nobility and clergy marched with him; Highlanders joined the Lowland levies he had summoned a month before, and a ponderous artillery train moved slowly southward. The king's first objective was the castle of Norham, which surrendered after a six days' siege, and another week was spent on the reduction of some lesser fortresses. It would have been rash, of course, to leave such strongholds behind him, but a fortnight's delay let the English commander, the earl of Surrey, complete his mobilisation.

Surrey had made arrangements for a muster of the northern levies a year before. He mobilised forces in London in July, and sent his artillery to Durham by sea. By the beginning of September the men of the northern counties had assembled, and after receiving a reinforcement of a thousand men from the fleet, commanded by his son, Lord Howard, he took the field on the 5th. His army may have numbered nearly 20,000 men, and the Scottish army was perhaps as large.

There was some going to and fro by heralds from either side, and Surrey challenged the king to give battle before Friday the 9th. It was a curious preliminary to a conflict between embattled nations, and Surrey, who was clearly alarmed by the possibility that James might retire, and expose the English to the ardours of a long advance, was certainly gambling on his knowledge of the king's romantic temper. James, as he had anticipated, accepted the challenge.

The river Till flows into the larger Tweed about three miles south-west of Norham, and Surrey found the Scottish army occupying a position, in hilly ground, west of the Till, that was manifestly too strong to attack. James had chosen his ground too well. His position gave him too great an advantage: it was practically unassailable. The only approach was narrow and covered by the Scottish artillery. Surrey, who was no romantic, declined the invitation, and took the dangerous decision to cross to the east side of the Till and march north. James, with a numerous artillery and Highland troops in his army who were capable of rapid movement, could have attacked him at the river-crossing, but did not. Surrey was allowed to cross to the west again, by Twizel bridge and a convenient ford. He moved south from there towards Branxton Hill, north-west of Flodden Edge. But James, moving fast from his impregnable position, got there first.

Surrey had placed himself between the Scots and their own country, and James dared not allow him too much freedom of movement. But in his haste he failed or was unable to make proper disposition of his artillery. For when the English guns opened fire from the low ground immediately north of Branxton Hill, the Scots could make no effective reply. Their guns, it may be, were so placed that they could not be sufficiently depressed to hit an enemy on lower ground; or they were, perhaps, still being manhandled from their original positions.

The Scottish infantry on the hill were being badly mauled, and instead of retreating to the reverse slope and waiting till their artillery could be properly sited, they were ordered to charge. But now, though still armed with long, eighteen-foot spears, they were not disposed in the disciplined, closely drilled schiltrons that had given Robert Bruce the victory at Bannockburn, but loosely arrayed in a great front that lost cohesion as it plunged down the wet slope of the hill. And waiting for them were Surrey's well ordered ranks, armed with eight-foot bills that carried heavy axe-blades short of the point; and they were better weapons than the Scots' unwieldy spears. Worst of all, perhaps, was the king's behaviour in placing himself in the centre of his line and, if not leading the attack, in being among the foremost: the reckless fault that Ayala had condemned. By indulgence in gallantry he left his army without a commander.

The battlefield became a slaughterhouse. The Scots did not yield, but fought too stubbornly. The bishop of Durham declared that great, strong men among them fought on though struck by four or five of the English bills. But strength was not enough to win a battle so grotesquely mishandled, and a brave king's folly cost his country—if English accountancy can be trusted—some 12,000 dead, among whom were James himself and Alexander his son, a dozen earls, more barons, and sons or sires of almost every good family in the land. As for the common folk; there were burghs, such as Selkirk, that stood aghast when only one man returned of the many who had joined their king.

> I've heard the lilting at our yowe-milking,
>   Lassies a-lilting before the dawn o'day;
> But now they are moaning in ilka green loaning:
>   'The Flowers of the Forest are a' wede away.'

On the left of the army a division commanded by Lord Home had been commanded to take some high ground, and had taken it. There he remained, fulfilling his instructions, and covered the flight of those who survived the slaughter. The following day he withdrew in good order. By some he was harshly blamed for failing to commit his division to general disaster, but in the detached and sober judgement of a later day he seems to have stood alone in his assertion of good sense on a day of national calamity. Nor can any account of the battle be concluded without undiluted praise for Surrey's superb generalship, and for the hardihood of the English soldiers who, half-starved and with nothing to drink but water—about which they bitterly complained—marched and manoeuvred so vigorously, and fought with such stout discipline against their impetuous enemy.

Book Four

THE
LATER
STEWARTS

Chapter 1

IN the story of Scotland, from the death of Alexander III to James VI's accession to the throne of England, there is a recurrent resemblance to drama rather than history: a violent reversal of fortune, balanced by a persistent faculty of survival, can hardly be denied an element of drama. But domestic drama must be seen in its larger context, and in the sixteenth century, as Scotland became increasingly involved in continental policies and movements, so to a great extent its history was shaped by them.

Defeat at Flodden had an impact on Scotland far greater than defeat at Bannockburn had had on England. But Scotland, though its defeat had been overwhelming, was not vanquished. In Edinburgh immediate preparation was made for defence, and public grief, for national calamity or the loss of relatives, was sternly discouraged. The capital, however, was in no immediate danger. Scotland was disabled and Flodden was the end of the campaign. The menace of assault from the north had been dispelled, and Henry VIII could pursue his continental policy without fear of Scottish intervention.

Villages to which a solitary young man had returned from the battle-field—the only survivor of perhaps a score who had marched out—could breed another score within as many years; but the psychological impact of disaster was profound and had effects that lasted longer. Though the 'Auld Alliance' was renewed, it lost popular favour, and increasingly France was regarded as an ally who used her lesser friends only for her own advantage. As the century grew older, there began to emerge a pro-English party, which was enormously strengthened when the Reformation broke an old pattern of society and created new political divisions in Europe.

Flodden was fought on 9th September, and at Stirling the new king was proclaimed as James V on the 21st. He was an infant barely eighteen months old, but its king was Scotland's symbol of unity and independence—a unity ever precarious, an independence always threatened—and the monarchy was hallowed by faith in its antiquity. James's mother, Margaret Tudor, sister of Henry VIII, became regent, and her councillors were James Beaton, archbishop of Glasgow, the earls of Huntly, Angus, and Arran. Alexander Gordon, earl of Huntly, was the greatest of the northern magnates; Archibald Douglas, earl of Angus, was head of the 'Red Douglases', and bitterly hostile to James Hamilton, earl of Arran, a grandson of James II. It appears, however, that the council was distrusted, for an invitation was sent to John, duke of Albany, a son of James III's exiled brother Alexander. Albany, who had been brought up in France and served in the French army, had the disadvantage of speaking no English; but he was close to the throne, and about the end of 1515 he became heir presumptive.

In April, 1514, the queen-mother gave birth to a posthumous son. Margaret was still in her early twenties, and a few months later she married Archibald Douglas, earl of Angus. Albany was now more urgently invited to come home, and by assent of a general council became regent and guardian of the infant king. After the death of Margaret's posthumous child Albany stood next in succession, but showed no improper appetite for advancement. His presence in Scotland was resented by Henry VIII, who tried, but in vain, to compel the Scottish parliament to dismiss him and send him back to France.

In Europe the power of France had been circumscribed by the phenomenal growth of Spain. The Emperor Charles V, king of Spain, grandson on his father's side of the Emperor Maximilian, and on his mother's of Ferdinand and Isabella, ruled not only Spain and the south of Italy, but the vast Hapsburg lands in central Europe and most of the Netherlands; and to enhance his rule he enjoyed the rich tribute of the New World with which Ferdinand and Isabella had endowed him. Encircled by this sprawling empire, France sought the neutrality of England, her old enemy, and was ready to sacrifice her old ally, Scotland, in the sacred cause of self-preservation. Charles V also wanted England's friendship to let him use the English Channel for easy communication between Spain and the Netherlands; and Henry VIII and his great minister, Cardinal Wolsey, saw the advantage to England of establishing a balance of power between the rival thrones of Charles V and Francis I. Spain was the first to be favoured, but when France was heavily defeated and Francis captured at the battle of Pavia, the danger of a weakened France made England her ally.

A peace treaty, of policy rather than intention, was concluded between France and England in 1515, in which provision was made for protection of England against border raids, but none to punish an

English raid into Scotland. Albany approved the treaty, and advised maintenance of peaceful relations; but later appears to have changed his mind. Having provided safe-keeping for the young king, and appointed a broad-based council of regency to govern the realm, Albany returned to France in 1517 and negotiated the treaty of Rouen, by which France and Scotland pledged mutual assistance should England attack either, and a daughter of Francis I was to be given in marriage to the infant James. The promise of a marriage alliance was ignored, and Albany, who had intended to stay in France for four months only, was detained there for four years. There can be little doubt that his detention was demanded by England as a condition for the renewal of an Anglo-French agreement in 1518; for two years later when Henry VIII and Francis I met near Guines at the Field of the Cloth of Gold—a sumptuous and rather silly parade of rival splendours—the order for Albany's detention was renewed in spite of Scottish protest.

In the short period of his regency in Scotland, Albany had shown himself strong, shrewd, and tolerant. Of several turbulent barons only Lord Home was executed, and he came of a family notoriously troublesome. In France too, during his enforced residence, Albany had been able to serve Scottish interests both in matters concerning the church's relationship with the papacy, and in securing certain concessions to Scottish merchants trading abroad. What Scotland lost by his absence is revealed by the turmoil that ensued. In Lothian, after the execution of Lord Home, Albany had left as his lieutenant a Frenchman, de la Bastie, who was murdered by a Home of Wedderburn. The queen-mother, Margaret Tudor—apparently a volatile young woman—had been briefly banished, then allowed to return to Scotland; she celebrated her return by divorcing her husband, the Red Douglas. Douglas, earl of Angus, associated with Homes and other unruly borderers, and stirred up trouble in Edinburgh, where he and his kinsmen were popular.

James Hamilton, earl of Arran, and James Beaton, archbishop of Glasgow and lord chancellor of Scotland, were now at the head of government, but their government was unable to repress the exuberant opposition of the Douglases and their border allies. The two factions met in headlong battle in the long High Street of Edinburgh. The Hamiltons, it appears, had packed the town, and their leaders were gathered in the chancellor's palace. To them came Gavin Douglas, bishop of Dunkeld—scholar and poet as well as uncle to the Red Douglas—in a last effort to keep the peace. The archbishop of Glasgow, replying vehemently that he knew nothing of any evil intended by the Hamiltons, struck himself on the breast as if to demonstrate his untroubled conscience; and his hand beat loudly on the armour he wore beneath his vestments. 'A poor conscience,' said Gavin Douglas, 'for I heard it clatter.'

The Douglases, it is said, stood ready for battle in the High Street, and the Hamiltons assailed them from the narrow wynds and closes that opened off the street. There was furious scuffling, and the climax came when a troop of border horsemen, having broken down one of the town gates with sledge-hammers, rode up the causeway under David Home of Wedderburn—who had killed de la Bastie—and fought hotly on the side of their Douglas allies. The Hamiltons were so decisively driven out that the citizens christened and remembered the brawl as 'Cleanse the Causeway'.

Albany returned to Scotland in 1521. After his demonstrative meeting with the French king at the Field of the Cloth of Gold, Henry VIII had had conversations of a different sort with Charles V, in consequence of which they decided to attack France jointly. Having lost his English ally, the French king once again besought the goodwill of Scotland, and at Roslin Albany mustered what seems to have been an exceptionally large army for an invasion of England and assault on Carlisle. It was well equipped with artillery, and troops from some of the small French garrisons who were now stationed in Scotland may have marched; but Francis had refused to send an expeditionary force. Realising that the French king had no intention of helping them—and possibly remembering Flodden—the Scots nobles would not cross the border, and the army dispersed, having accomplished nothing.

Albany went back to France to demand support, and in the early summer a force of some 500 men was landed in the Firth of Forth. Albany followed in late September with a considerable French army of perhaps 4,000 infantry, 500 cavalry, with guns and money and supplies. There was immediate mobilisation for an autumn campaign, but the Scots showed no enthusiasm for war, though English raiders under the duke of Norfolk—son of the earl of Surrey, the victor at Flodden—had lately crossed the border to burn Kelso and Jedburgh and leave wide desolation. The Franco-Scottish army marched as far as the Tweed, crossed it reluctantly, made a hesitant and unsuccessful attack on Wark castle—in which the French did the fighting—and hurriedly withdrew. Flodden was too close for comfort, and as allies the French had lost their old appeal.

Parliament decreed that the French troops must return to their own country, and in May, 1524, Albany went also. He did not come back, and a politic change in England's relations with France may have decided him to stay in the country where he had been brought up, and which, after some recent experiences in Scotland, he probably preferred. To maintain a balance of power in Europe after the major defeat that France suffered at the battle of Pavia, south of Milan, it was necessary for England to go to the aid of France; and in 1527 an Anglo-French treaty was signed that temporarily put a stop to France's interest in Scotland. The way was opening by which a pro-English party could pursue its policy, and such a party was not slow to emerge.

In spite of his discomfiture at 'Cleanse the Causeway', Arran was still powerful, and he and the queen-mother were both in favour of alliance with England. They contrived a ceremony called the 'erection' of the king, and at the age of twelve James V was invested with crown, sword, and sceptre, and from his uncle of England acquired a bodyguard of 200 men. Parliament approved all that Arran and the queen-mother had done, and Angus, the Red Douglas, who had fled to France after the affray in Edinburgh, was restored to his former lands and dignities. He too was of the English party, and disrupted it; for Angus and Arran were still at odds, and Angus and his former wife, the queen-mother, were not to be reconciled. An English party might be confident of existence, but it was unlikely to find a policy on which its members could agree. The queen-mother appeared to escape from politics by marrying Henry Stewart, afterwards Lord Methven, and Angus, taking advantage of a nobility divided in pursuit of individual gain, acquired a dominating position.

It had been decided by parliament that custody of the king should be the responsibility of the more prominent lords and prelates in turn; but when it came to Angus's turn he retained possession of the boy and refused to give him up. A subservient parliament declared that authority lay in the king's hands; and Angus exercised it. Beaton the archbishop ceased to be lord chancellor, and Angus took the Great Seal. He made his kinsmen officers of his household, and appointed his uncle, Archibald Douglas, as treasurer and provost of Edinburgh. But as the Red Douglas grew in strength and arrogance, so increased in number those whom he had offended. His power was unassailable so long as the king remained his prisoner, and more than one attempt was made to rescue James. A border foray failed, and a coalition of lords and prelates, led by the earl of Lennox, was defeated in battle and Lennox killed. It was James himself who at last contrived his escape, with the assistance of his still energetic mother.

In Edinburgh, or perhaps in Falkland palace—there is no certain knowledge of how the escape was made—he eluded the vigilance of those who guarded him, and rode to Stirling castle, which seems to have been in the keeping of the queen-mother. To his support there rallied a powerful group of magnates, not all of whom were moved by hatred of the Douglases, and to Edinburgh he led a force whose leaders included the border lords Home, Bothwell, and Maxwell; the earls of Argyll, Rothes, and Eglinton; Moray and Keith from the north; and Arran who had lately been a humble ally of his old enemy Angus. Angus was summoned for treason and put to the horn; but in his castle of Tantallon, on the Lothian shore, he defied the royal army for three weeks, and for the price of their forfeited castles the Douglases were then allowed to retire to England. James, at the age of sixteen, was king in his own realm. He was precocious, physically strong, and well-made; he may have been poorly educated, but if so he was quick to learn and acquired a sound knowledge of the laws and institutions of his kingdom.

The immediate problem facing the new king and his counsellors was financial. Both Albany and the queen-mother had been extravagant, and crown rents had not profited from disorder or the private needs of those who collected them. There was no general system of taxation, and the value of money was still falling. The Church, however, was inordinately rich, and in 1531 King James solicited the pope for an annual subsidy of £10,000, to be extracted from the revenues of the church in Scotland, for defence of the realm. In the circumstances of the time the demand was not impolitic, nor was James's expectation unrealistic. In much of Europe heresy was spreading fast, and the church of Rome would need all the friends it could muster. Pope Clement VII was a prisoner of the Emperor Charles V, and the emperor, whose delegates had lately concluded a commercial treaty with Scotland, would not be displeased to offer alternative benefits to the Auld Alliance with France. Scotland, too, might expect some favour when England was so hostile to both pope and emperor— hostile and contemptuous of old authority—for Henry VIII had defied the pope by declaring the whole body of English clergy guilty of treason and *praemunire;*[1] while still insisting on his divorce from Catherine of Aragon, who was the emperor's aunt.

The pope finally consented to James's demand when it was agreed that the subsidy should be used for the establishment of a College of Justice, or supreme court, half of whose members were to be church-men, and which, by the maintenance of law and order, would be serviceable in protecting the church against the assault of unruly heretics. The Scottish prelates, who had to find £10,000 a year from their own revenue, were less than enthusiastic about the bargain, and persuaded James to accept, instead of annual tribute, the sum of

[1] *Praemunire:* to assert or maintain papal jurisdiction in England.

£72,000, to be paid over four years without condition as to its use, and thereafter £1,400 a year for the College. As there were to be fourteen members of the College, the salary of a judge was thereby fixed at £100—not sterling, but Scots—and even in the sixteenth century that was hardly adequate. But Scotland was given a supreme court and a paid judiciary, even though it was poorly paid.

Another potential source of income was marriage. Though James V was a minor figure on the European stage, in the alternating balance and imbalance of power a marriage alliance with the king of Scots had its value, and a bride with a handsome dowry would bring welcome relief to an impoverished kingdom. In his infancy James had been promised a daughter of Francis I, but in an ebb-tide of Franco-Scottish friendship that promise had been forgotten. There were, however, other potentates with available daughters, and as if they were certificates of eligibility James received from Henry VIII the Order of the Garter; from the emperor the Order of the Golden Fleece; and from Francis I the Order of St. Michael. The possibility of marriage to Henry's daughter Mary was considered; the emperor suggested princesses of Denmark and Portugal; and in 1536, after long negotiation, a business-like contract was made for a marriage with Mary of Bourbon, a daughter of the duke of Vendôme, whose dowry was to be 100,000 crowns. Having inspected the lady's portrait James asked also for a pension of 20,000 livres, and permission for Scottish merchants to trade freely in certain French ports. His conditions were accepted, and in September he sailed to Dieppe. But when he saw the duke's poor daughter he was so displeased by her appearance that he broke off the match.

He did not return unwed, however. Francis I had a daughter called Madeleine whose suitability as a royal bride had often been discussed; but Madeleine was delicate and Francis unwilling to let het go from him. To Madeleine, however, James at last was married, on 1st January, 1536, and he took her with a dowry less than half of that offered with the duke of Vendôme's daughter, and the rental on 125,000 livres. In May they returned to Scotland, and unhappy Madeleine died in July. But a French bride was now what James wanted, and negotiations soon began for his marriage to another. While he was in France James had met Mary of Guise-Lorraine, then married to the duke of Longue-ville. But Longueville died a few weeks before Madeleine, and there was no obstacle to her marriage with James other than a proposal from Henry VIII; who, having divorced Catherine of Aragon, beheaded Anne Boleyn, and survived the death of Jane Seymour, was again a widower. James was preferred, however, and in June, 1538, Mary of Guise-

Lorraine, already married by proxy, came to Scotland with a dowry of 150,000 livres.

That James was greedy for money cannot be denied. The poverty of his kingdom can in part excuse him, and the Tudor blood of his mother may have made him avaricious by descent. But at the expense of many of his nobles he added to his wealth by seizure and forfeiture of their lands, by penalties and exactions of various kinds, in a way that shows him to have been not merely rapacious but vindictive. In his early life as a ward and then a prisoner of self-seeking provincial autocrats lie probably the seeds of later behaviour, and his unremitting hatred of the Douglases is at least comprehensible. But not only the Douglases suffered. He acted with impolitic rapacity. He vindictively despoiled the earls of Bothwell and Morton, the young earl of Crawford, a Scott of Branxholm, a Colquhoun of Luss, a Colville of East Wemyss, and others too. He added to his wealth the lands he took and the fines he exacted, but naked avarice roused contention when loyalty was needed, and when he wanted friends he found enemies.

There was, in Scotland, persistent need of a strong ruler. Both in the Highlands and on the borders were people of exuberant temper and contemptuous of authority, to whom the concept of general law and order imposed from the centre was profoundly alien; and there—as indeed in all parts of Scotland—law and order had occasionally to be enforced. James V was fortunate in that control of the Highlands, during his legal infancy, had been exercised by the earl of Argyll and the earl of Huntly. Argyll, the chief of Clan Campbell, ruled not only his own county and some of the nearer isles, but, through kinsmen, Breadalbane and various Lowland properties from Ayrshire to the Moray Firth; while Huntly, chief of the Gordons, was dominant in the highland parts of Aberdeenshire and Banffshire, had extended his influence by marriage into Sutherland, and still held lands in Berwick-shire where the family had first settled. The strength of Argyll and Huntly was almost unassailable, and though, as lieutenants of the king, they might not bring him much profit, they prevented any grave aggression by lesser chiefs, any major threat to the stability of the realm.

In the middle and lowland parts of the kingdom where such great families as the Hamiltons and Douglases were perhaps even more closely knit than a Highland clan, there had been, after Albany's departure, no power capable of preventing, or impartially suppressing, the disgraceful fracas called 'Cleanse the Causeway'. A strong king had good reason for asserting his strength where royal authority might be challenged; but no king could depend wholly on reverence for the

[176]

monarchy. To rule effectively he had to enjoy general consent and the active support of a majority of his principal subjects.

The borders presented a very difficult problem, because it could be argued that their traditional unruliness offered a permanent defence against English aggression. Though their defence was often permeable, it had the advantage of being cheap: it cost the crown nothing. A border laird, on the other hand, found it easy to intrigue with England, and a border foray might provoke English retaliation when policy required peace. It was, presumably, to prevent such provocation that James, in 1530, undertook an expedition which, because it inspired a famous ballad, became the most notorious event of his reign, save only his ultimate defeat at Solway Moss.

His punitive campaign was directed primarily against Armstrong of Gilnockie, popularly known as Johnnie Armstrong, a freebooter of formidable ability who lived near Langholm, in Eskdale in the south-west, and on both sides of the border plundered those who would not pay blackmail for his protection; though England, it seems probable, provided most of his revenue. In the years of his ascendancy the Red Douglas had made six attempts to capture or disable Johnnie Armstrong, and on each occasion had been baffled or defeated. There was reason to believe that Armstrong gave shelter to English fugitives, and had illicit connexions with the greater lords of the border; and as a pre-liminary to his campaign James seized and imprisoned the earl of Bothwell, the Lords Home and Maxwell, Scott of Buccleugh, and other local magnates. Armstrong was summoned to meet him near Hawick, and apparently unaware of the king's hostility—in his own mind, perhaps, innocent of any fault—he came in state, attended by a well-attired retinue of twenty-four bold friends or kinsmen. There was some debate between them, but the king would listen to no defence nor condescend to bargain. Johnnie Armstrong and his twenty-four moss-troopers were taken by force and promptly hanged from the nearest trees. There was justification for so ruthless a punishment, and there is no proof that the king had treacherously written 'a loving letter'—as the ballad declares—to bring Armstrong to their rendezvous; but leniency might have been more politic. The immediate effects, however, of visible and condign punishment were so striking that James felt it safe to release the greater lords whom he had arrested.

In the west Highlands and Islands there was some confusion after the death, in 1329, of the third earl of Argyll; who in his lifetime had been all-powerful. Fighting broke out between Campbells on the one side, and on the other Macleans and the MacDonalds of Islay; the expansionist policy of the Campbells had fostered the enmity of lesser clans, and personal relations were always liable to the disruption of violent emotion. The chief of Maclean, Lachlan of Duart, had married a daughter of the second earl of Argyll, and having grown tired of her exposed her to the sea on a tidal rock. Happily she was rescued, but when Maclean was given a safe-conduct to Edinburgh, to discuss Highland policy, he was murdered in his bed by Campbell of Cawdor, the lady's brother. The fourth earl of Argyll wrote to the council, claiming experience in 'the daunting of the Isles', and offered himself as lieutenant over those in the south; but he was already too powerful, and falling from favour was deprived of some of his lands.

MacDonald of Islay was given the lieutenancy for which Argyll had asked, and James himself made several progresses to the west. For some years there was peace in the Highlands, but in 1539 a rebel movement was initiated by one of the Skye chieftains, Donald Gorm of Sleat, who was killed under the walls of Eilean Donan, the castle that guards the dark waters of Loch Duich in Kintail; and this new symptom of unrest persuaded James to embark on a notable voyage. In 1540, with Huntly, Arran and the archbishop of St. Andrews in attendance, he led a fleet of twelve well-armed ships on a circumnavigation of his kingdom. They sailed from the Forth to Orkney, where he installed Oliver Sinclair, of the great house of Roslin and Caithness, as his sheriff and tacksman, and thence through the Pentland Firth to Lewis, Skye, Mull and Islay, and rounding the Mull of Kintyre came into the Firth of Clyde and landed at Dumbarton. With him the king brought chiefs from all those parts where he had found signs of disaffection, and left behind him so peaceful and obedient a mood that it was even possible to collect his rents.

James was active in the maintenance of law. His justice ayres, or circuit courts, were regularly held, and he himself often attended. Malefactors were rigorously punished. But he continued to alienate those who, by inherited authority, could have helped him to establish order and respect for law. In the latter years of his reign it was said that his council consisted only of churchmen, and the great nobles appear to have boycotted both parliament and council. In 1540 he confirmed a previous revocation of all grants, of lands and privileges, that had been made during his minority, and in the same year he further aggravated the ill-humour of his nobles by putting to death, on a dubious charge of treason, a somewhat unscrupulous but important member of the house of Hamilton, known as the Bastard of Arran. As if life was a Greek tragedy, he seems to have been impelled to the very actions and the destined road that led him to his doom.

Tragedy darkened his private life, for in 1541 the infant sons that

Mary of Lorraine had borne him both died within a few days of each other; and the kingdom was left without an heir. But the kingdom was not a land impoverished by James's exactions, and among the ordinary people he was still popular. In that year he and his queen made a triumphant progress to Perth and Aberdeen and Dundee, where sedulous preparation was made for their entertainment. In Aberdeen, indeed, they remained for fifteen days, and the town and the university regaled them with plays, disputations, and orations 'in Greek, Latin, and other languages'. On their return to Edinburgh, however, politics replaced these amiable diversions.

Under the gathering clouds of heresy, or zeal for reformation, James had declared his resolution to maintain the Roman church and the Auld Alliance; and as if to demonstrate his allegiance he had twice married into France. Henry VIII, who had boldly asserted and successfully proved his independence of the papacy, was still anxious to reach an understanding with James, and the year 1541 seemed propitious for a meeting; David Beaton, cardinal archbishop of St. Andrews in succession to his uncle James, had gone abroad, and Beaton was foremost among those who stood for the French alliance. In his absence James consented to meet Henry at York in September, and Henry went there at the agreed time. It was his first and only visit to the city, and he was naturally indignant to find he had gone in vain. His privy council had refused to let James undertake a journey that might have been doubly dangerous. It was rumoured that Henry had had conversations with dissident border lords, to discuss the possibility of kidnapping the Scottish king; and what was more important for the churchmen on his council, it was feared that James might be persuaded to follow Henry's example, and renounce the authority of Rome. They would have been wiser to remember that Rome was far away, and England near. Henry's anger was never passive, and in the following year he mobilised his northern levies, and Sir Robert Bowes led them over the border into Teviotdale; where they were defeated by the energetic earl of Huntly.

A second foray, under the duke of Norfolk, was more successful, and according to a well-established convention burnt Roxburgh, Kelso, and some smaller places. Henry reasserted the old English claim of suzerainty over Scotland, and James mustered a Scottish host, and marched as far as Fala Moor on the road to Lauder. Farther than that his army would not go. Though supplies may have been insufficient, the real reason was that the nobles would not agree to undertake a war on behalf of France. The army dispersed, but within three weeks James had mobilised another, and that he did with the help of Cardinal

[179]

Beaton; James Stewart, earl of Moray, his lieutenant in the north; and Oliver Sinclair, his new favourite, whom he had lately made his sheriff and tacksman in Orkney.

They marched from Edinburgh on 21st November, with an army that may have numbered 10,000. Beaton and Moray moved to Haddington, apparently with the purpose of threatening the eastern border, while James led the main force to the west. Sinclair halted at Langholm, the king went as far as Lochmaben, from where he proposed to cross the sands of Solway when the tide was out. Sinclair advanced southward from Langholm, and at Solway Moss met Sir Thomas Wharton, the English deputy warden, who had marched from Carlisle with a force of some 3,000 men. What happened next can only be explained by the supposition that again there was dissension among the Scottish leaders, that few were willing to fight for a king in whom they had no confidence, and that Oliver Sinclair's command was not accepted. What should have been a battle became a rout. The Scots turned tail and fled, and Wharton took 1,200 prisoners.

James withdrew to Edinburgh. He spent some time at Linlithgow, where on 8th December his queen gave birth to a daughter. The king had already retired to his favourite palace of Falkland, and died there six days later. He was only in his thirty-first year, a man of sturdy build and energetic habit, and yet it appears that he died, not of any physical ailment or injury, but of that spiritual despair which is commonly excused as a broken heart. The shame of Solway Moss haunted his last hours. 'Fled Oliver?' he cried. 'All is lost!' When he was told of the birth of his daughter he took no pleasure in the news, but only remembered an older king's daughter, by whom the hapless Stewarts had been advanced to the throne: 'It cam' wi' a lass, it will go wi' a lass.' And he turned his face to the wall.

From James I to James VI, none of the royal Stewarts was a simple character, easy of comprehension—none lacked charm, ability, or virtue —and none left to posterity a more enigmatic memory than James V. In almost all his reported dealings with his nobility he was rapacious, and often cruelly intent on revenge. Some account has been given of his merciless greed, and there were darker episodes than the expropriation of broad estates. In July, 1537, the Master of Forbes and Lady Glamis were executed, the former because he had had the 'abominable imagination' of shooting the king in Aberdeen; the latter, who had several times been accused of offence, because she was suspected of an attempt to poison the king. She was burnt on the Castle Hill of Edinburgh, and the Master was drawn, hanged, and beheaded: an English doom previously unknown in Scotland. Lady Glamis, it must be noted, was a sister of the Red Douglas, whom James never forgave; the Master of Forbes was Douglas's brother-in-law.

In stark contradiction of brutality and vindictiveness, however, is the undoubted fact that James was fondly remembered as 'the poor man's king'. Like his father, James IV, he was fond of wayfaring in a humble disguise. Leading down from Stirling castle was a steep pass called Ballengiech, and James *incognito* would describe himself as the Good Man of Ballengiech—the tenant, that is—and if legends are to be trusted, his behaviour, on such occasions, was friendly and genial and showed a taste for gaiety and simple humour. He was licentious, and that may have been an aspect of his gaiety. He left five natural sons for whom, while they were mere children, a complaisant church found accommodation in some of its richest benefices; and the evidence of so sturdy a common appetite may have done much to make him popular among the common people of his country. The belief that he was the author of *Christ's Kirk on the Green*, which vulgar tradition for long maintained, was probably due to the fact that those robust, good-humoured verses seemed to reflect what common memory preserved of the luckless king.

If, moreover, a taste for architecture is to be written on the better side of a mortal balance-sheet, James must be given credit for the building he did at Stirling, Falkland, and Linlithgow. At Linlithgow he raised a palace of extravagant splendour for Mary of Lorraine, and though only a noble ruin now remains—it was burnt by Cumberland's troops in 1746—it suffices to give some substance for the queen's flattery when she told James it was 'the most princely home she had ever looked upon'.

Can the contradiction between the Good Man of Ballengiech and the tyrannous oppressor of his nobility be resolved by admitting the possibility that many Scottish nobles in the sixteenth century were indeed so insufferable, so corrupted by local omnipotence and devoid of morality as to excite, in one who had more power than they, an inhumanity equal to their own? Much that happened in the reign of James's daughter Mary, who became queen of Scots, can hardly be explained except by an admission that the pursuit of power can become obsessive and utterly corrupting.

Chapter 2

MORE than a century before the regent Albany came to Scotland in 1515, the first duke of that title had governed his realm for the old, incompetent monarch Robert III; and of the elder Albany it was written that he was a resolute Catholic who hated all lollards and heretics. In 1406 the first of such heretics to become a martyr was James Resby, who was burnt in Perth for preaching the doctrine of John Wyclif, which included social criticism as well as theological commentary. Wyclif was offended by the wealth of the church and the profligacy of churchmen. He was so extreme in his views as to suggest that only an innate holiness could justify a man in becoming either priest or pope, and that for worldly possessions there was no true title but God's grace. His preaching, that is—apart from any theological content—was directed against constituted authority. In such a cause James Resby could not die in vain.

In 1516 Martin Luther, leader of the Protestant Reformation in Germany, began to preach against the sale of 'indulgences': the remission, that is, of the punishment due after sin by application of some small fraction of the church's alleged treasury of merit. The penitent expressed his sorrow by contributing to the treasury, and so in effect paid for his pardon. Luther was especially incensed by an indulgence proclaimed by Pope Leo X to provide money for building St. Peter's. The attempt to create capital by the sale of what, in modern terms, may be called 'futures', was too nakedly commercial, and Luther was impelled to question the whole concept of papal supremacy. His heretical views were condemned, and he published the treatises which may be regarded as the kernel of the Reformation. He appealed to the German people to resist the exactions of the Roman court and reform its own church; he rejected transubstantiation and accepted only baptism and the eucharist as scriptural sacraments; he proclaimed the priesthood of all believers, and justification by faith alone.

Seamen and continental traders carried news of that spiritual rebellion

[182]

to ports and harbours on the east coast of Scotland, and Luther's teaching was eagerly accepted by a people whose native instinct doubted all authority, and who were already critical of the faults of their own church and churchmen. The unity of the Middle Ages had broken apart. The totality of belief in God and His universal church was being replaced by an intense preoccupation with God's relation to the individual. The visible influence of the Renaissance on Scotland was small, but it had broken the coherence of the Middle Ages, it had quickened history with the embryo of individual consciousness, and the Reformation, that following wave, brought a spirit, both self-assertive and God-regarding, that would, after bitter conflict and vain dispute, reshape the character of the Scottish people.

In the sixteenth century the church in Scotland was too rich and too many of its clergy, indifferent to pastoral care and moral law, were idle; though some could plead illiteracy to excuse their neglect of duty. In earlier years, during the War of Independence, the church had been most valiantly patriotic, and had never been unduly subservient to papal authority; but about the middle of the sixteenth century its annual revenue was approximately £400,000,[1] and that disproportion grew more apparent as criticism, both of doctrine and practice, became more vocal. For several centuries the clergy had presumably satisfied a spiritual hunger that was more exigent then than now, and to a widely varying extent the institutions of the church had done something to mitigate the hardships of poverty in those ages when simple charity, at the door of monastery or castle, was needed to save simple people from starvation. Prelates and the pious magnates whose minds they dominated had built, by unworldly dedication of their wealth, churches and abbeys of ornate magnificence whose splendour—though nowadays it may only be the splendour of the ruins that rebels, Reformers, or the English left—still shows their builders' genius and the genius of a poor land that could find infinite riches to assert and exalt their sense of God's glory. To the church must be given credit for the creation of the three universities of St. Andrews, Glasgow, and Aberdeen in a country whose population was perhaps three-quarters of a million people.

The merit and the labours of the old church of Scotland may not be denied or demeaned; but in its latter days the parishes were bereft of care because their revenue, or the bulk of it, had been diverted to the maintenance of monasteries and cathedrals, and the king and the lordliest of his barons had found means to provide for their bastards or their younger brothers by endowing them with bishoprics and rich benefices. The papacy, defeated by distance, no longer appointed

[1] *Scotland: James V–James VII.* Gordon Donaldson.

prelates of its own choice, and made no attempt to prevent Scottish churchmen from raising capital by feuing their lands; by granting a perpetual lease, that is, in return for a cash payment and annual rent. Under new tenants the rural population found new discontents, and in the mercantile atmosphere of the burghs there was diminishing sympathy for an institution whose numerous servants contributed nothing to the material wealth of the country. But argument *against* the church must not obscure what appear to have been the dominating arguments *for* the Reformation. The doctrine of justification by faith had an obvious appeal; the elimination of intermediaries between the sinner and his Redeemer enhanced the self-importance of the sinner, and the moral earnestness of the reformers stood out in harsh contrast with the lax conformity of the old priesthood.

In St. Andrews in 1528 Patrick Hamilton, a young man of royal descent and nephew of the earl of Arran, was burnt at the stake for heresy. He had studied under Luther in Germany, and preached the alarming doctrine that man and God were made friends by faith. 'The reek[1] of Master Patrick Hamilton,' it was said, 'infected as many as it blew upon.' Among those whom it may have infected was Sir David Lindsay of the Mount, whose satire on *The Three Estates* buffeted the church with open abuse and hearty ridicule. The date of its composition is not known, but it was performed before James V and his queen at Linlithgow in 1540. The extraordinary freedom of Lindsay's language can in part be explained by the fact that he had lived on the most intimate terms with his king since James's childhood, but acknowledgment must be made of James's tolerance in permitting both raucous criticism of the church and public rebuke of his own sensuality. There is in the satire a Pardoner—one who sells indulgences—who introduces himself:

> I am Sir Robert Rome-raker,
> A public perfect Pardoner,
> Admitted by the Pope.
> Sir, I shall show you for my wage
> My pardons, and my privilege,
> Which you shall see, and grasp.
> I give to the devil, with good intent,
> This mischievious wicked New Testament,[2]
> With them who translated it:
> Since humble men have known the truth,
> Pardoners get no charity
> Unless they argue about it

---

[1] The smoke of the fire that burnt him.
[2] Now printed in the common tongue.

Among the women with tricks and cunning;
As my associates beguile all men
By our fair false flattery,
Yes, every sort of craftiness I know by heart
As I was taught by a friar Called Hypocrisy.
But now, alas, our great discomfiture
Is made clearly known, to our confusion,
Which I may fairly deplore:
Of all trust I have been deprived,
Everyone now despises me
Who studies the New Testament.
May grief befall those who made it,
And those who brought the book home,
And I wish by the Cross
That Martin Luther, that false rogue,
Black Bullinger and Melancthon,[1]
Had been smothered in their mothers's bowels. . . .

More surprising, perhaps, is the fact that among the *dramatis personae* is one called John the Common Weal, a representative of the common people who is treated with great respect. Robustly he begins his speech:

Sie, I complain against the king and all the Three Estates.
As for our revered Fathers of Spirituality,
They are led by Covetousness and Sensuality.
And, as you see, Temporal Power has need of correction,
Which for long has been led by public Oppression—
Look where the rogue lies lurking behind him!
Get up, I hope to see your neck break in a rope!
Look, here are Falsehood, and Deceit, well do I know them,
Leaders of the merchants and foolish tradesmen:
What's surprising if the Three Estates go backwards
When such a vile company lives among them,
That has ruled all the crowd for many distressing days,
And robbed John the Common Weal of all his warm clothes?[2]

There is much more of the same sort, and John the Common Weal is allowed to savage all in authority with what may seem to be the quite premature voice of enfranchised democracy. It must be noted, however, that freedom of speech is traditional in Scotland. Difference in degree has never imposed a servile reticence, and the socially inferior have always felt at liberty to criticise their betters; their betters, indeed, have usually admitted the impossibility of silencing criticism. When Lindsay of the Mount used John the Common Weal to fortify his own denunciation of abuse, he was merely acknowledging a permitted custom of the country.

[1] Swiss reformers; associates of Calvin.
[2] These quotations have been slightly modernised.

There were, then, social, economic, moral, and spiritual arguments for a new order; but the new order became the Reformation because England, isolated by Henry VIII's rejection of papal authority, required a Protestant neighbour on its northern frontier. The ambition or idealism of the Scottish reformers had the good fortune to find an ally in English policy.

When James V died in December, 1542, he left as his heir a female infant barely a week old. The child's nearest male kinsman was her great-uncle, Henry VIII, who had a son, Edward, aged five. In 1286 Alexander III had died and left his throne to the Maid of Norway; her great-uncle was Edward I, and he too had had a son. What Edward I had proposed was repeated by Henry VIII, and negotiations began for a treaty of peace and the marriage of the infant Mary and the boy Edward. In Scotland, however, opinion was divided. There was contest for the regency between Cardinal Beaton and the earl of Arran: Beaton, archbishop of St. Andrews, stood for the Auld Alliance, and Arran, heir presumptive to the throne, was Anglophile and half a Protestant. The Red Douglas, earl of Angus, who had been an exile in England since 1528, returned to Scotland, and with him came nearly a dozen of the nobles who had been captured at Solway Moss. By force of principle or persuaded by bribes they had aligned themselves with Henry and the apparent benevolence of his policy. Arran became regent and governor of the kingdom, and Beaton was imprisoned. Parliament authorised the reading of the Scriptures in the vulgar tongue, and by the Treaty of Greenwich Mary, the infant queen of Scots, was betrothed to Edward, prince of Wales.

But Beaton, though imprisoned, was not wholly deprived of influence; and Henry VIII, though seemingly in command of the situation, was the captive of his temperament. Arrogance undid him. As if Scotland were already subject territory he demanded custody of the infant queen, proclaimed himself her successor should she die in infancy, and seized some Scottish ships at sea. He awakened the old hatred and distrust of England, and Beaton, having established communication with France, secured the return of two important exiles to balance the homecoming of the pro-English lords. One of them was Matthew, earl of Lennox, who would have a claim to the throne if Arran's legitimacy—about which there was some doubt—could be disproved; and the other was John Hamilton, abbot of Paisley, Arran's half-brother, and a much abler man than the governor. Beaton regained his liberty and was supported by Mary of Lorraine, the queen-mother. Opposition to the Treaty of Greenwich hardened, and Arran the half-Protestant suddenly regretted his apostasy and rediscovered his older faith. Beaton and the queen-mother became his fellow members in a new council of government, and the Treaty of Greenwich was denounced. The Auld Alliance was renewed, and Beaton was made chancellor, John Hamilton treasurer.

But the change of front did not produce unity. When Arran joined Beaton and the queen-mother, Lennox transferred his allegiance to Henry VIII, and the lords were again divided. Henry's anger at the failure of his policy was extreme, but not unnatural. Lennox, the Red Douglas, and others were his friends in Scotland, but their strength was insufficient for his purpose. Only by invasion could he punish his troublesome neighbour, and the instructions which his Privy Council sent to the earl of Hertford, the commander of the invading army, were explicit and ferocious. Hertford was ordered to 'put all to fire and sword, burn Edinburgh town, so razed and defaced when you have sacked and gotten what ye can of it as there may remain forever a perpetual memory of the vengeance of God lighted upon them for their falsehood and disloyalty. Do what ye can out of hand and without long tarrying to beat down and overthrow the Castle, sack Holyrood House and burn and subvert it and all the rest, putting man, woman, and child to fire and sword without exception, where any resistance shall be made against you; and this done, pass over to the Fifeland, and extend like extremity and destruction in all towns and villages whereunto ye may reach conveniently, not forgetting among all the rest so to spoil the cardinal's town of St. Andrews as the upper stone may be the nether, and not one stick stand by another, sparing no creature alive within the same.'

The Scots were taken by surprise. Hertford landed in the Firth of Forth, and burnt Leith, Holyrood, and Edinburgh; another force crossed the border and burnt Jedburgh and its great abbey. The violence of the English assault did little to recommend Henry's policy, and though Lennox was active in his interest, Angus changed sides and early in 1545 routed an English army, of considerable strength, at Ancrum Moor near Jedburgh. Under Beaton, Arran, and the queen-mother a façade of unity was maintained, but Henry was still determined to enforce his will by military action. Reports were received of preparation for assault by land and sea, and the French sent a military mission which quickly became unpopular and was of negligible assistance. Hertford crossed the border in September, in command of an army that included many foreign mercenaries, and subsequently boasted of having destroyed five market towns, two hundred and forty-three villages, and sixteen fortified places. His catalogue was probably exaggerated, but the year's harvest was burnt, and the ruined abbeys of Kelso, Dryburgh, Roxburgh, and Coldingham testified to the ardour of what came to be known as Henry's 'rough wooing'. In a campaign in the west Lennox was joined by several Highland clans—Macleans, Macleods, and Clan Donald under Donald Dubh—who had accepted English subsidies. The Highland rebellion was extinguished by the death of Donald Dubh, and Lennox found refuge in England: he had married Margaret Douglas, a daughter of the sixth earl of Angus and James IV's widow, Margaret Tudor, a marriage which gave him a relationship to the thrones of both England and Scotland.

The struggle for religious authority became more embittered when George Wishart, a popular preacher, was arrested for heresy in Haddington and executed in St. Andrews. He may be called a martyr, but almost certainly he was an English agent. Eight weeks later, at the end of May, 1546, a band of men, several of whom were lairds in Fife, broke into the castle of St. Andrews, and having adjured the cardinal to repent of Wishart's death, murdered him. There were many opposed to Beaton's policy, and for some time his life had been in danger from conspirators who had the sympathy and support of the English king. There is no need to believe that Wishart's arrest was anything more than an excuse for his murder; but whatever the motive, the consequences were grave.

The murderers seized the castle, and held it against an ineffective siege. They were reinforced by sympathisers, among whom was a priest called John Knox, who on the occasion of George Wishart's arrest had made himself conspicuous by carrying a two-handed sword. England and France had briefly been at war, but came to terms in June. England decided to help the besieged, and though Henry VIII died in January, 1547, there was no change in English policy. The new king, Edward VI, was only a boy, and the protector of the realm was the ruthless earl of Hertford, now advanced to the dukedom of Somerset. English pensions were voted to Beaton's murderers, but before more decisive action could be taken a fleet of French galleys arrived and bombarded the castle. Francis I, king of France, had died only two months after Henry of England, and been succeeded by Henry II, under whom Mary of Lorraine's two brothers, the duke of Guise and the cardinal of Lorraine, attained great power. Their policy, it was rumoured, was to arrange a French marriage for the little queen of Scots, and as a preliminary to courtship they followed the example of Henry of England's Rough Wooing. The castle of St. Andrews was battered into submission, and of its garrison the 'gentlemen' were consigned to French prisons, while the others, among whom was Knox, were condemned to the galleys.

French success brought English retaliation. In September the protector, Somerset, led an army that may have numbered 18,000 over the eastern border, and a fleet accompanied him to the Firth of Forth. In Scotland old enmities were momentarily forgotten, and summoned by the fiery cross an army larger than the English force was mustered. The two armies met near Musselburgh, a few miles from Edinburgh, and the Scots abandoned a strong position to give battle in circumstances that invited defeat. They found themselves between Somerset's artillery and the guns of the English fleet, and after initial advantage were routed with great loss. The battle of Pinkie was a major disaster, and the English augmented their victory by capturing and occupying Haddington and other important strongholds in the south-eastern parts of Scotland.

Deeply divided by religious and political schism, Scotland was incapable of expelling the English garrisons. Its only hope of assistance was from France, and the price of French help was the queen of Scots. Mary was to be sent to France, and in due course married to the dauphin. At Haddington, where a Scottish army was besieging the town, French commissioners concluded a treaty by which the five-year-old child was exchanged for an army of six or seven thousand men, and soon it seemed that France had both Scotland and the game in its hands. The English again invaded, were gradually defeated, and Haddington was recovered. In France the English held Boulogne, pending the payment of a French indemnity, and there too they were defeated. By the treaty of Boulogne the town was ceded to its natural proprietors, and the English retired from all their strongholds in Scotland.

But Henry II of France showed himself as exigent as Henry VIII of England. When Mary arrived in France, 'France and Scotland are one country', he said; the French garrisons were reinforced, and when Mary married the dauphin the Auld Alliance threatened extinction of the minor partner. That danger, indeed, was graver than it appeared. Though Mary and the dauphin Francis—a sickly boy of little account —had publicly asserted their intention to preserve and to respect the ancient laws and liberty of Scotland, there were secret documents by which Mary, should she die childless, had bequeathed to Francis both her kingdom of Scotland and her title to England. Mary was fifteen, a year older than her husband, when she was persuaded to sign those papers; it is easy to imagine the circumstances in which a pious girl, an orphan excited or alarmed by the prospect of marriage, would listen obediently to an uncle who was a prince of the church, and do her duty as he defined it. Mary may not be blamed, and only the

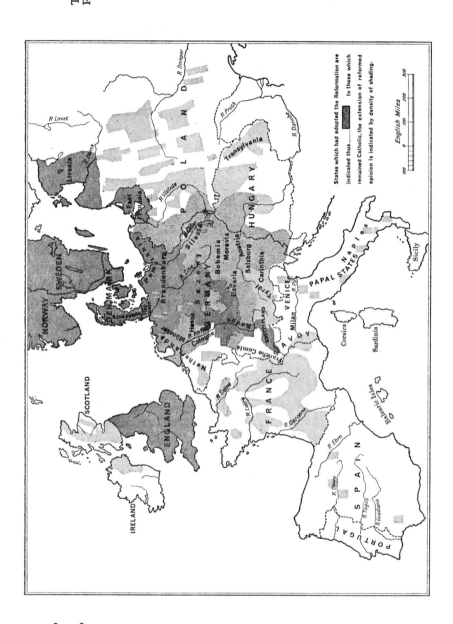

innocent will say that France's policy was odious. It was no worse than Henry VIII's deeply cherished purpose.

An unforeseen consequence of French policy was the transformation of the Reformers into the patriotic party of Scotland. The Auld Alliance and the church of Rome had been bulwarks against English aggression, but now bulwarks were needed against French ambition; and those who stood for the Reformation could also claim that they stood for liberty. Henry VIII had received his title of Defender of the Faith from Pope Leo X; but the Reformers, already confident of God's grace, needed no intermediate authority, and with manifest unction called themselves the Army of the Congregation of Christ.

Four years before Mary's marriage her mother, Mary of Lorraine, had become regent in Arran's place. The queen-mother was a handsome woman, of 'majestic stature and graceful proportions', who for eighteen years after the death of James V in 1542 maintained a position of varying authority, and with politic devotion sustained an unpopular policy in a land seething with discontent. Though one may deplore her influence, it is impossible to deny admiration for her strength of character and the skill with which she steered a course through conflicting tides. From Henry II she had obtained a promise of the dukedom and revenues of Châtelherault for the earl of Arran, and in 1550 she went to France with a distinguished company of the Scottish nobility and clergy whose previous inclination to take sides with England and the Reformers was quickly reversed by French gold. She failed, however, to persuade Arran to resign his regency. His half-brother John Hamilton was then archbishop of St. Andrews, and they were about to make a final attempt to disarm the Reformers' cause by reform of the old church. Hamilton published a catechism that was simply and sincerely written, and showed a generous willingness to accept, in some degree, the Lutheran teaching on justification by faith. The directions issued for its use, however, exposed a lamentable weakness in the priesthood for whom reform was pledged; it was to be read in church only by priests who could read without 'stammering and stumbling'. The catechism appeared too late, and when Mary in France legally came of age—at the mature age of twelve—it was possible to argue that she was entitled to choose and appoint her regent in Scotland. Arran was induced to resign, by a large addition to the revenues of Châtelherault, and Mary of Lorraine acquired the authority she had long sought.

More French troops came to Scotland, and the queen-mother was assisted in her task of government by French officials. In the summer of 1553 Edward VI, the young king of England, had died at the age of fifteen, and his half-sister Mary, the daughter of Catherine of Aragon, succeeded him. Mary, a devout Catholic, married Philip II of Spain a year later, and a papal legate absolved England from the sin of schism. An anti-lollard statute of 1401 was renewed, and at Smithfield the burning of heretics began. In Scotland the queen-mother pursued a policy of toleration, and English Protestants, fleeing from Roman Catholic persecution, found refuge under the Catholic regent and her French advisers. She could afford to be tolerant, for the death of Edward VI and the succession of Mary Tudor had deprived the Congregation of Christ of their Protestant ally: England could no longer be called on to redress French influence. Toleration, indeed, went further than the offer of asylum to refugees, and pastors of the reformed church were permitted to preach without hindrance. Quietly and with pertinaceous skill the queen-mother won to her side anglophile lords and mercantile interest in the burghs; but toleration could not seduce the more earnest and resolute Reformers, and their organisation grew apace under the shelter of laissez-faire.

One of the pastors who came home to preach was John Knox. He had survived his servitude in a French galley, and spent some time in England, in whose Reformation he played an active part. He had retired to the continent after Mary Tudor's accession, and in Geneva had been closely associated with Calvin, whose theology he approved. In Berwick he married Marjorie Bowes, an English woman, and for almost a year remained in Scotland, where he made himself known to Argyll and the Lord James Stewart, an illegitimate son of James V, who favoured him; and he may have influenced a brilliant young man called William Maitland of Lethington, who became, for a little while, secretary of state to Mary of Lorraine, and for a longer period to her daughter. Knox then returned to Geneva.

The queen-mother was faced with grave financial difficulties, and got little help from France. She was generous with her own resources, but when new taxes were imposed the inevitable response was hostile, and the nobles bluntly refused to march with a French expedition across the border. There was some danger of rebellion in 1557, and John Knox in Geneva was invited to come home for the comfort of those who were ready to jeopardise life and goods for the further glory of God. The invitation was premature, and Knox came no nearer than Dieppe. But before the end of the year the Protestant nobles who called themselves Lords of the Congregation of Christ signed a covenant that bound them to use every endeavour to establish 'the most blessed word of God, and to renounce the congregation of

Satan'. In alliance with the reforming pastors they had resolved to establish a Protestant Church.

In 1558 Mary Tudor died childless, and was succeeded by her half-sister Elizabeth, the daughter of Anne Boleyn and the last surviving child of Henry VIII. Elizabeth was twenty-five, unmarried, a woman of massive ability sometimes marred by petty calculation, and of instinctive genius in the art of government. She had, however, the disability of being illegitimate in the opinion of Rome and the great continental powers, which had never admitted the validity of Henry's divorce from Catherine of Aragon. In Catholic opinion the rightful queen of England was Mary, queen of Scots, the granddaughter of James IV and Henry's sister Margaret. Mary herself had no doubt of her title, and a few weeks after Elizabeth's accession she and the dauphin Francis assumed the arms of sovereigns of England. In England a new Act of Supremacy made Elizabeth 'Supreme Governor' of the church in England, and an Act of Uniformity restored Edward VI's second Prayer Book and made church attendance compulsory. England was again defiantly isolated from Catholic Europe, and for her security Elizabeth could depend only on her Englishmen—whom she knew so well how to manage—and on the Protestant groups in Scotland. The Reformation was essential to Elizabeth's safety and the well-being of her country, and to that end, among others, the Reformation was established.

After the marriage of her daughter Mary to the dauphin Francis, Mary of Lorraine began to tire of politic toleration. France and Spain had been at war, but made peace and showed a common front against heresy. In Scotland Protestant preachers were now threatened with expulsion but continued to preach, and in 1559 John Knox returned to Scotland. In Perth he preached a rabble-rousing sermon, and the rabble rose. The monasteries of the Black and the Grey Friars and the Carthusians were sacked, and when the regent mustered an army to suppress disorder, the Army of the Congregation of Christ gathered to oppose it. The Reformation came to life as rebellion, but there was little fighting until the English arrived.

The French troops in Scotland were too few to essay war, and the Army of the Congregation was untrained. The French fortified Leith; the Army of the Congregation, after sacking friaries in Stirling, Dundee and Linlithgow, and spoiling churches, occupied Edinburgh. Demands and defiances went to and fro, and the Lords of the Congregation declared that the regent had been deposed; but when their army launched an attack on Leith it was driven back and fled at Stirling; from where some returned to the west, and others into Fife.

Then England intervened. Her fleet sailed into the Forth, blockading Leith and cutting communications between the French garrison and a detached force which had followed that part of the Reformers' army which, under Lord James Stewart, Argyll, and Kirkcaldy of Grange, had retired into Fife and was still fighting. The French were compelled to retreat, and Scottish commissioners went to Holy Island to confer with the duke of Norfolk and devise a treaty by which England would undertake the preservation of Scotland's freedom.

Queen Elizabeth's principal minister was William Cecil, later Lord Burghley, with whom emissaries of the Congregation had for some time been in contact. Cecil saw clearly that French authority in Scotland and Mary's claim to Elizabeth's throne were a menace that had to be removed, but Elizabeth, warned by Tudor caution or her native genius, had been reluctant to stir up rebellion for fear of its infecting her own subjects. She had allowed money to be sent to sustain the Reformers—much of which crossed the border only to fall into the earl of Bothwell's hands—but had not permitted military action. Now, however, the menace of France had come a little closer, for Henry II was dead, and Francis and Mary were king and queen of both their countries. Elizabeth was still cautious, but let Norfolk, as earl marshal of England, sign with the representatives of Châtelherault—*ci-devant* earl of Arran, whom the Scottish parliament recognised as regent—a contract for the expulsion of French troops. Their contract, known as the Treaty of Berwick, was in effect a pact of mutual assistance against a danger common to both. Nothing was said about religion, and there is substance as well as criticism in the statement that what finally assured the Reformation in Scotland was 'the doubtful state of Elizabeth's birth-certificate'.[1]

An English army commanded by Lord Grey moved into Scotland in March, and the siege of Leith was renewed. The French resisted manfully, and counter-attacked boldly. It seemed as if the siege might be a long one, but the French were unable to reinforce their garrison, and sent envoys to discuss peace. They were in Berwick when, on 11th June, Mary of Lorraine died in Edinburgh castle, where she had found sanctuary some weeks before. For nearly twenty years she had, with valour or discretion, maintained in a foreign land the cause of France and her church, and with exquisite tact she died at the very moment when her death removed the last obstacle to peace. The English and French commissioners met in Edinburgh in July, 1560, and concluded a treaty by which it was agreed that French and English troops should withdraw from Scotland; that warlike preparation, in England

[1] *A Short History of Scotland.* George Malcolm Thomson.

[194]

against France and in France against England, should cease; and that Mary, queen of Scots, and Francis her husband should forego the title and arms of England, and recognise Elizabeth's title to its throne.

Almost immediately the English army withdrew, the French embarked in English ships—as glad to be gone as were the Scots to see them go—and the fortifications of Leith were dismantled. Elizabeth of England had won recognition and security, and though the Treaty of Edinburgh had made no ruling about religious matters, the Army of the Congregation of Christ was in no doubt about its victory. The Reformed parliament met in August, and though a codicil to the treaty had declared its inability to make decisions about religion—parliament might only submit its proposals to Mary and Francis—'That we little regarded', wrote Knox, and a Confession of Faith became the law of the land. The authority and jurisdiction of the pope were abolished; the seven Sacraments were reduced to baptism and the eucharist; the celebration of Mass was forbidden and made punishable by death for the third offence; and whatsoever the Confession of Faith did not approve, was condemned.

The Lords of the Congregation could indeed congratulate themselves on victory. Scotland and England, both Protestant countries, were in alliance; Rome and the Auld Alliance had been cast off. The long, destructive warfare with England had come to an end, but cause would be found for wars of another sort. Victory was not complete, for Mary, when she came to Scotland, neither ratified the treaty of Edinburgh nor accepted the Confession of Faith: religion was still a matter for dispute. The Reformed parliament, moreover, had disappointed Knox and other ministers of the Congregation by declining to accept their Book of Discipline.

By the Confession of Faith the new kirk of Scotland arrogated to itself an authority independent of, and superior to the conventional authority of the state. In the years to come, when Andrew Melville, a stronger man than Knox, returned from Geneva, he plainly told James VI that in Scotland there were two kings and two kingdoms, and the senior were 'Christ Jesus the King, and his Kingdom the kirk, whose subject king James VI is'; and the source of that assertion was the Confession of 1560. It claimed, moreover, that what distinguished the kirk was the true teaching of the Word of God; that truth, to be learnt only from the Bible, could only be interpreted by the spirit of God; and that spirit reposed only in the pastors of the kirk.

The Book of Discipline went further. It was a prospectus for a theocracy to be administered by the pastors and elders of the kirk; and much of what it proposed was good. It had an idealistic plan for

[195]

education, by which every parish should have its schoolmaster able to teach grammar and Latin, and in the principal towns there were to be colleges teaching Latin, Greek, Logic, and Rhetoric. The universities, as well as offering a general course in Arts, would have schools of Medicine, Law, and Divinity. And the whole process of education would be so directed that men—the education of women seems not to have been considered—would be the better able to serve both church and state. Between church and state, indeed, there was to be little difference. Ministers and elders were to be elected by their congregations, and ministers would be subject to the inspection of the elders, who would yearly report on their manners and diligence. There would be no bishops, but 'superintendents' would have an inspector's authority, and as the pastors who were to rule the state would be informed by the spirit of God, the 'superintendents' would be chosen by the light of the spirit. Special provision was made for assistance to married ministers, for pensions to their widows and orphans, and for bursaries for poor boys who could not afford to pay university fees. In other respects provision for the poor was less specific, though the relief of poverty was to be the burden of each church within its parish.

Such totalitarian benignity would be expensive, but the Roman church possessed vast wealth, and with a curiously naïve optimism the Reformers expected to acquire all the revenue of the church except monastery rentals. In that they were disappointed. The church had disposed of so much of its property that a great number of rich or well-to-do tenants had a vested interest in its lands and benefices, and were by no means inclined to impoverish themselves for the mythical benefit of a Judaic theocracy administered by self-elected Calvinist 'superintendents', the manners and diligence of whose junior ministers would be subject, once a year, to the jealous criticism of Calvinist elders. Scotland had reason to be grateful for the simple, narrow selfishness that saved it from such a rule; though a school in every parish would have raised memorable monuments to the Reformation, and might have made Latin the language of democracy.

Chapter 3

Francis, that sickly boy, died in the late winter of 1560. 'Unhappy Francis,' wrote Knox complacently, 'suddenly perisheth of a rotten ear—that deaf ear that never would hear the word of God.' It was, presumably, a mastoid abscess that made Mary a widow at the age of eighteen, and after seventeen months as queen of France and Scotland, left her queen of Scotland only. In the courts of France she had been praised for her beauty, her wit, and her dancing, but from a society in which profligacy was politely commonplace she emerged with a reputation quite unsullied. She had been educated by her grandmother, Antoinette de Bourbon, a devout and austere old lady, and young as she was, her political or dynastic ambition was strong and deeply rooted. Maitland of Lethington, who had briefly been her mother's secretary of state, wrote of her: 'The queen my mistress is descended of the blood of England, and so of the race of the lion on both sides. I fear she would rather be content to hazard all than forgo her right.' And Throckmorton, Elizabeth's ambassador in France, had written: 'Since her husband's death she hath showed (and so continueth) that she is both of great wisdom for her years, modesty, and also of great judgement in the wise handling of herself and her matters, which, increasing with her years, cannot but turn greatly to her commendation, reputation, honour and great benefit of her and her country.' But he suspected her ambition. 'The queen of Scots,' he wrote, 'doth carry herself so honourably, advisedly, and discreetly, as I cannot but fear her progress.'

She had refused to ratify the Treaty of Edinburgh, and Elizabeth refused her permission to travel through England. A belated safe-conduct was sent to France, but before it arrived Mary had put to sea with a fairly numerous and distinguished company that included three of her uncles, of the house of Lorraine, the gifted seigneur de Brântome, and a luckless young man called Chastelard. There were English ships that watched for her passing, not to intercept her, but, apparently, to prevent her landing in the north of England. The French galleys reached the Firth of Forth on 19th August in a thick fog of the sort known locally as a *haar*. So dark was it that Knox was able to see in the inclement weather an omen of disaster. 'The very face of heaven,' he wrote, 'did manifestly speak what comfort was brought into this country with her; to wit, sorrow, dolour, darkness and all impiety; for in the memory of man, that day of the year, was never seen a more dolorous face of the heaven, than was at her arrival, which two days after did so continue.'

It is evident that Knox's mind was even more unfriendly than the sky, and the welcome offered to their young queen by the people of Edinburgh can only be called equivocal. They serenaded her with psalms, and presented her with a Bible covered in fine purple velvet: a gracious gift, indeed, but it was less than gracious to tell her:

> A gift more precious could we none present,
> Nor yet more needful to your Excellence.

There was a tableau representing the burning of Korah, Dathan, and Abiram for the sin of idolatry, and the earl of Huntly prevented the showing of another in which the effigy of a priest was to be burnt while elevating the Host. On the Sunday following her arrival there were riots at Holyrood when Mass was celebrated for the queen and her household, and the Lord James Stewart prevented the infuriated crowd from breaking in to kill the priest.

That Mary should rouse fear and anger in the mob was inevitable. To the majority of people in the south of Scotland she was not only a Catholic, *croyante et pratiquante*, but virtually a foreigner: French by upbringing as well as by her mother's birth. She had come attended by French courtiers only a few months after Scotland had painfully got rid of the French troops whom they had hated for their foreign ways and the danger they invited. In her own person, because she was tall and elegant and graceful far beyond the common fortune of women, she woke fear and suspicion in some who might have known better. John Knox was not an untravelled man, but in Knox's troubled mind, as if he were a provincial curate suddenly translated to Versailles, she woke dark misgivings. 'We call her not a hoor,' he wrote doubtfully, 'but she was brought up in the company of the wildest hoor-mongers, yea, of such as no more regarded incest than honest men regard the company of their wives.'

It was manifest from the beginning that her reign would be difficult. It is a matter of history that her reign was short, and came to a conclusion of lurid tragedy. From one point of view it may be regarded merely as an interlude in the long-drawn dispute between constituted authority and the Reformed church's claim to supersede such authority. But for six years Scotland was of more interest to Europe, and potentially more important, than it had ever been before, or was ever to be again. For that brief eminence in the world it was indebted, in part, to the critical state of affairs that existed in several European countries—to an atmosphere pregnant with crisis—and in part to Mary's own personality and her unwedded state. She was, moreover, the last monarch of a wholly independent Scotland, for her son and successor, without sacrificing the regality of Scotland, took it into a larger context in which, inevitably, it lost much of its old individuality. It is right and proper, then, to provide more room for an assessment of Mary and her reign than would be warranted by its mere length in time.

In France the leaders of the Catholic party were still aware of their influence over the daughter of Mary of Lorraine, but France was no longer a Catholic country. There too the Protestant faction had become a political party, and France was on the verge of a series of civil wars that would be fought with the utmost bitterness, and, because Catholics and Huguenots were almost equally balanced, with appalling loss of life and property. The French Protestants got help from England, and might have got more but for the possibility that Mary's Catholicism might still be obedient to her French uncles.

In Spain Philip II had made his peace with France, but added to the complications of ruling a vast, untidy empire by attempting to suppress heresy in the Netherlands, and accepting the leadership of a Catholic crusade against England. That Mary might become a weapon in the crusade was a possibility that could not be ignored, and if Mary failed in her Catholic duty she might find that Philip's disappointment would grow into enmity. The grand inquisitor, Michele Ghislieri— Fra Michele dell' Inquisizione, who made his name a thing of terror before he became pope as Pius V—was a fanatic who encouraged fanaticism in Philip; and the growing power, the increasing activities of the Jesuits, whose great founder had seen the church as living in a state of war, showed clearly that Catholicism had no intention of retreating before the mounting attack of Calvin's Protestantism.

But England, that lay nearer Holyrood than any of the others, had closer concern with Mary. Elizabeth, who before her death was to make her throne the very heart of England, sat in doubtful security in the early years of her reign. Her title was suspect, her younger rival had not renounced her claim, the church of England was not yet rooted in the soil, and among her Catholic subjects, who were powerful and numerous, there were some of uncertain temper. There was, too, a personal rivalry between the neighbouring queens. Elizabeth, unmarried, had many suitors, and as a woman she took a more than dynastic interest in Mary's prospects of a second marriage. Elizabeth and her England were to advance in triumph, with their sailors on every sea and their poets colonising realms more splendid than the Indies, while Mary, utterly defeated, was to die beneath the axe; yet it was Mary's son who inherited Elizabeth's throne. It seems, indeed, as if history, for a generation, were dissatisfied with the customary disorder of its progress, and chose to move with the tauter steps and the more deliberate manner of drama.

The first act opened quietly, despite Scotland's surly welcome to Mary. In the interregnum before her return the Lord James Stewart and the duke of Châtelherault seem to have assumed the authority of government, assisted by the ingenious Maitland of Lethington. Dynastic hopes may have stirred in both, for the Lord James was a bastard son of James V, and Châtelherault, next in line to the throne, had a son, the earl of Arran, who had been offered as a Protestant husband to Elizabeth of England, though his sanity was very doubtfully balanced. After the death of Francis the Lord James had gone to France and given his half-sister good advice. By several Catholic bishops she had been invited to land in the north of Scotland, where they and the earl of Huntly would find an army with whose aid she could rule a Catholic country; but the Lord James had persuaded her to use discretion in the matter of religion. It is probable that Mary, in the first few months of her reign, owed much to the prudent counsel of her half-brother and Lethington, who became her secretary. She refrained from advertising her claim to the English throne, and the extreme Reformers were dissuaded from pressing their demand that she should renounce Catholicism and accept their new interpretation of the word of God. The reformed religion, she proclaimed, would be maintained, but there must be no interference with her own devotions and the religious practice of her servants. Lethington may have told her what to say, but in the way she said it there was an enchantment to which many yielded.

She could accept advice of which she approved, but equally she could show a lordly temper. There was a provost of Edinburgh, a Douglas of Kilspindie, who on being re-elected in the autumn of 1561 issued a wantonly offensive order to expel from the city all adulterers, fornicators, drunkards, Mass-mongers, and obstinate papists. In Geneva his edict would have been applauded, but Mary immediately ordered the arrest of Kilspindie and his bailies.

[200]

The ministers of the Reformed church were constantly her critics, some of whom declared openly that her subjects owed no obedience to an idolater. She could not dance in Holyroodhouse, it was said, without dancing being condemned in St. Giles, and when the winter skies of Scotland discharged a shower of hail, John Knox saw it as a sure sign that heaven disapproved of her ways.

She had several conversations with Knox, which he himself reported, and they are of the greatest interest, not merely for the incidental light they let fall on the character of the disputants, but for their revelation of a state of mind, presumably common to the pastors of the Congregation of Christ, and apparently accepted as reasonable by a majority of people in the south of Scotland.

Knox had acquired notoriety by the publication of his book entitled *A First Blast of the Trumpet against the Monstrous Regiment of Women*: a tract directed against the two Roman Catholic rulers, Mary of Lorraine and Mary Tudor of England. His opinion of female sovereigns was made forthright in such sentences as: 'To promote a woman to bear rule, superiority, dominion or empire above any realm, nation or city is repugnant to Nature; is contumely to God, a thing most contrarious to his revealed will and approved ordinance; and, finally, is the subversion of good order and of all equity and justice.' In conversation with Mary, however, he did not restrict himself to denunciation of a woman's government, but nakedly exhibited the Reformers' claim to dominate all temporal authority.

His first interview with the queen was at Holyrood. Present with them were the Lord James and two gentlewomen. There was some talk about *The Monstrous Regiment*, and in wider discussion of a sovereign's rights Knox spoke of Israel's stubborn opposition to their rulers in Egypt, of Daniel's defiance of Nebuchadnezzar, and of the Early Christians in Rome.

To which Mary replied: 'Yea, but none of these men raised the sword against their princes.'

'God, Madam, had not given unto them the power and the means,' said Knox.

'Think ye that subjects having power may resist their princes?'

'If their princes exceed their bounds, Madam, no doubt they should be resisted, even by power. For there is neither greater honour nor greater obedience to be given to kings or princes than God has commanded to be given to father and mother. But, Madam, the father may be stricken with a frenzy, in which he would slay his own children. Now, Madam, if the children arise, join themselves together, apprehend the father, take the sword or other weapons from him, and finally bind his hands, and keep him in prison, until his frenzy be overpast; think ye, Madam, that the children do any wrong? Or think ye, Madam, that God will be offended with them that have stayed their father from committing wickedness? It is even so, Madam, with princes that would murder the children of God that are subject unto them. Their blind zeal is nothing but a very mad frenzy: and therefore, to take the sword from them, to bind their hands, and to cast them into prison until they be brought to a more sober mind, is no disobedience against princes, but just obedience, because it agreeth with the will of God.'

The queen, says Knox, listened to this remarkable speech and stood amazed. It is, indeed, a speech that demands attention, for its temper was to dominate much of Scotland's thought and a large part of Scottish policy in the years to come. But Mary's amazement, at her first hearing of the Reformers' pretensions, can elicit nothing but sympathy, and her reply was a precise analysis of their portent.

'Well, then,' she said, 'I perceive that my subjects shall obey you, and not me; and shall do what they like, and not what I command; and so must I be subject to them, and not they to me.'

With some humility Knox told her that his task was to make both princes and people obey God. God, he said simply, would like kings to be foster-fathers to the kirk, and queens to be nurses to the people.

'But ye are not the kirk that I will nurse,' said Mary. 'I will defend the kirk of Rome, for I think it is the true kirk of God.'

No true believer could keep his temper at mention of the Scarlet Woman, and Knox's reply exhibited his anger.

'Your will, Madam, is no reason!' he shouted. 'Neither doth your thought make of that Roman harlot the true and immaculate spouse of Jesus Christ. Wonder not, Madam, that I call Rome a harlot; for that church is altogether polluted with all kind of spiritual fornication, as well in doctrine as in manners.'

The queen answered, 'My conscience is not so.'

'Conscience, Madam, requires knowledge: and I fear that right knowledge ye have none.'

'But I have both heard and read.'

'So, Madam, did the Jews that crucified Christ Jesus read both the Law and the Prophets, and heard the same interpreted after their manner. Have ye heard any teach, but such as the pope and his cardinals have allowed? Ye may be assured that such will speak nothing to offend their own estate.'

'Ye interpret the Scriptures in one manner,' said the queen, 'and they interpret in another; whom shall I believe? And who shall be judge?'

Terrible in its perverted simplicity was Knox's answer. 'Ye shall believe God, that plainly speaketh in His Word,' he said. 'And, farther than the Word teaches you, ye shall believe neither the one nor the other.'

There is the substance and there the mood of the argument that bedevilled James VI's relations with the kirk, and that dominated tempers in the civil war that wasted so much of the seventeenth century, and made Charles I a culprit or a martyr. The bigoted assurance of God's grace and their own unassailable virtue, that characterised the Reformers and their Presbyterian successors in the war between Cavaliers and Roundheads, was never matched until Communism revealed the gospel according to Marx and the inspiration of Lenin's teaching. Between Calvinism and Communism there are, indeed, remarkable similarities, but perhaps the intransigence of both is sufficient to cast doubt, not only on the truth of their doctrines in a world where absolutes are rare, but on the value of their message to a human society that has bred its finest products from non-conformity and individuality.

One cannot dismiss the debate between Mary and Knox, however, without some comment on their persons and personalities; because their debate, to a large degree, was a miniature of the quarrel between Mary and her realm of Scotland.

Knox's age is unknown. He may have been born in 1505 or 1513. He was, that is, between fifty and fifty-seven when Mary was about twenty. He was a fanatic with the obsessed eyes of a fanatic, and a rabble-rouser with the excessive beard of an exhibitionist. Like the Communists who, in a later century, adopted the manner of his argument but diverted it to another end, his arguments were tortuous but his premises inflexible. Mary, his opponent, was uncommonly tall and marvellously graceful. She had very beautiful hands and fingers. Her face was long and oval, her skin of an exquisite pallor. Under a high forehead her nose was strong and long, her lips exquisitely moulded. Her eyes, under heavy lids, shone with a curious warmth, deeper than amber, and the French called her hair *blonds et cendrez*: or fair with auburn tints.

Add to the enchantment of her person a mind that was quick and lively, gaiety and a willing friendliness. She was brave and resolute, and could write minor verse of an agreeable sound. Her thoughts were wise, her talk witty, and she could ride out a rough campaign without complaint. She could pursue a prudent policy, and break out of it with fierce and swift delight. From her mother—Mary of Lorraine, of 'majestic stature'—she had inherited not only her tall and slender height, but pertinacity; and yet—perhaps because of the many illnesses she had suffered in her youth—she was subject to sudden collapse. There were times when she could respond to danger, or the challenge of adventure, with a hard and glowing spirit; but at other times, as if some bodily weakness betrayed her, she surrendered to girlish fears and childish weeping. After one of her conversations with Knox she wept bitterly. 'I have borne with you in all your rigorous manner of speaking, both against myself and against my uncles,' she cried; 'yea, I have sought your favour by all possible means: I offered unto you presence and audience, whensoever it pleased you to admonish me, and yet I cannot be quit of you: I vow to God I shall be once revenged.'

And having uttered this threat, as Knox complacently reports, 'Scarce could Marnock, her secret chamber boy, get napkins to hold her eyes dry, for the tears and the howling, besides womanly weeping, stayed her speech.'

Her conversations with Knox are revealing in several ways, but they occupied only a fragment of her time. In the early years of her reign she was well advised by the Lord James and Lethington, and shrewdly accepted their advice. For the skill with which she balanced her own adherence to Rome, with recognition of the Reformers' claim to determine the worship of others, she was certainly indebted to them; but she may be given credit for listening to counsel that she cannot always have found palatable. Some provision was made for the payment of ministers, some priests were prosecuted for their public celebration of Mass, and Archbishop Hamilton was imprisoned for it. In 1562, moreover, she set out on a progress to the north which turned into a campaign against the earl of Huntly. He, the most powerful figure beyond the Highland line, was Catholic and conservative, and no friend to the Lord James.

Mary had lately granted the earldom of Moray to her half-brother, though for some time it had been administered by Huntly. The situation was complicated by the fact that one of Huntly's younger sons, Sir John Gordon, had become enamoured of the queen, and was suspected of a design to kidnap her. Like many of his family, he was an unruly young man, and when he was imprisoned for assaulting Lord Ogilvie and taking possession of some of his lands, he promptly escaped. When Mary, riding with a small army, reached Inverness in September, she was refused admission to the castle, which was held by the Gordons. But the local gentry rallied to her side, not to Huntly's, and the castle was forced to surrender. Its captain was hanged, its little garrison pardoned.

Huntly mustered his clan, but other clans gathered about the queen's standard, and though there seemed an imminent prospect of fighting, Mary and her following crossed the Spey without hindrance, and rode to Aberdeen. Thomas Randolph, an English agent at her court, endured the hardships of the campaign and bitter weather—it was 'extreme fowle and colde'—and in a report to Cecil wrote of the queen: 'In all these broils I assure you I never saw her merrier, never dismayed, nor never thought that so much stomach to be in her that I find. She repented nothing but (when the lords and others at Inverness came in the morning from the watch) that she was not a man, to know what like it was to lie all night in the fields, or to walk on the causeway with a jack and knapsack, a Glasgow buckler, and a broad sword.'

Huntly, moved by the recklessness of Gordon blood, marched on Aberdeen, but the queen's army under the Lord James—now earl of Moray—was stronger than his, and the Gordons were soundly beaten at Corrichie, some twenty miles west of the town. Huntly died, perhaps of a stroke; Lord Gordon his heir, the earl of Sutherland his cousin, and the young Sir John were formally condemned to death, and Sir John was executed. Mary consented to his execution, and was present, though unwillingly, when by a clumsy headsman he was put to death. Such severity, in an age when armed rebellion was not uncommon, appears excessive, and can most plausibly be explained, not merely by Moray's hostility to the Gordons, but by Mary's remembrance that Sir John had been suspected of a plot to kidnap her. He had been guilty, if only in intention, of *lèse-majesté*; and that was unpardonable.

In the following year there was an incident, of no political importance, that seems also to exhibit the intensity of feeling with which Mary regarded any assault, or attempted assault, on her royal person. Among those who had accompanied her from France was the young man called Chastelard. He was so unfortunate as to fall in love with the queen, and a short time after his return to France, came again to Scotland, where Mary showed him some favour which he misconstrued. One evening, to the queen's surprise, he appeared in her bedchamber: an indiscretion for which he was reproved and forgiven. But he repeated his folly, and Mary, in a state of fury that seems to have been close to hysteria, summoned Moray and commanded him to kill her importunate suitor. Moray demurred, the queen insisted, and Chastelard, after trial and conviction, was beheaded. It is impossible to say whether the extremity of Mary's anger was due to maidenly fear and resentment of Chastelard's intrusion, or to her suspicion that he was an agent employed to sully her reputation and reduce her value in the eyes of foreign suitors. She was not cruel by nature—certainly

[205]

no sadist—but a real or imagined threat to her person or her name, and so to the stability of her throne, could rouse her to unrelenting sternness.

From a stable throne she could look forward to her inheritance of England: her cousin was nine years older than she, and still unmarried. But Elizabeth was stubbornly averse to naming Mary as her successor —averse, indeed, to admitting that she must have a successor—and Mary's position was at no time really secure while she remained a Catholic monarch whose task was to rule a Protestant country. She might appease her Protestant subjects by imprisoning a Catholic arch-bishop, but only at the cost of displeasing her Catholic sympathisers abroad. Her refusal to use her royal authority in support of the Roman church angered the militants of that church, but did not reconcile the militants of the Congregation of Christ to her insistence on her own liberty of worship. And yet, for four years, she was able to prevent any gross division between her nobles, or grave infraction of her peace; and in the history of Scotland four years of peace must be acknowledged as an achievement worthy of record. It is agreeable, moreover, to know that in these years Mary herself found pleasure and entertainment to mitigate her burdens. She enjoyed hunting, hawking, and golf, she practised archery; she liked needle-work, music, and dancing; she made an obeisance to scholarship and read Latin with that renowned scholar, George Buchanan, of whom more will be heard; and she had the company of her 'four Maries'—Fleming, Beton, Livingstone, and Seton—the children who had sailed to France with her, and came home with her.

It was her second marriage that destroyed both peace and pleasure, and for that her own folly and English policy may both be blamed. Of suitors, and rumours of impending marriage, there had been a variety since the death of her first husband. Châtelherault's son, the earl of Arran, had been resolute to wed her. He had persuaded the earl of Bothwell to join him in a plot to capture her, but the plot had been discovered, Bothwell sent into exile, and Arran had relapsed into such stark insanity that he had to be confined. Don Carlos of Spain and other princes had been offered as candidates or considered as potential dangers: the kings of France, Sweden, and Denmark, a pair of Austrian archdukes and two lesser dukes, had all been canvassed for the vacant half of Mary's throne. The most serious contender was Don Carlos, son and heir of Philip II, but his candidacy had to be withdrawn when he, like Arran, fell into hopeless insanity.

Elizabeth of England told Lethington that she would make Mary her heir if she approved of Mary's choice of a husband, and suggested that a suitable consort would be Robert Dudley, earl of Leicester. Dudley, who was thought to have murdered his wife, had long been Elizabeth's 'favourite', though whether that formidable queen's favour included the ultimate familiarity may still be matter for speculation. Her suggestion was tactless, if not deliberately an insult, and her next move in the game defies explanation. It was unlike Elizabeth to be negligent, and miscalculation was typical neither of her nor Cecil; but one is reluctant to believe that she was so unscrupulous as to offer Mary a suitor of the very sort to tempt her into marriage, and of the very kind to make their marriage disastrous. Yet that is what happened, and Mary fell headlong into temptation.

For some twenty years Matthew Stewart, earl of Lennox, had been an exile in England, banished for his treasonable association with Henry VIII. In September, 1564, Elizabeth let him return to Scotland, and by Mary's will—Lennox was a Catholic—his forfeited estates were restored. Early in the next year he was followed by his son Henry, Lord Darnley. He was the grandson, by her second marriage, of Margaret Tudor, sister of Henry VIII, and on his father's side a descendant of James II. English by birth and upbringing, he was next after Mary in succession to the English throne. He was very tall, well-proportioned, and good-looking in a soft, feminine way. He had the superficial graces which may, for a little while, conceal a fatuous vanity and total irresponsibility; and at nineteen he was three years younger than Mary. At Stirling castle he fell ill with measles, and Mary, much accustomed to a sickroom, nursed him and fell in love with him.

As they were both grandchildren of Margaret Tudor a papal dispensation was required for their marriage. It was publicly celebrated, according to Roman Catholic rites, in the chapel of Holyroodhouse on 29th July, 1565; but the dispensation had to be antedated, for they were already married. To the Lords of the Congregation their union appeared to have joined two papists in wedlock, though in England Darnley had attended the Anglican church, and may well have had little enthusiasm for either. Lethington had protested hotly against the marriage; for him and Moray it was defeat—they could not expect a wedded queen to be guided by them—and their hope of collaboration with England seemed to be dissipated by Elizabeth's hostility to the match which she had permitted if not promoted. The Hamiltons and their friends were antagonised by the elevation of a Lennox Stewart, and when the heralds proclaimed Darnley king, none of those present added *Amen* save old Lennox only; who loudly cried, 'God save his Grace!'

Rebellion followed, but the rebels were divided. Moray and Knox had fallen out, and though Moray was promised help by Elizabeth he had lost the support of many of the Protestant lords—among them Morton, Cassilis, Lindsay, and Ruthven—who had been mollified by Mary's reiterated promise to protect the Reformed church, and may not have been insusceptible to her charm. She released from his prison old Huntly's heir, and recalled Bothwell from exile. When the rebels mustered in Ayr she quickly gathered her own forces in Edinburgh, pawned her jewels to pay them, and marched to the west. The rebels eluded her, and came to Edinburgh, where they found no welcome. They retreated to Dumfries, and Mary raised more troops, but had no need to use them. Moray had not got the help he expected from England, the rebellion collapsed, and when Moray took refuge across the border he found little comfort in his reception. She had never meant to help the rebels, said Elizabeth.

In this crisis Mary showed the highest spirit. She was utterly determined to punish the rebels, despite Elizabeth's plea for clemency. She outlawed Rothes, Kirkcaldy of Grange, and the provost of Dundee because they would not take orders from her, and Dundee, Perth, St. Andrews, and Edinburgh were persuaded or compelled to contribute to the maintenance of her army. It saw no fighting, but there was hard marching in foul and fearful weather, and the queen's courage grew with the storm. She wore a secret coat of mail, a steel cap on her head, and had a pistol at her saddle. In the Chase-about Raid, as it was called, she appears to have been celebrating her release from Moray's tutelage. She proved herself to be Scotland's queen, and enjoyed the demonstration.

She was guilty, too, of some duplicity. Before receiving the dispensation for her marriage, she and Darnley had promised to defend the Roman faith to the utmost of their power. When the rebellion at first seemed to threaten her safety she wrote to the king of Spain to ask his help in saving the Catholic religion from ruin. She summoned her parliament, and her ambassador in France was told that something had been done towards restoring the old religion. Yet the purpose of that parliament, as publicly proclaimed, was to put away and abolish 'all acts, laws, and constitutions, canon, civil or municipal', that were prejudicial to the Reformed church. If Elizabeth had been disingenuous—she had both encouraged and disowned the rebellion— then Mary was something less than frank. Both were ruling queens, and had queenly problems.

In attendance on Mary, or employed by her, were several foreigners to whose presence Moray and some of his fellow rebels had taken exception. Only one of them roused enmity enough to make him notorious, and he was David Riccio, a Piedmontese who had come to Scotland with Morette, the ambassador from Savoy, in 1561. He was a musician who had first attracted the queen's attention by singing bass in a quartet of 'varlets of her chamber'; and by his cleverness had risen to be her secretary for French affairs. The Scots lords resented the promotion of a foreigner, less well born than they, and expressed or pretended their fear that he was a papal agent charged with some task for the emerging forces of the counter-Reformation. Before his marriage Darnley had been friendly with Riccio, and Riccio is supposed to have done what he could to encourage the queen's rash wooing. None of Darnley's friendships was of long tenure, however, and before the year was out he was showing his jealousy of Riccio. Now Mary was his friend, and she showed her liking for him too plainly for prudence. In such a court as hers, in an entourage of surly Calvinists and ruffian lords, it was not unnatural that she should have been attracted to a clever, decently educated Italian, and in the absence of Lethington—who had discreetly retired until he could make up his mind which side was likely to win—she must have needed advice, or at least discussion with someone capable of rational discourse. But any favour shown to such a one as Riccio, in such a court as hers, was bound to provoke maligant gossip, and for the first time in her life her behaviour gave excuse for slander.

In October Thomas Randolph, the clever, gossiping, English agent, offered Cecil an explanation of the great enmity between Mary and her half-brother Moray. He knew, said Randolph, her guilty secret, and she hated him because of his knowledge. Later in the month he wrote to the earl of Leicester that Mary had been 'brought to that extremity, that the fame she had gotten through virtue and worthiness is now clean fallen from her. . . . Her country so evil guided that justice lies dead in all places, and her noblemen chased out of the country, and such others placed nearest her that are most unworthy. . . . He may well think what the matter means when so many mislike that a stranger, a varlet, shall have the whole guiding of his queen and country.'

Randolph, it is obvious, was writing with a double purpose. He wanted to please 'the noblemen chased out of the country' and their friends; and he wanted to supply Leicester with gossip for his royal mistress. In his report to Cecil he had been more skilful: to that most ingenious of men he had given an ingenious explanation of Moray's quarrel with the queen. It was an explanation both neat and satisfying. Its only defect was its manifest untruth. That Mary, the queen so jealous for her dynasty—so determined to preserve her reputation in the Catholic world—should commit adultery with one of her secretaries was utterly improbable; and it is beyond belief that she should look for sexual satisfaction from Riccio when the behaviour of Darnley, her young and pliant cousin, showed plainly that she had failed to keep alive in him a passion that should have been natural to them both, but was lacking in her. In later years the elegant Latinist George Buchanan preserved the scandal in Book XVII of his *Rerum Scoticarum Historia,* and there gave it a form appropriate enough for one of Balzac's *Contes Drolatiques,* but not conducive to belief. Buchanan was either repeating a fiction he had heard, or inventing one.

But hatred of Riccio, assisted by an uncomely willingness to think evil of the queen—or pretend to such thought—made ground on which could be built an alliance between an already discredited Darnley and those who represented the rebellious Protestant lords. Moray, Argyll, Rothes, Kirkcaldy of Grange, and others had been summoned to stand their trial before parliament in March, 1566. It was Darnley's marriage that had prompted their rebellion, but now they and their friends offered to support his claim to the crown matrimonial, and promise him succession to the throne should Mary die without issue, in exchange for their pardon and permission to return to Scotland. As a preliminary to their homecoming Riccio was to be murdered, and if necessary Mary would be coerced into granting the pardon. Randolph, writing again to the earl of Leicester in February, told him that Darnley and his father had plans to secure the crown, that Riccio was to have his throat cut, and that Mary's own life might be in danger.

The iniquitous bond was duly made, and in or near Mary's private chamber in Holyroodhouse Riccio was brutally murdered on the evening of 9th March. The details of what happened are confused by differing accounts, but Darnley joined the queen's supper party, which was small and quiet because she was pregnant and the season was Lent. James Douglas, the rapacious earl of Morton, surrounded Holyrood with his troops; and Lindsay of the Byres, with Lord Ruthven and his son, were the other ringleaders. Riccio sang for the last time, the queen's chamber was roughly invaded. Riccio clung to the queen for protection, but was killed either in her presence or at an outer door, and Darnley's dagger was left in his side. Mary's life, and the life of her unborn child, were indeed in peril; but this was one of the occasions when her spirit rose to the challenge of danger, and defeated it. Her life was dominated by a dynastic purpose, and to serve that purpose she and the child in her womb had to be saved alive.

The alarm was raised, and the provost with townsmen in armour hurried to the palace. Darnley assured them that Mary was safe, and was able to pacify them; but Mary was told that if she herself tried to speak she would be cut 'in collops' and thrown over the wall. Bothwell and the earls of Huntly and Atholl were all at Holyrood, but they had been taken by surprise, and were powerless. Bothwell, however, succeeded in escaping.

Mary was alone among her enemies. But there was a weak link in the chain that confined her, and she knew it. Darnley came to see her in the morning, and very bitterly she reproached him. But he was persuaded to let some of her ladies attend her, and with the help of Lady Huntly she sent a message to Bothwell. That evening Moray visited her, to offer his sympathy and protest his innocence. It is unlikely that she believed him, but she may have been glad to see him. Darnley returned, to plead for the conspirators and those who had been in exile, and with a composure that proved how small a place in her affection poor Riccio had held, she was coldly realistic and accepted a *fait accompli*. Morton, Lindsay, and Ruthven remained doubtful of her goodwill, and when she had sent for Lethington, that astute and prudent man, they demanded that she sign a document absolving them of evil in act or purpose. She approved of the document but postponed signing it; and the soldiers by whom she was guarded were withdrawn.

Darnley remained with her, and to him she spoke of her misery and the danger into which he had fallen. Were he to deny his spiritual allegiance to Rome, as the Protestant lords required him to do, how would he appear to his fellow sovereigns abroad? Shallow as a puddle and pliant as a reed, Darnley listened to her, and later she wrote demurely to the archbishop of Glasgow: 'He was induced to condescend to the purpose taken by us, and to retire in our company to Dunbar, which we did under night.'

The first stage of the road to Dunbar was a secret or little-used stair that led down to dark kitchens, and beyond them the fugitives hurried through a cemetery to a gate where horses stood and Arthur Erskine, esquire of the stables, waited for his queen. She mounted behind him, and her woman, Margaret Carwood, rode pillion behind another loyalist. There were horses for Darnley, an equerry and a servant, and for ten miles they rode hard to Seton on the Firth of Forth, where they saw soldiers waiting for them. Darnley fell into a panic and bade them ride faster. The queen spoke of her heavy pregnancy, and Darnley told her brutally that if she lost the child they could make more. They had, however, no cause for alarm. The soldiers had been posted by Bothwell. He and Huntly were there, and they were sure that no safety could be found nearer than Dunbar, fifteen miles away. So they rode on, and when they arrived, as dawn was breaking, the queen cooked eggs for the soldiers' breakfast.

James Hepburn, fourth earl of Bothwell, was a man of thirty or thirty-one, descendant of a noble border family, who had lived a life of burly adventure and played his part in the rough politics of the time. He had travelled, he had lived in England, France, and Denmark. He enjoyed the favours of women, and his experience of women's favour was not inconsiderable. He lacked the vision of a statesman, the constructive ability of a statesman, but he was more honest than many of his titled compatriots. Most of the Protestant lords were venal men, and gladly accepted English pensions in payment of their service to Protestantism and England; but Bothwell, who was not rich, seems never to have taken bribe or fee. In the crisis that now confronted him and his queen he showed the genius of his kind—that genius which had kept the great border clans alive in a debatable land where danger was incessant—and in his own country raised a force of three or four thousand, troopers and spearmen. He gave Mary an army, at the head of which she returned to Edinburgh.

She came as a prudent queen, to pacify and rule, not to exact revenge. Most of the rebels submitted. Moray declared on oath that he had parted company with the murderers of Riccio, but took the trouble to arrange asylum in England for Morton, Lindsay, and Ruthven. Morton and some others were outlawed, and two men were hanged; but the queen pardoned more than she punished, and from Darnley accepted in public his protestation of innocence. He had signed two documents that convicted him of murder and what could be construed as treason—the bond that condemned Riccio to death, and the other that was to have given him the crown matrimonial—and Mary had seen them both. But Darnley was the father of her child, and for his sake had to be given, for as long as he would wear it, a disguise of respectability.

The discreet Lethington retired to the Highlands, and Knox, after uttering a defiant word of praise for those who had so rightly punished 'that knave David', fled to Ayrshire. His first wife had died, and in 1564 he had married a daughter of Lord Ochiltree, a girl of fifteen. His remaining years, part of which he spent in England, were largely devoted to writing or rewriting his *History of the Reformation in Scotland*, without which his subsequent reputation might not have bulked so large and tall in Scottish minds.

With Elizabeth of England Mary had some diplomatic exchanges that revealed her growing accomplishment in the art of conciliation. Randolph, the English agent and entertaining letter-writer, had been

[212]

betrayed by one of his accomplices, who confessed that Randolph had given him three thousand crowns to aid the rebel cause. Randolph had been expelled from Scotland, and Elizabeth had declared her ignorance of the whole matter. She had sent no help to the rebels, she said. Mary accepted her denial, and offered the mollifying suggestion that Randolph must have been acting in a private capacity. Then Mary was told that if she would not pardon Moray, there would be room for him in England. Moray, Argyll, and Glencairn had already been pardoned, and with Bothwell, Huntly, and Atholl now formed Mary's council; but tactfully she replied that she had exercised her clemency to please her dictatorial cousin.

For a little while there was peace in Edinburgh, and in that peace, which Mary's wisdom and strength of mind had created, her son was born in the castle between ten and eleven in the morning of 19th June, 1566. Her labour had been long, and she was in a state of feverish excitement when Darnley came to see her in the early afternoon. She spoke to him with some bitterness and twice referred to the slander he had circulated about her and Riccio. James Maxwell, later Lord Herries, one of Bothwell's neighbours who had joined her at Dunbar, was present in that small and crowded room, and in his *Memoirs* recorded a part of their conversation.

'My lord,' she said, 'God has given you and me a son, begotten by none but you!'

The king stooped to kiss the child. She took it in her arms and said again: 'Here I protest to God, and as I shall answer to Him at the great day of judgement, this is your son and no other man's son. And I am desirous that all here, with ladies and others, bear witness; for he is so much your own son that I fear it will be the worse for him hereafter.'

To Sir William Stanley, an Englishman who was also there, she said: 'This is the son who (I hope) shall first unite the two kingdoms of Scotland and England.'

Popular applause, hundreds of bonfires, and volleys of ordnance celebrated the birth of Prince James. Messengers were hurriedly despatched to France and England, and Elizabeth, dancing after supper, was made mournful by the news, but soon recovered, and for the boy's christening sent a gold font big enough for him to bathe in. But six months later it had to be melted down to replenish the mint. For a little while the queen's peace endured, and du Croc, the French ambassador, wrote: 'I never saw Her Majesty so much beloved, esteemed, and honoured; nor so great a harmony amongst all her subjects, as at present is by her wise conduct, for I cannot perceive the smallest difference or division.' On the last day of September the lords of the Privy Council told Darnley he should thank God for giving him so wise and virtuous a wife.

But Darnley was deaf to advice. That Mary, with a woman's obstinacy, still thought of him with some affection—still, perhaps, had hope that his mind and manners might improve—seems evident from the inventory she made for the disposal of her property should she die in childbed. There were fifteen separate articles that she bequeathed to him, including a diamond ring, enamelled in red, against which she wrote: 'It was with this that I was married to the king, who gave it me.' For part of that year, however, Darnley seems to have been in a mood that alternated between half-witted ambition and half-witted desperation. In May, when Philip II of Spain was planning a campaign in the Netherlands, Darnley had spoken of going there. Later there was talk of his going to France, and a rumour that he had a ship ready for the voyage. Lennox, Mary, and du Croc combined to dissuade him, and he retired to Stirling, where his pleasure in hunting may have deterred him from mischief.

Bothwell, as was right and proper, had been richly rewarded for his good service. He had been made sheriff of Edinburgh and Haddington, he was warden of the East, West, and Middle Marches, and master of several castles. He was flattered by the queen's friendship as well as by her gifts, and some while later there were those who remembered, or pretended to remember, that their association had been warmer than mere gratitude required. Foremost among those who propagated this new slander was George Buchanan. When Mary was accused of having been privy to the murder of Darnley, Buchanan wrote his *Detection* as part and parcel of the evidence to be shown to Elizabeth's commissioners in vindication of the Protestant lords' dethronement of their queen. The *Detection* is a curious document, the nature of which may be inferred from the quotation that follows. At some time in the autumn of 1566 Mary lived in Edinburgh in a house 'where the annual court called the Exchequer was then held'. It was a large house with pleasant gardens, and according to Buchanan it had, for Mary, an additional advantage:

'There lived nearby David Chalmers, a creature of Bothwell's, whose back-door adjoined the gardens of the queen's lodging. By this door Bothwell could come and go as often as he liked. Who cannot guess the rest? The queen herself had confessed the whole thing, to the regent and his mother as well as to many others. But she laid the blame on Lady Reres, a most dissolute woman, who had been one of Bothwell's whores and was at that time one of the queen's familiar attendants. By this woman, who in her old age had turned from the

[214]

profession of harlotry to that of procuress, was the queen, as she herself put it, betrayed. For Bothwell was introduced through the garden to the queen's chamber, and there forced her against her will. But how much against her will Lady Reres betrayed her, time, the parent of truth, has revealed. For not many days after, the queen—desiring, I suppose, to repay force with force!—sent Lady Reres (who herself had formerly made trial of the man's "forcefulness") to bring him captive unto her. The queen, in company with Margaret Carwood, a woman privy to all her secrets, let her down by a sash over the wall into the next garden. But in such warlike affairs all things cannot be foreseen that some inconvenience may not arise: behold the sash suddenly broke! Down with a great noise tumbled Dame Reres, a woman of ample weight in both years and body. But the old warrior, nothing dismayed by the darkness, the height of the wall or her unexpected flight to earth, reached Bothwell's chamber, opened the door, plucked him out of bed—out of his wife's embrace—and led him, half-asleep, half-naked, to the arms of the queen. This account of the incident has been confessed not only by most of those who were then with the queen, but also by George Dalgleish, Bothwell's manservant, a little before his execution.'[1]

It was stuff of that sort which the accusers of Mary offered as evidence against her; and stuff of that sort was still seriously regarded by serious historians of the nineteenth century.

It is true that Mary showed concern when Bothwell was wounded in an affray on the border, and rode a long way to see him. Somewhere near the great gaunt castle of Hermitage Bothwell had had a spirited encounter with a malefactor who got the better of him. Mary was attending a justice court at Jedburgh, thirty miles away. She heard that Bothwell's condition was serious, and with Moray and others rode to Hermitage and back within the day. It was obvious that she did not stay long at Bothwell's bedside, and so spirited and arduous a journey reminds one of the enjoyment she had found in hard riding on her little Highland campaign against Huntly, and in the Chase-about Raid. But Buchanan decorates the tale with his own furious fancy. 'When (Bothwell's injury) was reported to the queen at Borthwick, she flew madly by forced journeys, though it was bitter winter, first to Melrose, then to Jedburgh. Though she learned there on good authority that his life was safe, her affection could brook no delay, and she betrayed her infamous lust by setting out at a bad time of the year, heedless of the difficulties of the journey and the danger of highwaymen, with a

---

[1] *The Tyrannous Reign of Mary Stewart.* George Buchanan (translated and edited by W. A. Gatherer).

company such as no decent gentleman would entrust with his life and goods.'[1] The company 'that no decent gentleman' would trust included her half-brother Moray, and so far from her affection brooking 'no delay', it was not until five or six days after she had heard of Bothwell's wound that she set out to visit him, and then not from Borthwick but from Jedburgh.

Her long ride was too much for her, and in Jedburgh she fell desperately ill, and may well have suffered more from the appalling treatment of her doctors than from what seems to have been an intestinal haemorrhage. Bothwell, whose wounds healed rapidly, came to see her, borne in a horse-litter; and tardily, a week later, Darnley arrived, but stayed only for one night. Her convalescence was tedious, and appeared to be unwilling. She could not forget the grief that Darnley had caused. But by December she was well enough to make arrangements for the baptism of her son in Stirling. The service was conducted with some splendour and according to the rites of the Roman church; but Mary, despite her devotion and the fact that the officiating priest was Archbishop Hamilton, refused to let 'a pocky priest spit in her child's mouth'. Darnley was living in Stirling, but did not attend the ceremony.

About this time the possibility of obtaining a divorce was discussed with some urgency. There was a conference at Craigmillar castle, near Edinburgh, and according to Huntly the first to consider annulment of the queen's marriage, as a measure of policy, were Moray and Lethington. Bothwell, Argyll, and Huntly himself were sympathetic, and together they approached the queen. Lethington reviewed some recent events, and declared it was idle to hope for improvement in Darnley. Therefore, for the good of the country as well as for the queen's pleasure, they offered to arrange annulment of the royal marriage if Mary would agree to pardon Morton, Lindsay, and their associates. To which Mary is said to have replied that she would accept the bargain on two conditions: that the divorce should be legally obtained, and that it must not be prejudicial to her son.

There are different accounts of the conversations at Craigmillar, and in the so-called *Protestation* made by, or prepared for, Huntly and Argyll, Lethington is then alleged to have said, 'We shall find the means that your Majesty shall be quit of him'—Darnley, that is—'without prejudice of your son. And albeit that my lord of Moray here present be little less scrupulous for a Protestant, than your Grace is for a Papist, I am assured he will look through his fingers, and will behold our doings, saying nothing of the same.'

[1] *The Tyrannous Reign of Mary Stewart.*

[216]

Into that statement—if, indeed, they are Lethington's words—a sinister interpretation can be read; but Lethington was not the man to make even a covert threat of assassination, and it is difficult to know what was meant. To the queen's reply—again, if the words are hers—no exception can be taken: 'I will that ye do nothing through which any spot may be laid upon my honour or conscience, and therefore I pray you, rather let the matter be in the condition that it is, abiding till God of his goodness put remedy thereto; lest you, believing that you are doing me a service, may possibly turn to my hurt and displeasure.' 'Madam,' said Lethington, 'let us guide the matter among us, and your Grace shall see nothing but good, and approved by Parliament.'

How he intended to guide the matter will never be known. No steps were taken to obtain the divorce, but on the eve of Christmas Mary pardoned Morton and seventy others who were implicated in Riccio's murder. Darnley, in Glasgow, was in communication with the pope and Philip of Spain, and was said to be taking an unusual interest in the practises of the Roman church. To what extent he was implicated in a Catholic plot is another insoluble problem. Before he could reveal his intentions—if he had any—he fell ill with a distemper variously diagnosed as poisoning, scabies, smallpox, and syphilis. The first suggestion is Buchanan's, and need not be taken seriously. As for the second, a patient is seldom confined to bed by scabies. Signs of syphilitic lesion are said to be visible on a skull not certainly identified as Darnley's, and as a primary infection does not commonly leave such traces, that diagnosis may also be discarded. The disease was almost certainly smallpox.

While he lay ill it was rumoured that he and Lennox his father had been plotting to crown the infant prince and make Darnley regent. The rumour was strong enough to reach France, and echo back again. What substance was in it, and whether it had any connexion with Darnley's letters to Spain and the pope, are not known; but Mary grew anxious for the safety of her child, and on 14th January brought him from Stirling to Holyrood. On the 20th she wrote to her ambassador in France, asserting goodwill to her husband and complaining about his constant suspicion of her; and on the same day she set out for Glasgow to bring him back with her to Edinburgh. She was qualified to nurse a smallpox patient, for as a child in France she had had the disease, and escaped pocking by the skilled care of her doctor.

Her intention seems to have been to take Darnley either to Craigmillar or Holyroodhouse, but Robert Balfour, canon of Holyrood, had a house at Kirk o' Field, just inside the city wall, that was empty and in a healthier position than the low-lying palace. Robert Balfour had two brothers, Sir James and Gilbert, the older of whom had been implicated in the murder of Cardinal Beaton. After the taking of St. Andrews castle by the French he had, with John Knox, been condemned to servitude as a galley slave, and later in life, in the period before the murder of Riccio, he had served in the queen's court or household. In the opinion of du Croc, the French ambassador, James Balfour was the real traitor in the still mysterious calamity that was now imminent, and it may have been he who persuaded Darnley that Kirk o' Field would be more suitable for his convalescence than Craig-millar. Darnley was sensitive about his appearance, and wore a taffeta mask to conceal the signs of his disease.

By the end of the month, then, he lay in the old Provost's house of what had formerly been an ecclesiastical foundation. It was a solid, stone-built structure consisting of a long narrow hall connected by a spiral stairway to the two-storeyed main part of the building, which stood on a slope. In the top storey were Darnley's room, an ante-room, and a gallery that projected on to the city wall. The queen's room was in the lower storey, and a basement divided into servants' quarters, kitchen, and cellars may have occupied the full length of the building. A garden and a little orchard lay beside the house. The upper and lower bedrooms and the ante-room were furnished in sufficient comfort, and the queen slept in the lower room on 5th and 7th February.

On Sunday the 9th there was a wedding at Holyroodhouse, and bishop of Argyll was entertaining the ambassador from Savoy. Morette, who had brought Riccio to Scotland, had returned on another mission. The queen honoured the banquet with her presence, but strangely absent were Moray and Lethington. Then Mary left the bishop's house in the Canongate to ride to Kirk o' Field, where she had promised to spend the last night of Darnley's quarantine. The earls of Bothwell, Huntly, Argyll, and Cassilis were playing dice in Darnley's room, and the queen sat in a high chair. As well as Darnley's room, the whole house was probably crowded with people, for great nobles did not go unattended.

Then Mary remembered that she had promised to dance at the wedding party in the palace, where Bastien, a faithful servant, had been married that morning to one of her women. Darnley protested loudly, for he had expected her to sleep in the room below his, but she was determined to keep her other promise. To comfort him she gave him a ring from her finger, and said they would spend the next night together at Holyrood.

Darnley was left with Taylor his valet, who slept in his room. Two servants lay in the gallery that projected on to the city wall, and elsewhere in the house were a couple of grooms.

At two o'clock in the morning of the 10th a great roar, like thunder or the discharge of cannon, woke all Edinburgh and brought out the magistrates and frightened people. At Kirk o' Field they saw that the Provost's house had been utterly demolished, and among the tumbled stones lay a mutilated body. There was snow on the ground, and under a pear-tree in the garden beyond the wall lay the bodies of Darnley and Taylor his valet. Their bodies were quite unmarked. Darnley wore nothing but a night-shirt, a night-cap, and a slipper on his left foot. Near them in the garden lay a quilt, a dressing-gown, Taylor's belt and dagger, and a wooden chair.

Chapter 4

ON 10th February, the day of the murder, Mary wrote to the archbishop of Glasgow to say that she believed that what happened at Kirk o' Field had been intended for her death as well as her husband's; and the following day she received, from the archbishop, a warning to take heed to herself because of some enterprise plotted against her. The explosion that threw two bodies into a wintry garden raised more questions that corpses.

Mary offered a reward of £2,000 for information, and a free pardon to the informer. Within a week a placard was nailed to the door of the Tolbooth by someone who wrote that the reward had encouraged him to make inquiry, and he named the murderers as: 'the Earl Bothwell, Mr. James Balfour, Mr. David Chalmers, black Mr. John Spens, who was the principal deviser of the murder, and the Queen assenting thereto, through the persuasion of the Earl of Bothwell and the witchcraft of the Lady Buccleugh. And if this be not true, speir at[1] Gilbert Balfour.'

The author was presumably one of Bothwell's old associates, turned hostile, for the Lady Buccleugh was a remarkable and gifted woman with whom, when she was nearly twice his age, Bothwell had been in love. That the Balfours were guilty seems too probable to be doubted, but Spens and Chalmers had no other connexion with the crime than a libellous association with James and Gilbert on the poster. More placards denouncing Bothwell, and portraits of him under the rubric 'Here is the Murderer', appeared on the streets in the weeks to come, and it is difficult to believe that they were a spontaneous expression of general hatred and distrust. It is far more likely that they were inspired by policy and a particular interest; and the inference can hardly be avoided that the source of the attack lay not far from Moray and Lethington.

Bothwell, defiant, walked through Edinburgh with his hand on his

[1] ask.

dagger and fifty borderers behind him. He stood high in the queen's favour, but the queen was constrained to yield to old Lennox's demand for public inquiry into the crime when the Protestant lords made common cause with Lennox and his Catholic friends, and both were reinforced by the voice of England; for Cecil demanded, in sweeping terms, that God's honour must be maintained and the murderers punished. She promised that Bothwell and others should stand their trial, and Bothwell sat as a member of her Privy Council to make the necessary arrangements. To the rumours that he was guilty of Darnley's death was now added another; he was about to divorce his wife Jean Gordon, Huntly's sister, to be free for marriage with the queen.

Before the Lord Justice, the earl of Argyll, Bothwell was accused of 'art and part of the cruel, odious, treasonable, and abominable slaughter of the late, the right excellent, right high and mighty prince, the King's Grace', and for seven hours the court deliberated. Bothwell had filled Edinburgh with his supporters, but Lennox, having mustered almost as many, had been halted at Linlithgow. There was no one in court to swear the truth of the indictment or support its charges, and as there was no evidence for a conviction the jury, in which sat some of Bothwell's avowed enemies, had no choice but to acquit him.

When the queen rode to her parliament, a few days later, Bothwell carried the sceptre; and when parliament closed he carried the sword of honour. That evening, the 19th April, he invited a distinguished company of twenty-eight peers and prelates to supper, and after supper produced a lengthy document which they were asked to sign. Reference was made to his trial and acquittal, and in its second part the document took note of the queen's solitary state, her need of a husband, and the good qualities of the earl of Bothwell. His guests were then asked to further the marriage he proposed by their 'vote, counsel, and assistance'. Eight bishops, nine earls, and seven barons put their signatures on the paper.

The queen had gone to Seton. Bothwell, with Lethington in attendance, followed her and declared his suit, but Mary's answer was 'nothing correspondent to his desire'. She wrote to the bishop of Dunblane that in the preceding weeks he had shown his 'readiness to fulfil all our commandments' and his desire 'to entertain our favour by his good outward behaviour'; but when, at Seton, 'he began afar off to discover his intentions unto us and to essay if he might by humble suit purchase our goodwill', Mary's firm and judicious reply was that she had friends and he had enemies, and neither would permit a marriage for which, in any case, she herself had no liking.

There was, at that time, no one in Scotland who was strong enough, or had cause enough, to declare his active opposition to Bothwell. Moray, his devoted enemy, had discreetly retired to France. In the Hepburn family, moreover, there was something like a tradition of involvement with royal ladies. A Hepburn had been friendly with Joan Beaufort, widow of James I; another was the reputed lover of Mary of Gueldres. Bothwell, in his youth, had given lively support to Mary of Lorraine, and some years later had been associated with the mad earl of Arran in the latter's design to kidnap the queen who was now Darnley's widow. In preceding reigns the nobles of Scotland had never been averse to enhancing their power by possessing themselves of the person of a monarch in the years of his minority. In appropriate circumstances kidnapping had been a useful policy, and to a man of Bothwell's temperament the circumstances of 1566 must have seemed, not merely favourable to abduction of the queen, but to require her abduction if he himself were to have any hope of maintaining his precarious authority.

With Huntly, Lethington, Melville—sometime her envoy in England—and thirty horsemen Mary rode to Stirling to see the infant prince. On 23rd April she slept at Linlithgow. Ten miles away, at the House of Calder, Bothwell waited with eight hundred troopers. On the road between Edinburgh and Linlithgow Mary and her small escort were halted, and Bothwell politely told his queen that he had come to save her from a grave danger, and would take her to the safety of Dunbar, of whose castle he was captain. Some of Mary's company were willing to defend her, but she prevented them and said she would rather go with Bothwell than cause bloodshed and death. She managed, however, to send James Borthwick to the provost of Edinburgh with an appeal for help; which proved vain.

There, presumably, is the little foundation on which was built the story of her complicity in the abduction. Many have written, and more have believed, that the abduction was prearranged to give Mary an excuse for entering upon an association which would have to be resolved by marriage. It was devised, say historians, to save her face. But Mary may have surrendered to save her life. Historians have seldom been willing to admit the enormous influence that fear has so often pinned upon those of whom they write. Fear is a shameful emotion, and should be excluded from the orderly pages that tell so wholesome a story of human progress and the benign growth of human institutions. But from life itself fear has never been excluded. Fear has lost battles and ruined policy. Greed has done more, but fear has done enough, and when she was confronted by the swords of eight hundred troopers, and Bothwell inflamed by the arrogance of his border breeding, it is more than likely that Mary, softened by her visit to the infant prince, succumbed to simple fear.

In the accounts of what followed there is very little to suggest that she went willingly to Dunbar, or got much pleasure from her journey. At the castle there was a violent quarrel between Huntly and Lethington, in which Mary had to intervene to save her secretary's life. Bothwell wooed his captive with civil eloquence and some prolixity. Mary admitted, in her letter to the bishop of Dunblane, that when he spoke of marriage 'he joined thereto all the honest language that could be used in such a case'. But when honest language failed of its purpose he used physical argument. Mary's own words are: 'As by a bravado in the beginning he won the first point, so ceased he never till by persuasion and importunate suit, accompanied not the less with force, he had finally driven us to end the work begun at such time and in such form as he thought might best serve his turn.' Melville, who was at Dunbar, said plainly: 'The queen could not but marry him, seeing that he had ravished her and lain with her against her will.' Throckmorton, the English envoy, was told later of the queen's captivity and how she was 'by fear, force and (as by many conjectures may be well suspected) other extraordinary and more unlawful means, compelled to become bedfellow to another wife's husband'. The 'extraordinary means' were witchcraft, which Bothwell was thought to practise; and assisted by 'fear and force' it may have been effective.

Early in May, Jean Gordon was given her divorce from Bothwell on the grounds of his adultery with her sewing-maid, and the Catholic consistory court of the archbishop of St. Andrews announced that Bothwell's marriage had been null from the beginning; though the archbishop had given a dispensation for it—it was within the prohibited degrees—about a year before. The queen took advice from several Catholic bishops, who did not forbid her marriage. A Privy Council, at which Lethington was present, did not denounce it. And Mary herself, as after the death of Riccio, had apparently steeled herself to the acceptance of a *fait accompli*. Another sentence of her letter to the bishop of Dunblane reads: 'We saw no esperance to be rid of him, never man in Scotland once making an attempt to procure our deliverance.' There was no one to whom she could turn for help.

After ten days at Dunbar Mary went back to Edinburgh. On 14th May Bothwell had been made duke of Orkney and lord of Shetland, and the marriage contract was ready. John Craig, the bold and honest minister of St. Giles, had refused to read the banns, and

[223]

preached against a marriage that was 'odious and slanderous to the world'. But Adam Bothwell, bishop of Orkney, was less scrupulous. He was brother-in-law to James and Gilbert Balfour. By Adam Bothwell the marriage was celebrated, according to the Protestant rites, and as at her wedding to Darnley, Mary wore mourning. 'There was neither pleasure nor pastime used, as was wont to be used when princes were married'; and those who believe that Mary was driven into Bothwell's arms by a passion that would not be denied, must admit their disappointment, or at least perplexity, to find that there is no record or rumour of such wanton happiness at Holyrood as would surely have followed her wedding if passion had been its motive and fulfilment.

Lethington wrote: 'From her wedding day she was ever in tears and lamentations, for he could not let her look at anybody, or anybody look at her, though he knew that she liked her pleasure and pastime, as well as anybody.' Melville heard her ask for a knife to stab herself, and to du Croc, who was surprised by the change in her demeanour, she said: 'If you see me melancholy it is because I do not choose to be cheerful; because I never will be so, and wish for nothing but death.' Sir William Drury, the English marshal of Berwick, did indeed write to Cecil to tell him that the queen and the duke would ride abroad together and make an outward show of contentment; that he would come bareheaded before her, and sometimes she would politely bid him be covered. That is hardly the behaviour of a Cleopatra newly joined to her Antony; an Antony who, if gossip may be trusted, was already seeking comfort from his divorced wife Jean.

It was a deserted court that Mary ruled. Lethington remained with her for a little while, but early in June, having written to Cecil to beg English help for the rebels who were already gathering their forces, he left without ceremony to join the opposition, the 'Confederate Lords', whose headquarters were in Stirling. Bothwell, in a sober and responsible fashion, tried to pick up the reins of government; but the horse had slipped its collar. Aware of imminent danger, he took the queen to Borthwick castle, and within those formidable walls easily withstood the brief assault of rebel cavalry. But he could not rule Scotland from Borthwick, and he and Mary, in disguise, rode to Dunbar and issued a summons calling loyal subject to their aid.

Had Bothwell been able to hold Dunbar and Edinburgh, he would have had strength enough to negotiate with the Confederates. But he had lately removed a loyal governor from Edinburgh castle, and given its command to James Balfour. For that disastrous error there can hardly be found an explanation other than the supposition that

Balfour had blackmailed him.[1] Of what happened on the night of Darnley's murder—of what had been prepared for that night, and what had gone amiss—it is almost certain that Balfour knew more than most; and what was worth Edinburgh castle except the knowledge of him who had fired the fuse to blow up the house at Kirk o' Field? Balfour can have had no serious intention of holding the castle for Bothwell; after a little argument he surrendered it, for a good price, to Lethington. The Confederate Lords occupied Edinburgh, and Bothwell's cause was lost. He and Mary, with an army of no great strength and little heart, encountered the Confederates at Carberry Hill, near Musselburgh; but there was no fighting. There was debate and a little bluster, and Bothwell was allowed to ride away, unpursued. But Mary was made prisoner and taken to Edinburgh, where a roaring mob, inflamed with self-righteous anger, greeted her with villainous cries of 'Burn the hoor!'

Bothwell made determined but unsuccessful attempts to recruit a new following, and with a small fleet sought refuge in his nominal dukedom of Orkney. There he found another of the Balfour brothers, Gilbert whom the placard pinned to the Tolbooth door had denounced for his knowledge of Darnley's murder. Gilbert, who had been sheriff of Orkney since the beginning of 1566, held the strong castles of Kirkwall and Noltland, and refused shelter to Bothwell. He fled to Shetland, and from there to Denmark and a Danish prison.

Mary was imprisoned in the island castle on Loch Leven, where on 24th July, 1567 she was compelled to abdicate in favour of her son, and to name as regent the earl of Moray. The infant James VI was crowned at Stirling on the 29th, and Moray, who had left Edinburgh the day before Darnley's murder, and retired to France two days before Bothwell's trial and acquittal in April, returned to Scotland on 11th August. At about the same time as her abdication, some three months after her abduction, that is, Mary is reported by Claud Nau, sometime her private secretary, to have been prostrated by the miscarriage of twins.

[1] *Lord Bothwell.* Robert Gore-Browne.

Chapter 5

THE official account of Darnley's murder was issued in a report by the Justice Clerk compiled after two of Bothwell's kinsmen and two of his servants had been captured and tortured in the Tolbooth of Edinburgh. The unhappy men were John Hepburn of Bolton, John Hay of Talla, Geordie Dalgleish who was Bothwell's tailor, and Willie Powrie his porter. If the agonies they suffered from rack, boot, and pincers persuaded them to tell the truth, as far as they knew it, the truth was suppressed; for the official story is wholly unacceptable.

According to it, Bothwell had brought gunpowder from Dunbar to Holyroodhouse, from where it was taken, packed in bags, in a leather portmanteau, a trunk, and a barrel, to the Provost's house at Kirk o' Field. A grey horse was used and two trips were necessary. The operation began at ten o'clock on the night of that busy carnival Sunday, the 9th of February, when there was a wedding party at Holyrood and in James Balfour's house in the Canongate the bishop of Argyll was entertaining Morette, the ambassador from Savoy. The conspirators were admitted to the Provost's house by Bothwell's page, known as French Paris, and the powder was emptied in a heap on the floor of the queen's bedroom, where John Hepburn and Hay of Talla remained in charge.

French Paris went up to Darnley's room to tell Bothwell that all was ready. The queen, it is known, left the house to return to Holyrood, and was escorted by Bothwell and torch-bearers. At Holyrood Bothwell put off the splendid clothes he was wearing, and in workaday dress went back with French Paris to Kirk o' Field, where at two o'clock in the morning John Hepburn and Hay of Talla lit the fuse.

It is, of course, a nonsensical story. That Bothwell should store a quantity of gunpowder at Holyrood is, for a start, improbable. That his servants could load a horse, and without attracting attention twice lead it through streets which, on that lively night, were certainly not deserted, is not to be believed. That bags of powder could then be carried up to the queen's bedroom, in a house where guests and inquisitive servants were free to come and go, is manifestly impossible. And that Bothwell, on his return to Kirk o' Field, should let himself be identified as often as the report pretends, is frankly incredible.

It has been calculated, moreover, that the maximum weight of gunpowder which, with a trunk, a portmanteau, and a barrel, a horse could carry on two journeys was about two hundred and twenty pounds.[1] But that weight of powder—the indifferent powder of the sixteenth century—dumped in a heap on the floor of a lower room was ludicrously insufficient to wreck and demolish the solid, stone-built Provost's house. There is unequivocal testimony, however, that the house and all its ponderous masonry were brought down in total ruin and collapse; and to produce that effect a cellar beneath the house must have been closely packed with so much powder that, when it exploded, it had the force of a land-mine. The house, which belonged to James Balfour's brother, the canon of Holyrood, had been prepared for demolition; and that could not have been done on Sunday evening.

Who, then, loaded the cellar, and who were the intended victims? It is at least possible that there was more than one plot in being. Some mention has been made of Darnley's curious behaviour, and reported conversation, in the months before his death: his apparent wish to cross over to the Netherlands at a time when Philip II of Spain was meditating an offensive there, his correspondence with France and Rome, his late revival of interest in the practices if not the faith of the Roman church. That Mary, by her prudent decision to sustain the Reformed church of Scotland, had deeply disappointed those who had hoped to find in her a militant champion of Roman Catholicism can hardly be open to doubt; and Major-General Mahon, in a work already cited,[1] has assembled a great deal of circumstantial evidence for the existence of what has been called the 'Paris Plot', the purpose of which was to remove Mary and substitute for her tolerance a bold and forceful policy in the restoration of Roman discipline. Pope Pius V, the zealot of the Inquisition, had chosen Vincenzo Laureo, bishop of Mondovi, as his legate to Scotland, who recognised the difficulties confronting him, but thought they could be overcome. On 23rd August, 1566, he wrote to the cardinal of Alessandria: 'These difficulties might be obviated if the king of Spain should come, as is hoped, with a strong force to Flanders or, as certain people of weight believe, if justice were executed against six rebels whose deaths would effectually restore peace and obedience in (Scotland).' The victims of the assassination he proposed were the earls of Moray, Argyll, and Morton; Lethington,

[1] *The Tragedy of Kirk o' Field*. R. H. Mahon.

Bellenden, the Justice Clerk, and another official. Darnley, he thought, 'could execute it without any disturbance arising and with the assured hope that afterwards the holy Catholic and Roman religion could soon be restored.'

Laureo, however, did see a major obstacle ahead of him. 'The danger,' he wrote, 'is that the Cardinal of Lorraine and the Queen in their excessive kindness, would not consent to such an act.' What he failed to see was that Darnley was not the man on whom anyone could rely for the prosecution of a bold and secret enterprise. Darnley had an unbridled tongue and told Mary what was proposed; who promptly warned her half-brother of the danger that threatened. But Laureo sent the bishop of Dunblane and the Jesuit Edmund Hay to Scotland, and the arrival of Morette from Savoy may seem significant. Savoy, a buffer-state between France and Spain, had lately reasserted its allegiance to the latter; and it is curious that Morette, who had previously introduced David Riccio to Edinburgh, now brought his brother Joseph. The Spanish ambassador in Paris told his colleague in London that 'he had news of a plot forming in Scotland against the Queen'; and Mary herself, after Darnley's death, believed that she had been the intended victim.

There, in outline—or the shadow of an outline—is the 'Paris Plot'. Now the English interest in the conflict between Mary and her Protestant lords has been evident from the beginning of her reign; and England had good reason for supporting the Protestant cause. That Cecil, Elizabeth's devoted secretary of state, was closely watching the uneasy situation in Scotland is shown by the existence[1] of a drawing of the scene at Kirk o' Field, made by an English agent in Edinburgh on the morning after the explosion, and sent by him to London. It is a composite drawing that shows the rubble left by the explosion, the bodies of the victims, and lying beside them a quilt, a dressing-gown, and a wooden chair; as if all had been blown out pell-mell by the monstrous blast. Long before the fuse was lighted that touched off the eruption, Moray and Lethington had removed themselves from Edinburgh with the smallest of excuses for their conspicuous absence: Moray's wife was pregnant, Lethington was newly married. Within a very short time they were working urgently to proclaim and establish Bothwell's guilt; and after Mary's abdication, when their English pay-masters required reasons for their insurrection, they showed them-selves even more resolved, and took more ingenious measures, to implicate her in the crime. Against Bothwell they had good cause for action, for not only was there old, unhealing enmity between him

[1] in the Record office, London.

[228]

and Moray, but Bothwell was certainly a guilty man; though not the only one. But the evidence they presently offered to incriminate Mary was all fabricated; and the nature of that evidence, and the manner in which it was presented, evince so plainly the fear of those who fabricated it that their own guilt can scarcely be disputed.

What happened at two o'clock on the morning of 10th February cannot be told. Guesswork may suggest that James Balfour, principal agent in the 'Paris Plot', had prepared the house at Kirk o' Field for demolition, and when the plot was discovered by Darnley's babbling he had been suborned or bribed by Moray and Lethington to let them use the land-mine, which he had planted, for their own purposes. They may have hoped to rid themselves of Mary, Darnley, and Bothwell too; a project very helpful to Moray's ambition for the regency, and a stroke of policy—if blame could be diverted—that would not gravely displease their master in London. But Bothwell, perhaps by accident, perhaps by Balfour's double-dealing, discovered with little time to spare what was intended, and with the genius of a brutal opportunism saw his chance to use the plot which had miscarried for his own advantage. He lighted the fuse, he murdered Darnley, and made Mary a widow whom he could wed.

That, of course, is supposition. But in the narration of what followed there are facts which clearly indicate the deep unease that affected Scotland, and the profound anxiety that animated Moray and his associates.

It can be argued, fairly enough, that after Mary's surrender at Carberry the Confederate Lords were justified in imprisoning her in the castle on Loch Leven: she had escaped her captors after Riccio's murder, she might escape again. But they exceeded the need for caution when, a few weeks after her surrender, they compelled her abdication and hurriedly crowned the infant James. When Moray returned from France, moreover, his assumption of the regency was patently anomalous, for the insurgent lords had risen to punish Darnley's murderers, and the regent himself, as well as some of his associates, can hardly have escaped the suspicion that they, in some degree, had been implicated in that murder.

Moray, though regent, was not the leader of a united nobility, and when, at the beginning of May, 1568, Mary escaped from Loch Leven, she was quickly at the head of a considerable army. But there was no one who knew how to order and command her voluntaries, and at Langside near Glasgow she was outmanoeuvred and defeated by Moray. She fled southward and crossed the Solway into England; whose queen, she hoped, would welcome her as a friend. But to

Elizabeth she was not merely a fellow monarch in distress, but a source of embarrassment.

After the fiasco at Carberry Elizabeth had, indeed, sent her envoy Throckmorton to negotiate Mary's release; but Mary still obstinately retained her claim to the English throne. Elizabeth, however, had no inclination to support rebellion against the queen of a neighbouring country, and when Mary fled into England Elizabeth wrote to offer her help on condition that Moray, who was accused of rebellion, should be given liberty to show cause for rebellion. Moray should stand his trial, that is, but Mary must answer such accusations as he chose to bring against her. To that Mary agreed, and Moray, who depended on English recognition, had no choice but to acquiesce.

The conference, or court of inquiry, assembled first at York in October, 1568; was removed to Westminster; and finally met at Hampton Court in December. Moray, it seems, attempted to vindicate the rebellion of the Confederate Lords, and his assumption of the regency, by producing that indictment of Mary called the *Detection*[1] by George Buchanan, or an early version of it; and a set of documents, remarkable in character and obscure of origin, known to history as the Casket Letters.

Two samples of the *Detection* have been quoted, and in the excitement of their fiction one can almost hear the voice of a defendant, fearful for his own safety, who is trying feverishly to exculpate himself by monstrous inventions that must inculpate another. Buchanan was a scholar—the finest Latinist of his age—but he was Moray's creature, obedient to Moray's will and truly convinced, it may be, that Moray was the man whom Scotland needed as its ruler. But in the cold air of four hundred years' distance Buchanan's voice does not inspire belief.

The story of the Casket Letters is more interesting. According to the earl of Morton they were discovered on 19th June, 1567, in a silver box which Geordie Dalgleish, Bothwell's tailor, was accused of having removed from Edinburgh castle and hidden under his bed in his lodging in the Potterrow. Its alleged contents included nine letters in French, said to have been written by Mary to Bothwell, and some French 'sonnets'. In June, 1568, when Moray was required to justify the rebellion of which he was the leader, he informed Elizabeth that his secretary John Wood, then in London, had been sent 'that which we trust shall sufficiently resolve her Majesty of anything she stands doubtful unto'. Buchanan's *Detection* may well have been in the parcel which Wood received; that it contained a translation of the Casket Letters appears evident in the instructions issued to him. He was told

[1] See pages 214-15.

to ask 'if the French originals are found to tally with the Scots trans-lations, will that be reckoned good evidence?' The inference, that the 'originals' could be altered if necessary, is plain enough.

There are extant Scots, English, and Latin translations of the letters, as well as French translations from the Latin; but the original letters are not known to have been seen by any man—they or the silver casket —after the death of the earl of Gowrie; who died in 1600. No one knows precisely what was seen and studied by the commissioners who assembled at York and later removed to Westminster; and for two reasons the surviving translations cannot be accepted as evidence. If they are indeed literal translations of genuine letters, written by Mary to Bothwell, then they prove beyond question that she was guilty by association of Darnley's murder; but there is no proof that they are what they pretend to be, and in them are so many contradictions, inconsistencies, and improbabilities that a critical judgement can hardly explain them except by admission that they were fabricated for the express purpose of incriminating Mary and vindicating Moray.

The court of inquiry delivered its verdict on 10th January, 1569. It was a verdict that solved nothing, but avoided trouble. It acquitted Moray and his adherents of rebellion, and affirmed that nothing had been proved against Mary. But the Casket Letters had very usefully blackened her reputation.

For nineteen years she was a prisoner in England, and in all that time she formed no association of a sort that could provoke scandal or suspicion. She was only twenty-five, and a very attractive young woman, when she fled across the Solway; she was not kept in close confinement; and in England there was no lack of mettlesome young men. If Mary had been the sort of woman that her enemies pretended —if her friendship with Riccio had been adulterous, if passion had driven her into Bothwell's arms—it is more than likely that she would have found lovers to complicate or enliven the sad story of her exile. But her dominating interests had always been dynastic and political, and so they continued.

It cannot be denied that Mary, while she lived, was a menace to the peace of England. She was aware of conspiracies to procure her freedom, and did not rebuff the conspirators. The duke of Norfolk, who had been Elizabeth's commissioner at the court of inquiry—and therefore knew all that had been said or written to implicate Mary in Darnley's murder—aspired to her hand in marriage, and for his im-prudence was committed to the Tower. He was later involved in a plot which, for its success, required the invasion of England by Spanish troops; and was executed for treason. Parliament demanded a like penalty for Mary, but she was saved by Elizabeth's clemency. A northern rising, led by the earls of Northumberland and Westmorland, came so near her prison at Tutbury in Staffordshire that she had to be removed in a hurry to Coventry. Then she was taken to Sheffield, where for fourteen years she remained under the care of the earl of Shrewsbury. The Massacre of St. Bartholomew excited the English Protestants against her; but again Elizabeth refused to sign her cousin's death-warrant.

There was indeed an ingenious proposal, behind which Cecil may be detected, to release Mary and send her back to Scotland on condition of her being executed there. But the earl of Mar, then regent, died before negotiations could be completed, and was succeeded by the earl of Morton. In the shifting allegiances that gave to Scottish policy a tidal aspect, Mary's cause found new champions in Lethington and Kirkcaldy of Grange: Lethington was indeed a kind of chameleon, and Kirkcaldy, one of the Lords of the Congregation, had been involved in the murder of Riccio, and was mainly responsible for Mary's defeat at Langside. But now they held Edinburgh castle for their exiled queen, and Morton was given English help to reduce it. Lethington died soon after its surrender, and Kirkcaldy was hanged.

For some years Elizabeth was untroubled by conspiracy, and Mary consoled herself with needlework, her lap-dogs, and a vast correspondence. But in 1586 she became involved in the Babington plot, the purpose of which was to liberate her, foment a Roman Catholic rising with the assistance of Spain, and murder Elizabeth. Anthony Babington was an accomplished and enthusiastic young man who in his boyhood had served Mary as a page when in her wandering imprisonment she was taken to Sheffield. In England, however, an elaborate and very efficient system of secret intelligence had been built up by Francis Walsingham, one of Elizabeth's most devoted ministers, and it is fairly certain that Walsingham had, from its very beginning, a detailed knowledge of the plot. The conspirators were arrested, Babington was executed, and in September Mary was taken to Fotheringhay castle in Northamptonshire. Three weeks later she was tried for complicity in the plot.

She denied the jurisdiction of an English tribunal, and defended herself with a high spirit and considerable subtlety. She denied absolutely her complicity in any plot against Elizabeth's life, but admitted conspiring to escape. She was found guilty, and both Houses of Parliament recommended her immediate execution. Elizabeth temporised, but on 7th February, 1587, the earls of Kent and Shrewsbury arrived at Fotheringhay with the necessary warrant, and

Mary, retaining to the end a most queenly grace and composure, was beheaded on the following morning.

In her own consciousness she was a martyr for her religion; but it is not unfair to see her also as the victim of a dynastic purpose that never wavered. Sixteen years later that purpose was achieved when her son, James VI of Scotland, succeeded to the throne left vacant by Elizabeth's death, as James I of England.

Chapter 6

THE face of Scotland was still the countenance of a poor and primitive country, but the wealth of the burghs was perceptibly enhancing the comfort in which the new middle classes had begun to live. Edinburgh, Dundee, Aberdeen, Perth, Glasgow, and St. Andrews were the largest of the small towns in which the profits of trade and commerce had become more and more visible as stone-built houses replaced old wooden dwellings; and when the seventeenth century came in there were, in Edinburgh, a few rich men. Prospering merchants, indeed, probably lived better than the lesser nobility who drew their rents in kind and had an embarrassing number of servants and followers, but no means of making money. There were, as yet, no signs of improved agriculture. Oats and a coarse barley were the staple crops, and fields were still unkempt, undrained, without shelter of hedgerows. But food was plentiful, except in time of famine, and as wool, skins, and coarse cloth were among the principal exports of the kingdom, the rural populace may well have been stoutly clad in the ill-lighted cabins of turf, or stone and turf, in which it lived. The cottages of the poor can have been no colder than the castles of the nobility.

The dominating topic of the age was religion, and except in the remote parts of the north and the west the majority of people seem to have responded with a quickly increasing goodwill to the new doctrines and discipline; though in the beginning the Reformation was curiously permissive. Despite the fervour of Knox's preaching, and the occasional savagery of his followers, the Roman church remained in being, and bishops and priests lived much as before, though papal authority had been denounced and the Mass forbidden. Ministers of the Reformed church were too few in number to replace immediately the old incumbents, and there was difficulty in paying them while two-thirds of the revenue of church lands were still drawn by Roman prelates or the laymen of noble birth who had acquired their benefices. It was not until 1573 that a start was made in ejecting from their benefices those who would not accept the Protestant Confession of Faith.

The Reformers, however, established a parliament of their own when the general assembly of the kirk of Scotland first met in December, 1560; and the Lutheran doctrine of justification by faith was sharpened and hardened by the teaching of John Calvin. In Geneva his autocratic rule had created what John Knox described as the most perfect school of Christ since the days of the apostles; though some complained of tyranny. His teaching was founded on the sovereignty of God who reveals himself through the scriptures, and from mankind chooses those who shall have the saving faith to attain salvation. Salvation may not be attained by merit, but only by God's grace, and God in his justice and mercy has chosen to save some from perdition, while others are left to their deserts. Calvin's system of church government was characterised by a puritan simplicity, a strict discipline, and a form of public worship in which the main feature was the sermon. It was anti-clerical, it vested much authority in elders, and Scotland found the system to its liking. Predestination was also accepted, and faith in the inviolacy of Election may have been general until, rather more than two hundred years after Calvin, Robert Burns derided it:

> O Thou, that in the Heavens does dwell,
> Wha, as it pleases best Thysel,
> Sends ane to Heaven an' ten to Hell,
> A' for Thy glory,
> An' no for onie guid or ill
> They've done before Thee!

In 1574 the Reformation was reinforced by the return to Scotland of Andrew Melville. He, a precocious scholar, learnt Greek from a Frenchman living in Montrose, and had the pleasure of introducing that unknown tongue to his preceptors in the university of St. Andrews. He studied and taught in Paris and Geneva, and after an absence of ten years came home to be appointed principal of Glasgow university, which had fallen into sad disrepair. He recreated it, established new faculties, and attracted many students by the brilliance of his teaching. Six years later he was transferred to St. Andrews, where his influence over young men studying for the ministry was supreme. For the church's government he advocated a strict presbyterianism: all ministers, that is, were to enjoy equal status, untroubled by the discipline of bishops or superintendents, but responsible only to committees consisting of other ministers; and the general assembly of the kirk, which until his time represented the Three Estates, should, he contended, consist only of ordained ministers, teachers like himself, and elders elected for life. He was moderator of the Assembly in 1582.

He compiled or gave his authority to a second Book of Discipline in which he made aggressively evident his belief that the kirk's authority was derived directly and exclusively from God, and was therefore superior to the authority of civil magistrates. In his opinion, indeed, the kirk had a duty to instruct the civil authority in all matters of conscience and religion. Here was the origin of his challenge to the power of the sovereign which became explicit when he told James that there were two kings and two kingdoms in Scotland, and one of the kings was Christ Jesus, whose kingdom was the kirk, of which King James was 'not a king, nor a lord, nor a head, but a member'.

Conflict between the learned king and his arrogant and scholarly subject was inevitable, and by repetition became tedious. James was as stubborn as Melville himself, and by critics has been much maligned. It is often recorded that Melville once called him 'God's silly vassal'; but less often remembered that in those days 'silly' did not mean foolish, but weak and defenceless, as James and all other mortal men were under the dominance of such a God as Melville worshipped; it is also recorded that the rector of St. Andrews university had called Melville, then a young student, 'My silly fatherless and motherless boy.' James himself had grown up fatherless and motherless, under a brutal teacher, and lived much of his young life in circumstances that were sometimes acutely dangerous. His later life was far from exemplary, but much that he said or wrote or did was wise and laudable; and nowadays, when some knowledge of psychology is common property, there can be no difficulty in finding a source for the weakness and grossness of his later years in the extraordinary conditions of his childhood.

It is necessary to return in time to the years immediately after his mother's flight to England.

Chapter 7

THE regency of the earl of Moray did not establish peace. There were again two parties in Scotland, for now, when it was too late, there was strong support for Mary, and considerable hostility to Moray. He was regent for three years only, and then was murdered in a street in Linlithgow by one of the Hamiltons. There was trouble on the border, and in retaliation for a raid a small English army captured the town and castle of Hamilton. A few months later the strong castle of Dumbarton was taken by bold assault, and Archbishop Hamilton—head of his powerful family and perhaps the most formidable enemy of the infant king's party—was made prisoner and hanged for his alleged complicity in the murder of Moray. The old earl of Lennox, Darnley's father, had become regent after Moray's death, and he was killed at Stirling when a gathering of the king's men was attacked by the queen's men. The earl of Mar took the regency, and died within a year. He was succeeded in 1572 by James Douglas, earl of Morton, who had held the approaches to Holyroodhouse to let Riccio's murderers do their work; and Morton, ruthless, competent, and assisted by England, broke the queen's party and re-established order. He did not, however, escape his proper fate; and belatedly, in 1581, was executed, on evidence conveniently discovered, for connivance in the murder of Darnley.

In uneasy conjunction with the rising power and increasing wealth of the middle classes in its few small towns, such was the political state of Scotland while the Reformation was being established and the infant James—son of a murdered father and an exiled mother—grew into boyhood and adolescence. To make him, moreover, the most learned prince in Christendom, and to darken his childish spirit, there was appointed, as his principal tutor, that scholarly old sadist, the perjurer of his mother, George Buchanan.

James's guardian, for the first six years of his life, was the earl of Mar; and the home of his boyhood, Stirling castle. George Buchanan

[237]

became his tutor before James was four, and by harsh treatment instilled in him both learning and a deep regard for scholarship. He and a junior tutor, Peter Young, gathered for their pupil a library of six hundred volumes, most of them written in Latin, but others in Greek, French, Spanish, and Italian. The boy was extremely intelligent, and his masters drove him hard. He learned Latin before he could speak his native tongue, and at the age of eight he was able to translate *extempore* the Latin Bible into French, then French into English. His health was preserved by physical exercise, and from an early age he was allowed to indulge his love of hounds, horses, and hunting. Buchanan lived till his royal pupil was sixteen, by which time James had escaped from tutelage and found a precocious maturity in the more dangerous world of politics.

He was only twelve when the earls of Atholl and Argyll persuaded him that Morton's regency had exceeded its term of usefulness, and he should rule in his own name through an appointed council. But the authority which Atholl and Argyll attempted to assert was disputed by the young earl of Mar—son of James's first guardian—who was of Morton's party and claimed custody of the king by hereditary right. The Highland earls were discomfitted, and Morton's authority was re-established. But in the following year there came from France a cousin of James's father who quickly established his influence over the young king, and so weakened Morton's power that the regent could be accused and arrested for complicity in Darnley's murder.

Esmé Stewart, seigneur d'Aubigny, was a nephew of Darnley's father, the earl of Lennox. A Catholic, brought up in France, d'Aubigny may have been a French or papal agent; but it is more likely that he was merely an ambitious man who saw an opportunity to exploit a blood-relationship to the king, and his remote interest in the succession. Some twenty years older than James, d'Aubigny soon won the heart of a boy who had never known affection; and was lavishly rewarded. He was made duke of Lennox, keeper of Dumbarton castle, and a privy councillor. Another Stewart—James, son of Lord Ochiltree whose young daughter John Knox had married—also attracted favour, and it was he who brought about Morton's downfall by accusing him of complicity in the murder of Darnley. James Stewart, who claimed a Hamilton descent, became earl of Arran, and Lennox found other supporters. To Catholic militants in France and Spain it seemed possible that Lennox and his party might be used in their interest, and Mary from her English prison suggested, through the duke of Guise, the feasibility of her restoration to a throne that she would share with James. Neither James nor Lennox welcomed her proposal, and Jesuit agents in Scotland found no support. But the ministers of the Reformed church remained stubbornly suspicious of Lennox and obdurately opposed to his policies; if policy he had. The earls of Gowrie, Angus, and Glencairn were the leaders of the Anglophile and Protestant faction, but behind the action that dislodged Lennox were personal motives at least as strong as policy or religious zeal.

In Scotland the readiest means to power had always been possession of the king's person, and in August, 1582, James fell into the hands of Lennox's enemies. When he was hunting near Perth he was invited to Ruthven castle, a seat of the earl of Gowrie, and there he had to remain. James wept, and never forgot his humiliation; and Lennox, returning to France, died a few months later.

Gowrie and his party found partisans in Edinburgh and the kirk, whose ministers took unscrupulous advantage of the freedom of their pulpits to abuse the king; but Elizabeth, who had promised help, gave none, and the great barons of the north—Huntly and Argyll, Crawford, Rothes and others—came to James's help when, by his own wit, he escaped his captors in the summer of 1583. James Stewart, the adventurer who had become earl of Arran, was released from prison and restored to power and the Privy Council; Gowrie was executed; and James had the satisfaction of receiving Walsingham, Elizabeth's secretary of state, who showed both anger and agitation, and of corresponding with the duke of Guise, who again was hopeful of enlisting the young king's interest. But Arran's policy offered no threat to England, no hope to France. He was an educated adventurer who had soldiered both in France and Sweden, and his splendid presence was fortified by an independence of mind so sturdy and judicious that he could reject alike both English dictation and the pretensions of the kirk. Arran became chancellor, Maitland ef Thirlstane—a brother of Lethington—was made secretary, and in May, 1584, Andrew Melville's *Second Book of Discipline* was firmly refuted. The power of the king and the authority of bishops were reaffirmed to the consternation of a hundred indignant presbyteries, and a score of ministers sought refuge in England, where Melville had already fled. Elizabeth, who did not underrate her monarchical privilege, was apparently still deaf to the extreme presbyterians' denial of royal authority.

The complex negotiations between Scotland and England which then ensued can be described, without impropriety, as political bickering, and the conclusion was a league of friendship established by agreement in July, 1586. Scotland got an annual subsidy of £4,000, but Arran, discredited, had fled, and the Protestant lords who found refuge in England when Gowrie was executed had returned. Elizabeth was still

[239]

reluctant to admit that James must be her successor, and a Scottish application for the naturalisation of Scots in England, balanced by a like privilege for the English in Scotland, had been rejected.

Three months after conclusion of the league of friendship Mary, sometime queen of Scots, was accused of conspiring with Babington and his fellow-plotters against the life and throne of Queen Elizabeth; and in November, when Mary was found guilty, the English parliament demanded her execution. Much has been written about the apparent indifference with which James heard of the imminence of his mother's death; he has been condemned, with scorn and disgust, for his callous acquiescence in her execution; and his behaviour, his attitude, certainly require critical scrutiny. Before essaying comment on his observed demeanour and known conduct, however, it may be useful to consider a careful report made by Fontenay,[1] a French visitor, in 1584, when James was eighteen.

Fontenay, a brother of Mary's French secretary, had been sent by her to inquire if James would support her should she appeal again to be acknowledged as his associate on the throne of Scotland. Fontenay found the young king elusive in debate, a diplomat perhaps too accomplished for his years. But he did not restrain his admiration for the boy whom he described as, 'for his years, the most remarkable Prince that ever lived. Three qualities of the mind he possesses in perfection: he understands clearly, judges wisely, and has a retentive memory. His questions are keen and penetrating and his replies are sound. In any argument, whatever it is about, he maintains the view that appears to him the most just, and I have heard him support Catholic against Protestant opinions. He is well instructed in languages, science, and affairs of state, better, I dare say, than anyone else in his kingdom. In short, he has a remarkable intelligence, as well as lofty and virtuous ideals and a high opinion of himself.'

He was timid, said Fontenay; but in common with most timid men wanted to be thought courageous. He still suffered, in a social way, from the deprivations of his upbringing; from the narrow and appalling discipline to which, in his childhood, the unspeakable Buchanan had subjected him: 'He dislikes dancing and music, and the little affectations of courtly life such as amorous discourse or curiosities of dress, and has a special aversion for ear-rings. In speaking and eating, in his dress and in his sports, in his conversation in the presence of women, his manners are crude and uncivil and display a lack of proper instruction. He is never still in one place but walks constantly up and down, though his gait is erratic and wandering, and he tramps about even in his own

[1] Hatfield House mss. Quoted in *King James VI and I*. D. Harris Willson.

chamber. His voice is loud and his words grave and sententious. He loves the chase above all other pleasures and will hunt for six hours without interruption, galloping over hill and dale with loosened bridle. His body is feeble and yet he is not delicate. In a word, he is an old young man.

'I have remarked in him three defects that may prove injurious to his estate and government: he does not estimate correctly his poverty and insignificance but is over-confident of his strength and scornful of other princes; his love for favourites is indiscreet and wilful and takes no account of the wishes of his people; he is too lazy and indifferent about affairs, too given to pleasure, allowing all business to be conducted by others. Such things are excusable at his age, yet I fear they may become habitual.' And contrary to the reputation which his countrymen subsequently acquired, he was extravagant in his poverty, and monstrously careless about money.

He was twenty-one when his mother was beheaded at Fotheringhay castle on 8th February, 1587. He can have had no memory of her, and little knowledge other than the preposterous tales that Buchanan may have told him, or that he had read in the *Detection*. There were those in Scotland who had thought that Mary's death would inevitably mean war with England; but James, though earnestly pleading for his mother's life, was equally earnest in his insistence that nothing should be said or done that would endanger his prospect of succession to the English throne. That prospect, that dynastic purpose, had dominated Mary's life; there is little reason for surprise at the discovery that he had inherited her purpose. He went so far as to write to Elizabeth and say that Mary's execution would involve his honour, and already the people of Scotland were so deeply incensed that he hardly dared to walk abroad; but his envoy in London told the earl of Leicester that Mary's death would not so incense the king as to make him break his league of friendship with England. He wrote again, his envoys pleaded and argued again; but neither plea nor argument had any effect because it was evident that James had no intention of yielding to a romantic or impetuous emotion in a manner that would have been characteristic of his great-grandfather James IV.

When news of Mary's death reached him, he appears to have been deeply grieved; though accounts of his behaviour vary widely, and one asserts that he openly rejoiced. There seems to be no record of his feelings, if he had any, for his murdered father; yet he may well have known the portrait of Darnley, painted in 1563 by Lucas de Heere,[1] that shows so strikingly their close resemblance—a portrait of James

[1] Now in possession of H.M. the Queen.

[241]

himself, at the age of eight,[1] makes this evident beyond question—and if that is so, it is hardly possible that James did not, to some extent, identify himself with his father, and so admit, by inheritance, a certain animus against the mother who, according to his old tutor and the impressive history that Buchanan had written, was deeply implicated in his father's murder. If James was only lightly and briefly moved by the dire news from Fotheringhay—if, indeed, he had shown himself callous to tales of Mary's unhappiness—there may be excuses for him of a sort that few historians deign to observe.

Had James been such a man as his great-grandfather, he could have mustered an army for war against England; but what he did, more prudently, was to let some of his wild borderers lead punitive raids into the debatable lands, and accept with diplomatic credulity an English assertion that Elizabeth had neither intended nor authorised his mother's death.

In the following year, 1588, Philip of Spain launched his Great Armada to achieve Catholic victory, the triumph of Spain, and England's subjugation. Since the early days of Mary's return to Scotland in 1561, both Spain and France had seen the northern kingdom of Britain as a pawn that might profitably be used in the somewhat chaotic game known as the Counter-reformation; and from time to time the interest of one or the other had caused embarrassment. In some of the Catholic and conservative northern counties there was still a stubborn or romantic pretence of loyalty to the Spanish cause, but James, as well as being a non-Presbyterian Protestant—who sensibly believed that a ruling king needed bishops to cushion the conflict of church and state—was a political realist who clearly saw that if Philip of Spain conquered England, he would proceed to conquer Scotland without hindrance or delay. He did nothing to antagonise the pro-Spanish magnates of the north, whose strength, though insufficient to menace the throne, was too great to be wantonly provoked, but he stood firmly behind the Protestant league with England, and was rewarded for his good sense by a useful addition to his subsidy. The Catholic crusade was defeated by English seamen whose arrogant and splendid queen grudged the cost and maintenance of their ships; the Great Armada was scattered by an opportune storm; and the Protestant cause was firmly established in Britain.

James was now in search of a wife. His choice, to begin with, lay between Catherine, the sister of Henry of Navarre, and Elizabeth, the elder daughter of Frederick II, king of Denmark. Henry of Navarre was the Huguenot heir to the French throne, but he could not afford

[1] Now in the National Portrait Gallery, London.

to give his sister a dowry, and she was eight years older than James. The merchants of the south of Scotland, whose trade was with northern Europe, were much in favour of the Danish match, but James offended his prospective father-in-law by asking too large a bounty and military aid as well, should he be tempted to military adventure. Elizabeth of Denmark, moreover, was already promised to the duke of Brunswick. But she had a sister, Anne, who was barely sixteen, and the bookish young man—Scotland's pedantic king, whose boyhood had been austere and loveless, but for his devotion to hounds and horses—fell suddenly in love, if not immediately with Anne, at least with the idea of marriage to a tall and lively, well developed and very fair young Danish princess. He forgot his demand for a large dowry, and waited impatiently for the bride whom his proxy married in Copenhagen on 20th August, 1589.

He waited until he heard that Anne, having met with bad weather and put back, was storm-bound in Oslo. He had been writing bad poetry to occupy his mind and fend off frustration, but now his patience was exhausted, and without reference to Maitland, his very able chancellor, or consultation with his Privy Council, he nominated governors for his realm and put to sea to find his bride. He left Leith on 22nd October, and married Anne in Oslo a month later. He was in no hurry to return to Scotland, and from Oslo travelled leisurely to Gothenburg and crossed over to Hamlet's castle of Kronborg in Elsinore. There and in Copenhagen his new Danish relations, with their traditional deep-drinking hospitality, entertained him until April weather could promise a pleasant voyage to Leith.

Much has been written about James's ineptitude as a king, much about his perversity as a man. At the age of twenty-three, however, he was so whole-heartedly in love with a gay and pretty Danish girl that he left his kingdom to look after itself for six winter months while he played with her and drank with her uncles; and so substantial was the reputation he had made for himself in Scotland—so wise and prudent had been his provision for its government—that his turbulent realm was still whole and entire when he came back to it, and gave him and his bride a tumultuous welcome. He deserves, indeed, more respect than he has usually been given, and it is idle to suppose that he could have survived the recurrent crises and perpetual difficulty of his years in Scotland had he not possessed, as well as the dynastic purpose he inherited from his mother, a shrewd judgement and the ability to keep his balance in both action and inaction. His Danish bride was no match for him in intellect, but in Edinburgh or Stirling the court must have been enriched by her fund of gaiety, and their

The spheres of influence of clans and families in the Highlands and Brae
Country in the sixteenth century.

[244]

life together retained a kindly intimacy until seven children had been born.

Foremost among the northern magnates who, with grave indiscretion, had expressed their loyalty to Philip of Spain was George, earl of Huntly, an attractive young man, rash and lively in the way of the Gordons, who had married a daughter of Esmé Stewart, seigneur d'Aubigny and briefly duke of Lennox. Huntly, the head of a great Catholic family, was a convert to Protestantism, or pretended to be; and he had been made captain of the king's guard. He was so foolish as to condole with Philip of Spain when his Great Armada was defeated, and had promised his help should Philip try again; worse than that, he chose a messenger who let himself and his incriminating letter be intercepted and captured before he left England. Huntly, in disgrace, was imprisoned, but soon released. His arrogance was unabated, and with the earls of Errol and Crawford he threatened to march on Edinburgh; but surrendered when James, that unwarlike king, mustered an army and marched to Aberdeen. Huntly and Crawford were lightly punished and easily forgiven. Then Huntly was involved in a violent affair which achieved the immortality of a ballad. He instigated the killing, and assisted in the death, of the earl of Moray. The ballad, which is well known, begins:

> Ye Hielans and ye Lawlans,
> Oh, whar hae ye been?
> They hae slain the Earl o' Moray,
> And laid him on the green.

> Now wae be to you, Huntly!
> And wharfore did ye sae?
> I bade you bring him wi' you,
> And forbade you him to slay.

The death of the earl of Moray roused a storm of anger, and the ballad is evidence of the deep impression it made on contemporary minds and popular memory; but one cannot accept so naïve an assessment of the killing, and the anger it provoked, as that offered, a few years ago, by the erudite American historian[1] who wrote: 'Men felt it insufferable that the brave Protestant earl should be thus slaughtered by the cruel Catholic potentate of the north.' There is no evidence that Moray was braver, or Huntly more cruel, than other of their titled contemporaries, and it is mere sentimentality to see them as champions of Rome and the Reformation. What divided them was not only the dogmatic self-interest of every member of the

[1] D. Harris Willson.

Scottish nobility, but their inheritance of a long-established, particular animosity. The murdered Moray was a Stewart who, by marriage to a daughter of the regent Moray—the illegitimate half-brother of Mary, queen of Scots—had acquired the title to his father-in-law's earldom; and between old Moray and the Gordons of Huntly there had been no junction of love or sympathy. Antagonism was inbred, and the circumstances of Moray's killing were precisely of the sort to create the matrix of a ballad.

In February, 1592, Moray was at the castle of Donibristle on the north side of the Firth of Forth. Huntly, having crossed the Forth from Edinburgh, laid siege to the castle and set it on fire. Moray broke out through the encircling flames, and reached the winter darkness of the shore. There he was overtaken and stabbed to death, receiving—according to popular belief—the *coup de grace* from Huntly himself; whom he is said to have mocked with his dying speech, 'Ye hae spoilt a better face than your ain, my lord!' Add to that a rumour, for which there is no known foundation, that he was Anne of Denmark's lover, and the earl of Moray's posthumous fame can easily be explained. The real importance of the affair subsists in its demonstration of the lordly anarchy that could still disrupt the peace of Scotland in the decade immediately preceding James's transition to the English throne. A king of Scots who lacked the military resources, or the intrinsic strength of character, to rule by sheer power, could only retain his throne by exercising the poise and agility of a royal acrobat.

The perils and perplexities among which James lived, and managed to assert a precarious authority, are even more vividly revealed by the extraordinary behaviour and bewildering career of Francis Stewart, earl of Bothwell. His father, a bastard son of James V, was a brother of the regent Moray; his mother was a sister of the Bothwell who abducted and married Mary, the mother of James VI; and his emotional inheritance included an ancestral feud with James's good chancellor, Maitland. Bothwell enjoyed a superior education, a cultivated mind, an arrogant assurance. James feared him, and could not deny him respect. As an iceberg ponderously conceals its true size and shape, so may Bothwell have hidden from his contemporaries the submerged but dominating fact of his insanity.

Though professing the Reformed religion, and posing indeed as a leader of the Protestant faith, he had associated with the northern earls in their small and foolish rebellion, and tried without success to rouse insurgence on the border against his cousin the king. Early in 1591, when one of his Liddesdale men was about to be tried for some indefensible outrage, he had abducted a witness from the Tolbooth in

[246]

Edinburgh, and ridden to Kelso to foment more trouble. Later that year he acquired an infamous notoriety as the leader of a cult which, however ludicrous it may now appear, was then able to evoke fear and horror, not only in Scotland, but throughout western Europe. The earl of Bothwell was said to be a warlock who commanded the obedience, if not the worship, of several covens of witches.

By later critics King James has often been derided for his belief in witchcraft, but in his own time there were few who did not share both his credulity and his dread. For several centuries the church had been much concerned with Satanism and sorcery, and when Goya, who died in 1828, drew a picture of witches flying naked on a broomstick through darkened skies, he was commemorating a popular belief at least seven or eight hundred years old. The Reformation, that assailed and divided Rome's venerable authority, released, in many parts of Europe, what appears to have been a suppressed or hidden allegiance to old pagan faiths or rituals, most of them associated with fertility rites; and witches, so-called, appeared or were alleged to have appeared, in alarmingly increased numbers, to subvert the decent laws of nature and indulge in abominable practices. On the continent of Europe the Inquisition burnt them in thousands; in England and Scotland they were sought out, and persecuted, with an errant or local zeal which, however hateful it may appear to a contemporary mind, must be excused as less destructive, less malignant, than, for example, Germanic practice.

King James, who was profoundly interested in theology, could not possibly have escaped interest in the Satanism which was traditionally associated with witchcraft; and in April, 1591, he was naturally attracted to the trial of several suspected women in North Berwick when one of them boasted that she could repeat his pillow-talk to Anne of Denmark on their wedding-night. The women confessed to the common practices of their kind. The Devil, in the likeness of a black man, had preached to them from the pulpit of the parish kirk of North Berwick, and they had worshipped him with customary indecencies. Their confession became truly alarming when it emerged that the purpose of the unholy congregation was to bring about the death of the king, who was then on his way to Oslo in quest of his bride; and the leader who accepted the witches' blasphemous worship was none other than Francis, earl of Bothwell.

Bothwell was captured and imprisoned; and promptly escaped. James pursued him to the borders, but Bothwell had many friends and openly defied the king. James was terrified of the rebel earl, and powerless to restrain him. At Christmas Bothwell raided the palace of

Holyroodhouse and tried to break into Maitland's room, then, with fire and hammers, into a tower where James had taken refuge. The alarm was raised, the townspeople hurried to the palace, and Bothwell fled. The king went to St. Giles to give thanks in public, and was snubbed for his pains. John Craig, the minister of St. Giles, rebuked him from the pulpit, saying that God in his providence had despatched a noise of crying and hammers 'to his own doors' as a warning to him. James in his familiar way tried to answer, but the insolent Craig would not listen. In church as on the borders the king was mocked, his impotence made evident. Yet James survived, and after a fashion contrived to rule his undisciplined land. No one, however, need pretend surprise to discover that when the English throne fell vacant, James responded with alacrity to the invitation to a kinder climate.

Bothwell tried to kidnap the king, and at Falkland, at the head of three hundred men, nearly succeeded. Again he invaded Holyroodhouse, to demand trial on the charge of witchcraft, and was rebuffed. Then, as superstitious fear abated, James was again perplexed by the political irresponsibility of the northern earls. A man called George Kerr, a Catholic, was stopped on his way to Spain, and in his possession were found several sheets of paper, blank but for the signatures of the Catholic earls of Huntly and Errol, of the recusant earl of Angus, and Gordon of Auchindoun. Kerr, under torture, confessed to yet another plot, initiated by the Jesuit, William Crighton, to offer assistance to Spain if the Spanish king could be persuaded to send an invading army to the Atlantic coast of Scotland.

The affair of 'the Spanish blanks' reveals, with unsparing clarity, not only the irresponsibility inherent in the Scottish aristocracy, but an ineptitude even more distressing; for what could be more devastatingly stupid than to give the equivalent of blank cheques—cheques drawn against an account lodged by treason—to an agent so incapable of his task as to let himself be captured with the evidence upon him? If James had had a standing army strong enough to exact respect, alike from nobility and churchmen, he might well have imposed the peace of law upon an acquiescent people; but he had no such army because he could not pay its wages. Poverty was a persistent blight on council chamber and the exercise of royal power: there were merchants in Edinburgh who grew rich by commerce and ingenuity, and nobles who could stiffen their native intransigence by the mobilisation of territorial levies; only the king lacked men and money.

He possessed, however, a curious self-confidence; a mind better than most contemporary minds; and a determination to live until he could enjoy the comfort and safety of the English throne. He managed to muster a force sufficient to put to flight and scatter the silly signatories of the Spanish blanks, but carefully refrained from any punishment so severe as to drive them into desperate antagonism. His politic leniency offended the kirk of Scotland and the queen of England, both of whom, as it appears, were equally unscrupulous in the measures they took to subdue and harness him to their own purposes: both encouraged Bothwell to continue his half-insane attempts to dominate the king by fear of his association with the powers of evil.

Again Bothwell invaded the palace of Holyroodhouse, and again bystanders watched the emotional, perhaps hysterical encounter of the challenged king and his brilliant but near-lunatic cousin. Bothwell's behaviour was theatrical; James was terrified, and in terror found the courage to defend his honour. Bothwell's supporters were outnumbered by the citizens of Edinburgh, who were always attracted to any source of trouble, and while James assured his people that all was well, Bothwell weakly consented to retire. He was forfeiting sympathy; he was, perhaps, losing confidence. Early in 1594 he led an armed attack on the king, and after that had failed he got no more support from England. He made a tentative alliance with the Catholic earls, and in consequence was abandoned by the kirk whose ministers had previously favoured him. A year later he left Scotland, and finding no occasion to return, died in Naples.

His association with the northern earls had provoked the king's displeasure, and the equal displeasure—fortunately for James—of the kirk, the emergent middle classes, and the minor lairds to whom presbyterianism made a pseudo-democratic appeal. With their help and approval James mounted a new offensive against his recalcitrant barons, and once more they retreated before him into the wilderness of the northern and north-western Highlands. A little while later, the earls of Huntly and Errol, who after submission had gone into exile, came back to Scotland, and turning their backs on Rome were received into the Reformed church of their native land. The menace of Catholic insurrection was now extinct, and James, who had been wooing his Presbyterians without making any large or material concessions to them, was soon in a position to rebuke and disarm the Protestant extremists.

The kirk, in its arrogance, had attempted to shape the country's politics. It had tried to prevent trade with France and Spain, it had presumed to dictate terms to England. It had rebuked the king for using intemperate language, and the queen for frivolity. The whole populace of Scotland was denounced for its failure to live according to the stern principles of the Reformation, and the minister of St.

Andrews announced his discovery that all monarchs were children of the devil. He called that doughty Protestant, Elizabeth of England, an atheist; and at Falkland Andrew Melville more mildly reminded King James that he was only 'God's silly vassal' and should be obedient to the kirk of Scotland that was now endowed with divine wisdom and divine authority. The Presbyterian pastors of Scotland anticipated, indeed, the policy of much later authoritarian states, and to obviate the perils of liberty of conscience demanded that ministers should constantly attend the king: Calvinism, as interpreted in Scotland, had close resemblances to the Communist practice of more recent times, and ministers of the kirk habitually attempted to assume the power of commissars.

But the ministers presumed too much and went too far even for James's tolerance. In Edinburgh, a little while before Christmas, 1596, they confected and pretended to discover a popish plot to murder the king and his council, and James was inspired to proclaim his wrath. The magistrates were daunted and the town was fined; the presbyterian conspirators were imprisoned in the castle and told they would not be released until the king should please to show his clemency. Bothwell had fled, and now Andrew Melville was discredited. The king, God's silly vassal, had shown his masterly patience; he had used, with great modesty, his native intelligence; he had exercised his elastic, pliant resolution to survive his enemies; and he was, in consequence—though still precariously—the master of his realm. He had had few resources outside his own mind and character; but so far they had sufficed him.

The contest between kirk and king is the most interesting feature of James's ruling years in Scotland—the anarchy and violence that tormented him were characteristic, not of his reign only, but of Scottish history as a whole—and the dominating new temper of the country is exquisitely revealed in the king himself. Andrew Melville and the angry ministers were hungry for power. In their reading of theology they were God's elect, his chosen agents and interpreters; but James was as learned and ardent a theologian as they, and according to his theology he was functionally nearer to God than any minister. A lawful and anointed monarch was responsible, not to his people, but only to God; and against such a monarch rebellion could never be justified. He, the king, was the author of law, and because he was the head of all three Estates, it was nonsense to say—as Melville said —that as Christ was the kirk's true king, supreme authority should be vested in a general assembly of the kirk; for only in him, James, lay the power to convene a general assembly. It was, in all probability, the temper and behaviour of Melville and his ministers that persuaded

James of the sheer necessity of bishops—men approved by himself and exalted by apostolic authority—while to such as Melville, who was sure that he stood closer to God than James could hope to come, a bishop was no better than a royal lackey, and a blasphemous intervention between God and his chosen Presbyterians. The pattern of the dispute which was to dominate and mortify so much of the seventeenth century was determined before the end of the sixteenth; and what helped to determine it was the fact that Scotland had a king who was as much concerned with God, and his relationship to God, as were the ministers of the Reformed church and an increasing number of those to whom they preached. Few of them, however, saw God as the author of justice and compassion. To most of the disputants—when dispute, a generation later, became lethal—God was valued as a king of Scotland had too often been valued: whoever could claim possession of him, enjoyed a political advantage that no rival could approach.

Accepted by the general assembly in 1578, Presbyterianism had been denounced in 1584, when Episcocacy was reaffirmed. But again the tide turned, and by 1592 the ebb had carried Episcopacy almost out of sight, and the Presbyterian system appeared to be an accomplished fact though bishops were not abolished, many parishes were still without a minister, and the general assembly acknowledged the king's right to summon it. After 1596 James decided not only when but where the assembly should be convened, and by politic exploitation of divisions within the kirk—not all of whose ministers trusted Melville —he added steadily to his regained authority. In 1600 bishops were appointed to the sees of Aberdeen, Ross, and Caithness: they had at first no local status, but they voted in parliament, and gradually acquired administrative functions. Only a few years now remained before James found a new throne in England, and during those years his power, in ecclesiastical matters, grew quietly and without offence.

He did not leave Scotland, however, without suffering a last demonstration of its curious temper. A tendency to break through the rational surface of existence—its daily rules and normal behaviour— had always characterised Scottish life, and on 5th August, 1600, James's life was endangered by what seems to have been violence of a quite irrational sort. Those involved with him were the young earl of Gowrie and his brother the Master of Ruthven, a youth of nineteen. James was hunting near Falkland when, according to his own statement, he was accosted by Ruthven, who told him a strange story of a man in Perth who had a pot of gold. He begged James to come with him to investigate, and later in the day James rode to Gowrie House with several attendants. He dined there, with Gowrie and Ruthven, and after dinner Ruthven took him to a room in a turret, where he found, no pot of gold, but a man in armour. Ruthven told him he must die, and after much altercation James struggled towards a window and shouted for help. His attendants rushed in, and a page called John Ramsay stabbed Ruthven in the back. Gowrie, sword in hand, came running up the turret stair, and Ramsay killed him too.

That was James's story, and many disbelieved it. But Gowrie was the grandson of Lord Ruthven, one of the murderers of Riccio, and son of the first earl of Gowrie, who had led the 'Ruthven Raid', to seize the king, in 1582. James's story may not have been wholly true, nor yet entirely false. There were some who thought it was he who began the quarrel—he owed Gowrie a large sum of money—but James was no fire-eater, and it seems improbable that he deliberately began brawling with Gowrie and his brother in Gowrie's own house. It is more likely that Gowrie, in alliance with the presbyterian extremists, was attempting to repeat the Ruthven Raid; for James summoned the five Protestant ministers of Edinburgh and commanded them to tell the story of the attempt on his life, and to lead their congregations in thanks for his safety. At first they refused, but James was insistent, and four of the five submitted. Throughout Scotland its ministers proclaimed a solemn thanksgiving, and the 5th of August, the day of his deliverance, was long celebrated with praise.

Before leaving Scotland the scholarly king found time to write a pamphlet entitled *The True Law of Free Monarchies*, in which he clarified and vigorously discussed his ideas on the divine right of kings; and another, more distinguished and better known, called *Basilikon Doron*. Henry, his elder son, was born in 1594; two daughters followed, Elizabeth and Margaret, the latter of whom died in infancy; and then, in 1600, came Charles. *Basilikon Doron* was a book of instruction for princes. Much of it was good instruction, and most of it was written in good, lively, vivid language: the young prince, indeed, was told to avoid 'pen and ink-horn terms' as well as vulgarity. Elsewhere he was told:

> Laws are ordained as rules of virtuous and social living, and not to be snares to trap your good subjects. . . .
> Learn also wisely to discern betwixt Justice and Equity; and for pity of the poor rob not the rich. . . .
> Where ye find a notable injury, spare not to give course to the torrents of your wrath. . . .
> But above all vertues, study to know well your own craft, which is to rule your people. . . .

Privately printed in 1599, *Basilikon Doron* was published in London about the time of Queen Elizabeth's death in 1603. It was immediately successful, and widely translated. It became evident, to his new subjects, that James was truly a man of letters; and in the high noon of English letters that was no small commendation.

Elizabeth had refused to name her successor, but in the last years of her reign there was general agreement that James would be England's next king. He had waited with what patience he could muster for his summons to London; and Robert Cecil—son of William, Lord Burghley, Elizabeth's chief minister—had made all ready for him. On Thursday, 24th March, the great queen died, and a few hours later James was proclaimed king in London, and Sir Robert Carey was riding to Edinburgh with the joyful news. He reached Holyroodhouse on Saturday night, and was rewarded for his promptitude with a post as Gentleman of the Bedchamber. Early in April, after listening to a sermon at St. Giles, James bade farewell to his people and rode south to a larger throne.

Chapter 8

IN spite of turbulent barons and a contumacious clergy, Scotland in the latter part of the sixteenth century was perhaps the most peaceful country in Europe, and in comparison with many others its people lived in enviable security. In France religious wars of the utmost savagery had erupted at brief intervals for nearly thirty years, from the massacre of Vassy in 1562 to the assassination of Henry III in 1589. In the Netherlands the duke of Alba's 'council of blood' had established so harsh a rule that despair turned into revolt and seemingly endless wars. In Italy and Poland religious enthusiasm had provoked bloodshed, and the Inquisition had crossed the sea to start new terror in the Indies. Even in England there were memories of economic chaos in the middle years of the century, of rebellion in Cornwall and Norfolk and Kent, and of the three hundred heretics burnt in Bloody Mary's reign; while in Ireland revolt was endemic and suppression merciless. In comparison with its neighbours Scotland had little cause for complaint.

James had hotly denounced the old raiding business of the border, which he saw clearly as an uncouth relic of more barbarous times, and a grievous danger to the friendship with England on which he set so much store. He was able to reduce the rough traffic of moonlit nights, but in 1596 his peaceful policy was rudely checked by the notorious affair of William Armstrong, known as Kinmont Willie. At a time of truce he was made prisoner by the English and taken to Carlisle, whose governor was Lord Scroope. This outrage against border law was made known to the laird of Buccleugh, who in the old fashion of his family determined that justice must be done without waste of time. As the ballad records:

> Now word is gane to the bauld Keeper,
>   In Branksome Ha', where that he lay,
> That Lord Scroope has ta'en the Kinmont Willie,
>   Between the hours of night and day.

[254]

He has ta'en the table wi' his hand,
    He garr'd the red wine spring on hie—
'Now Christ's curse on my head,' he said,
    'But avengèd of Lord Scroope I'll be!

'O is my basnet a widow's curch?
    Or my lance a wand of the willow-tree?
Or my arm a ladye's lilye hand,
    That an English lord should lightly me!

'And have they ta'en him, Kinmont Willie,
    Against the truce of Border tide?
And forgotten that the bauld Buccleugh
    Is Keeper here on the Scottish side?'

So the bold Buccleugh led forty troopers to Carlisle, and stormed the castle, found Kinmont Willie, and carried him back over the border before pursuit could overtake them. There was jubilation on the one side, furious remonstrance on the other; but both governments were sensible, and having appointed a joint commission to discuss better methods of administering justice, concluded a treaty which proved effective. A few years later, after James had gone to London, an armed constabulary was formed and many known thieves were hanged. When the border was no longer a frontier between hostile lands, its old traffic came to an end; and so did the ballads.

The Highlands and Islands had long been seats of dissent and a source of embarrassment to kings and their ministers who had never had the necessary power, or administrative machinery, to impose and maintain their rule in the farthest parts of Scotland. James had no respect for his Gaelic-speaking subjects: those on the mainland were, in his opinion, barbarians modified by some tincture of civilisation, but the men of the isles were like 'wolves and wild boars'. To demonstrate his authority he required Highland landowners to show their titles, and he made preparation to plant Lowland colonies in their midst. A company of gentlemen-adventurers, recruited in Fife, were given title to the island of Lewis and attempted to make a settlement near the present town of Stornoway: but the men of Lewis could not be conquered, were indifferent to bribes and deaf to persuasion, and the venture was a failure. More successful was the earl of Argyll's establishment of the burgh of Campbeltown, at the southern corner of the long peninsula of Kintyre, and his fortification with Lowlanders of the burgh of Inveraray.

The union of the crowns made more apparent a disability from which both kingdoms had suffered, at intervals, since Robert Bruce's

War of Independence. The Celtic people of Ireland and the Western Isles were related not merely by a common ancestry, but by antagonism to their more powerful mainland neighbours; Scotland, in consequence, had sometimes been able to take advantage of Ireland's native hostility to England, and England, especially during Elizabeth's reign, had made much use of the island clans' indifference to the Scottish throne's authority. From Antrim to Islay Clan Donald was dominant, and James's enlargement of Campbell power in the Kintyre peninsula was designed to separate the MacDonalds of Ireland from those of the Isles. The plantation of Ulster—its colonisation by Lowland Scots—which began about 1606 or 1607, completed the process and raised a dour, presbyterian barrier between the Irish Celts and their Hebridean cousins.

To authorise hostilities by one clan against another was the traditional method by which an impotent throne attempted to demonstrate its authority in Highland parts; and James, in the orthodox fashion, used Campbells against MacDonalds in the south-west, and Mackenzies against the Macleods of Lewis. The Mackenzies were more successful than the gentlemen-adventurers of Fife, and their chief, the earl of Seaforth, was hardly less powerful than Huntly or Argyll with their Gordons and Campbells behind them. But James was sensible enough to listen to good advice, and one of the bishops whom he had succeeded in imposing on the church was Andrew Knox, bishop of the Isles; who gave him very good advice. It was poor policy, said Knox, to exalt Clan Campbell at the expense of Clan Donald, for one was almost as pestiferous as the others. It would be wiser, he proposed, to put some trust in the chiefs of all the clans, and make them responsible for the behaviour of their people. His suggestion was the more feasible because in 1608 Andrew Stewart, Lord Ochiltree, on an expedition to the Hebrides, had succeeded in persuading many of the island chiefs to board his ship in the Sound of Mull; where he imprisoned them. And in the following year Bishop Knox—who had been with Ochiltree in the Sound of Mull—met the chiefs on Iona, and there induced them to promise, as well as obedience to the king, support for the Reformed church, the cause of temperance, and encouragement of the English language.

It is fairly evident that the success of royal policy, in the Highlands as on the border, was largely due to a general apprehension that James was about to acquire—or had newly acquired—a far greater power and authority and wealth than any previous Scottish king had known. There was widespread admission of his political advancement, and in many quarters, it is probable, a gratification comparable with his own.

[256]

It is pleasant, therefore, to record that in the enhancement of his power he listened to Bishop Knox's good advice, and was so prudent as to recognise—though perhaps reluctantly—a measure of social validity in the clan system. It was a system whose disadvantages were to become manifest in later years. It was static, it offered little opportunity for change, and none for progress. It prohibited—perhaps for Scotland's good—a union of all the Celtic clans, because its loyalties were too closely defined to permit of general union; and also, it may be, because there lingered in the Celtic ethos a stubborn mistrust of any larger association than was necessary to meet a momentary crisis. But within its limitations the clan was obviously a benign and satisfying association. Function was divided, but a basic unity was assumed. In daily practice there was no equality, or pretence of equality, but an organic relationship was an acknowledged thing and a binding thing. There were common memories, of song and story and an heroic past in the mythopoetic glens of Ireland; and in 1600, so far as anyone from the Mull of Kintyre to the Butt of Lewis could see, the future would be a common inheritance, as the past had been. Elsewhere there might be growth and change, but the Gaels of the west—who built nothing and made nothing but music—appear to have found an emotional stability in which they saw no need for change. The clans had earned the recognition that James had been persuaded to give them.

It would be entirely wrong to pretend that the Highlands and Islands had achieved an idyllic way of life, for poverty and hard weather were always too close to permit any sort of ease other than indolence, and any luxury more common than a few hundred good swords, and the wine and silver and velvet that were to be found in a score of grim castles. But it would be equally wrong to exclude from a picture of Highland Scotland a remarkable description of it left by a clever and amusing English visitor who was entertained there, in a lordly fashion, in the year 1618.

In the previous year James had revisited his northern kingdom, and gossip about it—or perhaps the king's suggestion—had roused in Ben Jonson's mind an eccentric resolution to follow his example. The great dramatist was forty-six, he weighed nearly twenty stone, and when he declared that he was going to walk to Scotland, the London wits decided to caricature so ludicrous a journey by sending after him, also on foot, a well-known local 'character' known as John Taylor the water-poet. A Thames boatman with a liking for travel and a rough-and-ready knack of versifying, Taylor had many friends and a genial temper, and in the Highlands he found a generous host in the earl of Mar. He was made welcome in a noble company that was gathered for some weeks of hunting near Braemar. As Taylor explains:

'Once in the year, which is the whole month of August, and sometimes part of September, many of the nobility and gentry of the kingdom, for their pleasure, do come into these Highland countries to hunt, where they do conform themselves to the habit of the Highland men, who for the most part speak nothing but Irish; and in former time were those people which were called the Red-shanks. Their habit is shoes with but one sole apiece; stocking, which they call short hose, made of a warm stuff of divers colours, which they call tartan: as for breeches, many of them nor their forefathers never wore any, but a jerkin of the same stuff that their hose is of, their garters being bands or wreaths of hay or straw, with a plaid about their shoulders, which is a mantle of divers colours, of much finer and lighter stuff than their hose, with blue flat caps on their heads, a handkerchief knit with two knots about their neck; and thus are they attired. Now their weapons are long bows and forked arrows, swords and targets, harquebusses, muskets, dirks, and Lochaber axes. With these arms I found many of them armed for the hunting. As for their attire, any man of what degree soever that comes amongst them must not disdain to wear it; for if they do, then they will disdain to hunt, or willingly to bring in their dogs: but if men be kind unto them, and be in their habit; then are they conquered with kindness, and the sport will be plentiful.'

After leaving Braemar they went for twelve days without seeing any inhabited place, but never lacked comfort. For kitchens would be dug in the side of a bank, fires lighted, and presently there would be 'many spits turning and winding, with great variety of cheer; as venison baked, sodden, roast, and stewed beef, mutton, goats, kid, hares, fresh salmon, pigeons, hens, capons, chickens, partridge, moor-coots, heath-cocks, capercailzies, and termagants (ptarmigans); good ale, sack, white, and claret, tent, or Alicante, with most potent Aquavitae.

'All these, and more than these we had continually, in superfluous abundance, caught by falconers, fowlers, fishers, and brought by my lord's tenants and purveyors to victual our camp, which consisted of fourteen or fifteen hundred men and horses. The manner of the hunting is this: five or six hundred men do rise early in the morning, and they do disperse themselves divers ways, and seven, eight, or ten miles compass, they do bring or chase in the deer in many herds, two, three, or four hundred in a herd, to such or such a place, as the Nobleman shall appoint them; then when day is come, the Lords and gentlemen of their companies, do ride or go to the said places, sometimes wading up to their middles through bournes and rivers. And then, they being come to the place, do lie down on the ground, till those foresaid scouts, which are called the Tinchel, do bring down the deer; but as the proverb says of a bad cook, so these Tinchelmen do lick their own fingers; for besides their bows and arrows, which they carry with them, we can hear now and then a harquebuss or a musket go off, which they do seldom discharge in vain. Then after we had stayed there three hours or thereabouts, we might perceive the deer appear on the hills round about us, their heads making a show like a wood, which being followed close by the Tinchel, are chased down into the valley where we lay; then all the valley on each side being waylaid with a hundred couple of strong Irish greyhounds, they are let loose as the occasion serves upon the herd of deer, so that with dogs, guns, arrows, dirks, and daggers, in the space of two hours, fourscore fat deer were slain.'

It was a lordly and enviable way of life that Taylor was allowed to see and share, and of which he wrote in his *Penniless Pilgrimage*. It was, admittedly, a way of life that could contribute nothing to the modern world which the Reformation had begun to shape and colour; but its continuing existence, in the first quarter of the seventeenth century, does much to explain the historical reluctance of the Highlanders to accept the authority of the central government; and Taylor's lively description of an heroic society in holiday mood certainly facilitates understanding of such a society's ability to threaten the established peace of the eighteenth century, as it did when Charles Edward Stuart landed and led a Jacobite rebellion as late as 1745. It was not until then that the last survivors of the antique world, whom Taylor had briefly visited, were finally defeated.

The fringes of that world were already sullied by contact with modern opportunity. In wild country about and beyond the head of Loch Awe lived the MacGregors, 'the Children of the Mist', in whose favour neither government nor their neighbours could find much to say. They lived largely on plunder and blackmail, and it was difficult to punish them because the great moor of Rannoch had been made for their protection, and in that watery wilderness, between quaking bog and frowning hill, it was impossible to find them. But in 1603, the year of James's removal to London, they went too far—in geography as well as outrage—when they embarked on a murderous raid against the Colquhouns of Glenfruin, near the south-western corner of Loch Lomond. That put an end to laissez-faire. The chief's name was proscribed, and to all Clan Gregor's neighbours a commission of fire and sword was given, with orders for the clan's extermination. In later years that dire punishment evoked a good deal of sentimental repining, but the Children of the Mist were indeed ruffians who could not be tolerated.

In the northern islands of Orkney and Shetland a little-regarded tragedy had been enacted. In 1564 Mary, queen of Scots, had granted a feu of their crown lands to her half-brother Robert, a bastard son of James V, who in his childhood had been made commendator of Holyrood. To the bishop of Orkney he gave the abbey of Holyrood in exchange for the bishopric lands in Orkney and Shetland; and having been appointed sheriff, was presently made earl of the former and lord of the latter. He was, in effect, their absolute monarch, and he and his successor in the earldom, his son Patrick, took ruthless advantage of their power, and the persistence of Norse law in Orkney, to enrich themselves and ruin the native landowners. They had a pretty taste for architecture, and indulged it with an extravagance that required for its support an ever more grasping tyranny. They reduced the islands to poverty, and not until 1609 was Earl Patrick summoned to Edinburgh to answer for suspected treason and his indebtedness to the lord provost of Edinburgh. He was imprisoned, and his gallant but imprudent son Robert raised a rebellion, seized Kirkwall castle, and for five weeks held it against a powerful artillery. He was betrayed, and taken to Edinburgh, where on 1st January, 1615, he was hanged at the Market Cross; and five weeks later his father was beheaded at the same place. Kirkwall castle was razed, the old Norse laws abolished, and for consolation the ruined islanders were left with two large, untenanted palaces, and two castles of great strength, that the iniquitous Stewart earls had either built or improved.

But Scotland, as a whole, lived in unwonted peace; and peace, by permitting trade and encouraging commerce, had begun to promote a prosperity which had outgrown the old qualifying adjective, 'modest'. There were rich men in Edinburgh—George Heriot and Robert Gourlay, Thomas Foulis and the richest of all, John MacMoran —who were merchants and commanded such sums of money as none of the great nobility could ever hope to see. The bulk of the population still lived on the land, and by the land, and paid their rents in kind. By husbandry and an agriculture that was sufficient though still primitive, the Scottish countryside bred beasts and grew corn enough to feed its people except in time of famine—and, be it noted, famine had more often been the consequence of war than of bad weather. A stable peace was the best defence against famine; and when prolonged good weather was added to peace, Scotland produced a surplus of grain that could be sold abroad. In good years agriculture did earn money; but it was designed and governed for subsistence rather than profit.

Commerce was almost confined to the east coast, where many harbours had been restored or improved. Wool and linen were exported to England, as were coal and salt in increasing quantities: on the coast of Fife coal was being mined from under the sea, and new methods had been discovered for draining pits and bringing coal to the surface. Leather was an important product, soap and glass were manufactured in small quantities. Scotland was surrounded by seas—and traversed by streams, inundated by lochs—that nurtured an incredible wealth of fishes; and Scotland did indeed export herring and salmon in appreciable quantities. But it was the Dutch who exploited the North Sea, from the Dogger Bank to the Shetlands, where yearly their fishing fleet numbered several hundred vessels. Both England and Scotland were curiously indifferent to the rich harvests that could be reaped at sea.

After some argument it had been agreed that the peoples of north and south Britain should enjoy common nationality, and that offered advantages which diminished the disadvantages of maintaining two parliaments and two administrative systems. Edinburgh seems to have suffered less than was probably expected by removal of the court to London, and John Taylor the water-poet pleasingly reports of the High Street that it was 'the fairest and goodliest street that ever mine eyes beheld, for I did never see or hear of a street of that length, which is half an English mile from the castle to a fair port which they call the Nether-Bow, and from that port, the street which they call the Kenny-gate is one quarter of a mile more, down to the King's Palace, called Holyrood House, the buildings on each side of the way being all of squared stone, five, six, and seven storeys high, and many byelanes and closes on each side of the way, wherein are gentlemen's houses, much fairer than the buildings in the High Street, for in the High Street the merchants and tradesmen do dwell, but the gentlemen's mansions and goodliest houses are obscurely founded in the aforesaid lanes: the walls are eight or ten foot thick, exceeding strong, not built for a day, a week, or a month, or a year but from antiquity to posterity, for many ages; there I found entertainment beyond my expectation or merit, and there is fish, flesh, bread and fruit, in such variety, that I think I may offenceless call it superfluity, or satiety'.

Though certainly a most genial man, Taylor's humour was a little ponderous, and to make it clear that he got enough to drink, as well as plenty to eat, he writes, with a pretended solemnity: 'The worst was, that wine and ale was so scarce, and the people there such misers of it, that every night before I went to bed, if any man had asked me a civil question, all the wit in my head could not have made him a sober answer.' This he can be forgiven, however, for his admirable account of the domestic economy of great houses in the northern parts of Scotland. It is, of course, an economy based upon a pastoral background and an almost absolute authority derived as much, one suspects, from Celtic tanistry as from feudal privilege; and it is a perfect complement to Taylor's picture of the hunting of the deer.

'I have been,' he writes, 'at houses like castles for building; the master of the house his beaver being his blue bonnet, one that will wear no other shirts, but of the flax that grows on his own ground, and of his wife's, daughters', or servants' spinning; that hath his stockings, hose, and jerkin of the wool of his own sheep's backs; that never by his pride of apparel caused mercer, draper, silk-man, embroiderer, or haberdasher to break and turn bankrupt. And yet this plain homespun fellow keeps and maintains thirty, forty, fifty, servants, or perhaps, more, every day relieving three or fourscore poor people at his gate; and besides all this, can give noble entertainment for four or five days together to five or six earls and lords, besides knights, gentlemen, and their followers, if they be three or four hundred men, and horse of them, where they shall not only feed but feast, and not feast but banquet, this is a man that desires to know nothing so much, as his duty to God and his King, whose greatest cares are to practise the works of piety, charity, and hospitality; he never studies the consuming art of fashionless fashions, he never tries his strength to bear four or five hundred acres on his back at once, his legs are always at liberty, not being fettered with golden garters, and manacled with artificial roses, whose weight, sometime, is the last reliques of some decayed Lordship. Many of these worthy housekeepers there are in Scotland, amongst some of them I was entertained.' A picture, too brightly coloured, of an idealised society? Yes, that is probable. But Taylor was a shrewd, travelled, hard-working cockney whose words and opinions deserve, perhaps, as much respect as has, more commonly, been given to Defoe, who came to Scotland a hundred years later. While commerce and wealth were steadily growing in the south and east of Scotland, did the rest of it live, without money, ambition, or desire of change, in a material sufficiency, rude enough, that music graced and a Celtic ethos gratified with notions of an organic unity?

It is a possibility that can neither be roughly rejected nor immediately approved. There are indications of dissatisfaction in several parts of Scotland: indications, it is clear, of a background too poorly furnished to give comfort to all it bred; of fields, perhaps, too small to feed all who lived beside them. In fairly large numbers young men either chose or were forced to go abroad to earn their living; but because many chose to earn it by military service, it remains doubtful whether their primary impulse was to escape poverty or to seek adventure. Over a period of several centuries the Celtic mothers of their race had been stimulated by the incursion of viking fathers, whose advent may or may not have led to a permanent relationship; and as the younger sons of viking chiefs found congenial occupation in the Varanger Guard of the eastern emperors, so, to their remote descendants, it may have seemed natural to take service in the armies of France, Sweden, and Holland.

The tradition of service to France went back at least as far as the battle of Baugé in 1421; and the *Garde Ecossaise*, after fighting for St. Joan, took precedence over all other troops in France. The Scots Guards were granted the Blessed Virgin herself as their honorary colonel-in-chief, and till the Revolution their captain stood by the king's side at his coronation. Scots by the thousand had fought and died under the lilies of France, and in the sixteenth century their range of action was greatly extended. The export of volunteer soldiers, under licence, to Denmark and Sweden and the Netherlands became a traffic comparable with the export, in later years, of gardeners, doctors, engineers, and university teachers. As early as 1572 some troops of Scottish cavalry were in Swedish service, and in that year a force of infantry, estimated at 4,000 men, sailed to Livonia under the command of Archibald Ruthven, a son of Patrick who played a leading part in the murder of Riccio. Sweden was at war with Russia, but the Scots fell out with their fellow-mercenaries, some regiments of German cavalry, and lost heavily in the subsequent fighting. The Scots were accused of mutiny, and Ruthven was sent back to Stockholm in irons. With him, also in irons, went Gilbert Balfour, who had been so deeply implicated in the murder of Darnley. They were accused of conspiring against the Swedish king, John III, and Ruthven died in prison, Balfour under the axe.

The long peace that rewarded James's patient skill upon the throne must have increased the birth-rate or largely added to an infant's expectation of life; for after 1600 the export of healthy young men advanced sharply. When the Thirty Years' War began in 1618, supply responded to a larger demand, and some distinguished action followed the expedition from Cromarty of a regiment levied by Lord Reay and commanded, for much of its service, by Colonel Robert Monro, under whom, with many of the same name, served another Robert, chief of the clan. They fought at first for Christian IV, king of Denmark, and covered themselves with glory, but suffered inordinately. Some years later, after reinforcement, they held Stralsund on the Baltic against a most furious assault by the redoubtable Wallenstein, commander-in-chief of the imperial forces. Again the regiment suffered grievously, but Wallenstein lost three times as many men, and was defeated. Lord Reay brought fresh reinforcements, and at its full strength of twelve companies the regiment entered the service of Gustavus Adolphus, Lion of the North, king of Sweden, and 'the Phoenix of his time', as Monro calls him.

In April, 1631, Monro commanded half the regiment at the storming of Frankfurt on the Oder. With three other regiments it formed the Scots Brigade, led by John Hepburn, a very gallant soldier. The Swedish king commanded his army in person, and committed it to battle with pomp and circumstance. The Scots Brigade assaulted one of the main entrances and fought superbly, but in a town whose streets were choked with corpses and the riches of the imperial baggage train, got out of hand. Five months later, at Breitenfeld near Leipzig, the imperial troops under Tilly were thrashed again, and of all his infantry Gustavus Adolphus praised most highly the Scots Brigade. At Lutzen, a year later, the Swedish army was again victorious, but Gustavus was killed; it was the first major action that he had fought without Scottish help, and to Colonel Monro the reason for his death was obvious.

There may have been as many as 10,000 Scots in the Swedish army; that is, indeed, a conservative estimate. Not all who fought in the Thirty Years' War were on the Protestant side, and not all confined their service to the honesty of formal battle. When the great Wallenstein was judged intolerable by the Emperor Ferdinand II—the magnificent and enigmatic Wallenstein, duke of Friedland, Sagan, and Mecklenburg—they who were commissioned to remove him were two Scots colonels, Gordon and Leslie, and an Irishman, Colonel Butler. Several of his supporters were murdered as a preliminary, and on 25th February, 1634, Wallenstein himself was assassinated at Eger (now called Cheb) in Czechoslovakia. Of the three colonels John Gordon was a Gordon of Gight, the family which, seven generations later, was greatly distinguished by the birth to Catherine, Mrs. Byron of Gight, of the poet Byron.

John Hepburn, who had commanded the Scots Brigade, later took what was left of it, reinforced yet again, into the French service, and le régiment d'Hébron distinguished itself in new battles under Turenne and Condé. Hepburn was made marshal of France, but was killed at the siege of Zabern before he got his baton. It is said that Mackay's regiment, in the Scots Brigade, had originally six-and-thirty pipers, of whom one only survived to go to France with Hepburn: if that is true—and the incidence of casualties makes the story not improbable —one must discard the notion that Scottish mercenaries went to war in search of a livelihood. Their circumstances at home may have been pinched and narrow, but when they went to war, in France and Sweden, in Denmark and Russia and the Netherlands—the Dutch and the Danes and the Swedes were all good paymasters—it was for pride and adventure, with a reasonable preference for service where rations were generous and accommodation weatherproof.

What is truly astonishing is to find evidence, repeated again and again, not only of the natural bravery of the Scottish soldiers, but of their capacity to accept discipline, and by the application of discipline to bravery and initiative, to become soldiers capable of meeting, and often beating, the best continental troops. In their own country, over the centuries, they had lost battle after battle against the English because of tactical errors for a start and then failure of discipline that made error irretrievable: courage was taken for granted, but intelligence was left at home. The reason for failure—whether political, strategic, or tactical in origin—was usually all too manifest: discipline was unfastened by jealousy, distrust was endemic, and the left wing rarely obeyed an order until it had seen what the right wing was going to do. In a foreign country, however, local jealousies diminished; distrust vanished when all the regiments in the Scots Brigade were subject to an alien voice; and Scottish pride, that would never submit to a neighbour, found no difficulty in taking orders from Condé or the good and careful Swedish general Horn. Only at home were the Scots deeply and persistently irrational. Released from the emotional confines of clan and family territory, they showed themselves able to use abilities previously unsuspected, and some possessed an intelligence which, though rarely gracious, was truly respectable.

In the eighteenth century—which, with the antique heroism of Bruce's War of Independence, offers the world some reason for admiration of Scotland's genius—it was native intelligence, deployed in many shapes and unexpected directions, that demonstrated to the world the quite improbable fact that Scotland had survived the loss of its parliament, the loss of a whole and independent throne, and was still a living reality—visible, palpable, *sui generis*, and recognisable. And as if to anticipate, or utter a warning of what was to happen, an intelligence as anarchic as any unruly noble revealed itself, in a flash of disconcerting brilliance, in the early years of the seventeenth century.

Intellectually, indeed, the age was fairly lively. Robert Reid, bishop of Orkney, died in 1558 and left 8,000 marks to buy land in Edinburgh for the foundation of a college; and twenty-four years later the Privy Council released his bequest for the purpose specified. Scotland's fourth university made its tentative appearance, and in due course received the blessing of King James. He granted a charter for the *academia Jacobi sexti*, but left its management and development to the town council. It became the 'tounis colledge', and its professors taught—at least in theory—all the subjects of the *trivium* (grammar, i.e. Latin, logic and rhetoric) and the quadrivium (arithmetic, geometry, music, and astronomy). The college of Glasgow had been restored and given new life by Andrew Melville; St. Andrews acquired a new constitution, King's college in Aberdeen a new foundation; and in Aberdeen George Keith, the earl Marischal, endowed a second college.

There were, in Scotland, a few scholars of international repute, and some attempt to establish new industries had attracted attention to the elements of applied science. But there is nothing to account for the meteoric emergence of John Napier, eighth laird of Merchiston, who was born in 1550, before Archibald, his father, was sixteen. His father's father was killed at the battle of Pinkie. His great-grandfather, whose father, grandfather and great-grandfather had all been provosts of Edinburgh, fought at Flodden. Archibald Napier was subsequently appointed master of the mint, an office he held for a quarter of a century; the wife whom he had married at a tender age was a sister of Adam Bothwell, some-time bishop of Orkney, who had married Mary, queen of Scots, to another Bothwell.

John Napier was educated at St. Andrews, travelled on the continent, and lived a private and secluded life until he was forty-three when he published a theological work entitled *A Plaine Discovery of the Whole Revelation of Saint John*. He was an ardent Protestant, and at that time there was fear of invasion by Philip of Spain; Napier busied himself therefore with the invention of new weapons of war, among them a burning mirror to set fire to ships, a gun to engage targets round the arc of a circle, and what seems to have been a primitive tank. It was not until 1614, when Napier was sixty-four, that he published a work which, it has been said, can be placed second only to Newton's *Principia*; and gave to the world the new word 'logarithms', which he invented for his discovery.

As a contribution to science, in that age, it stands alone; there is no one but Napier, of British origin, who may be compared with Kepler or Galileo or Tycho Brahe. His discovery, moreover, had been made in a solitude far removed from the assistance of congenial minds. It was a gesture of most laudable independence in a country where gestures of independence had too often been destructive.

[266]

Chapter 9

KING James's journey to London, in April, 1603, was a triumphal progress. Everywhere he was made welcome, feasted and applauded. Since Elizabeth's death he had been flattered by the attention of those who were quick to see that he had new and greater favours to bestow; and consciousness of unaccustomed wealth made him lavish with his favours. Before he reached London his subjects included three hundred new knights. Crowds awaited him, and in noble houses banquets sustained him. The enthusiasm with which he was greeted was perfectly genuine, for Elizabeth, though a great queen, had died old, unmarried, and childless; and a king with a growing family promised security of a sort that England had not known for nearly sixty years.

Throughout her reign Elizabeth had relied primarily, and principally, on William Cecil, Lord Burghley, her chief minister; he was a cautious man, virtuous without high principle, and his service to England was very great. His final benefaction was to beget upon his second wife a son Robert, who, before Burghley died in 1598, had already stepped into his father's shoes, and for a couple of years before James came to London was in secret correspondence with him. For the smoothness and ease of James's passage from one throne to another he was vastly indebted to Robert Cecil; and until his death Cecil served England and his sovereign as devotedly as his father had done. He was a little, misshapen man, with a grave and noble head, whom Elizabeth had called her pygmy, and whom James called his beagle.

James and Anne his queen were crowned at the end of July—in a ceremony curtailed by a raging epidemic of the plague—and he soon began to show himself impatient of the noisy multitudes who lay in wait to watch and applaud him. He had been a king for as long as he could remember, and though less contemptuous than Coriolanus of the common cry—'whose breath I hate as reek o' the rotten fens'—and less extreme than Jefferson Davis—'All we ask is to be let alone'—

he took no pleasure in the mere noise of loyalty, and was unimpressed by numbers. In a smaller, more carefully chosen company he was affable and easy of approach, simple and friendly in his manner, ready of speech and quick-witted. Foreign ambassadors were impressed by him, and by his knowledge of languages; and churchmen were filled with admiration of his close acquaintance with the scriptures and his willingness to discuss them. He was thirty-seven when he arrived in England, and observers found him a good-looking man, bland and ruddy, rather above the middle height, and simply dressed.

It soon became evident that James not only recognised his good fortune, but was determined to enjoy it. His passion for hunting found new scope in the well stocked deer parks which were among the notable amenities of English country life, and most of the labour of government was left to Cecil, his little beagle, and other able, well-intentioned men—of whom, in England, there was no lack—while the king, attended by a numerous retinue, rode from one lordly mansion to another, in quest of sport. His critics complained that he would fall into a bad temper if matters of state, or even foul weather, threatened to interrupt his hunting. When confronted by armed and rebellious Scotch earls he had sometimes betrayed so much consternation as to create an impression that he was preternaturally timid—though many of his contemporaries would also have quailed before an arrogant Huntly, a sinister Gowrie, or the near-maniac Bothwell—but James on horseback, following running hounds in pursuit of a stag through woodland or over open country, appears to have been, not fearless only, but quite reckless, and undeterred by falls and injury. And then, having killed and gralloched his stag, he would be ready for argument about original sin, or the Mosaic authorship of the Pentateuch, with any available bishop whose learning was sufficient for serious encounter and who had a head for wine.

Adverse criticism of James cannot all be accepted as true. In later life he was grossly self-indulgent, he lacked taste and discretion, but his manifest weaknesses were not so malignant as to provoke major calamity in either of his kingdoms, and his insistence that England should live at peace with Spain, and could promote a foreign policy based on pacific intention, does not suggest that he wholly ignored the council chamber and spent all his time in the hunting field. He invited adverse criticism because he was a Scot, and in England there have, for a long time, been those who believe or have believed that the voices, habits, mannerisms and ideas of less fortunate beings born north of Berwick, east of Calais, or west of the Irish Sea are slightly but inherently ludicrous. He demanded criticism because he advocated a policy of peace—of peace with Spain—that was hotly disliked and actively deprecated in England at a time when English seamen were sublimely confident of their ability to defeat and most profitably plunder the Spanish treasure-ships that carried in their holds the gold and silver of the New World. And conspicuous among those who criticised, and whose criticism has sometimes been taken seriously, was a lively gossip called Antony Weldon, whose motive was so obviously malicious that much of what he wrote deserves little consideration except as an expression of malice; while another was a celebrated wit, Sir John Harington. But Harington was clever, and is worth quoting.

He was a godson of Queen Elizabeth and is chiefly famous for his essays entitled *The Metamorphosis of Ajax* and *Ulysses upon Ajax*, which are commonly decried as Rabelaisan, and anticipate the mechanics of modern sanitation with an ingenious specification for a water-closet. Among his later writings was a description of some part of the entertainment offered to the Danish king Christian IV, James's brother-in-law, who was invited to London on a state visit in the summer of 1606. Robert Cecil, by then elevated to the earldom of Salisbury, was on one occasion host to both kings at his great house of Theobalds, and for their pleasure devised a masque of Solomon and the queen of Sheba; but, according to Harington, he had given, not only the actors and actresses in the masque, but all his guests, too much to drink, with calamitous results.

'The lady who did play the Queen's part did carry most precious gifts to both their Majesties; but forgetting the steps arising to the canopy overset her caskets into his Danish Majesty's lap and fell at his feet, though I rather think it was in his face. Much was the hurry and confusion; cloths and napkins were at hand to make all clean. His Majesty then got up and would dance with the Queen of Sheba; but he fell down and humbled himself before her and was carried to an inner chamber and laid on a bed of state, which was not a little defiled with the presents of the Queen which had been bestowed on his garments, such as wine, cream, jelly, beverage, cakes, spices and other good matters. The entertainment went forward and most of the presenters went backward or fell down, wine did so occupy their upper chambers. Now did appear Hope, Faith, and Charity. Hope did assay to speak but wine rendered her endeavours so feeble that she withdrew and hoped the King would excuse her brevity. Faith was then all alone for I am certain she was not joined with good works, but left the court in a staggering condition. Charity came to the King's feet and seemed to cover the multitide of sins her sisters had committed. In some sort she made obeisance and brought gifts, but said she would return home again as there was no gift which heaven had not already given his Majesty. She then returned to Hope and Faith who were both sick and spewing in the lower hall.' They were followed by Victory, who unhappily fell asleep; and by Peace, who, being out of temper, soundly thwacked her attendants with her olive-branch.

The Danes were notorious for the pleasure they took in deep drinking, and there is no reason for supposing that the Danish king was not liberally entertained; but Harington's description of the masque at Theobalds cannot be accepted as an objective account of what happened there. It is, quite simply, too good to be true. It is useful, however, as a reminder that James and his high-spirited queen became patrons of an art-form that grew quickly, lived in exotic splendour for nearly forty years, and was utterly extinguished by civil war. The masque found favour, as entertainment for the court, because Ben Jonson was able to use his hard and ponderous intellect in the confection of gay, whimsical, learned trifles of a sort to please a learned king; because Inigo Jones, first of the great English architects, was willing to turn his Palladian gifts to the designing of costumes and stage scenery; and—to a lesser degree—because the old queen, always acquisitive and even a hoarder, had left a huge wardrobe of rich dresses, about two thousand of them, that James's queen and her ladies could shape anew to clothe Jonson's erudite inventions. The masque outlived both James and Jonson—though only by a few years—but in the tale of English literature it survives only as a Jacobean ornament and a curiosity sponsored by a matching interest in the byways of scholarship on the one side, by Danish gaiety on the other, and by extravagance common to both.

Far from Whitehall and the magnificent fopperies that Inigo Jones confected, James's northern kingdom lived in a peace so little troubled, and so unfamiliar, that there is some excuse for likening it to suspended animation. Armed hostility between Scotland and England—though not between Scots and English in the disturbed loyalties of civil war—had indeed been permanently suspended; and James could boast, not untruthfully, that where his predecessors had failed to govern with the sword, he governed with the pen. His Privy Council sat in Edinburgh, received his orders, and promulgated them. His parliament met occasionally to elect the Lords of the Articles—an executive committee—and usually elected the king's nominees. His influence had grown by his removal from the fear of being kidnapped, from the humiliation of public rebuke by ministers of the kirk; and his prestige was magnified by the wealth and power of England. Scotland had never had a stronger king than James who ruled it from London.

[270]

He failed to bring about total union between his countries, because the English refused to grant the Scots equal trading rights, but the union flag was a patent of common citizenship and his own royal style was changed to 'king of *Great Britain*, France and Ireland'. He established almost complete authority over the general assembly of the kirk: Andrew Melville was sent into exile for stubborn disobedience, and in compliance with the policy and belief he condensed into the phrase 'No bishop, no king', more bishops were imposed on or insinuated into the kirk, and their ecclesiastical status was enhanced by consecration from their English colleagues. When, however, he tried to improve the order of church service, his Scottish subjects indignantly refused to kneel for the eucharist—in their opinion only papists would stoop so low—and James was too sensible to insist on a posture that roused so much feeling.

In England politics were more complicated, and his vastly augmented authority induced in James an ambition to play the peacemaker for all Europe which, though undoubtedly based upon an honest and honourable belief that peace in all ways was preferable to war, involved him in political contradictions which were irreconcilable. Peace was concluded with Spain in August, 1604, though many of his subjects had found hostilities profitable, and others, perturbed by the continuing Catholic menace to England, more gravely argued that war with Spain should be maintained until the stubborn champions of Catholicism had been decisively beaten. For that treaty James was indebted to the diplomacy of Robert Cecil, whose continuing service was subsequently rewarded with the earldom of Salisbury. He too was a peacemaker by temperament and conviction, and for a decade or more the peaceful policy that he pursued and his master advocated can be called successful. They were fortuitously absolved from suspicion of popish sympathies —that the treaty with Spain had evoked in minds prone to suspicion— by discovery, in 1605, of the Gunpowder Plot.

The most celebrated of all English conspiracies was characterised— as political conspiracy so often is—by naïveté and betrayal. The purpose of the plot was to destroy the king and his parliament, both Lords and Commons, on 5th November, the day of the opening of parliament, by exploding beneath them a cellar charged with gunpowder; and the conspirators may have been indebted, for their plan, to the explosion that demolished Kirk o' Field, and Darnley, in 1567. Casks of gunpowder were successfully installed, and Guy (or Guido) Fawkes, a brave but not over-intelligent Yorkshireman, was enlisted to detonate them. The English Catholics had anticipated, under James, some measure of toleration, and in Warwickshire a group of local gentry had resolved on violent protest against the government's decision to enforce Queen Elizabeth's penal laws. They were betrayed, and their plot was discovered. Its exposure created a vast excitement, but there was no evidence of any large-scale Catholic involvement, or, as was suspected at the time, of Jesuitical direction. It was, in fact, merely an ebullition of provincial dissent, and its only lasting effect was to enrich English life with the most popular of its anti-heroes, Guy Fawkes.

It was unfortunate for James that in her old age his great predecessor had been somewhat negligent of her kingdom and its problems. She had refused to name her heir; she had left the church of England uncertain of its policy and discipline in a society lately menaced by extreme Puritanism and still subject to its influence; and she had been unaware of, or indifferent to, those changing views of the inherent or constituted authority of the crown which the Reformation had sponsored and encouraged. With the authority of her years she had been able to manipulate or defy an increasingly restive House of Commons, but her successor's ability to deal with a new, emergent power was diminished by his intransigent belief in his divine right to suppress it. To a parliament that had acquired a great deal of power, and was stubbornly convinced of its importance, James declared that the state of monarchy was 'the supremest thing upon earth', and his faithful Commons might debate only what he proposed for debate. They must not try to teach him how to govern, and he alone could redress grievances. The House of Commons could talk of privilege, but a king was God's lieutenant on earth, and James had no doubt of the validity of his commission. On this, and many other subjects, he addressed his parliament with eloquence and learning; but he spoke too often and too long.

He quarrelled with Coke, the chief justice: It is I who protect the law, said the king; Not at all, said Coke, it is the law that protects you. The royal prerogative fell into larger difficulties when it proved incapable of coping with royal expenditure. The king was irrepressibly extravagant, and Salisbury—now treasurer as well as secretary—reduced his debts and raised receipts, but was unable to solve the problem posed by expenditure that still exceeded his augmented income. The king must seek help from parliament, he said.

In 1610 James met the Commons and agreement was almost reached that, in return for the surrender of certain feudal rights, he should receive an annual income of £200,000. But again James talked too much—appeared to threaten freedom of speech—and the Great Contract, as it was called, faded and vanished. James lost his temper, refused to negotiate further, and in January, 1611, dissolved parliament. That year, however, despite its inauspicious beginning, saw the completion of a task, undertaken seven years before, that was to create for the king the most enduring monument of his reign, and for England a literary masterpiece for which no compeer was ever to be found except in the mightiest works of the Elizabethan or Jacobean theatre. The Authorised Version of the Bible was very much the product of King James's absorbing interest in scholarship and theology, and essentially the creation of the age in which it came into being; for at no other time has the English language been at once so lyrical and so majestical, so deep and sublimely capable of all, and so brightly new from the mint.

It was at a conference, summoned by James to Hampton Court to resolve churchly differences, that a proposal was made, by Dr. Reynolds of the college of Corpus Christi, Oxford, for a new translation of the Bible; and James, immediately enthusiastic, declared that he had never seen a well-written Bible, and at once proposed that 'special pains' should be taken for a uniform translation 'to be done by the best learned in both the universities; after them to be reviewed by the bishops and the chief learned of the church; from them to be presented to the privy council; and lastly to be ratified by his royal authority'. Some fifty translators—prodigies of scholarship among them—were chosen without reference to party, about half being Puritans, and with elaborate rules of work before them sat down in six groups, two at Westminster, two at Oxford, two at Cambridge. Each man worked separately, offered his work for scrutiny by his colleagues, and remembered the king's injunction that for declarations of belief, clear, simple, comprehensive English was to be used. The accuracy of their translation has often been challenged by later scholars, but with consummate taste they avoided vulgarity, pedantry, and improper elegance; and the beauty of their translation has ensured for 'King James's Bible' not only the devotion of Fundamentalists who recognise in all its chapters the dictation of God, but the admiration of critics whose high regard for language may be justified by belief 'that in the beginning was the word'.

It may be noted that the official adoption and authorisation of the new version applied only to England, for the Scots Presbyterians repudiated a standard translation. But a nineteenth-century historian[1] wrote that 'it was in Scotland that the authorised version received in the end the warmest welcome. It became the absolute standard in some respects of literature as well as of religion. Many would read no other book; and throughout the Protestant community all who professed

[1] John Hill Burton.

a decorous walk in life counted it the court of absolute and last appeal from all other literature.' It is pleasantly ironical to think that King James, who was treated so roughly and with so little respect by Andrew Melville and many ministers of the kirk, achieved eventually by his work so profound and far-reaching an influence over the faithful that, in comparison, all the ministers and elders of all the presbyteries in Scotland built by their exhortations but a molehill beside the Ararat of piety that he had raised.

In 1612 he and England suffered two losses, the one irreparable, the other incalculable. Salisbury died in May, perhaps of overwork and consequent exhaustion; and in early November, of typhoid fever, Henry, prince of Wales. James's elder son was only eighteen, but a young man who promised uncommon ability. There survives a miniature of him, by Isaac Oliver, that shows a profile of daunting severity, a grave, wide-open eye, under thick, auburn hair: he was devoted to martial exercise, deeply interested in the naval shipyard at Chatham. He was thought to be ambitious, he appeared to be religious, he was reticent and fearless, and out of sympathy with his father. Had he lived, he might have led his two countries into ruinous, quixotic wars; he might, on the other hand, have prevented their futile wars of religion.

Before Salisbury died James had already made evident the first of those absurd sentimental attachments that disfigured his latter years. The young man on whom he lavished undeserved favours was Robert Kerr, son of a respectable border family—his father was Sir Thomas of Ferniehurst, his mother a Scott of Buccleugh—whose principal gifts were high spirits, a good temper, and a handsome appearance. It was not for long that he exercised any influence on the king, but he was ennobled as earl of Somerset; it may have been he who advised James to dismiss his parliament in 1610; and certainly he involved his royal master in the scandalous revelations that followed the murder, in the Tower, of Sir Thomas Overbury.

Somerset had allied himself with the Catholic Howards and the pro-Spanish party. There were numerous Howards of whom the oldest was the gallant admiral who had commanded against the invincible Armada, and the most important, at this time, Henry, earl of Northampton. His nephew, the earl of Suffolk, had a beautiful and vicious daughter, Fanny, who was married to the young earl of Essex, son of Elizabeth's favourite. When she became Somerset's mistress, King James was persuaded to intervene, on behalf of Somerset and Fanny, in her action to divorce Essex. A former friend of Somerset, a clever, insolent young man called Sir Thomas Overbury, had sturdily opposed Somerset's wish to marry Fanny, and a few days before she was granted her divorce, Overbury—who happened to be a prisoner in the Tower—was murdered. Fanny and Somerset were married at Christmas, 1613, with lavish ceremony paid for by the king, and in a little while Somerset, swollen by power, lost friends and grew arrogant. He fell out with the king, and in the autumn of 1615 the lieutenant of the Tower confessed his knowledge that Overbury had been poisoned. The king commanded an inquiry—Francis Bacon was one of the commissioners—and at the trial both Fanny and Somerset were found guilty, though Somerset maintained his innocence to the end. They were sentenced to death, but escaped the gallows and were committed to the Tower.

It is worth attention that James, so often accused of a besotted attachment to his favourites, was, in the matter of Somerset, entirely immune from the jealousy so commonly associated with homosexual association; Somerset's marriage to Fanny Howard was certainly not a marriage of convenience—which might have explained James's complaisance—but a union dictated by natural passion. Yet James, so far from opposing, did all he could to promote it; and the manifest inference is that the favours he showed to Somerset, foolish though they were, must be ascribed, not to perversity, but to mere sentimentality. Attracted to the young man's good looks and gaiety, he thought, after Prince Henry's death, that he could find in him a substitute for the gifted and handsome son of whom he had been so cruelly robbed.

Before Somerset fell from favour another young man, equally attractive and endowed with slightly more ability—a livelier though by no means adequate intelligence—had been brought to James's notice, and speedily found favour. He was George Villiers, son of a poor Leicestershire knight, who moved rapidly up the ladder of favour—as if titles were rungs on the ladder—until, in 1623 at the age of thirty-one, he was created duke of Buckingham; and as such he was closely involved in English policy, both foreign and domestic, until, in the third year of the reign of James's surviving son, Charles I, he was assassinated by John Felton, a soldier justifiably enraged by Buckingham's ineptitude as a military commander.

Here, however, one is concerned only with political measures that affected, or were to affect, the people and condition of Scotland, and with those aspects of the royal character that contribute to a portrait of the last king of Scotland to be born upon its soil and rule from an independent throne. His relations with his English parliament require attention in view of the increasing part that parliament, in the next

[275]

reign, was to play in the affairs of both England and Scotland; and the parliament that James was persuaded to summon in 1614 permitted little hope that his son Charles would establish an easy association with so democratic an institution.

James in his address was tactless and fulsome. He praised himself, he called for love and harmony, and asked for money. He got, in return, nothing but a loud recital of grievances, and within two months parliament was dissolved. Seven years later a major crisis in foreign affairs, and urgent need of money, compelled its return to Westminster; and for explanation of the crisis it is necessary to turn back to the year 1613, when James's daughter Elizabeth was married, with great ceremony, to Frederick V, the Elector Palatine, the leading Calvinist prince of Germany, nominal head of the German Protestant Union. The dynastic importance of the Princess Elizabeth will be explicated later; here it is sufficient to say that she was to become the link between the old royal families of Scotland and England, and the present monarch. In 1619 the Protestants of Bohemia revolted against Austria, and offered their crown to Frederick. When he was threatened by Spain his father-in-law failed to support him, but offered to mediate. Mediation was unsuccessful and the winter king of Bohemia was defeated by the imperial forces at the White Mountain outside Prague in 1620. A little while later the Palatinate was overrun by the Spaniards, and Frederick and his wife fled into poverty and exile.

In England there was profound and widespread anger: the larger part of England was hotly Protestant in sympathy, and Elizabeth, gay and beautiful, had been greatly loved. James, it appears, had been incapacitated by three factors: his long-cherished pacifism, an inability to act or reach decision that may be ascribed to the weakness of pre-senility, and his extraordinary belief in—his curious reliance on—Gondomar, the exceptionally able Spanish ambassador. His mind was still dominated by the idea that had been foremost when he first came to England: that a policy of general peace must be begun by making peace with Spain. He wanted his son Charles to marry the Infanta of Spain, while his parliament wanted to go to war against Spain. The House of Commons asserted its rights and privilege, and James replied that their rights were derived only from the generosity of his predecessors, and his prerogative dominated all. When the impasse became absolute, James asserted his royal authority, accepted the fact that a disobedient parliament would not vote him the financial supply he wanted, and dissolved it. That was a major rebuff to a tentatively emerging political realism that, had it been both encouraged and controlled by a king in sympathy with his parliament, might have led to

[276]

a constitutional monarchy strong enough to resist the disruptive forces already brewing where extreme Puritanism found support in the self-righteousness of the newly rich.

James was still urgently in favour of the Spanish match, but Spain was difficult and the Infanta disinclined to marry a heretic. In 1623 Buckingham absurdly proposed that he and Prince Charles should ride incognito through France to press their suit in person; and the king, ill with arthritis and the stone, reluctantly agreed. In their absence he was a prey to anxiety, and wrote to them with tearful affection: 'God bless you both, my sweet babes, and send you a safe and happy return.' He invited Buckingham's wife and sister to dine with him, and they discussed the teething problems of a Buckingham baby. It seems unnecessary to suspect him of any perversion other than sentimentality. When Charles and his bear-leader returned empty-handed from Spain they were welcomed with love and rejoicing, as if their mission had been triumphantly successful.

Early in 1625 the king, who was fifty-eight, fell ill with a fever, and on 27th March he died. The indolence and self-indulgence that disfigured his last years cannot be regarded as characteristic of his whole life, or of his rule in Scotland and England. The mere fact that he had been a king for fifty-seven of his fifty-eight years indicates a capacity for survival that must have been built on qualities of resilience and resolution, of intelligence and confidence; and it must be remembered that many who knew him when he was young were much impressed by his ability. By any pragmatic judgement he was certainly the most successful of Scottish monarchs, and there is no denying that he was the most learned and literate of British kings. It must be admitted, however, that the aggregate of all his good qualities and abilities was still insufficient to warrant his belief in divine right to rule as he pleased: a belief which left to his successor a disastrous heritage, and must finally be condemned because it was already out of date.

Book Five

THE
WASTED
CENTURY

Chapter I

THE reign of James VI and I may be regarded as the culmination of a story that began with Robert the Bruce's violent assumption of Scotland's crown; and the reign of his successor was the prelude to a return of violence and a new phase in the story which, for the better part of half a century, seemed likely to be its concluding chapter.

Charles I inherited from his father a fatal belief in the divine right of kings without the saving weakness which had protected James against the consequences of intransigence in error. When James encountered opposition too stubborn to be overcome, he often lost interest in his purpose—consoled himself with wine, theology, or the headlong pursuit of a stag—and so avoided the penalties of error. But Charles had few weaknesses other than lack of judgement. He was a grave young man, twenty-five when he succeeded to the throne, who had outlived childish illnesses and early disabilities to become, like his father, a good horseman. John Milton jealously complained that he spent too much time reading Shakespeare; and he developed an aesthetic taste that let him assemble a collection of pictures of outstanding beauty and importance. In 1625, before Charles's accession, Peter Paul Rubens wrote of him: *Monsieur le Prince de Galles est le prince le plus amateur de la peinture qui soit au monde.* And after his execution Cromwell proved the soundness of Charles's taste by selling many of his pictures for a sum of money that his arbitrary government sorely needed. If Charles's political judgement had been as perceptive as his eye for paint, he would have been a monarch of memorable achievement; but he was withdrawn and ill at ease in the world, friendless after Buckingham's death, and apparently a cold perfectionist who saw no prospect of achieving the ideal order for which he hoped save by the rigid application of episcopal discipline. He was a devoted churchman, and though his execution did not make him a martyr, the manner of his death illuminated the purity of his motives and the real nobility of his character. Before he died, however, he had had time to match his own high-minded obstinacy against the intractable zeal of the Puritans, and between them they inflicted on Britain the peculiar beastliness of civil war.

He first gave offence by marrying a Catholic princess, Henrietta Maria, daughter of Henry IV of France; and then alienated most of the Scottish landowners by an act of revocation that cancelled all grants of crown property since 1540, and all dispositions of church property. Such acts were common enough, but Charles was suspect because of his English upbringing and what was thought to be his excessive sympathy with Catholicism. In the event the act inaugurated prolonged and complicated negotiations, the purpose of which was to reform the finances of the church, and which finally made it possible to augment the stipends of the Reformed clergy from 'teinds'—a tax amounting to one-tenth of the produce of the soil—and from the lands of the old church. The measures undertaken for this laudable purpose were sound and sensible, but they may have been introduced with too brusque a show of authority; and Charles offended many of his nobles by restriction of their privilege and his extreme veneration of bishops, which exalted them above their usual station.

Not until 1633 did he visit Scotland, when in the abbey church of Holyrood he was crowned with unusual splendour and a ritual emphasised by Charles's command that the officiating clergy were to wear surplices. That was widely regarded as a sinister innovation, and before long there was talk of a calamitous innovation. English church-men—most influential of whom was William Laud, archbishop of Canterbury—were convinced that Scotland should accept the English prayer book, and Charles was inclined to agree with them. The Scottish bishops, however, were determined to compile their own, and in 1637 a liturgy was agreed upon that conceded much to Scottish practice. But the book appeared, and its use was commanded, by sole authority of the king, and in the office prescribed for Holy Communion the table was to be placed, as if it were an altar, against the east wall, and the minister would stand, during his prayer of consecration, with his back to the people. There, on the one hand, was the threat of absolutism, and, on the other—or so it was generally believed —the old menace of popery. When the prayer book was introduced at St. Giles, in July, 1637, it provoked a riot that had probably been rehearsed.

The tumult began as soon as the dean opened the new liturgy. There arose 'such an uncouth noise and hubbub in the Church that not any one could either hear or be heard. The gentlewomen did fall a tearing and crying that the Mass was entered among them and Baal in the Church. There was a gentleman who standing behind a pew and answering Amen to what the Dean was reading, a she zealot hearing him starts up in choler, "Traitor (says she), dost thou say Mass at my ear", and with that struck him on the face with her bible in great indignation and fury.'[1] That was the riot which, according to a long cherished tradition, was started by a pious woman called Jenny Geddes who was so infuriated by the impious words of the liturgy that she was impelled to throw her stool at the dean. But Jenny Geddes is not warranted by history, and some of the apparently female zealots may in fact have been apprentices in disguise; for it was observed that they threw their stools 'to a great length'.[2] But whatever the true nature of the congregation, the service closed in utter confusion; the efforts of Archbishop Spottiswoode to calm and quieten the rioters were ignored, and the bishop of Edinburgh was chased home with stones and abuse.

Throughout the autumn and early winter the Privy Council received from many parts of the country petitions from all classes of the community, and all burdened with the same plea: that the king by grace would rid them of the hated liturgy. The petitioners appointed four 'Tables'—committees, that is—to represent the four orders of noblemen, lairds, burgesses, and ministers, and in December the Tables presented a joint petition in which they demanded, not merely withdrawal of the liturgy, but the removal of all bishops from the Privy Council. In England Charles had decisively quarrelled with his parliament. For some ten years he had been ruling without it, and ruling with considerable success. He had found various ways of maintaining his revenue, and a recent legal decision had justified his imposition of a tax known as ship-money. Fortified by success, he rebuffed the Tables, declaring that the liturgy would be maintained, that their petition had been illegal, and a repetition of it would be punished as treason. In reply to the royal proclamation the Tables presented a formal protest, and to demonstrate the strength of their position a covenant was prepared, and to make good its title—the 'National League and Covenant'—the whole nation was invited to sign and enter into it. Bonds and covenants to bind refractory cliques in a common purpose had been familiar features of Scottish history, but this, by its very magnitude, became something new.

It repeated the covenant signed by James VI in 1581, to uphold the Presbyterian system and defend the state against Romanism; it recited

[1] *History of Scots Affairs, 1736 to 1641.* James Gordon.
[2] Quoted by J. Hill Burton.

various statutes, supporting Reformed religion, and so claimed history and precedent and the rule of law as its supporters; it pledged its signatories to mutual defence 'against all sorts of persons whatsoever' to maintain the Reformed religion to the utmost of their power, and to resist all contrary errors and corruptions. It was not a wholly logical document, for the signatories pledged themselves to defend the person and authority of the king, and at the same time made clear their belief that only parliament could frame and change the law of the land. A contemporary observer wrote: 'The sense of all was, that they would continue obedient subjects, so that the king would part with his sovereignty—which was in effect that they would obey if he would suffer them to command.'[1] The Covenant was ready for signature by 1st March, and to Greyfriars Churchyard, where it was exposed, the people of Edinburgh came in great numbers and with much exuberance to pledge their adherence to it. All over the country, except the Celtic north and Aberdeen, there were similar demonstrations, and the populous parts of Scotland in 1638 may have been nearer to unanimity than at any other period of their history.

There was more than one reason for concord and enthusiasm. The Covenant let the people of Scotland express, simultaneously, their refusal to accept unwelcome orders even from a king to whom they professed obedience; it offered them a chance to show their still-continuing distrust of England; and it was an exceptional opportunity to demonstrate their pride and confidence in a national church that was, as they believed, unique in its purity and distinguished above all others by its close, unsullied relationship to God: that the Scots, like the Jews, were a chosen people, they had long known; and now they had a church that was pleasing to the Lord and congruous with their virtue. From this mood of arrogant elation Aberdeen, however, stood aloof; there episcopacy flourished, and a sounder scholarship than was general in Scotland had nurtured more moderate opinions.

In November a general assembly—the first for twenty years—was summoned to meet in Glasgow; elections and nominations to it were manipulated, and Covenanters packed it. The moderator defied the marquis of Hamilton, the king's commissioner, and the assembly annulled the liturgy, deposed the bishops, and abolished episcopacy. Such contumacy created an open breach with constituted authority, and king and Covenanters both made preparation for recourse to arms.

The Covenanters could call upon Alexander Leslie, who for many years had served under Gustavus Adolphus of Sweden, and risen to the rank of field-marshal. He returned to Scotland, with many other

[1] Quoted by J. Hill Burton.

soldiers who had learnt their trade as mercenaries abroad, and brought his arrears of pay in the form of field-guns and small arms. Most members of the Scots peerage were Covenanters—they had not forgotten Charles's threat to their teinds and title-deeds—and the rich burgesses of Edinburgh could be relied on to fill their war-chest. Other veterans of Swedish service and the Thirty Years' War joined the king's party, but their military knowledge and a sound plan of attack were nullified by the poverty and poor equipment of the royal forces. The first phase of the so-called Bishops' War lasted only from the end of March to mid-June, 1639, and there was little fighting except two small engagements at Aberdeen. Inconclusive negotiation followed a dubious truce, and when the general assembly met in Edinburgh, episcopacy was again condemned, and the office of bishop was found contrary to the law of God.

In 1640 the war was renewed, but again there was very little action. Charles, in desperation, had summoned his English parliament, which refused to grant supplies before it had discussed grievances, and then declined aid until peace had been made with the Scots. It met on 13th April, was dissolved on 5th May, and was very properly known as the Short Parliament. An English army, ill-trained and undisciplined, was unable to resist a Scottish force under Leslie which entered Newcastle, and after negotiation remained to occupy the six northern counties of England in return for a subsidy of £850 a day. The Covenanters and the king's enemies in England were drawing together, and in Scotland, where neither Charles nor his friends showed sufficient will or aptitude to oppose them, the Convenanters were rapidly becoming a revolutionary party intent on promoting its own power at the expense of the royal prerogative. In the autumn of 1641 Charles visited Scotland but did nothing for the royal cause except to insist on the release from prison of James Graham, earl of Montrose, who, though he had signed the Covenant and served in the Bishops' War, was already doubtful of the Covenanters' honesty, and suspicious in particular of the earl of Argyll, whose angry appetite for power was combined with an unscrupulous ability to reap private profit from public policy. Leslie, the Covenanters' general, was raised to the peerage as earl of Leven; he entertained his king handsomely, and swore never to take arms against him again, but forgot his oath when expediency intervened.

In England, in August, 1642, civil war broke out between Charles and his parliament. In the Great Rebellion the material advantages all lay with the parliamentary side, which held London and most of the country's wealth, but when hostilities began both sides were handicapped by lack of experience. After a drawn battle at Edgehill, north of Oxford, in October, the fortunes of war flowed to and fro, as if they had been tidal, until the beginning of 1644, when the prospect of parliamentary victory receded beyond the visible horizon, and Scotland, with some reluctance, became involved in the struggle. Its original interest was neither political nor military, but dogmatic.

For more than half a century the Presbyterians of England and Scotland had been on friendly terms, and the general assembly of 1642 listened with sympathy to a request from their English associates— self-styled of godly temper and major importance—for help in establishing, throughout Britain, conformity in doctrine and worship. A commission was appointed and a delegate despatched to Westminster. But when Charles and the English parliament both appealed to Scotland for military assistance, Scottish opinion was divided. The general assembly, which met early in August, 1643, favoured intervention on the parliamentary side, and English commissioners arrived to make known their requirements. They were in urgent need of military aid, and they also wanted coal. By the middle of the month they had been promised the alliance they craved, and in earnest of it the Solemn League and Covenant had hastily been drafted. It was, in effect, a treaty for the preservation of the Reformed religion in Scotland, for the Reformation of the church in England and Ireland, 'according to the Word of God and the example of the best reformed churches'. The churches of the three kingdoms were to be assimilated, popery and prelacy once more abolished, peace and parliamentary rule established for ever. The treaty was approved by the English parliament— the Long Parliament—which in November was promised a Scottish army of 18,000 foot and 2,000 horse.

The general assembly enthusiastically associated itself with what appeared to be a project to establish presbyterian rule throughout Britain, and to the Westminster Assembly of Divines sent representatives who, though lacking the authority of full members, busily assisted in designing catechisms large and short, a confession of faith, a directory of public worship and form of church government; all of which the general assembly and the Scottish parliament obediently adopted. The Westminster Assembly was not an ecclesiastical court, but a council elected by the Long Parliament, and its labours had little effect on the national life and thought of England. By a curious irony, however, its dogmas were soon accepted as an essential element in the faith and habit of all Lowland Scotland, and for two and a half centuries the children of the northern kingdom were to have their minds drilled and hardened—or, it may be, dulled and daunted—by the metaphysical questioning and formulated responses of the shorter catechism, to which all were subject and very few recognised as an English product.

The earl of Leven had sworn that never again would he take arms against the king; but before the end of January, 1644, he had led his Scottish army of dedicated Presbyterians across the border: every soldier in it had pledged obedience to the new Covenant, and officially was committed to strict morality as well as to the normal military disciplines. In July it engaged in battle on Marston Moor, some seven miles west of York, and played a substantial part in the defeat of a weaker royalist army commanded by Charles's nephew, Prince Rupert. Oliver Cromwell and his strictly trained 'Ironsides' were mainly responsible for the parliamentary victory, and the Scots were disappointed to be given only minor credit. In October Leven withdrew to Newcastle, where he found winter quarters, and between the Scots and their allies differences were sharpened, dislike was aggravated, and the Scots became less active in what they had fondly believed to be a common cause.

Chapter 2

IN Scotland there presently emerged new hope for the royal cause—or, perhaps more accurately, hope for resolution of the quarrel in a solvent of sounder sense than either side had so far shown—and for a little season of splendid promise the northern kingdom was dignified, and seemed likely to be dominated, by the only man, on either side or in either country, in whom a statesman's judgement was allied with charm of manner, and military virtue with a poet's sensibility. Montrose, now created a marquis, commanded the king's forces, and Alasdair MacDonald, called Colkitto, had at long last landed in Ardnamurchan with 1,600 Irishmen. Montrose, after repeated disappointment in the north of England, now planned to join them, and from Carlisle rode in disguise, with only two companions, to Tulliebelton a few miles north-west of Perth. Earlier in the year, on an expedition that failed in its aim, he had declared his purpose to be defence of the Protestant religion and the king's just and sacred authority, of the privileges of parliament and the peace and freedom of the people: he was in arms, that is, for a constitutional monarchy and the people's freedom to worship according to their faith. It was perhaps unfortunate that for so benign a purpose he had to rely on Irish reinforcement: Colkitto, a son of MacDonald of Colonsay, was a kinsman of the earl of Antrim, and his little army consisted of Catholic MacDonalds who were said to be of wild appearance and savage temper.

Montrose arrived in time to prevent a disastrous conflict between Colkitto's Irish and the embattled clans of Atholl, who mistook them for enemies. He persuaded them to friendship and marched immediately against a Covenanting army at Perth. They met near the village of Tippermuir, and six thousand Covenanters, with guns to cover them and cavalry on either flank, were broken and scattered by the fury of a Highland charge, though the Irish and the Atholl men faced odds of more than two to one. But his army had weaknesses as well as virtues, and few of his troops would remain under command except of their own free will. To keep them together he had to keep them occupied, and less than a fortnight after Tippermuir he was in front of Aberdeen. He advised the magistrates to send their women and children to a place of safety. His advice was disregarded, and a drummer boy who had marched with his envoy was shot as they turned away. There was a garrison of three thousand Covenanters, but again the Irish broke their line, and Aberdeen paid heavily for its stubbornness and the death of a drummer boy.

Easily the most powerful of the Highland chiefs was Archibald Campbell—sometimes called 'King Campbell'—marquis of Argyll, a man of wile and boundless ambition, an old enemy of Montrose, and now commander, on behalf of the Covenanters, of some four thousand horse and foot. He marched north in angry haste, and Montrose led him a dance through Speyside and Badenoch, through forest and over the hills, to Atholl again and thence to his own town by the sea. He rested for a little while, and marched north to the castle of Fyvie in Aberdeenshire, where, though desperately short of powder and ammunition, he waited for Argyll, and drove him back from Fyvie with heavy loss. It was now November, and some who had marched most valiantly sought shelter for the winter. But Montrose and the hard core of his army kept the field, and through high hill-passes returned to Blair Atholl.

There he and Colkitto were joined by two chiefs of Clan Donald, Glengarry and Clanranald, and a plan of monstrous audacity was hatched: in the depths of winter they would march into the mountainous west and strike a deadly blow at the seemingly inaccessible heartland of Clan Campbell. Down by loch Tay, by Tyndrum to Glen Orchy and the head of loch Awe, and so to Inveraray, the capital of Campbell country, near the top of loch Fyne: that was their route, and Argyll in his castle was taken by surprise, but escaped down the loch and left his clan to the mercy of the MacDonalds. There was little bloodshed, but everything that would burn was burnt, and a great booty was taken.

In Edinburgh there was wrath and perturbation. The Covenanters gathered fresh forces for renewed attack, and Montrose, who had no safe and easy way of retreating from Inveraray, chose the most difficult. He marched northwards under grim Ben Cruachan, crossed loch Etive, and came to loch Leven through Glencoe. There he could find no boats. Argyll was now in pursuit again, and his ships were on the sea and searching the sea-lochs. With Seaforth, chief of the Mackenzies, and General Baillie he had contrived a trap into which, as it seemed,

Montrose must certainly fall. Between them they would close all ways of escape from the Great Glen, the long, steep-sided chasm that splits all Highland Scotland between loch Linnhe and the firth of Inverness.

Montrose at last found boats, and crossing loch Leven came to the fort at Inverlochy under tall Ben Nevis. He had, as it appeared, walked into the trap—and to escape walked farther in, deep into the Great Glen, and in violent weather under heavy snow turned right and climbed the trackless, hidden mountains, over Corryarrick to Glen Roy, marching day and night, to return over the shoulder of Ben Nevis, and descend on Argyll and all his Campbells at Inverlochy. Argyll was safe aboard his galley, but camp-fires showed where his clan lay. There were four thousand of them, and about fifteen hundred were to die. Montrose's white-hooded army broke its fast on a porridge made of snow and the last handfuls of oatmeal—the trumpet that had sounded the charge at Tippermuir blew again—and Highlander met Highlander in a very desperate affray. The Campbells fought valiantly and were defeated; and their chief in his galley fled before the battle was lost.

Baillie fell back on Aberdeen, Montrose marched up the Great Glen and arrived in Elgin. There he got reinforcement from the Gordons, but lost them again when Huntly grew jealous and called his clan home. Montrose played cat-and-mouse with Baillie, and then, because he was in great need of meal and powder, made a surprise attack on Dundee, with a hundred and fifty horse and six hundred foot, and took it. There, while they were still collecting their rations, Baillie arrived with unexpected speed and three thousand men. Montrose's little force marched out in good order, and were covered by darkness. But the only route open to them had been the coast road leading eastwards to Arbroath, and Baillie, on their inland flank, closed all lanes of escape into the hills. Montrose and his seven hundred had already marched fifty miles. Now he turned them about and marched them back towards Dundee—Baillie had never expected that—and by the sheer force of his leadership eluded capture.

Montrose moved into the central Highlands again, now opposed by Baillie's lively second-in-command, Colonel Hurry. In early May, at Auldearn near Nairn, Hurry was defeated after some confused fighting, and on 2nd July, at Alford on the Don, Baillie was utterly routed. Now, after nearly a twelve-month of victory in the Highlands, it was time to carry war south over the Forth and Montrose, with a considerably increased strength, forded the river five miles above Stirling, and on a hot August day marched over the Campsie Fells to the village of Kilsyth, some ten miles south of Stirling. There, to crush him in pitched

[290]

battle, came Baillie, with more than four thousand men, and Argyll with hot-headed Covenanters who overruled the general's tactics. The Irish were reckless, and endangered the issue, but Montrose had, for once, a wing of cavalry, commanded by his cousin, old lord Airlie, and Airlie's gallant charge restored the balance. Then Montrose threw in his remaining infantry, Baillie's foot gave way and Argyll, who was well mounted, fled at speed. The battle of Kilsyth made Montrose master of the country. He rode in triumph into Glasgow, and Edinburgh made formal submission. Neither city was plundered or penalised, and to all who pledged allegiance to the king, Montrose gave pardon. Such generous clemency may have been injudicious— he may have carried it too far—but how agreeable it is to record tolerance in a season of black intolerance, and charity to men who in their own habit were unforgiving and vindictive. It was little less than a year before that the Covenanters of Perth had marched to Tippermuir shouting their battle-cry, 'Jesus and no quarter!'

South of the border, the king's cause appeared to be in ruins, and Presbyterianism in little better shape. Milton had published *Areopagitica*, his great plea for freedom of the press, his denunciation of Calvinist intolerance and Presbyterian censorship. By 1645 Oliver Cromwell had not only proved himself to be a great soldier, an assured and skilful leader of cavalry, but emerged as head of those very individualistic Puritans who called themselves Independents, and were as much opposed to Presbyterianism as to Episcopacy. And in June of that year, a couple of weeks before Montrose defeated Baillie at Alford, Cromwell with his 'new model' army, which was nearly twice as large as the royalist array, had routed Charles and Prince Rupert at Naseby; and sullied his victory by permitting the massacre of female prisoners. No one remained to succour the king save Montrose, but Montrose was confident and making plans to cross the border and reverse the defeat at Naseby.

He found few recruits in the Presbyterian Lowlands, however, and many of his Highlanders went home at harvest-time. Colkitto had gone to fight Campbells in Kintyre when at Philiphaugh, near Selkirk, Montrose was surprised by David Leslie, a veteran of the Swedish service, whose army outnumbered the diminished royalists by five to one. The Covenanters confirmed their victory by a massacre of the prisoners and camp-followers they had taken, and Montrose, compelled to flight by a score of his friends, found refuge in the north, where he survived another winter. In England Charles gave up the struggle, escaped from Oxford in disguise, and at Newark-on-Trent surrendered to the Scottish army; which Leven promptly withdrew to Newcastle. The Scots could find sympathisers in the English parliament, which was still largely Presbyterian, but Charles's offer to establish Presbyterianism in England, for three years, was quite impractical in face of hostility from the Independents of Cromwell's army. His presence was embarrassing and would certainly provoke division of opinion if not absolute schism. What the Scots wished for their king was secure and honourable confinement somewhere in England; and they were also intent on obtaining from the Long Parliament their arrears of pay. Towards the end of December they got £200,000 with a promise, not honoured, for £200,000 more; and five weeks later withdrew from Newcastle, leaving Charles in English hands.

The English parliament, however, lost him on 31st May, 1647, when by Cromwell's order he was seized and taken to army headquarters at Newmarket. Cromwell had good reason for his action. In the growing bitterness of the contest for power between the Presbyterian Long Parliament and the Independents of the army, Cromwell had argued for the maintenance of parliamentary authority; but when parliament tried to disband the army, and disclosed its intention to enlist Scottish help and restore Charles under Presbyterian domination, the army mutinied and Cromwell took command to prevent anarchy. Possession of Charles's person was vital to his authority, which he skilfully maintained by denunciation of extremism and a judicious deployment of his cavalry. The Scots, however, established contact with Charles, in open imprisonment in the Isle of Wight, and in a secret 'engagement' offered armed assistance in return for his promise to create a Presbyterian regime and grant his Scottish subjects trading privileges equal to those enjoyed by Englishmen. The 'engagement' was realistic in that acceptance of the second Covenant was not made obligatory, but when the Estates met in Edinburgh, in March, 1648, they were less practical. Something very like an ultimatum was sent to the English parliament, with demands for the liberation of the king, disbandment of the army, and fulfilment of the Covenant; and to enforce these demands a large but badly equipped and ill-trained army was mobilised. Both Leven and David Leslie refused the command, and the duke of Hamilton led it into Lancashire, where Cromwell cut it to pieces.

In Edinburgh the extreme Covenanters, who had refused approval of the 'engagement', had now the upper hand, and in October Cromwell surprisingly arrived, to sup with Argyll and others at Moray House in the Canongate, where agreement was reached to make common cause against what was now called 'malignancy'; against those, that is, who supported or sympathised with the king. A month later the Long Parliament suffered the diminution known as Pride's Purge, and the surviving 'Rump' of Independents declared it high treason for a king to go to war with his parliament, and demanded that Charles be tried as the cause and source of the many misfortunes that had fallen on Britain. All Scotland was indignant, and Scottish protest was vehement but in vain. On 30th January, 1649, Charles was beheaded in front of the Banqueting House in Whitehall. He died with perfect composure and gentle dignity, declaring that he had desired the liberty and freedom of his people as much as any, but 'a subject and a sovereign are clean different things'. It was almost exactly sixty-two years since his grandmother, for comparable intransigence, had died, with equal composure, under the headman's axe at Fotheringhay.

Charles II, aged nineteen, was in Scotland proclaimed king on 5th February; and in England the 'Rump' abolished monarchy and the House of Lords. The Scottish Covenanters demanded of their new king that he accept both Covenants and the Westminster Confession of Faith; but there was a royalist party at the head of which the exiled Montrose would have Charles break with the Covenanters and stand again for constitutional monarchy. Though Argyll was the master of Scotland Charles preferred the hope that Montrose offered, and in his name Montrose went to Denmark and Sweden to provide himself with arms, ammunition, and ships for another desperate venture. Ill luck awaited him, and his king came near to betraying him. The young Charles was so foolish as to recognise the government in Edinburgh, and so gave to Argyll and his friends an excuse to put a price on Montrose's head and declare they had Charles's authority to do so.

From Gothenburg Montrose put to sea, and his small fleet was scattered by storm. But in Orkney he recruited about a thousand men— none of them trained to arms—and crossing the Pentland Firth marched south as far as Carbisdale by the Kyle of Sutherland; where his little army was utterly routed by a charge of horse. None of the simple islanders had ever seen a dragoon before, and fled in terror from so fearful a spectacle. Montrose was made prisoner and taken to his death in Edinburgh. It was a death that shamed only his captors, and the rancorous abuse of the vulgar mob was stilled by the manifest goodness of its noble victim. That day—21st May, 1650—Scotland lost the best man and the clearest redeeming feature of a wasted century.

At Breda in the Netherlands Charles decided to make terms with his Covenanting subjects, and taking ship to the Moray Firth signed both the Covenants while still at sea. The English, who had abolished monarchy, marched north against their neighbours' refusal to

acknowledge its demise. Cromwell had written to the general assembly
—'I beseech you in the bowels of Christ, think it possible you may be
mistaken'—and failing to receive a satisfactory reply, led 16,000 men
over the border to persuade the stubborn Scots that a king could not
advance the cause of godliness, and the Scots, as intent on godliness
as he, gravely weakened their own army by purging it of all suspected
of 'malignancy'. Their commanding general was David Leslie, who
repelled Cromwell's attempt on Leith and thwarted his subsequent
move towards Queensferry. Cromwell depended for supplies on the
fleet which had accompanied his invasion, and withdrew to Dunbar.
The weather, at the end of August, was bad enough to make the Scots
impatient. They had Cromwell trapped between Doon Hill and the
sea, but left a strong position to advance over broken ground where
they had no freedom of movement. Cromwell, whose piety had the
advantage of a tactician's eye, saw his chance and totally defeated an
army, twice the size of his own, which by its own folly had invited
disaster. Three thousand were killed, ten thousand taken prisoner, of
whom many were carried across the Atlantic to 'the Plantations'.

In December, 1650, Edinburgh castle surrendered, and before the
following summer Cromwell was master of most of the south of
Scotland. But Charles II had been crowned at Scone, where, a little
strangely perhaps, Argyll played a major part in the ceremony; and
in June Leslie held Stirling in strength. Cromwell was not tempted to
attack him, but crossed the Forth and marched towards Perth. The
road into England was left open, and Charles, with an army of about
15,000 men, recklessly invaded the larger kingdom. It was a fatal move,
for no recruits came to his colours, he was cut off from Wales, where
support had been expected, and at Worcester, on 3rd September,
the Scots were again defeated and Cromwell got his 'crowning mercy'.
But Charles escaped and found his way to France.

George Monk was the general whom Cromwell left in Scotland,
to complete its subjection, and Monk performed his task with punctual
efficiency. Military government, in practice if not in name, was based
on garrisons in Leith and Ayr, in Perth, Inverlochy and Inverness, and
on lesser military establishments in a score of other places; and for
their maintenance Scotland was heavily taxed. But Scotland, nominally
at least, became part of the single commonwealth of England, Scotland, and Ireland, in which all enjoyed the natural privileges of the
English and liberty of worship. No discussion was permitted about the
terms of union, and in the several parliaments which, with dubious
authority, met from time to time in London, Scotland was thinly
represented. The English governed fairly and well. They maintained

order, and Monk ruthlessly broke royalist risings led by general Middleton and the earl of Glencairn. The general assembly was dissolved in 1653, and not convened thereafter, but English Puritans were as zealous as Scottish Presbyterians, and religion could not fail to flourish when in every garrisoned town there were officers and non-commissioned officers able and eager to occupy its pulpits. The eight years of the Cromwellian usurpation made a season of peace and perhaps even of modest prosperity for 'the middle sort' of people; but it must be recorded that when it came to an end, with the death of Cromwell in 1658 and the restoration of Charles II in 1660, there was enormous jubilation, and the departure of the English garrisons, though it may have reduced the volume of preaching, was to the vast majority an occasion for great rejoicing.

Chapter 3

BY instinct and habit the Scots were royalists—it was monarchy which had held together the several parts of the realm—but the restoration of Charles II did little to fortify their respect for the throne or enhance affection for the person of the king. He did not visit his northern heritage, which with the collapse of the Cromwellian union again became a separate kingdom; and none of his successors was ever seen in Edinburgh until George IV's belated arrival in 1822.

Charles had spent his youth in poverty-stricken exile, and was determined never to 'go on his travels again'. He had great charm and natural dignity, and a wit too lively for the grave responsibilities of a throne. By the age of thirty he had learnt enough of the world—of its policies and passions—to excuse if not to justify his cynicism; and against a background so precarious as his had been, his self-indulgence may be regarded as philosophical. Unlike his devout brother James—who, said Charles, chose a mistress as if she were to be a penance—his gaieties had the grace of good taste, and his prejudices were founded on reason. He saw no need to enlarge parliamentary authority by the diminution of his own prerogative, but he seems initially to have favoured a larger degree of religious toleration than many of his Scottish subjects were prepared to accept. In the Declaration of Breda, of 1660, he agreed to parliamentary settlement of the innumerable claims for the restoration of confiscated property, and promised 'a liberty to tender consciences and that no man shall be disquieted or called in question for differences of opinion in matters of religion which do not disturb the peace of the kingdom'.

Religious opinion, and the division of opinion, were still matters of dominating interest in Scotland. In the last ten years the Presbyterianism of the majority had become more moderate as royalist sympathy relaxed the absolutism of the second Covenant, and the heirs of the old extremists were now, in the main, confined to the south-western parts of the country. When, in 1661, the Scottish parliament passed

[296]

the Act Rescissory, annulling all legislation since 1633, the kirk had to accept a return to the episcopal government it had known at the end of James VI's reign; and in the following year bishops were re-established as a parliamentary estate, the Covenants were denounced as treasonous and rebellious, and private conventicles were forbidden. There, it is obvious, was contradiction of the toleration promised in the Declaration of Breda, but in the altered mood of the country it is probable that a majority would have accepted bishops for the sake of unity, and let the Covenants go in return for peace, if the new order had been more leniently interpreted and lightly imposed. But that was not to be.

Lay patronage, always resented, had been abolished in 1649. Now parliament in its folly declared that every minister admitted since then must be approved by the patron of his living and his bishop. Out of a total of some nine hundred ministers, nearly three hundred rejected the demand, and about two hundred who persisted in their refusal were expelled. Their congregations met in the fields, and worshipped in defiance of a subsequent act that instituted fines for those who absented themselves from church. Ministers who had been dismissed were forbidden to live within twenty miles of their former parishes, and in the south-west the old Covenanting wrath was nourished in the conventicles that gathered to hear extempore prayer and interminable sermons under the open sky. If the right wing was impercipient, the left was utterly intransigent, and it is possible that even a government both prudent and powerful would have failed to prevent their collision; for the right wing thought its judgement impeccable, and the left was assured, by its consciousness of God's grace, that it could do no wrong.

In 1666 there was insurrection in the south-west. England was now at war with Holland, and because it was feared or suspected that the extremists of the left were planning to rise in support of the Dutch, a small force of dragoons or mounted police had been raised to watch the disaffected districts. It was commanded by Sir James Turner and an officer lately in the Russian service, Dalziel of the Binns; and in mid-November Turner was surprised and captured by a band of 'Whigs', as these sturdy dissidents were now called. Their numbers were increased by enthusiastic addition to about 3,000, and without discipline or plan of campaign they advanced on Edinburgh. They were, for the most part, God-intoxicated peasants led by the ranting zeal of pious but ignorant ministers, and their ineffectual little company, rapidly growing smaller, was finally scattered by Dalziel at Rullion Green in the Pentland Hills. Many prisoners refused to take the oath of allegiance, and of these thirty were hanged, others transported to Barbados.

The king's commissioner in Scotland was now the earl of Lauderdale, and under him there was a period of conciliation in which indemnity was granted for past offences and a hundred expelled ministers, who had been of good behaviour, were allowed to return to their churches. The result of these indulgences, however, was to stimulate opposition to the policy which dictated them, and those who refused to profit by them denied the spiritual authority of bishops and rejected the ministry of more moderate men. Most of Scotland's small standing army was disbanded, and the consequence was that more and more dissidents more openly attended conventicles, and 'Whiggery' became a brawling revivalism that spread from the south-west into Fife and the Lothians. To counter this renewed aggressiveness landowners were made responsible for their tenants' behaviour, and could be fined for permitting conventicles on their property; and unlicensed ministers became liable to the death penalty for preaching at field conventicles. When, in 1677, landowners were warned that they must accept the responsibility of suppressing conventicles, many in the south-west replied that it was beyond their power, and a little while later the increasing militancy of the preachers and their congregations persuaded the government to adopt an extraordinary device for their discomfiture. It mobilised what was called 'the Highland host'—a force of some 8,000 men, of whom 3,000 were Lowland militia—and billeted them in Ayrshire, to live on the country and disarm it. The Highlanders conducted themselves with propriety—that is to say they looted with practised efficiency, but refrained from murder—but their presence and behaviour roused the fiercest resentment, and the west was already on the verge of revolt when, on 3rd May, 1679, James Sharp, archbishop of St. Andrews, was killed on Magus Muir.

The archbishop had busily co-operated in the restoration of Episcopacy, and after making many enemies had lately attracted great hostility by insisting, it was said, on the execution of a man called Mitchell, who had once attempted to murder him. It was by chance that a party of fanatical Whigs, who near St. Andrews were looking for the sheriff of Fife, in order to murder him, heard that the archbishop was driving across Magus Muir. Recognising what they termed 'a call from God to put him to death', they stopped his coach, ordered him out, and having exhorted him to repentance and prayer, murdered him with great brutality in the presence of his daughter. His assassins then rode at speed to the west, and joining forces with the insurgent Whigs denounced all violation of the Covenants. John Graham of

Claverhouse, a soldier who had served with distinction under the Dutch, commanded a troop of dragoons, one of three that were engaged on police work in the south-west. On 1st June, when riding in search of an armed conventicle, he was anticipated by the Whigs who detached from their religious exercises a force of fifty horse and nearly two hundred foot, and defeated Claverhouse in a brisk engagement at Drumclog, south of Paisley.

He retreated to Glasgow, and the insurgents, vastly reinforced after their little victory, followed and occupied the town when Claverhouse again withdrew. The rebels made poor use of success, and before the end of June were routed at Bothwell Brig, on the Clyde, by an army half as big as theirs, which was commanded by the duke of Monmouth, who had no claim to military prowess. Twelve hundred prisoners were marched to Edinburgh, and confined without comfort in the kirkyard of Greyfriars. Monmouth obtained an indemnity for all who promised to live at peace, and a new indulgence that permitted conventicles in private houses. About three hundred of the prisoners from Bothwell Brig were recalcitrant, and condemned to the Plantations; but two hundred of them were drowned when a storm sank their ship in Orkney.

Charles's brother James, duke of York, replaced the lenient Monmouth, and repression again became official policy; again it was invited by those against whom it was directed. A young man called Richard Cameron, ordained in Holland, had returned to Scotland and found that among the true, die-hard Covenanters there remained only one active minister, Donald Cargill. But Cameron renewed the war, and such was the invigoration of his preaching that a year after Bothwell Brig he was able to lead a score of his followers into Sanquhar, a village between Dumfries and Ayr, where they declared war against the king and Episcopacy. Troops were sent against them, and at Airdrie Moss, near Auchinleck, their company was defeated and Cameron was killed. But for a little while Cargill survived, and with solemn assurance excommunicated the king, the duke of York, Monmouth and Dalziel of the Binns, and the lord advocate, Sir George Mackenzie. Cargill was caught and executed in 1681, but the Cameronians found a new leader in James Renwick, and for a few more years maintained a desperate guerrilla warfare against the government, boldly declaring that any servant of the government who sought to take their lives, did so at risk of his own. Foremost among their enemies were Graham of Claverhouse and Sir George Mackenzie, the lord advocate: 'bluidy Clavers' and 'the bluidy Mackenzie' not only to the Cameronians but to many thousands of those who, in later years, were moved to sentimental admiration of the last of the Covenanters. The Covenanters developed a remarkable genius for propaganda, and had no lack of zealous propagandists; but in fact 'bluidy Clavers' was a just and moderate man, and recent scholarship has assessed the number of fanatical lives he was forced to take at ten.[1] While sheriff of Wigtown he wrote: 'In the greatest crimes it is thought wisest to pardon the multitude and punish the ringleaders.' And on a later occasion: 'It will be more of consequence to punish one considerable laird than a hundred little bodies. Besides, it is juster, because these only sin by the example of those.'[2] He was, indeed, a man of great rectitude, a devout Episcopalian, who in battle had saved the life of William of Orange, and could be so contemptuous of politics—when most politicians were fanatical—as to marry, for love, into a Whig household. He was, incidentally, a man of outstanding physical beauty.

Charles died in February, 1685, and was succeeded by his brother James, a practising Catholic who had been a naval officer of high competence, but who failed disastrously as a politician; largely, it seems, because he was genuinely incapable of duplicity. He was fifty-two when he became king, and the apparent strength of the throne was quickly demonstrated.

The Protestant and popular duke of Monmouth asserted his legitimacy and right to the crown. In pursuit of his ambition he invaded the south-west of England with a few supporters, and in collusion with him Archibald Campbell, earl of Argyll, landed in Kintyre, but was quickly captured, sentenced to death, and beheaded in June, 1685. His father, Montrose's bitter enemy, had been executed twenty-four years earlier, for traitorous collaboration with General Monk. Both died with exemplary courage. James's first Scottish parliament asserted its belief in absolute monarchy, and throughout the country there was no visible opposition to him except that of the irreconcilable Cameronians who had now declared that it was no sin to kill servants of the crown. It must be noted, indeed, that opposition on religious grounds had for a good many years been confined to the south-west, and though religious dispute now appears to have discontented or dominated all Scotland, those parts of it beyond the Forth were, on the whole, little troubled. But to his second parliament James made an unforgivable proposal. He suggested that Roman Catholics should be set free from the laws against them, and as a *douceur* for his Scottish subjects he offered them free trade with England. There was immediate indignation, a loyal parliament rebuffed its king, and for its disobedience was dis-

[1] *Edinburgh History of Scotland* (Vol. III). Gordon Donaldson.
[2] Quoted in *The Passing of the Stewarts*. Agnes Mure Mackenzie.

solved. James, with a most maladroit exposure of his conscience and his purpose, had found the certain way to endanger his throne.

There were very few Catholics in Scotland—perhaps fifteen hundred, perhaps two thousand—and emancipation would not have been dangerous. But the thought of it provoked widespread fear. To Protestants of every sort and colour Catholicism was the enemy. Catholicism had meant the peril of Spanish invasion, it still meant Louis XIV, who said 'L'état c'est moi', and denied the right of life to Protestants. Now James showed favour to his Catholics, and looked for converts. He allowed them freedom of worship so long as they did not worship openly in the high street or the fields. At Holyrood the nave of the abbey was reconsecrated and became the Roman Catholic chapel royal. Then James went further, and in 1687 gave all his subjects liberty to worship according to their own wish, whether in private or in public. Presbyterianism grew again at the expense of Episcopacy, and loyal Episcopalians watched with equal displeasure the encouragement given to priests, and the toleration extended to Presbyters whose old ambitions and hope of power retained were nourished by their freedom. In June, 1688, his queen—his second wife, the Catholic Mary of Modena—gave birth to a son, and the menace of Catholic rule, maintained into another generation, became evident. But Scotland did not initiate revolution. That began in England.

Seven bishops had refused to obey the king's command to read from their pulpits his Declaration of Indulgence, granting freedom from restraint to both Catholics and Dissenters, and the seven bishops were arrested and sent to the Tower. They were tried for seditious libel, and acquitted to the accompaniment of public rejoicing. James had lost the monarchy's traditional shield, the sympathy of the Anglican church, and when his son was born there were those, of major influence in England, who were convinced that the time had come to ask for the assistance, already canvassed, of William, prince of Orange, whose wife Mary was James's daughter and heiress to the British throne.

William, about to be king of Great Britain as William III, was the posthumous son of William II of Orange by Mary, the eldest daughter of Charles I. As stadholder of the United Provinces he had waged heroic war against Louis XIV, and married Mary, his cousin. He had been in correspondence with those English aristocrats who felt impelled to engineer James's expulsion, and when he received their positive invitation he made his preparations with great skill and in perfect secrecy. In November, 1688, he landed at Torbay with an army of 15,000, both Dutch and English, and being received with general favour achieved rapid and bloodless success. James fled the kingdom, and in February, 1689, a convention parliament proclaimed William and Mary king and queen of Great Britain and Ireland. To restore parliamentary freedom to Britain had been William's professed intention, but he refused to share its government save as king in his own person and for the term of his life. In the Highlands of Scotland there was some resistance to so sudden and arbitrary a change of rulers, and James's continuing adherents were known as 'Jacobites': a name that was to survive, and carry overtones of deep emotion, until the middle of the eighteenth century.

Two other political labels, invented about this time and destined to an even longer life, were 'Whig' and 'Tory'. Originally a mocking name for Covenanters of the south-west, 'Whig' had been transferred, with equal opprobrium, to those Englishmen who, when James II was duke of York, had hoped to bar him from succession to the throne; and they in turn had called their opponents, the king's men, 'Tories', which is said to be Irish for an outlaw and brigand. In the course of time both labels acquired other shades of meaning.

Chapter 4

DESPITE a preoccupation with religious issues that had dominated much of Scotland and Scottish thought since the time of the Reformation, there is no evidence that religious experience anywhere induced that profundity of thought, or intensity of feeling, which elsewhere have created enduring expression of it. In England, equally tormented by sectarian strife, the first half of the seventeenth century was sweetened and elevated by the sacred verse of Herbert, Crashaw, and Vaughan—it was George Herbert who wrote 'A verse may find him who a sermon flies', and 'Let all the world in every corner sing/My God and King./The Church with psalms must shout,/No door can keep them out.' And Richard Crashaw wrote of 'Love's great artillery', and 'I sing the Name which none can say/But touch'd with an interior ray.' And Henry Vaughan wrote, unforgettably: 'I saw Eternity the other night/Like a great ring of pure and endless light.' But there is no one even distantly of their sort to show forth and commemorate what seems to have been, in Scotland, a ruling passion. There is nothing that resembles religious poetry save the Metrical Version of the Psalms, and those deplorable cadences were the product of the Westminster Assembly of Divines. It is a curious lack or gap, and perhaps the most charitable explanation of it is that Calvinist theology was an incentive to action rather than to contemplation.

Theology might dominate, but it did not exclude all other interests, and in the midst of angry disputing there were reasonable men who pursued their sensible vocations and steadily added to the strength of existing institutions or laid new foundations. Edinburgh was to become in time one of the medical capitals of the world, and before the end of the seventeenth century its school of medicine had visibly grown and the Royal College of Physicians had been established. In his great work *The Institutions of the Law of Scotland* Sir James Dalrymple elucidated the long-established practice of Scottish lawyers, and before the parliament of Scotland was submerged in the louder concourse at

[303]

Westminster Sir Thomas Murray compiled a register of all its Acts of the last three hundred years. Though the palace of Holyroodhouse stood empty, it was largely rebuilt to the handsome design of Sir William Bruce; and the early years of the Royal Society of London, founded in 1660, were materially assisted by several ingenious and learned Scots who had discovered that it was possible to live with more ease and a larger freedom in England. But the deciding temper of the country had been Presbyterian, and Presbyterianism was certainly the force behind Scotland's share in that exchange of rulers—the enforced flight of James II, the welcoming of William and Mary—which was called 'the Revolution' because William of Orange accepted the responsibility of administration at the request of an English parliament which had not been summoned by the king, and therefore had no authority other than its claim to speak with the voice of the people.

In Scotland the persistent division, of sentiment and opinion, between Highlands and Lowlands let Graham of Claverhouse—now elevated to the peerage as Viscount Dundee—denounce the Revolution and declare for James: on whose behalf he raised a small but useful army of MacDonalds, Camerons, Macleans, and the Stewarts of Appin. To counter this threat came General Hugh Mackay with some 4,000 men —English, Dutch, and Lowlands Scots—and after some weeks of rapid marching and counter-marching Dundee, with rather more than half as many, met him in the pass of Killiecrankie, in Perthshire, and in the shortest of battles routed him utterly in one storming, irresistible charge. But the cost of victory was bankruptcy for the Jacobite cause: Dundee was mortally wounded and died on the field. For a little while the Highland war continued, but the Jacobites found no other commander of Dundee's quality. A Colonel Cannon was appointed, and he was soon defeated in extraordinary circumstances. The Cameronians, those turbulent, embittered Whigs from the south-west, had warmly welcomed the Revolution and volunteered to serve—on their own terms and under their own officers—against any stubborn supporters of the king they detested. A regiment was formed, commanded nominally by the earl of Angus but in effect by a young man called William Cleland, who had fought against Claverhouse in the skirmish at Drumclog; and in August Cleland led his embattled Cameronians to Dunkeld, a village some fifteen miles south of Killiecrankie. There they were attacked by Cannon, who had the advantage of numbers, but Cleland found a strong defensive position in the cathedral and a neighbouring mansion-house, and after desperate fighting the Cameronians won a notable victory. But they paid for it as the Highlanders had done, and young Cleland was killed in the hour of his victory.

(Some fourteen or fifteen years later, in the War of the Spanish Succession, Marlborough made his daring and brilliant march to the Danube. In his army were the Cameronians, by then distinguished as the 26th Regiment of Foot; the Royal Scots and the Royal Scots Fusiliers; and a regiment of heavy cavalry, the Scots Greys. All of them fought in the four great battles of Blenheim, Ramillies, Oudenarde, and Malplaquet. A few years earlier the Scots Guards and the King's Own Scottish Borderers had served, under William, at the siege of Namur. The Revolution gave Scotland new uniforms for one of its oldest professions.)

In the summer of Dundee's death the Scottish parliament once again abolished Episcopacy, and the following year re-established Presbyterian government and discontinued lay patronage. The general assembly met, for the first time in nearly forty years, and Episcopalian parsons were driven from their manses for refusing to pray for William and Mary. Episcopalians, of whom there were many in the north and north-east, and Highland chiefs in the west, were far from pleased at the substitution of Dutch William for James and the old royal family —if James was stubbornly wrong-headed, William was perverse and coldly self-seeking—and, on the other hand, the English government was extremely anxious to avoid trouble in those parts of the island which, being least accessible, were most conservative. Money was advanced, to bribe the reluctant chiefs, but the agent for its distribution was Campbell of Breadalbane, and how much was actually distributed is doubtful. What seems to be certain is that there were those who wanted an excuse to teach recalcitrant Highlanders—the men of an older and different culture, the men who would not conform—so terrible a lesson, for non-conformity, that the old problem of the Highlands would be solved for ever.

To those who had not yet submitted to William and Mary, offers of pardon were extended till the end of the year. There would be no mercy for those who did not pledge their allegiance by 1st of January, 1692. The king's Scottish adviser in London was Sir John Dalrymple, the Master of Stair—son of the good lawyer Dalrymple who had written his *Institutions of the Law of Scotland*—and he was notoriously in favour of harsh measures for the Highlanders, especially for Clan Donald. With him, in London, were the two Campbell earls, Argyll and Breadalbane, and Dutch William cannot be absolved of blame for the notorious massacre of Glencoe, which, beyond any doubt, was deliberately contrived. The stalwart chief of the MacIans of Glencoe, a sept of Clan Donald, was late, through no fault of his own except procrastination, in offering submission to Dutch William.

[305]

Early in 1692 a force of regulars, who were Campbells led by Robert Campbell of Glenlyon, marched into Glencoe with the excuse that government accommodation at Fort William was overcrowded. For a couple of weeks they were hospitably entertained, and then, at a pre-arranged time, they rose in the darkness of night and the bitterness of a February snowstorm, to slaughter their unsuspecting hosts. Their plans were obstructed by the weather. Government troops who had been ordered to seal the glen, failed to arrive. In circumstances of appalling discomfort many of the MacIans—but not their heroic old chief or his gallant wife—managed to escape; and not more than forty were murdered. In comparison with European figures—with the casualties of the French religious wars and the habitual slaughter of the Thirty Years' War—the tale of the dead was insignificant; but the circumstances of the massacre made it heinous, and those unlikeable men, Dutch William and the Master of Stair, must accept with the managerial Campbells the stigma of nauseating guilt. What is truly remarkable is that in the climate of 1692 the behaviour of the English government and its auxiliaries was widely held to have been abominable. But no one was punished until, some years later, the Master of Stair lost his position as Scottish secretary.

Scotland was now approaching calamity of a sort unknown in preceding centuries. Defeat in battle had become familiar, internecine slaughter and the mourning consequent upon it were known in every quarter of the country. But until now—the last years of the seventeenth century, that is—Scotland had been spared the horrors of financial failure, because Scotland had never had finance enough to promote a major failure. But the years between the Restoration and the Revolution saw widespread recovery from the Cromwellian 'usurpation' and the troubled time before it, and the economy of the country showed a variety and liveliness which, though far from indicating wealth, were an improvement on the past. The old staples of the export trade had been hides and wool and fish, but now linen and live cattle were of more importance, coal and salt brought money in, and after a good harvest there was a surplus of grain for export. Despite the Dutch wars trade expanded, Glasgow grew and new harbours were built on the Clyde. The Baltic trade kept Leith busy, and for a little while Scotland shared with England the commercial advantages of neutrality at a time when there was widespread war on the continent. Scottish shipping had suffered badly under Cromwell, but now recovered and found profitable business abroad. The acquisition of a little money naturally stimulated a desire for more, and it had become apparent that Scotland could grow rich only by increasing its trade. Now trade seemed more important than the subsistence agriculture with which the greater part of the country had hitherto been content, and in particular there was a great interest in the possibility of colonial trade. England's navigation acts had forbidden commerce with her plantations on the Atlantic coast of north America, but Scottish merchants had not been completely deterred by legal difficulties, and with the connivance of colonial proprietors small settlements had been established, principally in New Jersey and the Carolinas, most of which were short-lived.

In 1695 the Scottish parliament authorised the creation of a company to trade in Africa and the Indies, and as it was first contemplated the company was to be Anglo-Scottish, finding half its capital and half its directors in England. To some extent, indeed, it was planned as a rival to the rich and powerful East India Company, which had been founded, nearly a century before, in Elizabeth's reign; and that purposed rivalry was ill-judged. The East India Company was influential enough to persuade the Westminster parliament to forbid English participation in the scheme, and instead of subscribing £300,000, to match a like sum from London, the Scots had to find the necessary capital from their own resources, and succeeded in raising £400,000, a sum said to be nearly half of the available national wealth. It was decided, moreover, that the most promising area for investment was not the great continent of Africa, but the isthmus of Darien or Panama, the narrow neck of land that joined north and south America and divided the Atlantic from the Pacific. He who was chiefly responsible for this decision was William Paterson, a native of Dumfries and one of the earliest of company promoters, who in 1694 had founded the Bank of England; his conception of a great emporium, strategically situated to engage, free from tariffs, the trade of the whole world, was truly inspiring to all who were unaware of Darien's pernicious climate, and ignored the sinister fact that Spain claimed possession of all that territory. The colonists, indeed, would encounter more than yellow fever and Spanish hostility. Dutch William was determined that Spain must not be offended, English colonists in the West Indies were forbidden to offer help of any sort to Scottish adventurers; and English refusal to share the enterprise became naked opposition to it.

In July, 1698, five ships sailed from Leith, and by November had founded on the isthmus the township of New Edinburgh. It was short-lived. The expedition was ill advised, ill managed, and had no defence against fever. Defeat was inevitable, but before the fact of defeat had been recognised at home, a second and a third expedition put out to reinforce a hopeless venture. The Spaniards attacked, and were defeated. But the Spaniards returned, by land and sea, and in March,

1700, the fever-stricken remnant of the adventurers capitulated. Scotland counted its losses—perhaps 2,000 men and a quarter of a million pounds sterling—and in furious anger blamed England for all it had lost. Anger was natural enough, but what had to be accepted was that English interests and Scottish interests had met in direct and open opposition, and the monarch who was king of both countries—but now, in consequence of the Revolution, a king compelled to listen to his parliaments—had heard from Edinburgh what Westminster forcibly denied. What was policy to one was poison to the other, and the continuing existence of two sovereign parliaments—as they now accounted themselves—sitting under one diminished king had become at best anomalous, at worst impossible.

William, that brave but unlikeable king, died in 1702. Mary, his wife and equal in sovereignty, had died in 1694. He had maintained a gallant opposition to Louis XIV of France, and because he was a foreigner had enabled parliament and the magnates of England—those of them, that is, who took an interest in politics—to assume and exercise a power in the land which was effective in substituting, for the previous tension between king and parliament, a more elastic tension between rival political parties which for the next two and a half centuries would be distinguished as Whigs and Tories. William, that staunch, perverted, and costive Protestant, was by default a great innovator, and died childless. He was succeeded by Anne, his sister-in-law, the younger sister of Mary his deceased wife and, like her, a daughter of James II and Anne Hyde. Anne, now queen, had married in 1683 Prince George of Denmark, of whom Charles II had said: 'I have tried him drunk, I have tried him sober, and can find nothing in him.' She had borne seventeen children, all of whom died at birth or in infancy, and it was considered unlikely that she would leave an heir capable of succeeding to the throne. The English parliament, anticipating her accession, had decided that her heir must be the Electress Sophia of Hanover, her nearest Protestant kinswoman: and to show forth Sophia's claim to the British throne it is necessary to go back to James VI of Scotland who became James I of England. His daughter, the beautiful Elizabeth who married Frederick the Elector Palatine, and very briefly was queen of Bohemia, had a daughter Sophia—sister of the dashing Prince Rupert who commanded Charles I's cavalry in the civil war—and Sophia married the German Prince Ernest, Elector of Hanover. She died in 1714, the year of Queen Anne's death, leaving a son George, fifty-four years old, who by virtue of descent from James I and his Protestant faith became king of Great Britain and Ireland. It was to ensure this that the English parliament negotiated its union with the Scottish parliament; which was compelled to acquiesce by the crippling poverty of the country it represented.

In the very last years of its life the Scottish parliament, stimulated by its new-found freedom from royal dictation, was lively, enterprising, and aggressive, and very clearly expressed the strong and general dislike of England, the dissatisfaction with the union of 1603, which were the direct consequence of the failure at Darien and the widespread belief that failure was due only to English machination. In the first year of Queen Anne's reign, England again opposed Scotland's natural desire to enjoy some share in its overseas trade, and the year after that, in 1703, the last Scottish parliament passed an Act 'anent Peace and War' in which it firmly declared its separate power to embark on war and conclude the terms of peace. It passed the Wine Act, which promoted trade with France and, while it might increase the revenue, would certainly exasperate the English, who were at war with France. And it passed the Act of Security and Succession, by which it asserted its intention to oppose the Hanoverian succession unless the crown of Scotland, her parliament, religion, liberty and trade, were given effective safeguards against interference by England or any other power. The total effect of these Acts was to create a threat, or the realistic appearance of a threat, to the union of the crowns which, for a century, had been precariously maintained; and in March, 1705, the English parliament's blustering reply was the Alien Act.

Scotland was instructed to accept the Hanoverian succession before the end of the year, or appoint commissioners to negotiate a parliamentary union. Otherwise Scots would be declared aliens, their English property would be liable to confiscation, their exports of cattle, coal and linen prohibited, and their foreign trade prevented. Anger was intensified, and the unfortunate captain of an English ship—the East Indiaman *Worcester*—was executed, along with two of his officers, for an alleged act of piracy, for which there was no evidence, against a Scottish vessel. Then, in November, the Alien Act was repealed and commissioners from both countries were appointed to draft a Treaty of Union. That any such treaty, however, would prove acceptable still seemed quite improbable.

But in spite of brave words and strong feeling Scotland was in no condition for effective bargaining. The period of comparative prosperity after the Revolution had been of short duration. The French war, which had begun again in 1701, made it difficult to trade with what had been an important market, and merchant ships were subject to the double menace of French privateers and the press-gangs of the

Royal Navy. Shetland, for example, has never been given credit for its very numerous, long continued, and usually unwilling contribution to the Navy. Added to these difficulties was the malignancy of nature; for in the late 1690's there had been such calamitously poor harvests as to create near famine, and following close on the blight and foul weather had come the financial blight of the Darien disaster. Yet many have been willing to believe that only by widespread bribery of the Scottish commissioners or parliament, or of both together, was union achieved.

The two commissions met in London, and on behalf of the English the following proposals were submitted: that the two kingdoms should be united under the name of Great Britain; that the United Kingdom should be represented by one parliament; and in accordance with the English Act of Settlement the succession to the Crown should devolve on the House of Hanover—England was at war with France, and could not accept a hostile neighbour ruled by a Catholic king. The Scots would have preferred a federal union, in which they could have preserved their own parliament, but the English would listen to no discussion, and Scotland had little hope of avoiding bankruptcy save by free trade, at home and abroad, which the union would ensure. So, rather than wreck negotiation, the Scottish commissioners agreed to the proposal for entire union of the two countries. There were twenty-two further articles in the draft of the treaty that was presented for discussion to the Scottish parliament in the winter of 1706, and as well as financial arrangements for the proper allocation of tax and other burdens, provision was made for freedom of trade and navigation, and the continuance within Scotland of its own legal system and courts of law; while supplementary statutes were to secure for one kingdom its Protestant faith and Presbyterian church, for the other its Anglican church and Episcopacy. The commissioners had differed angrily only on the matter of proportional representation in the united parliament, and the final agreement to give Scotland forty-five members in the House of Commons against England's five hundred and thirteen, with sixteen representative peers to sit in the Lords, could not be said to depress the balance unduly in favour of the northern kingdom.

The Three Estates met for the last time on 3rd October, 1706. and while heated and eloquent debate resounded in the parliament hall, there was furious excitement in the adjacent streets. The Edinburgh mob, violently and vociferously opposed to union, had to be quelled by a show of force. Argument continued into the New Year, and in mid-January, 1707, the whole treaty was approved by a hundred and ten votes to sixty-nine. In each Estate there was a majority for it, the nobles being most markedly in favour. Lord Seafield, the chancellor, pronounced his famous epitaph on the vanished kingdom—'Now, there's ane end to ane auld song'—but a later critic[1] was nearer the knuckle when he wrote that the union was 'a political necessity for England, a commercial necessity for Scotland'.

[1] Quoted in *Scottish Trade on the Eve of Union*. T. C. Smout.

Book Six

THE
REVIVAL
OF REASON

Chapter 1

As a nation, subject only to a government of its own choice, Scotland had ceased to exist. It did not, however, disappear. It was not destroyed. If it had lost a measure of identity, it had gained a new outlet for its vigour. Within another hundred years, indeed, it was to become more clearly visible to the world than ever before, and much more audible. No Scottish voice before 1707 had ever been so widely heard as would be the voices of David Hume and Adam Smith, of Robert Burns and Walter Scott. In the people of Scotland the sense of nationality was not diminished by abolition of the apparatus and the trappings of nationality, and though the Highland way of life, and the clan society it nourished, were manifestly doomed by the approach of the modern world, the old conservatism of the north would only be defeated in a calamity that seemed to have been designed to immortalise its archaic gallantry—and then would leave, as its heir, a ghost of curiously ironic temper.

For its survival as a recognisable though decapitated entity, Scotland was primarily indebted to those provisions in the Treaty of Union which preserved its church and its courts of law, its clergy and its advocates; and in alliance with them was the invincible temper of Edinburgh which—as may well be thought—simply refused to recognise that it had been deprived of its *raison d'être*, and continued to exist in stubborn denial of its altered status. There was, however, a long, unhappy period—some twenty-five years or so—before it became evident that Scotland and its capital city had not been mortally wounded, and the pains of traditional poverty were, at first, aggravated by fiscal innovation and the new conditions of life, as well as by the continuing war with France. Before Scotland began its remarkable advance to the prosperity and comfort of the latter part of the eighteenth century, it had to endure a good deal of humiliation, a period of doubt, and a season of anxiety. The English were disposed to regard themselves, not merely as senior partners in the united kingdom, but as purchasers of a commodity for which the Scots had been paid a handsome price. When Queen Anne died and the Whigs were succeeded by the Tories, the peace of Britain appeared to be endangered by widespread dislike of the new German monarch—George of Hanover could not even speak English—and by a surge of Jacobite enthusiasm that became apparent from Cornwall to Aberdeen. And then, when the Pretender's[1] standard was flown on the Braes of Mar, there was, for a little while, acute anxiety about the outcome of rebellion.

The rebellion failed because Louis XIV, who might have supported it, did not live to do so; because in England, where there was loud vocal support for the Pretender, there was no inclination to fight for him; and in Scotland, where the clans mustered beneath his banner, their commander was 'Bobbing John', the earl of Mar, than whom no cause has ever had a more inept and fatuous leader. He had supported the Treaty of Union, he had been secretary of state for Scotland till Anne died, and then he had written to the new king George, to ingratiate himself and appeal for re-employment. But the Hanoverian did not want him, and from pique or vanity Mar became a rebel chief without having formed a plan for rebellion. Those who responded to his summons were more numerous, and represented much broader areas of dissent, than their successors, in 1745, who rose for Charles Edward. To the standard on the Braes of Mar came Clan Donald, Camerons, and Mackenzies from the west and north; Ogilvies and Gordons from the east and north-east; Murrays, Robertsons, and Drummonds from Perthshire; Macphersons and Macintoshes from Speyside and the middle Highlands: as many as 10,000 may have mustered, and for two months, from early in September, the greater part of them did nothing at all. In October about fifteen hundred men under Macintosh of Borlum made a daring foray to the south—crossing the estuary of the Forth in small boats—and having joined forces with Jacobites of the border and the north of England, advanced as far south as Preston, where they were defeated with heavy casualties on 14th November. On the same day Bobbing John belatedly led his Highlanders against a much smaller Hanoverian army, commanded by the duke of Argyll, which had been holding a sound defensive position at Stirling. The two armies met at Sheriffmuir, near Dunblane, in a battle whose confusion is remembered in the rueful jingle:

[1] The son of James II and Mary of Modena was recognised as James III, of Great Britain and Ireland, by Louis XIV of France and by his Jacobite supporters. By others he was known as the Pretender (i.e. claimant to the throne) and later, to distinguish him from his son Charles Edward, as the Old Pretender.

There's some say that we won
And some say that they won,
And some say that nane won at a', man,
But ae thing, I'm sure,
That on the Sheriffmuir
A battle there was that I saw, man,
And we ran, and they ran,
And they ran, and we ran,
And we ran, and they ran awa', man!

When the rebellion had been suppressed, and the venture was manifestly doomed, the Pretender landed at Peterhead on 22nd December. In a dozen places he had been proclaimed as James III, and a sense of honour may have induced him to make his belated appearance. There was, however, nothing he could do, and with Bobbing John he embarked at Montrose and returned to France. The Jacobite magnates lost their estates, but from the forfeiture of some fifty properties, several of them very large, the government got little profit: so large were the debts and burdens on them—and so ingenious the claims against them—that little more than £1,000 was left for the Exchequer. By act of parliament the clans were disarmed, but most of them, it was thought, retained their more serviceable weapons. Those who really suffered for their Jacobite enthusiasm were the prisoners taken at Preston, many of whom were executed.

The Old Pretender was not the ideal leader of a lost cause—he was given to melancholy—but Jacobite loyalty was truly remarkable, and by his marriage to the Polish Princess Clementina Sobieska he became the father of a son, Charles Edward, whose character was such as to inspire a passionate devotion and, with smaller resources than his father could have commanded, to frighten a much more solidly established government than that of George I. It must be noted that Jacobitism still offered any European power, that cherished hostile intentions against England, an opportunity to menace its security. In 1708, for example, when the armies of Louis XIV were hard pressed by Marlborough and no troops remained in Scotland, the French had embarked, at Dunkirk, twelve battalions of infantry aboard a fleet of five battleships and a score of frigates, and attempted invasion. The Pretender sailed with them, and the fleet arrived in the Firth of Forth. There, however, an English squadron of superior strength, and subsequently a spell of adverse weather, prevented a landing, and the French had to return to Dunkirk, having accomplished nothing. After the failure of 1715 the Swedish king, Charles XII, was briefly interested in the possibility of attacking Hanover through a back-door in the

Highlands, and in 1719 an elaborate plan for Spanish intervention was reduced by mismanagement and March gales to a pathetic adventure in which the marquis of Tullibardine and the Earl Marischal led a few Highlanders and three hundred gallant Spaniards to inevitable defeat in Glenshiel.

The final attempt to restore the older dynasty was made in 1745, and that again was launched on a promise of French assistance which, in the event, proved worthless. France, once more, was at war with Britain, and it was to further her own ends that a large expedition was planned for the ostensible purpose of establishing Charles Edward the Young Pretender—'Bonny Prince Charlie' as he was widely known— in a position of strength to which Jacobites from all parts of Britain would naturally gravitate. But the Royal Navy was vigilant, the storms that so often had come to England's aid blew punctually again, and after the French fleet had been scattered France's enthusiasm for the Jacobite cause vanished also. Charles Edward was left to his own resources, and found a strength of purpose sufficient to let him challenge the established might of Britain with no more than seven companions to support him in his venture.

They landed on Eriskay in the Outer Hebrides on 23rd July. He raised his standard at Glenfinnan, and was joined by a few hundred clansmen: Lochiel's Camerons, and MacDonalds of Keppoch and Clanranald. He marched to Perth, gathering strength as he went, and having crossed the Forth reached Edinburgh, where his father was proclaimed king as James VIII. Towards the end of September a small regular army commanded by Sir John Cope was routed at Prestonpans —as so often before, the Highland charge broke all that stood before it—and if the prince had had his way he would then have marched immediately against the English general Wade in Newcastle. In speed of movement and relentless audacity lay his only hope of success, but caution prevailed and he remained in Edinburgh to recruit, if possible, more strength. It has to be remembered that even in the Highlands only a minority of the clans were in arms for King James, and against them were all the Whigs: Campbells in the west, the earl of Sutherland in the north, Mackenzies divided, Lovat on the fence, and Duncan Forbes of Culloden, the Lord Advocate—a devoted Highlander, a shrewd and kindly man—doing all he could to limit the scope of rebellion.

For five weeks Charles remained in Holyroodhouse, and the Hanoverian government was given time to bring home many of its regiments from Flanders and arrange the hire of Dutch troops. Not until the end of October did the Young Pretender lead his army into

England, and though English Jacobites were numerous—or had been so vociferous as to make it seem they were numerous—no attempt had been made to organise or bring them to action. Charles, at the head of four or five thousand men, marched by way of Carlisle and Preston, and in Manchester the Jacobites were warmly welcomed. General Wade was still in Newcastle, and an English army, of very doubtful value, lay just north of London at Finchley. The greatest danger confronting Charles was presented by the young duke of Cumberland, who commanded an army brought back from Flanders. On 1st December, when Charles was at Macclesfield, Cumberland with twice his strength was some forty miles to the south at Lichfield, where he stood athwart the road to London. By a pretended threat to Wales he was induced to move, and the Jacobites advanced as far as Derby. It was Charles's wish to press on—save the army of indifferent value at Finchley, the road to London was now open—but he was overruled, and foremost among those who advocated caution was Lord George Murray. Whether Murray was right or wrong has been hotly debated, but the gambler's chance of success was thrown away, and the decision to retreat was an admission of failure that no local success in Scotland could contradict.

The retreat was well conducted, and Charles could either have attempted to recapture Edinburgh, to give himself a capital, or withdrawn into the Highlands to create a new army. He did neither, but laid siege to Stirling, though its castle was unlikely to yield. Cumberland remained in England, where French invasion was falsely feared, and in Scotland general Hawley—an officer detested by his own people—marched to relieve Stirling with twelve battalions of foot and four of horse. At Falkirk there was a confused, untidy battle, in which some Irish troops who had come to Charles's assistance behaved with great credit, but no attempt was made to exploit the Jacobite victory. Many of Charles's Highlanders, in their customary manner, celebrated success by going home with as much booty as they could carry, and when Cumberland came north to take over command from the brutal and discredited Hawley, Charles was compelled to retreat again. He withdrew to Inverness, which he captured, and Cumberland, marching through Perth, reached Aberdeen on 27th February, 1746.

He left Aberdeen on 8th April, at the head of some 9,000 men and a well-served artillery, and reached Nairn six days later. The Jacobite army, half as strong, ill-fed, and mustered in haste, made a rash attempt to surprise Cumberland by a night march, and when that failed returned to a position of indifferent advantage on Culloden Moor. Battle was joined on 16th April, a day of bitter cold with a north-easterly gale that carried rain and sleet, and within less than an hour the Highlanders were beaten by the overwhelming superiority of their enemies' fire-power. Cumberland's tactical management of his army was sound, and he could have acquired much honour for his victory had his behaviour thereafter shown even common humanity. By his orders, however, no quarter was given, wounded and prisoners were killed, and subsequent to their abominable behaviour on the field his soldiers, under command, proceeded to a policy, throughout the accessible Highlands, of merciless persecution. The Hanoverian government had been badly frightened, and the duke of Cumberland took a very ugly revenge for the assault on his father's throne.

Charles Edward made good his escape from a battle that should never have been fought—his bravery was not disputed, but his judgement lacked the authority to disregard the advice of those about him —and for the next five months, of desperate flight and close pursuit, he lived a life of stark adventure that proved his manhood and his princely temper, and showed forth, for enduring memory, the absolute purity of Highland loyalty and its indefeasible strength. For most of the time he depended for his safety on the honesty of simple people in the western Highlands and the Outer Isles. There was a price of £30,000 on his head—in a poor land, a fortune of incalculable wealth —but none betrayed him. His life was preserved by those who constantly hazarded their own lives for him, and at last he found his way to a French ship which carried him to safety and the long remainder of a life quite singularly devoid of happiness.

The failure of his adventure demolished the structure of clan society and reduced Jacobitism to a sentimental memory. England, seriously perturbed, disarmed the Highlands, proscribed the tartan, and abolished heritable jurisdictions: the private or feudal courts of law, that is, which for centuries had bound tenants to landowner, clansmen to their chief, and whose abolition destroyed the authority on which the social stability of the north was traditionally founded.

Chapter 2

IN 1760, when George III succeeded to the throne, Edinburgh was an overcrowded, evil-smelling, friendly city, equally distinguished for intellect and conviviality; and it offered a remarkable demonstration of the creative faculty inherent in the will to live.

It had lost its royal court in 1603, its parliament in 1707, and those losses, as well as diminishing its importance and robbing it of prestige, had gravely reduced its income. In the last Scottish parliament the burghs were represented by sixty-seven members, the shires by ninety, and of the Scottish peerage—which numbered in all a hundred and fifty-four—no fewer than sixty-four, many of them numerously attended, rode up the High Street to that final assembly. With their families and attendants the representatives of the Three Estates were to Edinburgh the source of a considerable revenue which vanished utterly when their beggarly remnant was diverted to Westminster. Since the middle of the sixteenth century, however, the population had been rising fairly steadily, and the building trades flourished with the help of recurrent outbreaks of fire. Printing, brewing, and candle-making were old-established trades, and to them, by the early years of the eighteenth century, had been added sugar refining and distilling, paper-making, and soap-boiling. Leith, though its fortunes fluctuated, was a busy port, but its export trade was less than that of Fife. The business of the church and the law courts continued, unimpaired by the parliamentary union, and Edinburgh was still their capital. Edinburgh had the resources to sustain its loss of dignity, and presently, having found a new zest in life, diverted some of its returning energy to intellectual pursuits.

It was a sign of grace that the earliest manifestation of the new spirit appeared in the person of Allan Ramsay, a wig-maker turned book-seller, anthologist, poet, and impresario. He tried to establish a theatre in Edinburgh; he wrote a delightful dramatic pastoral, *The Gentle Shepherd*; and he opened the first circulating library in Scotland. As if promising better times to come, he was a truly genial man and he wrote to give pleasure: a revolution to bear comparison with that inaugurated by Dutch William. He died in 1758, two years before George III's accession, and by then his name had been made more famous by his son, the portrait painter, who before he was cajoled into painting royalty and the court, preserved for posterity, as none in Scotland had previously done, the good looks and liveliness of Scottish ladies. How enchanting is his own wife, young, brown-eyed, and cossetted by lace! With what an assurance of her gentle dignity does Mrs. Bruce of Arnot look firmly from her canvas! And what simple, true nobility—what strength of character and sweetness of character— lie in his grave portrait of Flora Macdonald! Allan Ramsay the painter was one of the great benefactors of his time.

In 1760 David Hume was forty-nine, Adam Smith thirty-seven, and James Boswell just twenty. Hume, the oldest of them, was another genial man: perhaps the most genial of all philosophers. He wrote the shortest of autobiographies and described himself as 'a man of mild disposition, of command of temper, of an open, social and cheerful humour, capable of attachment, but little susceptible of enmity and of great moderation in all my passions. Even my love of literary fame, my ruling passion, never soured my temper notwithstanding my frequent disappointments'. His philosophic system appeared to proceed from empiricism to a total scepticism about the rationality of everyday beliefs, but perhaps the philosophers of our own time are better able to appreciate the thought and reason of his *Treatise on Human Nature*, of his *Dialogues concerning Natural Religion*, than were his own contemporaries. It has been written that his intellectual curiosity stopped at nothing, and he thought 'the human intellect very well employed about the legitimacy of treating the origin of worlds as similar in kind to the origin of watches'.[1] It was Kant who said that Hume's ideas about causality had wakened him from sleep and compelled him to think again about everything he had previously thought; while Hume himself 'could altogether discard speculation about rational belief while he played a game of backgammon and drank a bottle of claret'.

Adam Smith was one of Hume's friends who opposed publication of his *Dialogues concerning Natural Religion*; and Smith's own *Wealth of Nations* gave him recognition as 'one of the master minds in the European tradition'. It survives as the source of all theorising about what has come to be called political economy, and to understand Smith as a product of his age and country it is essential to realise that the essence of his doctrine 'is semi-theological in character. It is that there

[1] John Laird in Chambers's Encyclopaedia, 1950.

is a "Natural Order" divinely ordained. As becomes an eighteenth-century Deist brought up in Scotland, Adam Smith is somewhat shy of calling God by his name. Yet the Almighty, by whatever name he may be called, has endowed man with inclinations which have purpose and design. In that somewhat too familiar phrase, men may be led by an invisible hand to promote an end that is no part of their intention. Moreover, God intends the happiness of mankind—indeed the maximum of happiness that is at any time possible. Restrictions of any kind almost inevitably impede the invisible hand in its beneficent guidance. The natural order is always struggling to assert itself; if all restrictions were removed, each one would "naturally" act (though he knew it not) in such a way as to promote most effectively the public good.'[1] That may seem an odd beginning for free enterprise, division of labour, and a capitalist system unrestricted except by God's implicit purpose; but no one can deny that the wealth of the modern world derived largely from the gospel according to Smith.

He was only intermittently an Edinburgh man. A posthumous child, born in Kirkcaldy, in infancy he was stolen by gipsies, but except for that lived an uneventful life. Educated in Glasgow and Oxford, his most formative period was probably the thirteen years he spent in Glasgow as professor of Moral Philosophy. Before writing the *Wealth of Nations* he had made his name well and favourably known by an earlier work called *The Theory of Moral Sentiments*, and the morality underlying the economic analysis of his more famous essay is nicely illustrated in the following passage:

'The rich only select from the heap what is most precious and agreeable. They consume little more than the poor, and in spite of their natural selfishness and rapacity, though they mean only their own conveniency, though the sole end which they propose from the labours of all the thousands whom they employ, be the gratification of their own vain and insatiable desires, they divide with the poor the produce of all their improvements. They are led by an invisible hand to make nearly the same distribution of the necessaries of life, which would have been made, had the earth been divided into equal portions among all its inhabitants; and thus, without intending it, without knowing it, advance the interest of society, and afford means to the multiplication of the species.'[2]

The young James Boswell had to wait, for a proper appreciation of his genius, until, in the middle years of the twentieth century, so many judgements, theories, and opinions were recast according to the

[1] *Adam Smith*. Sir Alexander Gray.
[2] Quoted by Gray, *op. cit.*

lights of recent scholarship, modern psychology, or mere self-indulgence. He lives by virtue of his life of Dr. Johnson, and in his own lifetime and for many years after, he seemed little more than a tick-bird on a shoulder of that great buffalo of letters; but nowadays we know Boswell better than Johnson, and there are many to whom it must seem that the Lexicographer was merely the young man's happiest invention. It was Macaulay who declared, with the self-confidence native to him, that the *Life of Samuel Johnson* was the greatest biography in the English language—a verdict that even now cannot seriously be disputed—but its author was a fool and a sot. To-day, however, when much of his autobiography is widely known, Boswell is recognised as a genius who could expose himself—the whole fabric of his being—to ruthless experience, and record its impress with an artist's propriety and exactitude. Posterity, at long last, has admitted to fame the man whom neither Johnson nor Rousseau, Voltaire nor Paoli, could turn from their doors.

There were others in Edinburgh whom contemporaries much admired—men such as Principal Robertson, the historian; Hugh Blair, famous for his sermons; Lord Hailes, lawyer and historian; John Home the dramatist—but whose reputation has not kept its colour. Of those who had already taken the profitable road to England, the most useful, perhaps, were the brothers William and John Hunter, born in East Kilbride, Lanarkshire, and destined to raise to new heights the practice of surgery, the knowledge of human and comparative anatomy. Both were true scientists, notable teachers, and ardent museum-makers. William's *Anatomy of the Gravid Uterus* was his major work, and John has been recognised as the founder of scientific surgery. But London, not Edinburgh, was where the Hunters settled and made their name and built new systems of knowledge appropriate to the growing world; and another creative Scot, called Robert Adam, went farther than London before finding what he sought.

He was one of four brothers whose father William, born near Kinross in 1689, had acquired distinction as an architect in the Palladian style. Robert went to Italy in 1754, and beyond the Adriatic to Spalato where he studied, surveyed, and drew the ruined palace of the Emperor Diocletian. A magnificent book was the fruit of his labour, and the style he evolved from his studies—elegant, neo-classical, fluent, and gay —made him the most popular architect in Britain. He and his brothers established a family business in London, and built such great country houses as Harewood in Yorkshire, Osterley and Syon in Middlesex, and Kedleston in Derbyshire. But Edinburgh got its share of his genius, and as memorials to him can show the magnificent Register House at the east end of Princes Street, much of the University and Charlotte Square, and a great deal of interior design and decoration that owe almost everything to his example. By the time of his death, in 1792, the capital of Scotland had, indeed, been enlarged, transformed, and beautified by public spirit and municipal enterprise: an achievement which, in all sobriety, must be reckoned as one of the most romantic and creditable in Scottish history.

Forty years before Robert Adam died—in 1752, when he was living in Edinburgh before setting out for Italy—there was published a remarkable pamphlet entitled *Proposals for carrying on certain public works in the city of* EDINBURGH, the object of the proposal being 'to enlarge and improve this city, to adorn it with public buildings, which may be a national benefit, and thereby to remove, at least in some degree, the inconveniences to which it has hitherto been liable'. The 'inconveniences' were notoriously the cramped and confined circumstances of the old town, built so tall and narrow on the rocky spine that ran from the huge, proud eminence of the castle down the royal mile to the palace of Holyroodhouse under the cliffs of Arthur's Seat: a splendid Gothic spectacle, its old houses rising to a height of eight or nine storeys within a rich and daunting stench of history— the silks and satins of noble ladies stained by greasy stone walls under which Highland caddies slept—and the rich odours of oyster stew, strong ale, and thick hen-broth disputing for domination with a persistent faecal perfume that the absence of sanitation made inescapable. Some sixty thousand people, rich and poor, noble and nameless, lived in those high houses, above those narrow closes, and escape was imperative. What redounded so magnificently to Edinburgh's credit was that escape became a triumph. The flight from the old town created the cool and orderly splendour of the new town built on the open ground beyond the valley and the poisoned water of the loch that separated them.

Credit for the decision to build a second Edinburgh—not ruthlessly separated from the old, but manifestly a new creation appropriate for an enlightened century—must first be given to George Drummond, lord provost of Edinburgh, and to James Craig whose plan for the new town was judged the best of six submitted, and adopted in 1767; but the general temper of the age seems also to have been benign, for in the *Proposals* it is asserted that: 'At no period surely did there ever appear a more general, or a better directed zeal for the improvement and prosperity of this country. Persons of every rank and denomination seem at length to be actuated by a truly public and national spirit. Private men who adventure to propose schemes for the public good, are no longer ridiculed as vain projectors. When we consider the rapid progress which our trade and manufactures have actually made within these few years, and attentively compare the present state of this country as to these particulars, with what it was in former times, we are persuaded, that an attempt to enlarge and beautify this metropolis, will now at length be deemed necessary.'

Add, then, to talent and benignity the equally rare art of punctual execution; for 'What is astonishing about the *Proposals* of 1752 is that they outlined a scheme which, in the course of the following eighty years, was actually carried out. The connexion in history between splendid aims and grand intentions on the one hand and the subsequent pattern of events on the other is usually complicated, tenuous, difficult to understand. But in this case what was hoped for and intended was also what was done. Bridges were built and highroads repaired; the city was enlarged and improved and adorned with public buildings; people of rank came to live in it and it was constantly visited by strangers; Edinburgh indeed became a capital of "learning and the arts, of politeness, and of refinement of every kind". Seldom has the promised land glimpsed by one generation been so swiftly and accurately reproduced and entered into by another.'[1]

It was entirely appropriate that in 1771—four years after the adoption of Craig's plan, when the valley between the old town and the new had been drained and a solid earthen bridge was being raised across it —there should be born, in a house in College Wynd in the old town, a child of genius who was destined to create, for England, Scotland, and all the western world, a view and interpretation of Scotland as opportune, as influential, as radically new as the new capital of his country. Literary reputation is no more constant than the moon—it waxes, it wanes, and if there is substance behind it, waxes again—and in the curious literary firmament of to-day the great planet called Walter Scott is obscured by cloud and little regarded. But fashionable neglect, and the failure of contemporary vision, cannot hide the fact that Scott was one of those writers who transcend the ordinary terms of literary reference, and must be accepted, in accordance with a Platonic theory, as demiurges or makers of the changing world. The literary merits of Walter Scott may be argued, and faults in his writing can easily be found; but the magnitude of his creation will be recognised again when current fashions have faded; and his historical importance cannot be disputed. Like James Craig he created something new, and that was a vision, or romantic interpretation, of Scotland and its troubled history. Within Scotland the author of *Waverley* did much

[1] *The Making of Classical Edinburgh.* A. J. Youngson.

to reconcile the educated Scots of Lowland parts to their national relationship with the breechless savages of the Celtic north. In England, to a largely hostile and generally condescending audience, he presented for the first time an acceptable picture of a society which, despite manifest imperfections, deserved honourable attention for its quality of valour, the wry shape of its wit and its ironic humour, its stubborn idiosyncrasies and burly sense of individuality. For France and Germany and Italy, for Spain and Scandinavia, he drew romantic landscapes and peopled them with heroes appropriately clad—the landscapes of *Marmion* and *The Lady of the Lake*, the people of *Quentin Durward*, *The Heart of Midlothian*, *The Fortunes of Nigel*—and there he was accepted as the patron of a new school of romance. For this enlargement of his fame and influence the way had been prepared by a writer whose reputation has dwindled steeply with the years.

James Macpherson was born in 1736 and at the university of Aberdeen showed a promise of brilliance which time was to substantiate. But it was brilliance of a specious sort, though founded on a genuine attachment to Gaelic poetry and what fragments remained of the Ossianic tradition. He was not satisfied, however, with actual relics, but thought he could improve them; and when, in 1760, he published *Fragments of Ancient Poetry collected in the Highlands of Scotland*—said to be translated from the original Gaelic—the book was so favourably received that Macpherson was encouraged to search for larger fragments, and in 1762 he published *Fingal*, which was described as 'an ancient epic poem in six books'; and was followed, a year later, by *Temora* in eight books. The heroes celebrated in these spurious epics are Caledonian champions who are supposed to have resisted—and successfully resisted—the march of Roman imperialism; and Macpherson's motives were undoubtedly patriotic. His practice, however, was less honourable, and neither Fingal, the conqueror of Roman armies, nor Ossian, the Gaelic Homer, has an ancestry that will bear scrutiny. But Macpherson had literary gifts which cannot be despised, for he concocted a rhythmical prose that captivated many of his contemporaries, and conspicuous among his professed admirers were Goethe and Napoleon Buonaparte. *The Works of Ossian* were translated into most of the European languages, and having stimulated the literary movement known as the Romantic Revival, they can be given credit for preparing a welcome for Walter Scott.

Though nowadays he may be the least read of Scottish writers, Sir Walter is unquestionably the greatest, and the nature of his achievement may be compared or contrasted with that of his slightly older contemporary, Robert Burns. Scott created an image of Scotland

These maps give some idea of the reduction of the Gaelic-speaking area of Scotland. The left-hand map shows the situation in the sixteenth century; the right-hand map, in which the percentages may be somewhat exaggerated, refers to 1944. It should be noted that there are in fact no 100% Gaelic speakers—no monoglots—in Scotland today, except for a few Old Age Pensioners, perhaps, and young children in the Outer Hebrides.

Gaelic-Speaking Areas shown thus .... [70-100% Gaelic]

Partly Gaelic-Speaking Areas shown thus .... [1-69% Gaelic]

English Miles
0   50

Gaelic-Speaking Part of Scotland shown thus ....

English Miles
0   50

which, though not always true to fact—he knew little about the Highlands and the Highlanders—was acceptable to the general opinion of his age; and having become part of that opinion, won for Scotland a kindlier interest and a warmer favour than had been customary in the past. Robert Burns, on the other hand, breathed life into the dead body of Scots poetry and by his genius gave it a universal temper and a vernacular tongue. What the Reformation had apparently killed, Burns revived, and a barren century was followed by a renascence that gave Scotland such a wealth of song as few countries can challenge. Burns was no innovator. He created nothing new, except in the lavish and inimitable way of nature herself, who yearly refurbishes alder and ash, birch and beech, and decks them out in the mere novelty of spring. He wrote of country people and country places, and in many respects he was extraordinarily limited; but what he made, he made with classical perfection and total comprehension. There is a sort of simplicity that only genius dares to use, and when used by genius may be translucent as dew and seem to show an infinite perspective.

> Had we never lov'd sae kindly,
> Had we never lov'd sae blindly,
> Never met, or never parted,
> We had ne'er been broken-hearted—

That is the undoubted voice of Robert Burns, but it was a voice which could tune itself, with equal purity, to piety and ribaldry, to scorn and jollity and familiar song. In his own country he was soon adopted as a folk-hero, he became the centre of a cult that was more convivial than poetical; for he had the grace to flatter common appetites by asserting his own pleasure in them. 'Freedom and Whisky gang thegither', he wrote; and 'The sweetest hours that e'er I spend,/Are spent amang the lasses O!'

Though Burns and Scott dwarf all their neighbours-in-time, a chronicle of the eighteenth century—which, as a cultural season, spills over into the nineteenth—should not omit the novelists Smollett and Galt, the poets Fergusson and Hogg. Tobias Smollett, born in 1721 between Dumbarton and loch Lomond, was an early emigrant. He went to London, he joined the Royal Navy and sailed to the West Indies, he travelled in France and Italy, and his splendid picaresque novels—*Roderick Random, Peregrine Pickle*—introduce the British sailor to English literature. Brilliant and ill-tempered, Smollett was incontestably a Scot, and beyond question became an English novelist, and a very good one. Wholly different was John Galt, born in Ayrshire in 1779, who is known for the admirable detail with which he describes rural life in Scotland, and for the firmly drawn and shrewdly observed characters who animate the pages of *The Ayrshire Legatees*, *The Entail*, and *Annals of the Parish*. He travelled as widely as Smollett—he must be regarded as one of the makers of modern Canada—but as a novelist he never moved from Ayrshire.

Robert Fergusson, who died in 1774 in an Edinburgh lunatic asylum —being then only twenty-four—was equally bound to St. Andrews and Edinburgh, and is unsurpassed, even by Burns, in the richness of his Scots vocabulary and the rollicking fun of such poems as *Leith Races* and *The Daft Days*. Marvellously observant is *Auld Reekie*, and for a very young man his picture of rural life, *The Farmer's Ingle*, is wonderfully kind without ever lapsing into sentimentality. Fergusson's genius, shown so generously at so early an age, may have lacked only the robustness, of mind and body, necessary for its support in a town so convivial as old Edinburgh. James Hogg, who was born in 1770 in the Forest of Ettrick, had no difficulty in maintaining health and high spirits in company of the most demanding sort, though he had spent his boyhood in circumstances so pinched and narrow as to make the poverty of Robert Burns's background seem richly furnished. Hogg was a protégé of Walter Scott, and had the supreme gift of enjoyment as well as a talent so varied that he could write 'mountain and fairy' poetry as enchanting as *Kilmeny*; a sophisticated and exquisitely exact parody of Wordsworth; and that darkly imaginative terror-in-prose (which André Gide admired) *The Confessions of a Justified Sinner*.

Henry Raeburn, born near Edinburgh in 1756, used an exuberant palette to illustrate the spirit of the Romantic movement, and left to posterity many superbly drawn and dramatically lighted portraits of his rich or fashionable contemporaries. There are nowhere more splendid-looking Highlanders than his 'Alastair Macdonnell of Glengarry' or 'The McNab'; and nowhere more dauntingly handsome women than the best of his female portraits. Raeburn was a giant of his age who has left ample proof of his strength and stature. Less fortunate was his contemporary, once famous as he, the philosopher Dugald Stewart, whose students at the university included the Earl Russell, Lords Jeffrey, Cockburn, Brougham, and Palmerston; Sir Walter Scott, Sir James Mackintosh, and James Mill, the father of philosophic radicalism, and John Stuart Mill. All were men of distinction in their own fields, and to-day their names, and some knowledge of their importance, are the only remaining evidence of their teacher's great renown.

Forgotten, too, by all except those with a special interest in their time or trade, are the rough-tongued reviewers and coruscating critics who made the *Edinburgh Review*, first published in 1802, and *Blackwood's Magazine*, fifteen years younger, organs of authority, new in kind and savage in temper. The *Edinburgh Review* was founded by Constable the publisher, and long edited by Francis Jeffrey, one of the most brilliant ornaments of the Scottish Bar, and happily remembered for his introduction to a review of Wordsworth's *Excursion*. 'This will never do,' he wrote. Sydney Smith, Brougham, and Scott were among his contributors until the *Edinburgh* became too nakedly Whiggish, when Scott very properly withdrew. *Judex damnatur cum nocens absolvitur* was the *Review's* merciless motto—'The judge is condemned with the criminal who's acquitted'—and it was Brougham who provoked Byron into writing that fine, fierce satire, *English Bards and Scotch Reviewers*, by his ruthless condemnation of the young man's *Hours of Idleness*. As reckless, as hard-hitting, and sometimes as wrongheaded as the *Edinburgh* was William Blackwood's *Magazine*, a Tory counterblast to the *Review*, whose chief contributors were John Gibson Lockhart, Scott's son-in-law and—as Tacitus to Agricola—his superb biographer; James Hogg of the Forest of Ettrick; and the athletic philosopher John Wilson, who took the pen-name of 'Christopher North', who first wrote of 'His Majesty's dominions, on which the sun never sets', and having warned a companion to beware of national prejudice, asserted that it gave him true pleasure 'to declare, that, as a people, the English are very little inferior to the Scotch'. Edinburgh, for a short while, not only claimed a tyrant's right to judge and abuse the world of literature, but exercised it with a boisterous spirit and frequent gaiety. How well for the world of fashionable writing to-day if there were still critics so erudite, so arrogant, so fearless and unfair!

It must not be thought, however, that Scotland's liberated genius revealed itself only in what are now sometimes called the liberal arts. The Lowland Scot is essentially a practical person, and there were several Lowlanders, of notable distinction, who promoted access to the modern world, now looming ahead of them, by their contribution to the business of locomotion. James Watt, born in Greenock as early as 1736, so reduced the cost of steam-power by inventing the separate condenser that he gave the steam-engine its modern form and ensured its economic employment in all the new industrial areas. John Macadam, an Ayrshire man, devised a system for the smooth surfacing of roads—published books on the new art and spent a fortune, all his own money, on its development—and in 1827 was voted a parliamentary grant of £10,000 and appointed surveyor-general of metropolitan roads. Travel was expedited by him, and greatly extended by the science and labours of Thomas Telford, son of a shepherd in Eskdale and Macadam's contemporary, who built bridges, dug harbours and canals—the Menai suspension bridge, the Dean bridge in Edinburgh, and the Caledonian canal are among his enduring monuments—and earned, very honestly, his facetious title, the 'Colossus of Roads'. From them to John Rennie of East Lothian, who in London built the old Waterloo bridge, the East and West India docks—to William Murdoch of Ayrshire, who in 1792 lighted his house and office with coal gas, and ten years later celebrated the peace of Amiens with a larger illumination, from the same source, in Soho—to Robert Stevenson, born in Glasgow, the pioneer builder of lighthouses—or to Sir James Young Simpson, a more sedate pioneer in the use of chloroform and other anaesthetics, there were, in abundance, Scots of this period who, endowed with the imagination and practical abilities necessary for the emergence of a modern world, seemed to appear at need and prosper accordingly.

They prospered, of course—and Britain prospered with them—because the parliamentary union of 1707 had given them a greatly extended area for the profitable use or practice of their crafts, and assured them of peace to prosecute their trade. It is tempting, moreover, to suppose that individual talents had benefited by their release from those political tensions which had never been wholly absent while England and Scotland were separate nations; and freed from the burdens of nationalism, gifted men found a liberty in which their talents could take wing and soar. So it must seem, at any rate, for in the century that followed the failure of the second Jacobite rebellion there erupted from Scotland so many men of outstanding ability that no explanation can be found for its sudden fecundity other than the removal of ancient prohibitions, of which some may have been social, others economic, while the larger ones were undoubtedly political.

Before that century came to an end, there was born in Edinburgh one whose contribution to the known structure of our contemporary world can hardly be overesteemed. James Clerk Maxwell proceeded from school and university in Edinburgh to Cambridge, thence to chairs of natural philosophy in Aberdeen and London, and a period of retirement in which he wrote his *Treatise on Electricity and Magnetism*; which was published in 1873. Before then he had returned to Cambridge as the first Cavendish professor of experimental physics, and of his many contributions to physical science perhaps the most momentous was his theory of electro-magnetic radiation. His work led Max Planck to enunciation of the quantum theory. It has been said, indeed, that if

[332]

you 'trace every line of modern physical research back to its starting-point', you come to Clerk Maxwell.[1] 'He achieved greatness unequalled,' said Planck. The possibility must be admitted that of all who were born within a hundred years of Culloden, the most influential was Clerk Maxwell.

[1] *People* in the series *People, Places and Things*, edited by Geoffrey Grigson and C. H. Gibbs-Smith.

Chapter 3

E SCORTED by his young friend Boswell, Dr. Johnson travelled through parts of the western Highlands in 1773, and to his satisfaction found there the remnants of a patriarchal way of life. It was, however, a way of life already doomed and rapidly decaying. Clan society had been founded on the accepted authority of the chief, who was closely supported by a related class of tacksmen, or principal tenants. The chief and they depended for the necessary services of peace and duties of war on a peasantry related to the chief by sentiment, interest, or blood; and the rights or privileges of the clansmen, which may have been slender, were assured by tradition and the knowledge of common interest instinctive in a closed community. But after the '45 the clans were disarmed, the tartan was proscribed, and the abolition of heritable jurisdictions knocked out the linchpin of Highland society. The chief of a clan was no longer the potential commander of a little regiment of armed men, confident of their obedience, but merely the landlord of a large territory—perhaps a very large territory—which produced very little revenue because the Highland way of life, though reasonably well adapted for social comfort and military service, had never been seriously organised for financial gain. The Highland chiefs had lost authority, the clansmen had lost their function; and to aggravate the problem, the population in many parts of the Highlands was rapidly increasing.

Among those whom Boswell and Johnson met on their Highland tour were Flora Macdonald and her husband, Allan Macdonald of Kingsburgh in Skye: in 1746 Flora had contrived the escape of Charles Edward from the Outer Isles, when the Hanoverians had almost cornered him, and her husband's parents had sheltered him at Kingsburgh. Allan and Flora Macdonald belonged to the upper classes of clan society, and in 1773 they were able to entertain Dr. Johnson in a manner befitting his dignity. But like all their kind they were suffering from the collapse of traditional values, and a year later were compelled to emigrate. In 1774 they settled in North Carolina, joining an exodus that, in the dozen years from 1763 to 1775, is reckoned to have numbered between 20,000 and 25,000 people. The earliest émigrés were people like the Macdonalds of Kingsburgh, who, with sufficient knowledge of what was happening and the intelligence to foresee a future growing steadily darker, had money enough to escape before circumstances became intolerable, and resettle themselves beyond the sea. There were tacksmen who took with them, not only their immediate families, but some of their subtenants to form in another land the nucleus of a new but familiar society. In 1791 it was reported on good authority 'that since the year 1772 no less than sixteen vessels full of emigrants have sailed from the western parts of the counties of Inverness and Ross alone, containing, it is supposed, 6,400 souls, and carrying with them in specie at least £38,000 sterling'.[1]

From counties in the central or south-western parts of the Highlands there was an exodus, less spectacular but probably at least as numerous, to those middle parts of Scotland where an expanding agriculture offered employment, and new industries were looking for recruits. Not all who fled early, however, fared as well as their enterprise deserved. The so-called industrial 'revolution'—which, in fact, had no violent, dramatic beginning, but was evolutionary in the slowness of its earliest stages—had some ugly consequences for those not clever enough to profit by it; and some of the migrants to America were deeply shocked when the thirteen impatient colonies asserted their independence and became the original thirteen states. Allan Macdonald of Kingsburgh, whose father, at the risk of his life, saved Bonny Prince Charlie from the soldiers of George II, risked his own life by fighting for George III, and when the rebellious colonists emerged as the winning side, he and Flora returned to Scotland. Thousands of others, as discontented as the Macdonalds, moved northward into Canada to settle, both east and west of Quebec, in the wildernesses of Nova Scotia and Ontario. Of the pro-British colonists, known as United Empire Loyalists, many were Scots, and for the remaining quarter of the eighteenth century and the first half of the nineteenth, Canada was the chosen haven for Highlanders who fled from hunger and affliction in their own land.

The Highland counties were over-populated, the great majority of those who lived in them had no remunerative work to do, and in the circumstances of the time landowners had become conscious, as never before, of their need of money. Their southern neighbours were ostentatiously growing richer, and money had clearly become more

[1] Quoted in *The Highland Clearances*. John Prebble.

important than the dignity of going to town with a tail of forty fighting men. There was very little money to be made from land that had to feed a swarm of indigent clansmen and their sprawling families, but a new and profitable form of husbandry was being evolved, and in due course it became evident that many a poor Highland estate could be made rich by the introduction of sheep. The price of beef had been doubled by war and the growing population of the south, but better than the small black Highland cattle were wool and mutton; for ingenious farmers had bred a hardy sort of sheep that could graze happily on the northern uplands. There was one difficulty, however, which would have to be overcome before turning the Highlands into money-making sheep-runs. There was no room for sheep and human beings too—human beings whose primitive agriculture was deplorably inefficient—and to make strath and glen and the better sort of hillside profitable, they would have to be cleared of their wasteful inhabitants.

The native sheep which for centuries had grazed the Cheviot hills of the eastern border had been improved beyond recognition by intelligent cross-breeding; as well as being a much heavier, better looking, and more thickly coated animal than its predecessors, the new Cheviot was hardier and could thrive where even black cattle failed. By 1760 the Cheviots were in Perthshire, and thirty years later they reached Caithness, where an admirable proprietor, Sir John Sinclair, who was a man of the highest intelligence, put forward plans for the gradual introduction of a new economy which, by the exercise of patience and intelligence, might transform the country without dislodging its population. But Sinclair's advice was ignored, and many proprietors were in a hurry to be rich. In one way or another, tenants were persuaded or compelled to leave the land where their fathers and forefathers had immemorially lived, and into many a deserted glen came instead a few Lowland shepherds and two or three thousand Cheviot sheep.

The clearances were widespread, and not all were overtly brutal. In the beginning, when the richer tenants left, the flight from the Highlands was, if not voluntary, at least unforced. There were proprietors who helped their poor neighbours to emigrate, and paid their passage-money. There were others who raised their rents to a figure that no tenant could afford to pay, and when the landlord lived elsewhere and left a factor, or agent, in charge of his estate, eviction was often merciless. Eviction might be summary if the proprietor gave an order that no tenancies were to be renewed, and there were unfortunate people who were driven from their homes with violence. In Strathglass and the lands of Macdonnell of Glengarry there was ruthless eviction, and from Easter Ross to the Outer Isles the country was cleared of its redundant population with an ease that is subject to explanation. The clans had been accustomed to leadership and become dependent on it, and now their natural leaders had abandoned them; they were, for the most part, a deeply religious people, and for reasons best known to themselves the majority of Highland ministers in the kirk of Scotland took sides with the proprietors. For the proprietors themselves an excuse can be found in a widespread readiness to believe that what they were doing was designed for the ultimate improvement of their country: from 1780 till the middle years of the nineteenth century they posed as the progressive party, and the most notorious exponents of their policy were active in the large county of Sutherland.

From Cape Wrath to the Dornoch Firth most of the land belonged to Elizabeth, countess of Sutherland in her own right, who in 1785 married George Leveson-Gower, marquess of Stafford, a dull man but the richest landowner in England. For more than twenty years he showed little interest in the vast estate he had acquired by marriage, but when his attention was drawn to the possibilities of improving it, he employed as his commissioners two men, William Young and James Loch, who in the course of time attracted a great deal of unfavourable criticism by the drastic measures they employed to bring about improvement. There was very little good arable land in Sutherland, but many thousands of acres of natural pasture on which sheep could profitably graze; and to make room for sheep, perhaps as many as five thousand people were evicted. In some parts of the county—notably in Strathnaver—they were brutally evicted, and their little houses burnt above them as they were driven out. Stafford spent large sums of money on building roads, bridges, and harbours, and it is probable that neither he nor his countess ever realised the appalling cruelty of the policy they encouraged, but which they never saw in operation. They were enislanded in their wealth, and the clansmen remote in their uncomprehended poverty. Equally uncomprehended was the economic policy which had been so enthusiastically adopted, for the prosperity which the sheep had brought was wearing thin by the 1840's, and some estates were already seeking a new source of income from shooting-tenants. In the course of time many sheep-runs were turned into deer forests, and the red grouse—that excellent and most succulent of game-birds, native to Scotland—became an object of veneration and a source of unexpected wealth.

Shooting-tenants able to pay handsomely for the several pleasures of deer stalking, grouse shooting, and salmon fishing were, by mid-century, readily available in the now numerous class enriched by the industrial revolution. Better farming, a growing linen trade, and the import of Virginian tobacco to the Clyde had, by the middle of the eighteenth century, brought a perceptible new prosperity to Scotland, and by 1760 a start had been made in the building of ironworks at Carron, near Falkirk, and in a project to deepen and improve the navigable channel of the Clyde. Heavy industry, which was to fatten and darken so much of Scotland, had been introduced, and the growth of Glasgow had begun. For a long time, however, agriculture continued to be the country's basic industry, and by the application of new skills and new machinery the land gave a vastly increased yield. Before the end of the first quarter of the nineteenth century the linen industry was more than three times as productive as it had been in 1760, and cotton-spinning, introduced in the 1780's, had grown so rapidly that in Lanarkshire and Renfrewshire, where most of the cotton-mills had been built, it had completely ousted linen, and in Scotland's economy the importance of cotton was secondary only to farming. The tobacco lords of Glasgow, who had become more successful than their competitors in Bristol and London, in 1772 imported 49,000 hogsheads out of a total, shipped to Britain, of 90,000[1]; and by far the greater part of their purchase was exported again to France and Holland and Germany. The great wealth of the tobacco trade vanished in 1775, however, when the American colonists began their war of independence; and having won their war, they then traded direct with Europe.

Of major importance was the use made of James Watt's improved steam-engine. In 1802 it provided power for the experimental tug-boat *Charlotte Dundas*; five years later the American Robert Fulton installed a Watt engine aboard the *Clermont*, and for the first time made steam navigation profitable; and in 1812, when Henry Bell launched his *Comet* on the Clyde, steam power began to drive, not only ships, but a new industry. The number of Scottish ships increased rapidly, the Clyde was deepened and Glasgow became a seaport. Sugar from the West Indies and raw cotton began to compensate for the loss of the tobacco trade, and new banks were founded to meet the demands of an expanding commerce.

In the textile industries machines began to displace manual workers, and though cotton kept its importance, the old-fashioned weaver at his hand-loom might now earn only a few shillings a week. In the central Lowlands, between Ayrshire and Midlothian, the heavy industries were developed where great deposits of coal and iron ore

[1] *Scotland from 1603 to the Present Day.* George S. Pryde.

were waiting for capital and labour to exploit them; and much labour was supplied by evicted peasants from the north. Coal-mines were dug deeper, new machines were invented for them, and the production of coal was vastly increased; while the output of pig iron, stimulated by the discovery of a cheaper process, was multiplied by twelve in the twenty years between 1835 and 1855. Coal, iron, and steel dominated the enlarging century; railways and canals gave access to the farthest as well as the busiest parts of the country; and great shipyards lined the banks of the Clyde. Sailing-ships with iron hulls grew larger, and made faster passages, and still outnumbered the steamers by ten to one when Samuel Cunard's first trans-Atlantic liner, *Britannia*, was built on the Clyde in 1840. The sailing-ship came to maturity and the fullness of her beauty in the great clippers that raced from Canton with tea or to Melbourne for wool, and many of the finest and fastest were built in Scottish yards: *Thermopylae* at Aberdeen, *Cutty Sark* at Dumbarton, *Taeping* at Greenock. But the steamers were to win in the end, and the Clyde, where the first four of Cunard's ships were built, became the home of such globe-encircling enterprise as carried the flags of the White Star, the Clan, the Anchor, and the Donaldson lines. The Clyde became synonymous with shipbuilding and marine engineering.

Scotland prospered, and many thousands of those who laboured for its prosperity suffered an extraordinary degradation. In all countries subject to it, the Industrial Revolution did indeed create a vast extreme between wealth and poverty—wealth became more ostentatious, poverty more exacerbated by contrast—and to Scotland, which had a long history of violence, it may be that the so-called revolution came with an impetus and temper more cruel than elsewhere. Its attendant atrocities were certainly aggravated by the concentration of its effort and effects, for the area open to intensive industry was quite small; and it seems probable that native intensity of feeling, intensity of purpose—which, throughout their history, had recurrently distinguished the Scottish people—were again in action, and now their aim was material success, which for the first time in their history appeared to be within their grasp. To those who were in a position to achieve and enjoy success, it seemed impermissible that anything should hinder or delay their purpose, and they were, in consequence, too often indifferent to the misery and squalor that existed round the corner from affluence.

'But if in the Highlands the people were trying to exist upon a diet of boiled grass and nettles, the case was even worse in the city wynds. Within a circle of twelve miles of Glasgow there were ten thousand paupers receiving on an average not more than one shilling and sixpence a week . . . The child serfs in the West of Scotland bleachfields were being worked from eleven to eighteen hours daily in stoves heated from eighty to a hundred degrees . . . The Census Returns for 1861 showed that one-third of the population of Scotland lived in single-roomed houses, and seven thousand nine hundred and sixty-four of these houses had no window . . . In Glasgow fifty per cent of children died under five years of age . . . In the Spring Circuit Court in Glasgow, 1864, Hugh Gray, for stealing a woollen lorry cover, gets eight years penal servitude; Mary Love, for stealing three yards of drugget from a hedge, gets six years; a man, Dogherty by name, gets three years for stealing a cloth cap from a shop door; Jane Campbell steals fourpence-ha'penny in copper, and gets fifteen months; but Alexander Still, for killing a man with a poker, gets off with six months . . . Property was sacred, not life . . . The pit bottoms are like common sewers, slush and water, with an inclination of one in three, and along these common sewers the women, half-naked, crawl on hands and knees, harnessed like horses to their bogies of coals; little boys, aged four or five, sit all day in the darkness at the trap-doors, cold and shivering, begging for a candle-end for light.'

These quotations are taken from a valuable and unpleasant book called *The History of the Working Classes in Scotland*, by Thomas Johnston, who later in his life became secretary of state for Scotland, and a very good one. They reflect a condition of affairs which may seem the more extraordinary when it is remembered that Scotland was again a deeply religious country. The broad-mindedness or laxity, the deism or scepticism, which had characterised some part of the eighteenth century had not endured, and the prevailing temper of religious thought was sturdily evangelical. Religion, however, had its obligations, and a selective reading of the Bible could provide proof that piety and prosperity had a natural affinity, as had poverty and sin. It was notorious that the poor were often intemperate, though they had been clearly warned that 'he that loveth pleasure shall be a poor man—he that loveth wine and oil shall not be rich'. Joseph, on the other hand—Joseph the son of Jacob, whom his brothers sold to the Ishmaelites—was clearly beloved of Jehovah, and in consequence 'gathered up all the money that was found in the land of Egypt'. The Shorter Catechism is buttressed by a verse from St. Paul's epistle to Timothy: 'If any provide not for his own, and specially for those of his own house, he hath denied the faith, and is worse than an infidel.' It needed no great extension or extravagant application of this text to bring within its condemnation the poor men of Sutherland and the poor men of the slums of Glasgow: they were guilty of poverty, they had failed to provide for their own, and were worse than infidels. If

[340]

the Bible—verse by verse and chapter by chapter—were literally inspired, as so many still believed, it was illogical to blame those who accepted its teaching, word by word, and truly believed that Joseph the son of Jacob had been authorised, by God's love, 'to gather up all the money that was found in Egypt'.

In the temper of to-day, when social inequalities are deprecated and social injustice is harshly censured, it is easy to say that the Scottish clergy were lamentably indifferent to the appalling social chaos that accompanied the swift ascent to prosperity of the more fortunate minority in Scotland; but in 1843 there occurred an event, of improbable dignity in so materialistic an age, that conclusively proved the high seriousness and devotion to principle of a majority of the ministers in the kirk of Scotland, indifferent though they might be to a prevalent destitution of which neither they, nor the champions of 'the auld kirk' against whom they rebelled, had taken cognisance.

The old dispute about patronage had reappeared. Those who dissented from the idea of a church in official association with the state saw in such a church both injustice and spiritual fault; and no minister, they said, could be appointed to an unwilling congregation. The evangelicals grew in power, stiffened in spiritual independence, summoned the privilege of democracy to their support, and at the general assembly of 1843 asserted the right of heads of families to prohibit the appointment of a minister whom they did not want. In so doing, they defied the law of the land, and the law courts condemned what they had done. But the rebels stood firm, and in 1843, in that momentous schism of the Scottish church called the Disruption, a third of all its ministers, numbering nearly five hundred, marched out with no promise of stipends or sustentation other than the goodwill of equally independent worshippers; and with a courageous temper and absolute conviction of the rectitude of what they did, formed the Free Church of Scotland. In doctrine it did not appreciably differ from the parent church. But its ministers and their congregations had accepted a great sacrifice in order to assert a principle of freedom, and freedom, as Dunbar had said long since, is a noble thing. The new churches that were built for the heroic seceders were less handsome than those they had abandoned, but, on the whole, were more enthusiastically attended.

Chapter 4

PATRICK GORDON, who became a Russian general and rendered memorable service to Peter the Great, was born in 1635, a cadet of the distinguished family of Gordon of Haddo in Aberdeenshire. At the age of sixteen he was entered, unconventionally, at a Jesuit college in Prussia, but disliking the education he was offered there, joined the Swedish army and for some years, being taken prisoner by each in turn, fought alternately and with equal goodwill for the Swedes and their Polish enemies. He distinguished himself on both sides, and presently took service under the Czar Alexis I. He fought against Turks and Tartars, and in 1679 was appointed to the chief command in Kiev. Ten years later, after a Crimean campaign against the Tartars, he suppressed in Moscow a rebellion against the young Czar Peter—whose step-sister Sophia was the mischief-maker—and thereafter commanded the capital during Peter's frequent absences abroad, reorganised his army, and became general-in-chief.

In Scotland to-day his name and achievements are virtually unknown, and wholly unknown are the circumstances in which a Barclay of Towie—Towie is on Donside, in the upland parts of Aberdeenshire —settled in Russia in the seventeenth century and bred Michael, Prince Barclay de Tolly, who devised the Russians' strategic retreat in 1812, and in 1815 entered Paris as commander-in-chief of the Russian army. More familiar, though not within common knowledge, is the name of Sir Samuel Greig, called the father of the Russian navy. In 1770 a Russian fleet sailed surprisingly out of the Baltic, through the Channel and the Straits of Gibraltar to the eastern shores of the Mediterranean, and there—even more surprisingly—found and defeated a Turkish fleet under the island of Chios. In nominal command was Count Orloff, lately the favourite of the Empress Catherine, but they who were responsible both for navigation and victory were Samuel Greig and two other Scots, Elphinstone and Drysdale.

That many Scots served in the armies of Sweden, Germany, and the

Netherlands is generally known, though who they were and what they did cannot readily be told; and most of them cannot be named. Reference has been made[1] to the ten thousand or more who fought for Gustavus Adolphus, the Lion of the North. Lord Reay took several thousand Mackays to the Netherlands, others served in Denmark and Prussia. In the Swedish navy, in the seventeenth century, there were several high-ranking officers of Scottish birth, but connexion with, and migration to, the Scandinavian countries may have started much earlier than that; for when the great Birger Jarl was steering Sweden towards unity in the thirteenth century, he had in his service a Scot called James Tait, whose descendants are said to be still living in Finland. Mercenary soldiers, of course, are necessarily foot-loose, but men who soldiered for Sweden often settled down to live and rear families there. In the sixteenth century there was a citizen of Stockholm, known to be Scottish and called by the Swedes 'Blasius Dundee', who was so rich that he acted as banker to their King John III. In the following century one of Sweden's principal diplomats was Alexander Erskine, and James Robertson of Struan in Perthshire was physician to Gustavus Adolphus. More curiously, perhaps, there were, at a slightly later date, goldsmiths and silversmiths of Scottish birth in Stockholm. Living there, at about the same time, were a James Clark, a Sanders Clark, a John Halliday, and an Alexander Fife.

The fact is that from an early time—perhaps from the thirteenth century, when James Tait took service with Sweden's Birger Jarl—Scotland had never been large enough or prosperous enough to sustain all the able and energetic male children born behind her frontiers; and if the true story of a country is the story of its children, then the story of Scotland cannot be confined within its geographical outline, but must be extended to include the activities of those active or restless Scots who took service abroad, and led creative lives in regions far distant from their native parishes. After the incorporating union of 1707, the opportunities of service in Russia and Sweden, in Prussia and Poland, were cut off, but as compensation employment became available in trade, politics, and the army, in the even larger regions ruled by the British crown. Scotland responded eagerly, and in the eighteenth and nineteenth centuries there was no lack of recruits from the north for the commerce, government, and fighting forces of the empire.

Empire-building, when Britain's empire-building began, invited no moral reprobation, and so far from being deliberate aggrandisement was, for the most part, the consequence of a reluctant government's acquiescence in the demand, by adventurous merchants abroad, for

[1] See p. 264.

protection of the precarious businesses they had tentatively established under the frowning walls of an oriental autocrat's forbidding capital. In Canada the French had to be subdued to allay the fears of the American colonists—to give them, indeed, the security in which they could successfully wage their War of Independence—and in India the collapse of the Mogul empire had left an anarchy so intemperate that if commercial relations with the western world were to be established, the first necessity was the introduction—the imposition by force, where force was required—of some degree of law and order. Competing for an empire in the East was England's old enemy France, and for war against France, the Union of 1707 had given England a new recruiting area of marvellous value.

William Pitt, earl of Chatham, told parliament in 1766: 'I sought for merit wherever it was to be found, it is my boast that I was the first minister who looked for it and found it in the mountains of the north. I called it forth and drew into your service a hardy and intrepid race of men, who when left by your jealousy became prey to the artifice of your enemies, and had gone nigh to have overturned the State in the war before the last. These men in the last war were brought to combat on your side; they served with fidelity as they fought with valour, and conquered for you in every part of the world.' Some twenty years before that, the quality of Highland soldiers had been effectively demonstrated at the battle of Fontenoy by the first High-land regiment to be raised for service of the crown. In 1725 six independent companies, or 'watches', of military police had been formed in the Highlands; and because they were clothed in kilts of a very dark tartan they were collectively called *Am Freiceadan Dubh*, or The Black Watch. In 1739 four additional companies were raised, and The Black Watch became a regiment of a thousand men. Six years later it fought its first battle, and in the epic struggle at Fontenoy—where the French under Marshal Saxe beat an allied army of British, Hanoverians, Dutch, and Austrians—it was magnificent in attack and in retreat covered the exhausted allies with exemplary steadiness and skill. In the next half-century thirty-two Highland regiments were raised, most of which, having been formed for some specific purpose, were disbanded within a few years; but permanent additions to the army list were the Highland Light Infantry, the Seaforths, the Gordons and the Camerons, the Argyll and Sutherland Highlanders. Superlatively good in battle—fierce and dashing in attack, stubborn and formidable in defence—most of these regiments were unusually well-behaved in their happier seasons of peace; crime was almost unknown, because in the closely knit communities from which they came their relations would suffer if it were said that a son or a brother had conducted himself in a way unworthy of his name. In one of his earlier stories[1] Rudyard Kipling has written: 'A powerfully prayerful Highland Regiment, officered by rank Presbyterians, is, perhaps, one degree more terrible in action than a hard-bitten thousand of irresponsible Irish ruffians led by most improper young unbelievers.' Though now it may be difficult to believe, in the nineteenth century many soldiers in India were indeed 'powerfully prayerful', and senior officers were inclined to regard their duties to God and the queen with an equal, evangelical fervour.

It would be tedious to catalogue even the more distinguished Scottish names that punctuate the tale of British expansion in India, of the substitution for war and anarchy of the rule of law. It is agreeable, however, to record that the founder of the Indian National Congress —the party or organisation which eventually provided an independent India with its first government—was a Scotsman called Allan Octavian Hume. A member of that most learned and dedicated of governing bodies, the Indian Civil Service, Hume wrote 'to all the graduates of the Calcutta University asking for fifty volunteers to join in a movement to promote the mental, moral, social, and political regeneration of India. "There are aliens, like myself, who love India and her children . . . but the real work must be done by the people of the country themselves. . . . If fifty men cannot be found with sufficient power of self-sacrifice, sufficient love for and pride in their country, sufficient genuine and unselfish patriotism to take the initiative and if needs be devote the rest of their lives to the Cause—then there is no hope for India. Her sons must and will remain mere humble and helpless instruments in the hands of foreign rulers. . . ." '

'The result of this letter was the first Indian National Congress of 1885.'[2]

Hume was a man of vision, but they who created stability in India, from which a long view became possible, were soldiers; and the story of India-in-transition amply demonstrates what Scots in exile contributed to the process. Sir Hector Munro, for example, who with eighteenth-century liberality was both a general and a member of parliament, won the great battle of Buxar which in 1764 decided the political future of Bengal and Bihar, and in 1778, in command of the Madras army, he took Pondicherry from the French. Another of the same clan, Sir Thomas, served an arduous apprenticeship in hardfought campaigns against the adventurer, Hyder Ali of Mysore, and

[1] *The Drums of the Fore and Aft.*
[2] *The Guardians.* Philip Woodruff.

Tippoo his son; and finally became a sagacious, sympathetic, and progressive governor of Madras. There were others of comparable distinction—Mountstuart Elphinstone and John Malcolm, who pacified the wild Marathas, and some of eccentric genius such as Samuel Macpherson. He was a son of the professor of Greek at Aberdeen, and as a young officer he was sent to survey a difficult and unhealthy area north of Madras. As recently as 1840, when Macpherson began this major work there, it was in effect unknown country, inhabited by a primitive people, the Khonds, who came originally from Orissa, and whose lives were dominated by what Macpherson called 'a weak, incoherent theism, with a subordinate demonology'. There were monthly fertility rites, at which the Khonds sacrificed human beings —infants, prisoners of war, and others bred for sacrifice—with revolting cruelty; and when the facts belatedly became known, public opinion, or British opinion, was deeply shocked. For various reasons it was impossible to suppress the Khonds and prevent their horrid practices by physical force. Reformation could be effected only by moral force, and only Macpherson knew enough about the Khonds to reason with them. He was instructed to do what he could, and by guile and goodwill, by sympathy and understanding, he was marvellously successful. He was a delicate man who did not live to enjoy much fame, but he pacified the Khonds and cured them of their murderous habit.

In July, 1857, when news of the revolt of the Bengal army reached England, command of the forces in India was given to Colin Campbell, an officer whose range of experience had been truly remarkable. He had fought under Wellington's command and Moore's in Portugal, he had sailed with the ill-fated expedition to Walcheren. He had served and twice been wounded in the Peninsular war, he was so unfortunate as to be ordered to America and learnt the taste of defeat at New Orleans. Garrison service in the West Indies was followed by war in China in 1842, and the Sikh war of 1848. He had no political or family influence to help him in his profession, and promotion was slow; but in the Crimea in 1845, after forty-six years of active service, he commanded the Highland Brigade, and after distinguishing himself at the battle of the Alma he stood with his 'thin red line' of Highlanders—the 93rd, Argyll and Sutherland—and broke the attack of the Russian cavalry trying to force their way through to Balaklava. He was sixty-five when he accepted his last command, in India, and added to his fame by relieving the long-besieged Residency at Lucknow. His sometime commanding general, Sir John Moore, was also a Scot—son of a Glasgow doctor—whose ideas were much in advance of his time; for he treated his soldiers like reasonable beings and trained the infantry whom Wellington led to victory. He and Campbell were soldiers of the sort who rose to high command under Gustavus Adolphus and Frederick the Great; it was Britain's good fortune that the incorporating union had given her a monopoly of Scotland's military talent.

At sea, in 1797, a sanguinary battle was fought off Camperdown, on the Netherlands coast, between a Dutch fleet of sixteen ships under de Winter and a British fleet of the same size commanded by Adam Duncan. Born in Dundee to a family said to have been distinguished for centuries for its peaceful and domestic virtues, Duncan entered the Royal Navy at the age of sixteen, and after many years of dull service had energy and initiative enough to cripple the Dutch by blockading the Texel; to survive the perilous mutiny of the Nore; and to crown his career with overwhelming victory at Camperdown.

More brilliant by far was the life of Thomas Cochrane, heir to the impoverished earldom of Dundonald, who in 1800 at the age of twenty-five commanded the small brig *Speedy* of fourteen 4-pounder guns and fifty-four men, and in the course of fifteen months, in the western Mediterranean, captured over fifty privateers and merchantmen, and the Spanish frigate *El Gamo*, of thirty-two guns and a complement of three hundred. Cochrane was then captured by three French line-of-battle ships, but was soon exchanged, and for some months resumed his studies at Edinburgh University. When he went back to sea he made a fortune in prize money, and after a stormy political career undertook, and almost instantly secured, the liberation of Chile from Spanish suzerainty, and subsequently fought with almost as much success for the freedom of Brazil.

In service abroad, in India, the Peninsula, and on several oceans, there were Scotsmen capable of high enterprise and willing to shoulder large responsibilities; but in Scotland itself, in the sphere of politics and government, there was a state of mind which can only be described as apathy. Archibald, third duke of Argyll, died in 1761, and for nearly forty years before his death—in the intervals of amassing a library of great value—had so successfully managed the affairs of Scotland as to be called its 'king'. His nephew John, third earl of Bute and sometime prime minister, succeeded him and for a few years controlled Scottish appointments; and in 1774 a new era began when Henry Dundas, the son of an old-established legal family, was returned as member of parliament for Midlothian. In the following year he was made lord advocate, and the weakness of the political constitution that Scotland had accepted in 1707—by which, in the whole country, there were only about four thousand qualified electors—gave him the opportunity to exercise an aptitude for power which made him, for some thirty years, the general manager of Scotland. In the British parliament, in firm alliance with the younger Pitt, he was advanced to high office; he was raised to the peerage as Viscount Melville; he survived impeachment for the misappropriation of public funds; he governed Scotland with suave assurance; and when he died in 1811 his son Robert succeeded him as general manager, though with reduced powers. In 1815, at the battle of Waterloo, the Scots Greys and the Gordons charged together—Highlanders holding by one hand to the troopers' stirrup-leathers—with a great cry of 'Scotland for ever!' The idea of Scotland, the belief in a nation which, though deprived of sovereign power, retained a sovereign image, was probably stronger and more definite in its forces afloat or oversea, and among individuals of an eccentric or idiosyncratic sort, than in the great majority of its domiciled population, many of whom were enjoying the benefits of the industrial revolution while many others were bemused and emasculated by it.

Throughout their history Scots had disclosed the stimulating effect, on their nerves and imagination, of foreign travel, and certainly there is significance in the fact that during a prolonged period of political lassitude at home, there was considerable activity among Scots abroad, whether in British service or in the discontented colonies. After Cromwell's victory at Worcester, there were several members of the Clan Munro among the royalist prisoners deported to America, and at Lexington in 1755 a descendant of one of them, who sired a large family, is said to have fired the first shot in the War of Independence: of the seventy-seven 'Minutemen' involved in that skirmish, no fewer than sixteen have been identified—if only tentatively—as Munros.[1] There is, moreover, circumstantial evidence that James Monroe, twice president of the United States, was descended through a cadet family from a Munro of Foulis, chief of the clan.

Of conspicuous interest is the case of John Paul Jones, born in 1774 in the stewartry of Kirkcudbright, and by repute the son of John Paul, a gardener. It was commonly thought, however, that John Paul's employer, a Mr. Craik of Arbigland, was in fact the boy's father. At an early age he determined to be a sailor, and in 1760 went to sea as an apprentice in the ship *Friendship*, bound for the Rappahannock in Virginia, where his elder brother had settled. He found the New World attractive, and after a dozen years at sea—during which time, after being mate on a slaver, he rose to command—it became 'the country of his fond election'. His brother died, childless, and Paul Jones—as he now called himself—settled down on his estate. But not

[1] *The Clan Munro.* C. I. Fraser of Reelig.

for long. When war was declared he quickly joined the insurgent colonists, and under a new flag showed his wonderful audacity and achieved spectacular successes. He spread terror in the Solway, he threatened Leith, and off Flamborough, in command of a very small squadron, he took two British men-of-war, homeward bound from the Baltic. When that war had been won he joined the Russian navy and served the Empress Catherine. From his father, whoever he was, he had inherited independence of mind, and he must be acknowledged, not only as an ornament to Virginia, but a credit to Kirkcudbright.

After the French wars, emigration to Canada increased, and many parts of Canada acquired new names from Scottish counties. The Hudson's Bay Company recruited largely from Orkney to man lonely stations that reached across the continent from Labrador to the Pacific. In 1803 Thomas Douglas, earl of Selkirk, had led eight hundred Highlanders across the Atlantic to a settlement in Prince Edward Island, and some years later he essayed the ambitious colonisation of a great tract of land on the Red River that flows into Lake Winnipeg; the colonists encountered many difficulties, but after confused conflict and Selkirk's death achieved a modified success. A generation before Selkirk showed interest in Canada, a native of Stornoway, Alexander Mackenzie, explored the country of the Great Slave Lake and followed a river, to which he properly gave his own name, to the Arctic ocean. Simon Fraser, whose father had fought with the Empire Loyalists, christened the great river that flows from the Rockies into the Pacific, and as if British Columbia were a larger substitute for the western Highlands, great numbers of Scottish emigrants crossed the mountains to Vancouver.

Later in the nineteenth century there was a numerous emigration to Australia and New Zealand, where there was an abundance of good land which, by the application of hard labour, would sustain life and eventually declare a profit. It is to be observed, however, that Scottish settlers in the Antipodes—even those who greatly prospered, and the sons and daughters of prosperous men—have habitually retained and frankly shown a continuing attachment to their native soil—of Sutherland or the Mearns, of Caithness or Perthshire—which, though it may be discounted as sentimental, cannot be denied an essential truth.

More interesting, perhaps, and possibly more indicative of a Scottish tendency to extra-polarity, is the fact that within eighty years there were born to a very small population at least three distinguished explorers of what, for many years, was romantically known and realistically described as 'the dark continent' of Africa. In 1755 the population of all Scotland may have been a million and a quarter; by 1820 it had grown to just over two million. It was in 1730 that James

[349]

Bruce was born, the gifted eccentric son of a county family, and having reached the mature age of thirty-eight Bruce set off on an ill-prepared expedition to Abyssinia in search of the source of the Nile. He survived extraordinary hardships and perils, and when at last he published an almost truthful account of his adventures, he was mortified by the general disbelief with which it was received.

Mungo Park, a farmer's son from the forest country near Selkirk, was born in 1771, qualified as a doctor, and dedicated himself to exploration of the course of the Niger. His intermediate reports have been described as 'classics of travel', but he died untimely in 1806. Greatest of the three, and born in 1813 in the humblest circumstances, was David Livingstone, whose father, a working man with studious habits and literary interests, was typical—not, of course, of the majority of working men in Scotland, but quite certainly of an influential minority. Young David worked in a cotton-factory for fourteen years, and studied Latin. He determined to become a Christian missionary, and with a practical realisation of the difficulties of his proposed vocation, decided to qualify as a doctor. He embarked for Africa in 1841, and for more than thirty years laboured in unceasing danger but with recurrent success for the establishment of geographical facts and Christian truths in some of the most beautiful and savage parts of that perilous and exciting continent.

In Africa to-day the virtues and achievements of David Livingstone are probably discounted or denied; but when historical judgements are reasserted his greatness will not be disputed. He combined, with a passion typical of his age, a fervour to propagate the Christian gospel with a very practical desire to introduce some of the small, available benefits of modern science; he wanted desperately to chart and map the difficult, enchanting country he had discovered; and to mitigate an ancient, pitiless conservatism he tried to introduce the enlightenment of Christian compassion. David Livingstone was a great man, a great explorer, and a martyr to the conscience of his age. His name and some account of the work he did should not be omitted from a story of Scotland and its people.

It is a very small country, but few small countries have exercised a greater influence on larger parts of the world; and as, within its own boundaries, individuals have been of more consequence than institutions, so, in those expansions of its history that lie beyond its native seas, have individuals made their mark and contributed to the national legend.

The history of Scotland is the history of its people, and cannot be confined to a map.

Chapter 5

IN the 1890's the population of Greater Glasgow was about 1,800,000—more than the population of all Scotland a hundred years earlier—and Glasgow was one of the largest cities in Europe. Elsewhere growth has continued, and in many places has been enormous. But Glasgow, though its appearance has altered, has shown no numerical increase. Its population to-day is approximately what it was seventy years ago.

Glen Strathfarrar in Inverness-shire is one of the most beautiful, and now one of the most desolate of all Highland glens. It is commonly said that two hundred men from Strathfarrar fought at Waterloo, fifty in the Crimea, but in the Great War of 1914 only two; because only two men of military age then lived there.

The present population of Scotland is more than five million, but by a current trend appears to be slowly decreasing. There is, at present, an emigration rate of about 45,000 a year, and more serious than the gross diminution that figures can show is the unfortunate fact that many of the liveliest and most intelligent young people are leaving because England offers more opportunities for advancement and facilities for amusement. Throughout the country there has been, for perhaps the last twenty years, a decline in rural population due in part to the increasing mechanisation of agriculture, in part to that preference for congregation rather than segregation—for city streets rather than country lanes—which is typical, not specifically of Scotland, but generally of the twentieth century. For rural depopulation reasons can be found, but it is difficult to explain Glasgow's failure to grow in a period when rapid growth had been characteristic of so many cities.

It has been suggested that Glasgow never fully recovered from the zeal with which it volunteered for military service in the first Great War: that too many of its ablest, most energetic and imaginative young men were killed at Gallipoli and Loos, on the Somme and at Passchendaele. It is probable, indeed, that many parts of Scotland, with a long

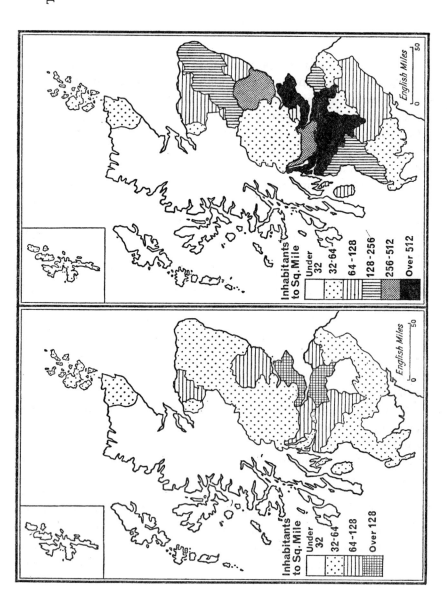

The density of population by counties, in 1755 and 1931.

tradition of soldiering behind them, contributed far beyond their strength to their local regiments, Lowland or Highland, all of which had to raise many battalions to meet the ever repeated demand for infantry in that long and abominable war. On the other hand it should be remembered that Glasgow, the great centre of heavy industry and so of the necessary war-time industries, became notorious for its militant socialism, for the angry strikes that threatened the production of new shipping and more shells, and for its election of parliamentary representatives who were even more disruptive of reasoned debate than pre-war Irish members. The river Clyde, the mother of ships, became widely known as the Red Clyde, and not many observers of the confused scene realised that the enthusiasm which had filled the ranks of the Highland Light Infantry and the Cameronians was closely related to the hot-blooded indignation with which munition workers denounced the injustice of having to make shells for their employers' benefit.

In the early 1920's Glasgow seemed to lose confidence in itself, but whether that was due to its losses in war or to embarrassment caused by its political complexion, cannot easily be decided. A generation later, when a great task of slum-clearance and rehousing was undertaken, uncommon difficulty was encountered; the slums of Glasgow had been built like fortresses and were as hard to demolish. Nowadays the scene has changed dramatically, and slab-sided, many-storeyed blocks of flats rise to a great height in almost smokeless air. The city's old foundation on heavy industry has to a large extent been replaced by a more varied economic base, and it appears that initiative has been regained.

Only in degree and local detail can the recent history of Scotland show differences from the rest of Britain, but twice within the last half-century such differences have been broad enough—or so have seemed to many—to provoke dissatisfaction and give it a political voice: the Scottish National Party was founded in 1928 with the explicit purpose of abrogating the Treaty of Union of 1707 and re-establishing by 'home rule' some degree of independence. For several years the Nationalists enjoyed a lively existence, but in 1939 their cause was obscured by the second Great War, and till recently their arguments made no great impact on the majority of people in Scotland. Within the last few years, however, there has been a growing interest in their proposals, and several of their candidates in the last general election were substantially supported.

In 1928 there was much cause for discontent. Scotland had very little control over her own affairs, and even before the American financial collapse infected the rest of the world, its economy was thin-ribbed and shrinking in comparison with England's. Some time after the first Great War the economists had proposed, for the ailments of British industry, a remedy called 'rationalisation', the purpose of which was to eliminate its unprofitable parts; and in Scotland it seemed that Scottish parts were usually the first to be declared unprofitable. In Scotland the disillusionment which followed the military victory of 1918 was bitter. It was more bitter than in England because Scotland, a far smaller country, was more aware of its losses, which most people believed to have been proportionally much higher than England's; and because Scotland, with its military tradition, had been immensely proud of the fame that Scottish soldiers had earned—especially the splendid 51st (Highland) Division—and was in consequence deeply disappointed when the only rewards of valour were neglect and a growing poverty. Scotland, perhaps, was hyper-sensitive, but for a little while Nationalism prospered—though its leaders were without skill or experience in the art of politics—because, in one way or another, native pride had been hurt, as well as native pockets; and conspicuous among its supporters were three eminent literary figures.

Their senior was Robert Bontine Cunninghame Graham, an aristocrat, a romantic who had lived as a gaucho in South America and served a prison-term in England for 'riotous assembly' in Trafalgar Square. Cunninghame Graham was gallant and erudite, the last cavalier; and in happy companionship with him was Compton Mackenzie, who had written *Sinister Street*—one of those novels called seminal—and after establishing a literary reputation on the involutions and ornaments of a style which Henry James had publicly admired, proceeded to a different success, in the first Great War, as a Royal Marine officer in charge of counter-espionage in the eastern Mediterranean. The third of the trio was Christopher Grieve, more generally known by his pen-name, Hugh MacDiarmid, who combined a fierce and flamboyant Nationalism with an individual variety of Communism and a remarkable poetic talent. He devised a literary dialect that drew freely from the full Scots vocabulary of Dunbar, and for some years wrote with such splendour that he was widely and justly recognised as a major poet, though his chosen dialect—which he called 'Lallans', and others 'synthetic Scots'—attracted much adverse criticism and the scorn of the conventional.

MacDiarmid's poetry, indeed, had a much longer life, and perhaps a more lasting influence, than the Nationalist temper of the 1920's. He was flattered by disciples and imitators who adopted his dialect, though none made any great advance in its use, and several writers,

[354]

of different sorts and talents, combined with him to add the gaiety of their literary compositions to political dispute. James Bridie, a Glasgow doctor, emerged as a gifted, original, and prolific dramatist and in Glasgow founded his own theatre. Neil Gunn was a novelist who wrote of Highland scenes with deep understanding and great sensitivity. Edwin Muir, who was born in Orkney but lived much abroad, was a poet who could express profoundest thoughts in an English so clear, so fresh and limpid, that often it seemed a language flowing, for him alone, from some secret spring. And there were others.

The more recent exposure of Nationalist feeling—and the reappearance in some strength of the National Party—have several causes. After a period of general prosperity it became evident that the average of earnings and income in Scotland was lower than in England; the incidence of unemployment tended to be a little higher; and Britain's new and humbler position in the world had deprived Scotland of such favoured fields of employment as Ceylon and Assam, where Scots tea-planters had, in happier times, almost established Scottish colonies. The persistent emigration of many of its cleverest and most energetic young people was not only a visible loss, but a source of exasperation because it showed clearly that Scotland neither had the resources to pay, nor the social, aesthetic, and intellectual rewards to satisfy the demands of those whom, in all probability, it had most reason to keep at home. And, in the changing economy of the world, the prospect—however distant—of Britain's entry into a European 'common market' led some to suggest that an independent Scotland might be better able to negotiate the export and sale of specific Scottish products.

The arguments for separation, for independence, have a larger foundation in emotion than in fact—they are derived from a persistent pride, from an enduring memory that Scotland was once a free, separate, and unruly nation, and no longer is—but the price of independence would be high, and the fruit might well be sour. While it would be blatantly dishonest to claim that 'all is well' with Scotland, it has to be admitted that the majority of its population enjoy a larger freedom and a greater degree of comfort than ever before. Its intellectuals—the upper classes of its native intelligence—have ample reason for complaint, for pessimism and anger; but in its population, of rather more than five million, there is only a small minority that can complain of the sort of poverty and physical unhappiness that were common as recently as the beginning of this century.

Here it may be opportune to explain why the lofty reputation of Scottish education, on which all Scotland used to pride itself, has lately declined. It has fallen because of our contemporary addiction to

[355]

egalitarianism, and to the excessive bureaucracy which now determines and controls the common forms of education. The Scots 'dominie'—the village teacher, that is—used to be a man of unchallenged authority, and he, in his wisdom, used to choose and select from his half-hundred pupils the four or five who were manifestly more gifted than the others, and to them he would devote the larger part of his time and attention, while the others imbibed what they were fit for, a merely elementary knowledge of reading, writing, and arithmetic. Under such a regimen Scottish teaching and its products were rightly praised, and many a village boy rose to well-paid eminence. But then bureaucracy crept in, and notions of egalitarianism. The village dominie lost his power, and education was spread more evenly, but more thinly. The basic problems of education—the problems of how, why, and to what end—are problems still unsolved, and they may be insoluble; it is possible, however, that the old-fashioned dominie had an understanding which has not been bettered.

Freedom for teachers—freedom from constituted authority and the insufferable interference of parents—might, within a generation, or two, create an insurgence of properly instructed intelligence large enough even to cope with the appalling problems which await the next generation but one.

Reference, more than once, has been made to Scotland's activities in other parts of the world; to soldierly achievement in France or under Gustavus Adolphus of Sweden, to conquest in India, to arduous and heroic exploration of the unknown darkness of Africa, to patient and laborious development of vast but unused lands in Nova Scotia and New Zealand. To an unbiassed observer, indeed—to a critic un-influenced by Highland blood or Lowland sentiment—it might well seem reasonable to compare the Scots with the Jews, and decide that Scotland's achievements beyond the surrounding seas of Scotland should be judged in comparison with the effects on the world of the Jewish *diaspora*. The dispersal of the Jews—the *diaspora*, as it was called —had effects on the western world that cannot yet be calculated or esteemed; and it may be suggested that the less advertised *diaspora* of the Scots—to Sweden as merchants as well as soldiers, to France and the Netherlands when they were needed, to India and the farther East, to Australia and New Zealand, to England and many parts of America —has had consequences which may for ever be farther than measurement can go. It is not beyond the scope of reasonable speculation to suppose that Scotland's ultimate importance may repose on the activities of its farthest or most forgotten exiles.

Of Scotland as geography defines it, and a contemporary judgement may esteem it, there are four things that demand expression. The first is that under the general flattening of national differences which the speed and increasing use of modern communications have imposed, Scotland more closely resembles its immediate neighbours than ever before, but retains so strongly a sense of separate identity that many of its reasonable inhabitants can contemplate, despite an economic disadvantage, a reassertion of political independence.

The second is that several parts of northern and western Scotland, previously of small value, may largely benefit from the world's latest industry, which is tourism. Many countries on which poverty has been imposed by basic geological facts are picturesque; and the Highlands of Scotland, where long sea-lochs come in to take the knees of the mountains in their arms, are of handsome shape, delectable colour, and still retain such ancient inhabitants as red deer, grouse, and salmon. Increasingly they are attracting visitors, and thereby earning some addition to the national income.

The third thing is the increasing demand for that product of Scotland which is often regarded as a symbol of the country, and about which little is usually known. In 1965 almost forty million gallons of whisky were exported, and the British Treasury got from Scotland's unique and not-to-be-emulated industry the useful sum, in foreign currency, of nearly £110,000,000 sterling. Most of those who drank the exported whisky drank the widely advertised blends; which are, in fact, a carefully adjusted mixture of several pot-still whiskies with a larger proportion of patent still spirit.

The traditional pot-still had been evolved in those Highland parts where sweet water, full-grained barley, and good black peat were all available; and the patent still, which delivered alcohol continuously and quickly, was invented about a hundred and thirty years ago. From a combination of their products came the spirit which, internationally, is called 'Scotch'; and the best of the blends are very good indeed. But by those who know them it is usually thought that better than any blend are the single whiskies, the pure malts of individual distilleries, each of which has its own flavour and distinctive character. How admirable, for example, are the robust and feudal flavour of Talisker, distilled in the Isle of Skye; the gentle orchard-bloom of Lagavulin from Islay; the distinctive, almost Irish geniality and persisting glow of Highland Park from Orkney; the little known but lyrical Glenmorangie from Easter Ross; the great whiskies of Banff and Moray, by many thought the noblest of all, from jovial Glenfiddich to the suave valour of Smith's Glenlivet. These whiskies—and there are many others—are not well known outside the remote places of their origin; but greater knowledge—and it may be growing—would certainly award them a dignity comparable with the esteem enjoyed by the great wines of France. Everyone knows by name the Château wines of Margaux, Lafite, and Latour; and Talisker, Glenlivet, and Highland Park deserve an equal fame.

Finally it should be said that the Highlands—for so long the most neglected and still the emptiest parts of Britain—may acquire other industries than tourism and distilling, and for the first time in their history wear a prosperous and busy look. The very fact of their emptiness could be an inducement to industries which need room for expansion, and for atomic power plants there is the advantage of an inexhaustible water supply. The old Celtic parts of Scotland have already taken a curious revenge for the humiliation they suffered in the eighteenth century, when their society was disrupted and their clan tartans proscribed. For when tartan was again permitted it was welcomed with sentimental enthusiasm; its few and simple patterns were multiplied by inventive tailors; it became fashionable, and the kilt which had been the garb of Highland peasants was proudly worn by Lowland converts to a romantic faith and the male members of the royal family for whom Queen Victoria had found a new home and old employments at Balmoral. As the banished tartans were restored to unexpected favour, so may the northern counties, emptied in the name of progress, be filled again by a second industrial revolution. To romantic minds such a prospect might not be welcome; but it cannot be excluded from speculation about the future.

THE RULERS OF SCOTLAND FROM THE UNION OF THE PICTS AND SCOTS TO THE UNION OF THE CROWNS OF SCOTLAND AND ENGLAND, 850–1603

843–860	Kenneth I (Kenneth mac Alpin)	1165–1214	William I (the Lion)
860–863	Donald I	1214–1249	Alexander II
863–877	Constantine I	1249–1286	Alexander III
877–878	Aedh	1286–1290	Margaret (the Maid of Norway)
878–889	Eocha		
889–900	Donald II	(1290–1292	Interregnum)
900–943	Constantine II		
943–954	Malcolm I	1292–1296	John Balliol
954–962	Indulf		
962–967	Duff	(1296–1306	Interregnum)
967–971	Colin		
971–995	Kenneth II	1306–1329	Robert I (Robert Bruce)
995–997	Constantine III		
997–1005	Kenneth III	1329–1371	David II
1005–1034	Malcolm II	1371–1390	Robert II (Robert Stewart)
1034–1040	Duncan I		
1040–1057	Macbeth	1390–1406	Robert III
1057–1093	Malcolm III (Malcolm Canmore)	1406–1437	James I
		1437–1460	James II
1093–1094	Donald Bane	1460–1488	James III
1094	Duncan II	1488–1513	James IV
1094–1097	Donald Bane (restored)	1513–1542	James V
		1542–1567	Mary
1097–1107	Edgar	1567–1625	James VI (and James I of England and Ireland from 1603)
1107–1124	Alexander I		
1124–1153	David I		
1153–1165	Malcolm IV		

Thereafter the kings and queens of Scotland (and the Commonwealth) are the same as for England, with in some instances differences in style, e.g. James VII of Scotland but James II of England.

A GLOSSARY
for the several excerpts of old Scots poetry

Page 41: *le*, law; *sons*, plenty; *gamyn*, sport; *stade*, stayed.

Page 79: *wictaile*, food.

Page 80: *gert*, made; *bryn*, burn; *heryit*, harried; *menyt*, mourned.

Page 82: *herbryd*, harboured.

Page 83: *And of sa hey wndretaking | That he haid nevir heit abaysing | Off multitude of men*—these lines may be paraphrased as 'So great was his assurance that mere numbers never diminished his purpose'.

Page 96: *raucht*, reached; *dynt*, blow; *stynt*, stay; *dusche*, blow; *harnys*, brains.

Page 133: *pleyne*, play.

Page 134: *abate*, stops; *astert*, starts; *abaisit*, abashed; *takyn*, token; *deray*, disorder; *wowaris*, wooers; *kirtillis*, short gown; *dicht*, dressed; *laitis*, manners; *raffel*, doeskin; *straitis*, leather.

Page 135: *lincum*, linen; *nicht*, approached; *ysqueilit*, squealed; *gaittis*, goats; *meid*, reward; *gympt*, neat; *rude*, complexion; *lyre*, flesh; *skrippit*, derided; *murgeonit*, made faces at; *chreist*, rumpled; *bad ga chat him*, told him to go hang; *clokkis*, beetles; *sat*, suited; *rokkis*, distaffs (for spinning).

Page 136: *olyprance*, display; *crouse*, elated; *braid up the burde*, wake the boy; *wauch*, wall; *lauch*, amount due; *auch*, owe; *heydin*, scorn; *dunt*, blow; *broggit*, pointed; *winceand*, swearing (?); *wood*, mad.

Page 158: *schankis*, legs; *drowrie*, lover; *orloge*, clock; *walkryfe*, watchful; *curcheis*, kerchief; *lemman*, sweetheart; *makaris*, poets.

Page 159: *wichtis*, men; *pete*, pity.

Page 160: *mavys*, thrush; *merle*, blackbird; *peax*, peace; *scattis*, skates (fish); *carlingis*, old women; *fensum*, offensive; *flyttingis*, quarrels.

Page 161: *bot*, only; *crudis*, curds; *pansches*, tripe.

Page 166: *yowe*, ewe; *loaning*, lane; *wede*, withered.

A SELECTED BIBLIOGRAPHY

BOOK ONE

THE EMERGENT KINGDOM

Stuart Piggott	*Scotland before History*
R. G. Collingwood and	
J. N. L. Myres	*Roman Britain*
W. F. Skene	*Celtic Scotland*
Adamnan (edited by	
A. O. Anderson)	*Life of Columba*
F. T. Wainwright (Editor)	*The Problem of the Picts*
A. O. Anderson	*Early Sources of Scottish History*
——	*Scottish Annals from English Chroniclers*
A. B. Taylor (Editor)	*Orkneyinga Saga*
R. L. Graeme Ritchie	*The Normans in Scotland*

Early chapters in the general histories of Scotland by John Hill Burton, P. Hume Brown, Agnes Mure Mackenzie, J. D. Mackie, and William Croft Dickinson.

BOOK TWO

THE WAR OF INDEPENDENCE

John Barbour (edited by	
W. Mackay Mackenzie)	*The Bruce*
Walter Bower (edited by	
W. Goodall)	*Scotichronicon*
Sir Herbert Maxwell (translator)	*The Chronicle of Lanercost*
Sir Thomas de Gray (translated	
by Maxwell)	*Scalacronica*
Joseph Bain (Editor)	*Calendar of Documents relating to Scotland*
John Fordun (translated by	
W. F. Skene)	*Chronica Gentis Scotorum*
Lord Hailes	*Annals of Scotland*

Jean Froissart (translated by Lord Berners)	*Chronicles*
Evan Macleod Barron	*The Scottish War of Independence*
Sir James Fergusson	*William Wallace*
G. W. S. Barrow	*Robert Bruce*
W. Mackay Mackenzie	*The Battle of Bannockburn*
General Sir Philip Christison	*Bannockburn*

Relevant chapters in the general histories previously named; and an earlier study of Robert Bruce by the present author, of which—where it derives from prime sources—substantial use has been made.

BOOK THREE

THE ROYAL STEWARTS: ROBERT II TO JAMES IV

Joseph Bain (Editor)	*Calendar of Documents relating to Scotland*
E. W. M. Balfour-Melville	*James I, King of Scots*
H. Harvey Wood (Editor)	*Robert Henryson: Poems and Fables*
W. Mackay Mackenzie (Editor)	*The Poems of William Dunbar*
J. Sibbald (Editor)	*Chronicle of Scottish Poetry from the Thirteenth Century*
R. L. Mackie	*King James IV of Scotland*
I. F. Grant	*The Social and Economic Development of Scotland before 1603*
W. C. Mackenzie	*The Highlands and Isles of Scotland*
J. Storer Clouston	*A History of Orkney*

Relevant chapters in the general histories previously named.

BOOK FOUR

THE LATER STEWARTS

Gordon Donaldson	*Scotland: James V–James VII*
John Knox (edited by W. Croft Dickinson)	*History of the Reformation in Scotland*
Sir David Lyndsay (edited by David Laing)	*Poetical Works*
George Buchanan (translated and edited by W. A. Gatherer)	*The Tyrannous Reign of Mary Stewart*
T. F. Henderson	*Life of Mary Queen of Scots*
Andrew Lang	*The Mystery of Mary Stuart*
P. Hay Fleming	*Mary Queen of Scots*
Major-General R. H. Mahon	*The Tragedy of Kirk o' Field*
Robert Gore-Browne	*Lord Bothwell*
D. Harris Willson	*King James VI and I*

Relevant chapters in the general histories previously named.

BOOK FIVE

THE WASTED CENTURY

THE REVIVAL OF REASON

Relevant chapters in the general histories, previously named, continue to be of value; and to them must be added the second volume, by George S. Pryde, which complemented the earlier volume, by W. Croft Dickinson, of the *New History of Scotland* published in 1961 and 1962.

As the old story of Scotland came closer to the contemporary scene, so its records multiplied and publications became ever more numerous. For certain periods and special subjects it is still possible to compile short and useful bibliographies, but for a general survey of more than three centuries it is difficult to do more than suggest a few books that commend themselves by their intrinsic interest, or are landmarks of their own time. Biographies of Montrose by John Buchan (Lord Tweedsmuir) and Veronica Wedgwood may open the list with pure pleasure, and to Daniel Defoe's *History of the Union of Great Britain* should be added W. C. Mackenzie's *Andrew Fletcher of Saltoun* and a recent and very illuminating work by T. C. Smout: *Scottish Trade on the Eve of the Union*. Sir John Sinclair's *Statistical Account* (1791–1799) offers a solid background for H. Grey Graham's *The Social Life of Scotland in the Eighteenth Century*; and Sinclair himself (a man of great energy and ability) has been properly commemorated by Rosalind Mitchison in *Agricultural Sir John*. A great deal has been written about the two Jacobite rebellions, and Sir Charles Petrie's *The Jacobite Movement* is an excellent introduction to the subject; but the liveliest memories of it are to be found in the three volumes of speeches, letters, and journals that Bishop Forbes collected and published under the title of *The Lyon in Mourning*. To balance the view it is advisable to add Sir James Fergusson's *Argyll in the Forty-Five*, and *The Life and Letters of Duncan Forbes of Culloden* by George Meanary. The troubled scene of the Highland Clearances can also be regarded from two points of view: on the one side Donald Macleod's *Gloomy Memories in the Highlands of Scotland*, on the other James Loch's *An Account of the Improvements on the Estates of the Marquess of Stafford*. To these should be added the much later and far more objective account of the whole broad background of the Clearances: Malcolm Gray's *The Highland Economy 1750–1850*. Agreeably composed and authentic tales of Highlands and Islands are *A Description of the Western Islands of Scotland* by Martin Martin; *Memoirs of a Highland Lady* by Elizabeth Grant of Rothiemurchus; and *A Hundred Years in the Highlands* by Osgood Mackenzie of Inverewe. Edinburgh of course has a literature of its own, far too large to be recorded here; but for entertainment Lord Cockburn's *Memorials of his Time* can be recommended; as can the *Autobiography* of Dr. Alexander Carlyle, and Robert Chambers's *Traditions of Edinburgh*. For a modern, objective assessment of Edinburgh's achievement in the creation of its New Town, A. J. Youngson's *The Making of Classical Edinburgh* is essential. To that, perhaps, one should add that no just assessment of the people of the Highlands and Islands can be made without study of Alexander Carmichael's *Carmina Gadelica*; and some compendious history of the Scottish Regiments, Highland and Lowland, will be equally useful. And finally it must be said that the outstanding landmarks of Scottish history, during the last three centuries, are the written evidence of Scottish imagination or achievement from the calculations of Napier of Merchiston to those of Clerk Maxwell; from the arrogance and effrontery of Urquhart of Cromarty to the elegance and gaiety of Robert Louis Stevenson; from the gigantic creation of Walter Scott to the sudden blueprint for a native Scottish theatre that James Bridie so wittily drew; from the doomed genius of the boy Fergusson to the seasonal brilliance of Hugh MacDiarmid. I suppress mention of Hume and Adam Smith and Robert Burns. I suppress the mention of twenty lesser names. But I think it right to assert that so small a nation as Scotland has shown itself remarkably creative in the centuries that followed its abandonment of a specific political responsibility for the conduct of its own affairs.

Index